Education for Sustainab
Development in the Post
World

Education for sustainable development (ESD) lies at the heart of global, regional, and national policy agendas, with the goal of achieving socially and environmentally just development through the provision of inclusive, equitable quality education for all. Realising this potential on the African continent, however, calls for radical transformation of policy and practice. Developing a transformative agenda requires taking account of the 'learning crisis' in schools, the inequitable access to a good-quality education, the historical role of education and training in supporting unsustainable development, and the enormous challenges involved in complex system change.

In the African continent, sustainable development entails eradicating poverty and inequality, supporting economically sustainable livelihoods within planetary boundaries, and averting environmental catastrophe, as well as dealing with health pandemics and security threats. In addressing these challenges, the book

- explores the meaning of ESD for Africa in the context of the 'postcolonial condition';
- critically discusses the Sustainable Development Goals (SDGs) as well as regional development agendas;
- draws on a wealth of research evidence and examples from across the continent;
- engages with contemporary debates about the skills, competencies, and capabilities required for sustainable development, including decolonising the curriculum and transforming teaching and learning relationships;
- sets out a transformative agenda for policy-makers, practitioners, NGOs, social movements, and other stakeholders based on principles of social and environmental justice.

Education for Sustainable Development in the Postcolonial World is an essential read for anyone with an interest in education and socially and environmentally just development in Africa.

Leon Tikly is UNESCO Chair in Inclusive, Quality Education at the University of Bristol, UK.

Foundations and Futures of Education

Peter Aggleton, *University of New South Wales, Australia*
Sally Power, *Cardiff University, UK*
Michael Reiss, *UCL Institute of Education, UK*

Foundations and Futures of Education focuses on key emerging issues in education as well as continuing debates within the field. The series is interdisciplinary and includes historical, philosophical, sociological, psychological and comparative perspectives on three major themes: the purposes and nature of education; increasing interdisciplinarity within the subject; and the theory-practice divide.

For more information about this series, please visit: www.routledge.com/Foundations-and-Futures-of-Education/book-series/FFE

Education for Sustainable Development in the Postcolonial World

Towards a Transformative Agenda for Africa

Leon Tikly

Routledge
Taylor & Francis Group

LONDON AND NEW YORK

First published 2020
by Routledge
2 Park Square, Milton Park, Abingdon, Oxon, OX14 4RN

and by Routledge
52 Vanderbilt Avenue, New York, NY 10017

Routledge is an imprint of the Taylor & Francis Group, an informa business

© 2020 Leon Tikly

British Library Cataloguing-in-Publication Data
A catalogue record for this book is available from the British Library

Library of Congress Cataloging-in-Publication Data
A catalog record for this book has been requested

ISBN: 978-0-415-79294-3 (hbk)
ISBN: 978-0-415-79296-7 (pbk)
ISBN: 978-1-315-21134-3 (ebk)

Typeset in Galliard
by Apex CoVantge, LLC

For my amazing family who have shown me so much love and support and have put up with my absence for many months.

The book is dedicated to the memory of Vicki Gardner who provided invaluable support to me in preparing this manuscript.

Contents

Abbreviations

African Development Bank (AfDB)
African National Congress (ANC)
African Union (AU)
Asia-Pacific Economic Cooperation (APEC)
Association of African Universities (AAU)
Association for the Development of Education in Africa (ADEA)
Association of South East Asian Nations (ASEAN)
Common Market for East and Southern Africa (COMESA)
Common Underlying Proficiency (CUP)
Continental Education Strategy for Africa (CESA)
Decade for Education and Sustainable Development (DESD)
Development Assistance Committee (DAC)
Donors to African Education (DAE)
East African Community (EAC)
Economic Community of West African States (ECOWAS)
Education for All (EFA)
Education for Sustainable Development (ESD)
Education Sector Strategic Plan (ESSP)
European Union (EU)
Fast Track Initiative (FTI)
Forum for African Women Educationalists (FAWE)
Global Citizenship Education (GCE)
Global Education Monitoring Report (GEMR)
Global Monitoring Report (GMR)
Global Partnership for Education (GPE)
Great Lakes Initiative (GLI)
Human Capital Theory (HCT)
Incheon Declaration and Framework for Action (IDFA)
Indigenous Knowledge Systems (IKS)
Inter-Country Quality Nodes (ICQN)
Inter-University Council for East Africa (IUCEA)
International Institute for Educational Planning (IIEP)
International Monetary Fund (IMF)

Learner-Centred Education (LCE)
Lord's Resistance Army (LRA)
Low-Fee Private Schools (LFPS)
Millennium Development Goal (MDG)
Ministry of Education (MINEDUC)
North Atlantic Free Trade Agreement (NAFTA)
New Economic Partnership for African Development (NEPAD)
Open Working Group (OWG)
Organisation for African Unity (OAU)
Problem-driven Iterative Adaptation (PDIA)
Programme d'analyse des systèmes éducatifs de la Confemen (PASEC)
Regional Trade Agreement (RTA)
Southern African Consortium for Monitoring Education Quality (SACMEQ)
South African Democratic Teachers Union (SADTU)
South West African People's Organisation (SWAPO)
Southern African Development Community (SADC)
Southern African Development Coordination Conference (SADCC)
Southern and East African Consortium for Monitoring Education Quality (SACMEQ)
Stabilisation and Structural Adjustment Polices (SAPs)
Sustainable Development (SD)
Sustainable Development Goals (SDGs)
Trade in International Services Agreement (TiSA)
UN Economic Commission for Africa (UNECA)
World Commission on Environment and Development (WCED)
World Education Forum (WEF)

Acknowledgements

Over the three years that it has taken to write this book, the manuscript has benefited from the constructive input of numerous individuals. Ideas behind the book have been presented at several seminars and conferences around the world where they have also benefited from critical feedback. I am grateful for the input of colleagues in the Centre for Comparative and International Research in Education at the University of Bristol and at the Centre for Education Rights and Transformation at the University of Johannesburg where I am a visiting Professor. I would especially like to thank Angeline Mbogo Barrett and Joan DeJaeghere for their helpful comments on parts of the text. Thanks also to Vicki Gardner and Anna Kliampa who provided assistance with undertaking background research and to Sarah Cox for her excellent proofreading skills, humour, and support in helping me take this down to the wire. Thanks also to the series editors who exercised great patience and provided positive feedback during the course of preparing the manuscript. Finally, I would like to acknowledge the support of my department in providing funding to support the development of the book.

Foreword

The book is inevitably shaped by my own relationship with African education systems over many years. This has been in the form of a political activist in the struggle against apartheid during my formative years as the son of a South Africa political exile growing up in London. This was at a time when struggles against the racist system of bantu education were very much at the forefront of the wider liberation struggle. My relationship has also been informed by my experiences as a teacher of secondary school science both in London comprehensives and at the Solomon Mahlangu Freedom College established by the African National Congress on land donated by the Tanzanian government during the 1980s. The school catered for refugees from South Africa and brought home to me the realities of the damaging effects of bantu education on the capabilities of learners to learn natural science but also of the necessity and challenges involved in decolonising the curriculum and forms of pedagogy in the interests of these learners and of social transformation more broadly. (The use of examples from the world of science education in the second part of the book to some extent reflects these experiences).

My PhD, completed at the University of Glasgow, traces the development of education policy since the advent of apartheid and was my first effort to develop a critical analysis of education policy that is relevant for Africa. My work as a policy researcher in the Education Policy Unit at the University of the Witwatersrand which coincided with the first democratic elections in South Africa highlighted the need not only to critique but to transform policy and the enormous challenges involved in systems change on such a large scale. My empirical research subsequently has been largely on the identification of strategies to improve the quality of education for disadvantaged groups of learners on the continent who are taught often in difficult delivery contexts. I continue to seek to frame my empirical work however, within a broader, critical understanding of education policy on the continent as well as of the postcolonial condition and social and environmental justice. My recent research is especially shaped through my engagement with policy makers, activists, and practitioners in a number of African countries, including in particular South Africa, Tanzania, Rwanda, and Ghana, where I have conducted studies over many years. I am indebted to all of these individuals, my fellow researchers, and the learners I have taught for contributing to my understanding of the challenges involved in transforming education systems and for strengthening my belief in the possibilities for transformative change and my resolve to make a difference.

1 Setting the scene

Introduction

This book is about education for sustainable development (ESD) in Africa. It seems a timely juncture at which to write such a book. More than half a century after the euphoria following independence from colonial rule and despite the fact that the continent is blessed with immense natural and human resources as well as great cultural and ecological diversity, it continues to face enormous and apparently intractable challenges of unsustainable development that range from coping with the effects of deep-rooted poverty and inequality to climate change. The advent of the Sustainable Development Goals (SDGs) as well as of regional development agendas such as the African Union's *Agenda 2063* has provided new impetus to tackle Africa's problems and to embark on new pathways of sustainable development. Education is centrally implicated in these agendas as demonstrated by the launch in 2015 of the *Continental Education Strategy for Africa* by the African Union. Yet many learners are still excluded from access to a good-quality education and training at all levels of the system. The upshot is that the continent faces a shortage of the skills and competencies required for realising sustainable development.

Africa is a particularly significant region from which to consider the opportunities and challenges for low-income, postcolonial countries in implementing ESD given the enduring colonial legacy, its position in relation to the global economy and politics, and the extent of the sustainability challenges it faces. Thus, whilst the focus of the book is on sub-Saharan Africa, it is hoped that the analysis developed will have a wider resonance for considering ESD in other low-income, postcolonial settings. The aim of this introductory chapter is to provide some background context for the remainder of the book. It will start by presenting an overview of global and regional agendas that impact on education whilst the second part of the chapter will outline the aims and main arguments developed in the remainder of the book. The chapter will commence, however, by introducing the reader to some of the key concepts that inform the book and will be developed in later chapters.

The 'postcolonial condition'

It is worth summarising briefly what is meant by the term 'postcolonialism' and the 'postcolonial condition' in the context of this book (for a fuller account, see Tikly 1999, 2001, 2004; Crossley and Tikly 2004; Hickling-Hudson, Mathews, and Woods 2004; Rizvi 2007; Rizvi, Lingard, and Lavia 2006; Rizvi and Lingard 2006; Coloma 2009; Takayama, Sriprakash, and Connell 2017; Shizha and Makuvaza 2017). With its origins in the work of scholars such as Edward Said, Gyatouri Spivak, Homi Bhabha, Stuart Hall, and others, postcolonialism is often understood as a 'critical idiom' through which to consider issues of development.

Postcolonial analysis has been applied in diverse ways in the field of international and comparative education, although it is possible to identify some central themes that run through the scholarship. These include a recognition of the importance of the colonial legacy in understanding global and regional education policy. In the context of the present book, it will be argued that much of what will be described as 'unsustainable development' on the continent, including the persistence of extractive economic practices, the patrimonial nature of the postcolonial state, the many forms of social inequality, and the marginalisation of African cultures and languages, have their origins in the colonial period, although they have been exacerbated under contemporary globalisation. Education systems, it will be suggested, have been instrumental in reproducing many of these dynamics and that key features of modern education systems, including their elitist nature, the Eurocentric and content-driven nature of the curriculum, the prevalence of teacher-centred pedagogy, the neglect and marginalisation of African languages, and indigenous knowledge, are complicit in this process. The identification of the postcolonial condition is not intended, therefore, to imply that colonialism is 'over' in a temporal sense. This is to acknowledge not only that some countries continue to experience 'direct' forms of colonisation but also that the dominance of the former colonising powers continues to manifest in new forms of what Nkrumah initially described as 'neo-colonialism' and that has elsewhere been understood as the 'new imperialism' (Harvey 2003; Tikly 2004).

Secondly, analysis of the postcolonial condition involves appreciation of Africa's position in relation to processes of contemporary globalisation and this is the focus of Chapters 3–6. Thirdly, like much Marxist, feminist, queer, and other kinds of critical scholarship, postcolonial analysis is also intended to give voice to those groups who have been historically marginalised in economic, political and cultural terms. As will be suggested in Chapter 2, this involves understanding the co-evolution of intersecting 'regimes of inequality'. In particular, this will involve consideration of inequalities based on class, gender, race, ethnicity, and urban/rural location. In this regard, postcolonial scholarship builds on and takes forward the ideas of many generations of anti-colonial activists on the continent both in the context of anti-colonial struggles and subsequently. Many of these such as Nelson Mandela, Stephen Biko, Julius Nyerere, Walter Rodney, and others wrote a lot about colonial education, as will be discussed in Chapter 5.

This is significant because these critical scholars were not simply content with providing an abstract analysis of injustices involved in colonial education but were also deeply committed to identifying solutions in the context of struggles for national liberation. It is in this spirit that the present book seeks to not only analyse the nature of education for unsustainable development but also to propose how education systems in Africa can be transformed to support a vision of sustainable development linked to the idea of social and environmental justice. This vision will be set out in Chapter 7. In developing the analysis of the postcolonial condition, however, the book parts company with some of the more overtly poststructuralist emphasis within much recent postcolonial scholarship linked to the 'cultural turn' in the social sciences during the 1970s and 1980s. Rather, it adopts what has been described in Chapter 2 as a 'complex realist' approach that seeks to bring together materialist and discursive forms of analysis to understand complex reality (Bhaskar 2011). It is argued in this respect that the postcolonial condition itself needs to be understood both discursively, i.e. in terms of the constitutive effects of different discourses of development on the way that social reality and postcolonial identities are constructed, and materially, as an aspect of the impact of wider changes in relation to processes of economic and political globalisation.

An overview of global and regional policy agendas

Later chapters will seek to develop a more sustained analysis and critique of global and regional agendas that have as their focus achieving SD and ESD on the continent. For now, however, and by way of background to the book, it is important to provide an overview. In particular, attention will focus at a global level on the SDGs, including SDG 4 (the education SDG), and at a regional level on *Agenda 2063* and the *Continental Education Strategy for Africa* (CESA), which it has been suggested represent a regional response to the SDGs. For some, the focus on global and regional agendas might appear puzzling given that education policy remains primarily a national concern. As will be argued in later chapters, however, it is an aspect of the dynamics of contemporary globalisation that global and regional policy agendas have become increasingly influential in shaping national policy. Linked to this, and as discussed in Chapter 4, it is important to understand how policy-making processes at different scales of the global, regional, and national interact to 'produce' policy that is enacted at a local level. It is also important to recognise from the outset, however, the tremendous diversity in economic, political, cultural, and environmental terms on the continent. Through focusing on the impact of global and regional policy agendas, it is hoped to tease out some of the commonalities as well as differences with respect to understanding the challenges and possibilities for implementing ESD. In this respect, as Hoogvelt (1997) has argued, at a regional level, Africa can be perceived to exemplify a distinctive 'postcolonial formation' in its attempts to engage with the effects of globalisation, i.e. a distinctive mixture of economic, political, and cultural dynamics linked to Africa's position in the world and to the nature of regional responses to globalisation.

The SDGs

A key point of reference for contemporary debates about sustainable development are the recently adopted SDGs. A brief history of the origins of the SDGs is given in Chapter 3. Originally proposed by the Colombian government, they were given impetus at the Rio+20 conference on sustainable development in 2012 which mandated the creation of an Open Working Group (OWG) to come up with a draft agenda.[1] Alongside the OWG discussions, the United Nations (UN) conducted a series of 'global conversations', the results of which were fed into the working group's discussions. Although the SDGs provide continuity on the preceding Millennium Development Goals (MDGs), they also signal a decisive break in recognising the inextricable links between economic and human development on the one hand and environmental protection on the other. The SDGs are also more expansive in scope than the more minimalist MDGs, setting out a total of 169 targets compared to the 18 targets in the MDGs. For the first time, the SDGs are aimed at countries of the global North as well as the Global South which on the one hand recognises the global reach of issues such as poverty, inequality, and climate change and on the other hand the role of rich industrialised countries, both in perpetuating and in potentially overcoming these challenges.

From the perspective of this book, a key feature of the SDGs is that they set out what is described as a 'transformative' development agenda (although it will be argued in subsequent chapters that they do not go far enough in this respect). Specifically, the *Transforming our World Report* (UN 2015c) identifies five 'Ps' that lie at the heart of a transformative agenda:

People

We are determined to end poverty and hunger, in all their forms and dimensions, and to ensure that all human beings can fulfil their potential in dignity and equality and in a healthy environment.

Planet

We are determined to protect the planet from degradation, including through sustainable consumption and production, sustainably managing its natural resources and taking urgent action on climate change, so that it can support the needs of the present and future generations.

Prosperity

We are determined to ensure that all human beings can enjoy prosperous and fulfilling lives and that economic, social, and technological progress occurs in harmony with nature.

Peace

We are determined to foster peaceful, just, and inclusive societies which are free from fear and violence. There can be no sustainable development without peace and no peace without sustainable development.

Partnership

We are determined to mobilise the means required to implement this Agenda through a revitalised Global Partnership for Sustainable Development, based on a spirit of strengthened global solidarity, focused in particular on the needs of the poorest and most vulnerable and with the participation of all countries, all stakeholders, and all people. (UN 2015c, 2)

The 17 SDGs can be seen to correspond to these principles. They are set out in Box 1.1.

Box 1.1   The Sustainable Development Goals

Goal 1. End poverty in all its forms everywhere

Goal 2. End hunger, achieve food security and improved nutrition, and promote sustainable agriculture

Goal 3. Ensure healthy lives and promote well-being for all at all ages

Goal 4. Ensure inclusive and equitable quality education and promote lifelong learning opportunities for all

Goal 5. Achieve gender equality and empower all women and girls

Goal 6. Ensure availability and sustainable management of water and sanitation for all

Goal 7. Ensure access to affordable, reliable, sustainable, and modern energy for all

Goal 8. Promote sustained, inclusive, and sustainable economic growth, full and productive employment, and decent work for all

Goal 9. Build resilient infrastructure, promote inclusive and sustainable industrialisation, and foster innovation

Goal 10. Reduce inequality within and among countries

Goal 11. Make cities and human settlements inclusive, safe, resilient, and sustainable

Goal 12. Ensure sustainable consumption and production patterns

Goal 13. Take urgent action to combat climate change and its impacts

Goal 14. Conserve and sustainably use the oceans, seas, and marine resources for sustainable development

Goal 15. Protect, restore, and promote sustainable use of terrestrial ecosystems, sustainably manage forests, combat desertification, and halt and reverse land degradation and halt biodiversity loss

Goal 16. Promote peaceful and inclusive societies for sustainable development, provide access to justice for all, and build effective, accountable, and inclusive institutions at all levels

Goal 17. Strengthen the means of implementation and revitalise the Global Partnership for Sustainable Development

Source: United Nations (UN 2015c)

It will be argued in Chapter 3 that the SDGs 'quilt together' a range of sometimes contradictory economic and political interests and that this is reflected in the contested nature of the goals and targets (Sayed 2019). The SDGs have also been subject to criticism. For example, some wealthy governments initially criticised the number of goals which they claimed were unwieldy.[2] They have also come in for criticism on account of their proposed cost.[3] On the other hand, the SDGs have been widely praised by many member states of the UN and NGOs for embracing environmental and human rights issues in particular. They are in the process of being incorporated into the development plans and visions of many governments, including African governments. Indeed, although it will be argued in the book that Northern interests have predominated in global agendas about development including the SDGs, African governments have played a role in advocating for sustainable development and this is evident in *Agenda 2063*.[4] In this respect, Africa's commitment to the SDGs was recently underlined by the opening in Kigali of the Sustainable Development Goals Centre for Africa by Paul Kagame, the Rwandan President.

The education SDG

Education is accorded a central position in the SDGs. A recent analysis of UN flagship reports, for example, shows that education is implicated in realising all of the other SDGs as well as being affected by them. These relationships are summarised in Figure 1.1. In later chapters, it will be argued that the nature of the relationships between education and other domains of sustainable development is highly complex and there is a need to avoid seeing education as a panacea for development. Rather than being linear in nature, the relationship between education and

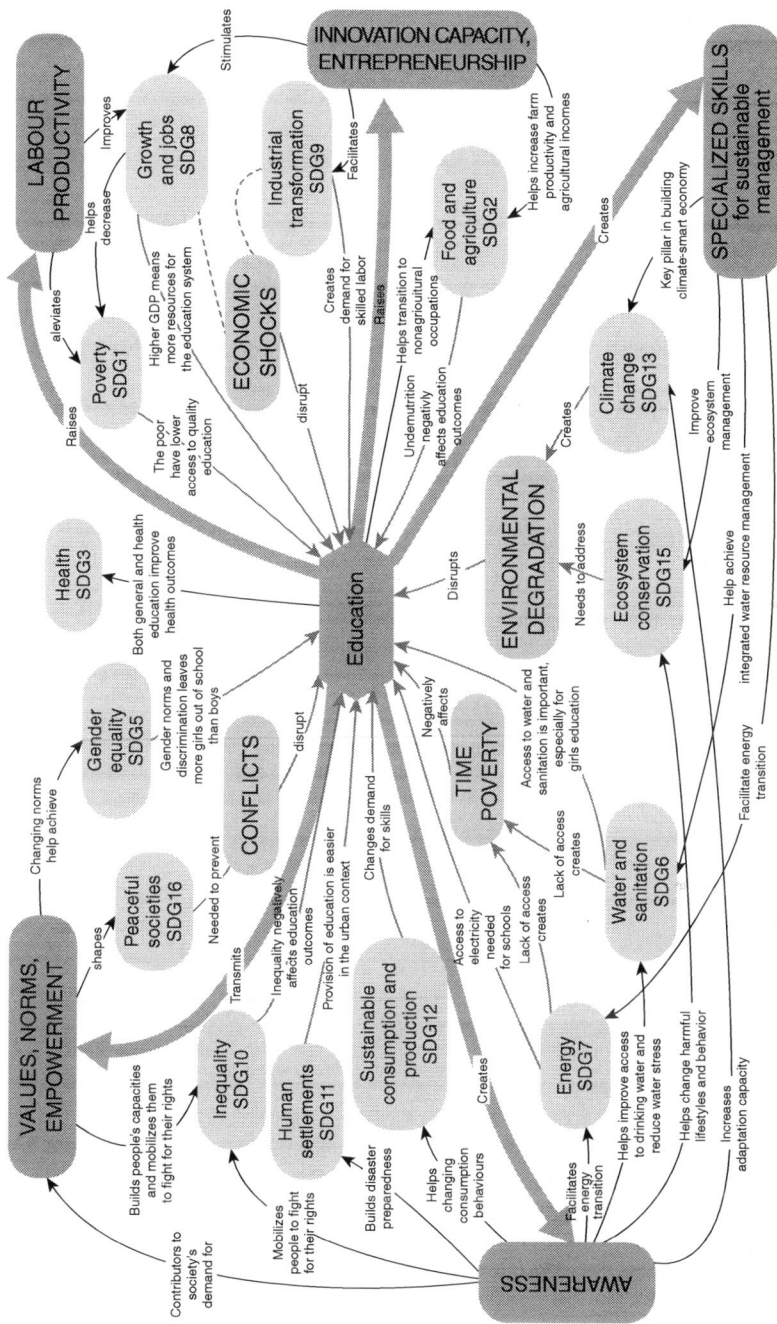

Figure 1.1 A simplified map of the links between education and other SDG areas, built from the messages contained in UN flagship reports.

Source: Vladimirova and LeBlanc (2015, 23)

other domains of sustainable development involves complex feedback loops and is multi-directional in nature. Change to education or indeed to any domain of development is therefore multi-causal and inherently unpredictable. Some of the implications for this view of complex systems are explored in Chapter 2.

As we have seen, the education SDG (SDG 4) aims to ensure inclusive and equitable quality education and to promote lifelong learning opportunities for all. As with discourses about SD, the education SDG also 'quilts together' different sometimes contradictory interests, discourses, and initiatives in the area of international education and development. Given its origins in both the *Education for All* (EFA) movement and global discourses on SD, the education SDG is much more expansive than the rather limited two MDG goals on education. The latter had been focused on achieving universal access to basic education and gender parity in access at all levels of the education and training system.[5] Unlike the MDGs, the education SDG is also concerned with promoting the attitudes and values required to support environmentally sustainable and socially just development. To this latter end, Target 4.7 seeks to

> ensure that all learners acquire the knowledge and skills needed to promote sustainable development, including, among others, through education for sustainable development and sustainable lifestyles, human rights, gender equality, promotion of a culture of peace and non-violence, global citizenship and appreciation of cultural diversity and of culture's contribution to sustainable development.

The education goal along with its related targets and indicators are set out in Box 1.2.

The box also contains data derived from the Global Education Monitoring Report (GEMR), which tracks progress in achieving SDG 4. It is worth indicating three points to emerge from an initial review of the data in Box 1.2. Firstly, in relation to virtually all of the indicators, Africa lags behind other regions of the world. To this extent, the data indicate the depth of the so-called 'learning crisis' on the continent (discussed in subsequent pages). Secondly, the indicators are themselves limited in their scope. For example, the indicators relating to learning outcomes deal principally with measures of cognitive achievement. Measures of affective outcomes, for example, attitudes towards environmental protection, peace, and global citizenship, are not included. Further, the indicators also relate largely to the basic education cycle which was the focus for monitoring progress under the more restrictive MDG regime, whereas the crisis in African education affects every subsector and level of the education and training system. Thirdly, at a more profound level, the figures themselves represent in the language of complex realism, a 'surface actuality' of the learning crisis. That is to say, they do not say anything about the underlying causes of the crisis. It will be suggested in subsequent chapters that understanding must involve getting behind the statistics to better comprehend the complex nature of causality, including the effects of power and of intersecting regimes of inequality in determining outcomes for different groups of learners.

Box 1.2 Progress towards achieving SDG 4 in Africa

SDG 4 target	*Indicators*	*Progress towards target in SSA against selected indicators*
By 2030, ensure that all girls and boys complete free, equitable and quality primary and secondary education leading to relevant and effective learning outcomes	GLOBAL INDICATOR 4.1.1 Proportion of children and young people (a) in Grade 2 or 3; (b) at the end of primary education; and (c) at the end of lower secondary education achieving at least a minimum proficiency level in (i) reading and (ii) mathematics, by sex THEMATIC INDICATORS 4.1.2 Administration of a nationally representative learning assessment (a) in Grade 2 or 3; (b) at the end of primary education; and (c) at the end of lower secondary education 4.1.3 Gross intake ratio to the last grade (primary education, lower secondary education) 4.1.4 Completion rate (primary education, lower secondary education, upper secondary education) 4.1.5 Out-of-school rate (primary education, lower secondary education, upper secondary education) 4.1.6 Percentage of children over-age for grade (primary education, lower secondary education)	Only 33% of countries in Sub-Saharan Africa guarantee free and compulsory education for nine years compared to 64% of countries globally. Regionally, out-of-school rates are highest in sub-Saharan Africa: 21% of primary school age children, 36% of lower secondary school age adolescents, and 57% of upper secondary school age youth are not enrolled. A relatively high proportion of learners in African schools are overage with more than 50% being overage in Burkina-Faso, Burundi, and South Sudan. Reliable, comparable assessment data are rare in many African countries. From available data, 87% of primary school age children in sub-Saharan Africa did not reach minimum proficiency levels in reading compared to a global average of 56%

(*Continued*)

(Continued)

SDG 4 target	Indicators	Progress towards target in SSA against selected indicators
	4.1.7 Number of years of (a) free and (b) compulsory primary and secondary education guaranteed in legal frameworks	
By 2030, ensure that all girls and boys have access to quality early childhood development, care, and pre-primary education so that they are ready for primary education	GLOBAL INDICATORS 4.2.1 Proportion of children under 5 years of age who are developmentally on track in health, learning, and psychosocial well-being, by sex 4.2.2 Participation rate in organised learning (one year before the official primary entry age), by sex THEMATIC INDICATORS 4.2.3 Percentage of children under 5 years of age experiencing positive and stimulating home learning environments 4.2.4 Number of years of (i) free and (ii) compulsory pre-primary education guaranteed in legal frameworks 4.2.5 Gross pre-primary enrolment ratio	African countries lag behind other regions of the world in introducing pre-school education. The gross enrolment ratio in pre-primary education in Africa is 32% compared to a global average of 49%. Children aged 36–59 months are more likely to lag behind their developmental age in Africa than in other regions. There is a strong correlation between the proportion of children lagging behind and income per capita. Pre-school children are much less likely to experience home activities that promote learning and especially father support for learning. Children from the poorest households are less likely to experience home activities that promote learning compared to children in other regions of the world. Many African countries also lag behind in introducing quality assurance processes in pre-school education

SDG 4 target	Indicators	Progress towards target in SSA against selected indicators
By 2030, ensure equal access for all women and men to affordable and quality technical, vocational, and tertiary education, including university	GLOBAL INDICATOR 4.3.1 Participation rate of youth and adults in formal and non-formal education and training in the previous 12 months, by sex THEMATIC INDICATORS 4.3.2 Gross enrolment ratio for tertiary education by sex 4.3.3 Participation rate in technical-vocational programmes (15- to 24-year-olds) by sex	Sub-Saharan Africa has the lowest levels of participation of 15–24 year olds in technical and vocational education than any other regions of the world and participation has stagnated since 2000. Sub-Saharan African countries also have the lowest gross enrolment ratios in higher education at 8% in 2015 compared to a global average of 36%. Enrolment ratios have increased more slowly in Africa than in other regions. Sub-Saharan Africa is the only region of the world where women do not enrol in higher education on a par with men. There are also much disparities between men and women in Science Technology, Engineering, and Maths degrees compared to other regions
By 2030, substantially increase the number of youth and adults who have relevant skills, including technical and vocational skills, for employment, decent jobs, and entrepreneurship	GLOBAL INDICATOR 4.4.1 Percentage of youth/adults with information and communications technology (ICT) skills, by type of skill THEMATIC INDICATORS 4.4.2 Percentage of youth/adults who have achieved at least a minimum level of proficiency in digital literacy skills	Most adults cannot perform even the most basic ICT functions. For example, from available data only 4% of adults in Sudan and Zimbabwe could copy and paste files

(*Continued*)

(Continued)

SDG 4 target	Indicators	Progress towards target in SSA against selected indicators
	4.4.3 Youth/ adult educational attainment rates by age group, economic activity status, levels of education and programme orientation	
By 2030, eliminate gender disparities in education and ensure equal access to all levels of education and vocational training for the vulnerable, including persons with disabilities, indigenous peoples and children in vulnerable situations	GLOBAL INDICATOR 4.5.1 Parity indices (female/male, rural/ urban, bottom/ top wealth quintile, and others such as disability status, indigenous peoples, and conflict-affected, as data become available) for all education indicators on this list that can be disaggregated THEMATIC INDICATORS 4.5.2 Percentage of students in primary education whose first or home language is the language of instruction 4.5.3 Extent to which explicit formula-based policies reallocate education resources to disadvantaged populations 4.5.4 Education expenditure per student by level of education and source of funding 4.5.5 Percentage of total aid to education allocated to least-developed countries	Sub-Saharan African countries lag behind the rest of the world in achieving gender parity in enrolments at all levels of the education and training system. Thus, only 49% of countries have achieved parity in pre-primary enrolment compared to a global average of 62% whilst 36% have reached parity of enrolment in primary compared to a global average of 66%. The picture at secondary level is even worse with only 26% and 9% of countries achieving parity compared to global averages of 45% and 25%, respectively. No African countries have achieved gender parity in higher education enrolments compared to 4% of countries globally. Available data also suggest disparities in learning outcomes between boys and girls in mathematics at the end of primary school. Boys outperformed girls in mathematics in eight out of ten countries surveyed. Household wealth is also a major

SDG 4 target	Indicators	Progress towards target in SSA against selected indicators
		predictor of inequality. In SSA, only 34% and 31% of males and females from the poorest households completed primary education compared to global averages of 72% and 71%, respectively. At secondary level, the figures were 17% and 13% compared to global averages of 54% for both sexes whilst in higher education the figures are 8% and 5% compared to global averages of 32% and 33%, respectively. The majority of African countries pursue policies in which there is an early exit from mother tongue to a European language. As is discussed in Chapter 6, more sustained use of mother tongue is linked to improved learning outcomes. There is a poverty of data relating to inequalities with respect to disability
By 2030, ensure that all youth and a substantial proportion of adults, both men and women, achieve literacy and numeracy	GLOBAL INDICATOR 4.6.1 Percentage of population in a given age group achieving at least a fixed level of proficiency in functional (a) literacy and (b) numeracy skills, by sex THEMATIC INDICATORS 4.6.2 Youth/adult literacy rate 4.6.3 Participation rate of illiterate youth/ adults in literacy programmes	More than one in four young pole in SSA cannot read or write. However, in systems that privileged local languages, 69% of adults with five years of education could read a sentence compared with 41% of adults educated partly or wholly in colonial languages

(*Continued*)

(Continued)

SDG 4 target	Indicators	Progress towards target in SSA against selected indicators
By 2030, ensure that all learners acquire the knowledge and skills needed to promote sustainable development, including, among others, through ESD and sustainable lifestyles, human rights, gender equality, promotion of a culture of peace and non-violence, global citizenship and appreciation of cultural diversity and of culture's contribution to sustainable development	GLOBAL INDICATOR 4.7.1 Extent to which (i) global citizenship education and (ii) ESD, including gender equality and human rights, are mainstreamed at all levels in (a) national education policies, (b) curricula, (c) teacher education, and (d) student assessment THEMATIC INDICATORS 4.7.2 Percentage of schools that provide life skills-based HIV and sexuality education 4.7.3 Extent to which the framework on the World Programme on Human Rights Education is implemented nationally (as per the UNGA Resolution 59/113) 4.7.4 Percentage of students by age group (or education level) showing adequate understanding of issues relating to global citizenship and sustainability 4.7.5 Percentage of 15-year-old students showing proficiency in knowledge of environmental science and geoscience	There is very limited data on the extent to which issues of global citizenship education, ESD, gender equality, and human rights are mainstreamed in policies, curricula, teacher education, and assessment. As is discussed in Chapter 5, most initiatives aimed at the above are provided in the form of extra-curricular activities by NGOs. The very limited evidence on the extent of sexuality education suggests that in ten African countries, fewer than half the curricula met global standards for all age groups with gender and social norms identified as the weakest areas. Recent studies in Ghana and Kenya provided evidence of inaccurate information on sexuality band sexually transmitted diseases in that 60% of teachers incorrectly taught that condoms alone can prevent pregnancy and 71% of teachers emphasised abstinence as the best ad only method to prevent pregnancy and sexually transmitted diseases

SDG 4 target	Indicators	Progress towards target in SSA against selected indicators
Build and upgrade education facilities that are child, disability, and gender sensitive and provide safe, non-violent, inclusive, and effective learning environments for all	GLOBAL INDICATOR 4.a.1 Proportion of schools with access to: (a) electricity; (b) Internet for pedagogical purposes; (c) computers for pedagogical purposes (d) adapted infrastructure and materials for students with disabilities (e) basic drinking water; (f) single-sex basic sanitation facilities; and (g) basic handwashing facilities (as per the WASH indicator definitions) THEMATIC INDICATORS 4.a.2 Percentage of students experiencing bullying, corporal punishment, harassment, violence, sexual discrimination and abuse 4.a.3 Number of attacks on students, personnel, and institutions	In sub-Saharan Africa, only 22% of primary schools have access to electricity, compared to 49% of lower secondary schools. Primary school access to clean drinking water is below 50% in at least four African countries whilst access to basic sanitation facilities was below 50% in 17 African countries. Although 69% of schools have toilets, many still lack separate sanitation facilities for girls and boys. Based on data from 65 developing countries, the median value of the percentage of schools with access to computers and the Internet for pedagogical purposes is above 70% in both primary and secondary education. However, the proportion drops below 40% for many countries in sub-Saharan Africa
By 2020, substantially expand globally the number of scholarships available to developing countries, in particular least developed countries, small island developing States and African countries, for	GLOBAL INDICATOR 4.b.1 Volume of official development assistance flows for scholarships, by sector and type of study THEMATIC INDICATOR 4.b.2 Number of higher education scholarships awarded, by beneficiary country	Only 17% of scholarship aid from OECD-DAC donor countries goes to sub-Saharan Africa. There is no available data relating to the BRICS economies

(*Continued*)

(Continued)

SDG 4 target	Indicators	Progress towards target in SSA against selected indicators
enrolment in higher education, including vocational training and information and communications technology, technical, engineering and scientific programmes, in developed countries and other developing countries		
By 2030, substantially increase the supply of qualified teachers, including through international cooperation for teacher training in developing countries, especially least developed countries and small island developing states	GLOBAL INDICATOR 4.c.1 Proportion of teachers in: (a) pre-primary education; (b) primary education; (c) lower secondary education; and (d) upper secondary education who have received at least the minimum organised teacher training (e.g. pedagogical training) pre-service or in-service required for teaching at the relevant level in a given country THEMATIC INDICATORS 4.c.2 Pupil-trained teacher ratio by education level 4.c.3 Percentage of teachers qualified according to national standards by level and type of institution 4.c.4 Pupil-qualified teacher ratio by education level 4.c.5 Average teacher salary relative to other professions requiring	Available data suggest that only 62% of primary school teachers in sub-Saharan Africa are trained compared to a global average of 86%. The situation is worse at pre-primary and secondary levels with 36% and 45% of teachers having been trained at these levels, respectively. The percentage of trained teachers has decreased since 2000 in several African countries, including Eritrea, Ghana, and Niger

SDG 4 target	Indicators	Progress towards target in SSA against selected indicators
	a comparable level of qualification 4.c.6 Teacher attrition rate by education level 4.c.7 Percentage of teachers who received in-service training in the last 12 months by type of training	

Source: Adapted from UNESCO (2017b)

Agenda 2063

Agenda 2063: The Africa We Want[6] adopted by the African Union sets out an aspirational 50-year programme of action for the continent framed within an overarching commitment to pan-Africanism, inclusive growth, sustainable development, and a vision of an African Renaissance. It can be treated as a regional response to the SDGs. The vision is for 'an integrated, prosperous and peaceful Africa, driven by its own citizens and representing a dynamic force in the international arena' (iv). It is based on a recognition of the enormous wealth of the continent in natural resources and the resilience and cultural resourcefulness of African peoples themselves. In highlighting the opportunities as well as the challenges faced by the continent in developmental terms, *Agenda 2063* stands in contrast to some of the more pessimistic accounts on development in Africa prevalent in the international development arena.

Agenda 2063 provides an analysis of the sustainability challenges facing Africa. It is worth setting out the main points of the analysis here as it provides important background context for the remainder of the book. However, it will be argued in later chapters that the analysis provided by *Agenda 2063 Framework Document* whilst useful in flagging key issues for development is also partial and limited, particularly in identifying the underlying causes of Africa's malaise and the nature of the global and indigenous interests that have shaped Africa's past development trajectory. The analysis in later chapters will instead draw on an analysis of the changing relationship between education and complex globalisation to seek to provide deeper insight. Secondly, the account that follows has been supplemented with material from other sources where this assists in portraying the full extent of the opportunities and challenges facing the continent.

The opportunities and challenges facing the African continent with
respect to sustainable development as portrayed in Agenda 2063

The *Agenda 2063 Framework Document* (AUC 2015a) (herewith referred to
simply as *Agenda 2063*) points out that African economies have been among the
fastest growing in the world in recent decades but with variation within countries and regions. Growth according to *Agenda 2063* can be attributed to an
expansion of foreign investment in extractive industries such as mining and oil
and to a lesser extent by the growth in the agricultural[7] and informal sectors, in
information technologies, and in remittances from the diaspora.[8] Amongst the
challenges, the document notes a decline in the export of manufactured goods
and a very small proportion of high-technology manufactured goods and a lack
of productivity in the agricultural sector. This is attributed to a variety of factors,
including poor infrastructure (roads, transport, electricity, etc.), the relatively
small size of African enterprises, a shortage of inter-firm linkages, and importantly
for our purposes, skills.

Agenda 2063 considers the links between the economy and social development on the continent, focusing in particular on demographic change, poverty
(particularly rural poverty), gender, health, and education. The *Agenda 2063*
notes dramatic changes in Africa's demographic profile.[9] In the period to 2063,
it is noted that the African population will increase far more rapidly than it will
in the rest of the world population. A key feature of development in Africa is
the rapid process of urbanisation. The document estimates that more than two-
thirds of the projected population of 2.5 billion will be living in urban centres
by 2063. It is also noted that Africa's population is young with a median age of
about 20 years in 2014, compared to a world average of 30 years. This is seen
in the report as both an opportunity and a challenge for education and training. A further demographic trend with implications is that of migration which
is intense, including rural–urban migration, opening up of borders, a growing
trend of young Africans seeking a better life in Europe and elsewhere, and forced
displacements, due to factors such as civil wars, droughts, water shortages, and
natural disasters.

In relation to poverty, *Agenda 2063* points out that there has been a reduction in absolute poverty in many African countries and that this is falling for
the first time in a generation.[10] However, the report notes that poverty has
worsened in several other countries and that 'overall, the gains remain fragile
and reversible due to rising inequalities and exposure to shocks (economic,
political, social and environmental)' (AUC 2015a, 31).[11] Linked to poverty is
the prevalence of disease.[12] The report highlights rural poverty as a particular
challenge. It links rural poverty in part to patterns of economic growth and
to the limited growth within the agricultural sector.[13] Linked to the issue of
rural poverty is the challenge of food insecurity. The report notes that with
60% of the world's arable land, agriculture is Africa's greatest potential and
can serve as the main engine to propel the continent's growth and transformation. However,

due to her high population growth, low and declining agricultural productivity, policy distortions, weak institutions and poor infrastructure, among others, Africa has turned into a net food importer, is currently importing nearly a quarter of her food needs. Consequently, one in four undernourished people in the world live in Africa.

(AUC 2015a, 31)

The report identifies the development of the agricultural sector as the key means for addressing rural poverty and food insecurity.

Agenda 2063 points to increases in the number of democracies on the continent and in multiparty elections. It also points out that most elections are now violence-free. The report highlights some improvements in economic governance,[14] including success in tackling corruption,[15] which it considers has a bearing on the sustainability of economic performance of African countries. However, it notes that policy making and service delivery remain compromised due to poor public institutions and administration at central, municipal, and local levels, leaving many citizens poorly served by their governments (AUC 2015a, 62). The report also argues that the quality of democracy remains a challenge with huge variability in the extent to which democratic norms are internalised and implemented.[16] In this context, *Agenda 2063* posits the notion of the 'developmental state' as a possible way forward for improving governance.

Significantly, the report addresses Africa's position in relation to processes of global governance. This is important because as an exporter of primary goods, the continent is exposed to externally imposed changes in the prices of commodities and is subject to a multitude of externally imposed agendas and initiatives. *Agenda 2063* is, however, relatively silent on the role of civil society in governance. It draws attention to the fact that 'civil society participation and contributions to democracy is frequently handicapped by their capacity and resources' (AUC 2015a, 62), but it does not delve more deeply into the issues involved. This is despite the fact that since colonial times, civil society organisations at national and global scales have played a prominent role in education as in other spheres (see Chapter 6).

Agenda 2063 goes some way towards highlighting major threats to Africa's peace and security. It notes increases in the propensity to resort to the use of violence within communities linked to 'cultural, political, social and economic gaps between the minority at the centre and the larger population – rural or urban and intergenerational disputes' and over 'failure to accommodate multiple community identities, especially at the local level, especially in fragile and conflict-affected areas'. At a state level, violence is linked in the report 'to ineffective credible and legitimate democratic governance institutions for the prevention of violent conflicts; such as the rule of law, democratic access to power and effective wealth distribution' and to 'limited state capacities leading to corruption, lack of accountability and impunity, which restricts the provision of services' (AUC 2015a, 66). The report also highlights new forms of criminal activity such as piracy and of religiously inspired conflict that cuts across national borders and to the 'ease of trading, acquiring and circulating weapons' (AUC 2015a, 66). Once again, it will be suggested in later chapters that the report does not go far enough in identifying the causes of violence and of conflict which, it will be suggested, lie primarily in competing interests at a global and national level over access to state power, patronage, and control over Africa's natural resources. Finally, the report draws attention to violence against women as a continent-wide problem. This is significant in the context of the book because it will be argued that violence needs to be understood in its full ontological depth, i.e. as encompassing not only state and civil society–sponsored violence but violence at a personal and psychological level as well. In this regard, education systems have been strongly implicated in perpetuating violence against girls and women as well as other marginalised groups (Chapter 6).

The pan-African influence in *Agenda 2063* is perhaps most evident in relation to discussions about the cultural domain. The report notes the effects of cultural domination during the slave trade and colonial era which it is claimed 'led to the depersonalization on the part of African peoples, falsified their history, systematically disparaged and combatted African values and tried to replace progressively and officially their languages by that of the colonized' (AUC 2015a, 68).[17] Education is singled out as having accelerated Africa's integration into a Western, global culture along with news media, music, and art. The report argues that while Western influences can enrich the African cultural heritage, 'they can also be a source of erosion and ultimately can supplant and replace African values and ethics'. *Agenda 2063* goes on to state that 'language is at the heart of a people's culture and the acceleration of Africa's socio-economic transformation is impossible without harnessing in a practical manner the indigenous African languages' (AUC 2015a, 68). Significantly, it goes on to argue that a 'major threat to African culture and heritage is the educational system which is marginalizing African languages', although, as we shall see in Chapter 8, this is not carried through in the CESA document. The document identifies poor management of Africa's diversity – ethnic, religious, cultural – as being a source of conflict on the continent. It also identifies religious extremism, including *Boko Haram* in Northern Nigeria and the *Lord's Resistance Army* (LRA) in Uganda as examples of what can happen on account of this mismanagement.

Agenda 2063 identifies Africa's natural resources as playing a critical role for vast segments of Africa's population who depend on the continent's biodiversity, forests, and land for their livelihoods directly or indirectly. The document points out that Africa is well endowed with biodiversity: both variety and abundance of species, ecosystems, and genetic resources. The document highlights the blue/ocean economy as having importance in environmental, economic, and social terms.[18] The report identifies natural resources as playing a critical role for vast segments of Africa's population who depend on the continent's biodiversity, forests, land, and waters for their livelihoods directly or indirectly. These natural resources, it is argued, also make a direct contribution to economic development through tourism, agriculture, logging, fishing, and other activities. However, the *Agenda 2063* notes that the continent's biodiversity, land, and forests are facing increasing challenges.[19] The report highlights unequal distribution of land, with small farmers pushed out to marginal areas by large investment programmes, severe soil degradation, desertification, and deforestation[20] accompanied by flooding and intermittent droughts. Significantly and in keeping with the analysis presented in Chapter 3, the document names the recent 'scramble for Africa's land' by big investors (mostly foreign) in biofuels, minerals, and oil, as well as food production for consumption abroad as a major risk to environmental protection and sustainable economic development.

In relation to the blue/ocean economy, the report states that the dumping of toxic waste, illegal trafficking, oil spills, degradation of the marine environment, and transnational organised crimes, among others, have seriously threatened Africa's oceans, seas, and lakes.[21] Finally, *Agenda 2063* draws attention to the abundance of energy sources on the continent, including crude oil and natural gas, with huge potential for hydropower, geothermal energy, and solar and wind power,[22] but it notes that Africa's energy profile is characterised by low production, low consumption, and high dependence on traditional biomass energy despite the huge energy resources.[23]

Missing from the document, however, is more recent evidence of the impact of climate change. The major causes of climate change lie in patterns of over-consumption in the global North. However, as a region, Africa is one of the most vulnerable to the effects of climate change (Masson-Delmotte 2018). Projections concerning climate change for the region point to a warming trend, particularly in inland subtropics. There is an increased likelihood of extreme heat events as well as increasing aridity and changes in rainfall, which is predicted to have a particularly pronounced decline in southern Africa and an increase in East Africa. Already high rates of infectious disease and malnutrition can be expected to increase compared to a scenario without climate change. Rises in sea levels will affect the livelihoods of coastal communities.[24] Agricultural systems that rely on rainfall on which the livelihoods of a large proportion of the region's population currently depend are particularly at risk. The increasing vulnerability of rural communities is likely to increase the rate of rural–urban migration, adding to the already significant urbanisation trend in the region. The movement of people into informal settlements may expose them to a variety of risks, including flash flooding, outbreaks of infectious disease, and increases in the price of food (Coumou 2016). Increasing competition over arable land has also been linked with increases in violent conflict.

Aspirations and priorities for sustainable development

In seeking to meet the above challenges, *Agenda 2063* sets out a number of aspirations for sustainable development on the continent. These are as follows:

> *A prosperous Africa based on inclusive growth and sustainable development.* Key to this priority is the eradication of poverty in one generation and building and sharing prosperity through social and economic transformation

and with the means and resources to drive its own development. This includes sustainable and long-term stewardship of its resources where African people have a high standard of living and quality of life, sound health, and well-being; well-educated and skilled citizens, underpinned by science, technology, and innovation for a knowledge society and where no child misses school due to poverty or any form of discrimination; cities and other settlements are hubs of cultural and economic activities; economies are structurally transformed to create shared growth, decent jobs, and economic opportunities; modern agriculture for increased production, productivity, and value addition contributes to prosperity and Africa's collective food security; and Africa's unique natural endowments, its environment, and ecosystems, including its wildlife and wild lands, are healthy, valued, and protected, with climate-resilient economies and communities.

An integrated continent, politically united and based on the ideals of Pan-Africanism and the vision of Africa's Renaissance. This involves creating a United Africa; a world-class, integrative infrastructure that criss-crosses the continent; dynamic and mutually beneficial links with her diaspora; and a continent of seamless borders.

An Africa of good governance, democracy, respect for human rights, justice, and the rule of law. Priorities here include Africa being a continent where democratic values, culture, practices, universal principles of human rights, gender equality, justice, and the rule of law are entrenched and where there are capable institutions and transformative leadership in place at all levels.

A peaceful and secure Africa. Priorities include a culture of peace and tolerance nurtured in Africa's children and youth through peace education; the more effective management of diversity; developing an entrenched and flourishing culture of human rights, democracy, gender equality, inclusion and peace; prosperity, security, and safety for all citizens; and mechanisms to promote and defend the continent's collective security and interests.

An Africa with a strong cultural identity, common heritage, shared values, and ethics. The *Agenda 2063* states that Pan-Africanism and the common history, destiny, identity, heritage, respect for religious diversity, and consciousness of African people and her diaspora will be entrenched and the African Renaissance has reached its peak by 2063.

An Africa whose development is people-driven, relying on the potential of African people, especially its women and youth, and caring for children. This is based on a vision that all the citizens of Africa will be actively involved in decision-making in all aspects, including social, economic, political, and environmental, and where Africa shall be an inclusive continent where no child, woman, or man will be left behind or excluded, on the basis of gender, political affiliation, religion, ethnic affiliation, locality, age, or other factors.

Africa as a strong, united, and influential global player and partner. The *Agenda 2063* affirms the importance of African unity and solidarity in the face of continued external interference, including attempts to divide the continent and undue pressures and sanctions on some countries (AUC 2015a).

Continental education strategy for Africa

The *Continental Education Strategy for Africa 2016–2025* (CESA) (AU 2015) was developed under the auspices of the African Union. It provides continuity on the central role accorded to education in *Agenda 2063*. Developing the priorities identified by African Ministers of Education set out in the *Kigali Declaration* that fed into the SDG consultation process, it can also be seen as a regional response to the education SDG. The vision is expressed in the following terms:

> Africa is ushering into an era that most observers and pundits are predict-ing will determine its destiny as the continent of the future. But to fulfil this promised bright future, the continent has to come to terms with its educa-tion and training systems that are yet to fully shed the weight of its colonial legacy and its own tribulations as a relatively new political and economic entity and player in the world arena. In the bid to 'create' a new African citizen who will be an effective change agent for the continent's sustainable development as envisioned by the AU and its 2063 Agenda, the African Union Commission has developed an Africa comprehensive ten-year conti-nental education strategy
>
> (CESA)(AU 2015, 7).

As will be discussed in Chapter 5, the vision seeks to rearticulate the idea of ESD in a way that is consistent with the Pan-African vision of an African Renaissance that underpins *Agenda 2063*. The document notes many of the challenges facing the education system identified in Box 1.2. It sets out a series of guiding princi-ples, pillars, and strategic objectives that are intended to address these challenges and are summarised in Box 1.3.

Box 1.3   CESA guiding principles, pillars, and strategic objectives

Guiding principles:

1   Knowledge societies called for by *Agenda 2063* are driven by skilled human capital
2   Holistic, inclusive, and equitable education with good conditions for lifelong learning is a sine qua non for sustainable development
3   Good governance, leadership, and accountability in education man-agement are paramount
4.   Harmonised education and training systems are essential for the realisation of intra-Africa mobility and academic integration through regional cooperation

5   Quality and relevant education, training, and research are core for scientific and technological innovation, creativity, and entrepreneurship
6   A healthy mind in a healthy body – physically and socio-psychologically fit and well-fed learners

Pillars:

1   Strong political will to reform and boost the education and training sector
2   Peaceful and secure environment
3   Gender equity, equality, and sensitivity throughout the education and training systems
4   Resource mobilisation with emphasis on domestic resources
5   Strengthen institutional capacity building through

    i   Good governance, transparency, and accountability
    ii   A coalition of actors to enable a credible participatory and solid partnership between government, civil society, and the private sector

6   Orientation and support at different levels and types of training
7   The creation and continuous development of a conducive learning environment

The 12 strategic objectives are as follows:

SO 1: Revitalise the teaching profession to ensure quality and relevance at all levels of education

SO 2: Build, rehabilitate, preserve education infrastructure and develop policies that ensure a permanent, healthy, and conducive learning environment in all sub-sectors and for all, so as to expand access to quality education

SO 3: Harness the capacity of ICT to improve access, quality, and management of education and training systems

SO 4: Ensure acquisition of requisite knowledge and skills as well as improved completion rates at all levels and groups through harmonisation processes across all levels for national and regional integration

SO 5: Accelerate processes leading to gender parity and equity

SO 6: Launch comprehensive and effective literacy programmes across the continent to eradicate the scourge of illiteracy

SO 7: Strengthen the science and math curricula in youth training and disseminate scientific knowledge and culture in society

SO 8: Expand TVET opportunities at both secondary and tertiary levels and strengthen link ages between the world of work and education and training systems

SO 9: Revitalise and expand tertiary education, research, and innovation to address continental challenges and promote global competitiveness

SO 10: Promote peace education and conflict prevention and resolution at all levels of education and for all age groups

SO 11: Improve management of education system as well as build and enhance capacity for data collection, management, analysis, communication, and use

SO 12: Set up a coalition of stakeholders to facilitate and support activities resulting from the implementation of CESA 16–25

Global and regional agendas and the 'learning crisis'

The term 'learning crisis' has been popularised by the World Bank amongst other organisations (Bank 2018). It will be argued, however, particularly in Chapter 10, that it is often used rhetorically in policy discourse when describing education systems in Africa in a way that elides the nature and origins of the crisis (see also Sriprakash, Tikly, and Walker 2019). It is, therefore, important to be clear what is meant by the term in the context of this book. Documents such as the *Continental Education Strategy for Africa* and the annual Global Education Monitoring Reports provide a statistical picture of the extent of the learning crisis against key indicators. These are summarised in Box 1.2. From here it can be seen that although there has been progress in improving access to primary education, learning outcomes (as measured in standardised tests of literacy and numeracy) remain very low across the continent. Worst affected are often learners from low socio-economic backgrounds, girls, minorities, and rural dwellers. As global and regional agendas make clear, the nature of the crisis is multifaceted. Although many countries are in the process of moving towards competency-based curricula, many curricula remain heavily content driven, linguistically and cognitively too demanding, and irrelevant to local contexts and the needs of learners. High-stake assessments aimed at filtering access to higher levels of education and to the limited opportunities in the labour market continue to drive both curricula and pedagogical processes which have, since colonial times, been formalistic, authoritarian, and teacher centres in nature. A key issue is the availability of suitably qualified teachers on the continent and a mismatch between teacher education and the realities of classrooms and other learning spaces. These issues are compounded by often very large class sizes as well as issues of a poor infrastructure and textbooks and other teaching and learning resources.

Opportunities to progress to higher levels of education and training are limited by inadequate basic skills, which further entrenches inequities and exacerbates the crisis. There is a shortage, for example, in technical and vocational skills that could potentially contribute to alleviating youth unemployment and assist processes of sustainable development in rural and urban areas (see Chapter 7). Access to higher education continues to be very limited, particularly for women and other marginalised groups. This also limits the capacity of universities to contribute to processes of African-led development through research and innovation. A major challenge is a lack of coherence between various parts of the education and training system.

Educational institutions are often sites for reproducing rather than reducing inequalities and for perpetuating physical violence in the form of corporal punishment, gender, and ethnically based violence as well as 'epistemic' violence through the marginalisation of local and indigenous languages and knowledge systems from the curriculum. Further, despite efforts to introduce forms of ESD into educational institutions, recent evaluations of the impact of the UN Decade of Education for Sustainable Development, for example, show that take-up has been partial and limited (UNESCO 2014b).

As with analysis of the wider sustainability challenges facing the continent, it will be argued that it is important to get behind the numbers, however, and to seek to better understand the causes of the learning crisis which, it will be suggested, are deeply rooted and mutually implicated in wider processes of unsustainable development. For this reason, a key argument that will be advanced in the book is that education systems alone cannot be expected to either 'solve' the learning crisis or wider development challenges as is sometimes implied in global and regional agendas. Rather, what is required are more fundamental and simultaneous processes of transformative change across all domains of development.

Aims and summary of main arguments

The book is motivated by a belief in the potential for environmentally sustainable and socially just development and of education's role in achieving this. It is also driven by a belief that a future transformative agenda is possible but must be based on a realistic analysis of the very real challenges facing the continent in realising sustainable development and in transforming its education systems. The first aim of the book then is to better understand the nature of the challenges involved if education is to play a genuinely transformative role. This requires going beyond the focus of the present chapter on simple description of the nature and scale of the various challenges and delving deeper to identify the underlying causes of the challenges facing Africa in relation to SD. As Karl Marx stated, however: 'The philosophers have only *interpreted* the world, in various ways; the point, however, is to *change* it'. The second aim of the book then is to build on analysis and critique in order to set out a transformative agenda that can serve as a guide for policy makers, practitioners, and civil society. It involves acknowledging the potential for social actors to transform their world in ways that are environmentally sustainable and socially just and identifying the conditions under which this might become possible. Rather than offering blueprints or magic bullets, however, the book will seek to sketch out an overall approach for reconceptualising ESD.

Chapter 2 will set out the conceptual basis for the book. Specifically, Chapter 2 will consider the implications of recent developments in complexity theory for understanding, at an ontological level, important characteristics of complex natural and social systems. It will present a view of education systems as complex, open, adaptive systems and of how education co-evolves in relation to other institutional domains that are traversed by power relationships and complex, intersecting regimes of inequality, including those based on class, gender, race, ethnicity, and rurality. The chapter will also set out the metatheoretical framework of complex realism. It will be argued that such a framework can underpin an approach to understanding education systems. This involves bringing together different kinds of evidence, including evidence derived from inter- and transdisciplinary research and forms of analysis that can be used by policy makers and practitioners to tackle 'wicked problems' such as those posed by unsustainable development and the learning crisis.

Continuing in the same vein, Chapter 3 will outline an approach for conceptualising the ethical basis for SD and ESD that informs the analysis and critique presented in the book. The chapter starts by providing a brief, critical overview of the genealogy of contemporary, dominant understandings of SD and ESD as they are portrayed in global and regional agendas. It then sets out an alternative means for conceiving the normative basis of SD and ESD. In so doing, it pulls together insights from the capability approach of Sen and Nussbaum with Fraser's views of social justice as well as work by Schlosberg that reinterprets the work of these authors through an environmentalist lens, drawing on the capability approach and based on principles of social and environmental justice. Drawing together the ideas of these authors, the chapter provides a definition of SD as *socially and environmentally just development that supports the capabilities (i.e. opportunity freedoms) of existing and future generations and of natural systems to flourish.* ESD is defined as *socially and environmentally just education that facilitates the capabilities of existing and future generations and of natural systems to flourish.*

Chapter 4 seeks to set out an understanding of the postcolonial condition that forms the backdrop for the discussion of global and regional policies in subsequent chapters. Drawing on recent work on globalisation, the chapter will provide an understanding of complex globalisation that is relevant for understanding Africa's marginal position in relation to contemporary global flows and networks. The chapter will set out an understanding of development in Africa since colonial times in relation to the co-evolution of six interrelated domains of the economy, the polity, civil society, violence, culture, and the environment. The chapter will consider how these domains are affected by the operation of different kinds of power that give rise to intersecting regimes of inequality. It is only through this kind of analysis, it will be suggested, that it becomes possible to fully appreciate the roots of unsustainable development on the continent. Subsequent chapters will consider the relationship between education and each of the domains of development introduced in Chapter 4.

Chapter 5 will focus on the relationship between education and the domains of the global polity and civil society. It will trace changing patterns in the global governance of education since colonial times. This involves taking account of not only global regimes of education governance where policy is officially 'sanctioned' at different scales but also of the nature of the role of civil society waves, including those of neoliberalism and pan-Africanism where much of the intellectual and moral energy for policy emanates. The chapter will analyse the changing patterns of global governance of education since colonial times. This involves consideration of changing regimes of global governance including the Education for All and, more recently the SDG regimes as well as related regimes such as the aid, trade, and security regimes that together constitute a regime complex that African governments must negotiate. The analysis will provide a basis for considering the emergence of contemporary global agendas. It will be argued that these agendas, although contested, have been shaped largely by dominant global interests (including Western interests and increasingly the Rising Powers) as well as by those of indigenous elites.

Building on the analysis in Chapter 5, Chapter 6 will turn the spotlight on the regional and national levels of governance. The chapter will consider the legacy of colonial forms of governance under British and French rule for shaping the current fundamental nature or (in the language of complex systems) path dependency of education systems. Consideration will be given to the role of developmental regionalism and of the postcolonial state in the post-independence era in shaping the policy-making process in the interests of global powers and indigenous elites and limiting the potential for democratic governance at different scales. This will involve understanding the often-contradictory role of different actors in the state and civil society in governing education, including not only policy makers and donors but also NGOs, social movements of different kinds, teacher unions, and the private sector. A focus for discussion is the increasing trend towards the privatisation of education at national level with implications for class and other regimes of inequality. The chapter will also consider the role of education and training systems in processes of political socialisation and in perpetuating violence. The chapter concludes by considering the possibilities for peace education in the context of the preceding analysis.

The focus of Chapter 7 is on changing discourses concerning the role of education in supplying the skills required for economic development. This, it will be argued, requires taking account of the changing relationship since colonial times between education systems and the domains of the economy as well as those of the environment and of culture. Drawing on the idea of 'skills formation' which emphasises the social nature of skills, the chapter traces the emergence of current discourses about skills for development as they have evolved in the context of contemporary globalisation. Attention will focus on the continuing influence of modernisation and human capital theories in shaping contemporary discourses relating to skills for development. It will be argued that current agendas are limited in their transformative potential. This is due to the contradictions inherent in the idea of 'inclusive growth' on which they are based and the predominance of neoliberal concerns with market-led growth over concerns for human development and the natural environment; through failing to fully acknowledge the implications of the causes of unsustainable development and of the learning crisis; and, through an emphasis on a narrow set of instrumentally defined skills and competencies that ignore the Eurocentric nature of global skills agendas and the need to develop skills that can support environmental protection.

Drawing on recent work on sustainable economic development, the chapter will present an alternative view of the economic domain that takes account of the environmental and social dimensions of economic production (including domestic labour) and seeks to balance meeting basic human needs with the need to operate within planetary boundaries. Drawing on the capability approach and on the idea of 'sustainable work', the chapter will present an understanding of skills and competencies that emphasises the social nature of skills and takes account of the barriers that prevent disadvantaged groups from developing skills and competencies that they have reason to value and that can assist in realising transformative SD. The chapter will illustrate the value of the approach through reinterpreting key priorities set out in regional agendas, including the development of basic literacy and numeracy and STEM-related skills and drawing out the implications of the analysis for policy makers.

Chapter 8 turns to a consideration of the relationship between education and the cultural domain. In particular, it considers the implications of contemporary debates concerned with 'decolonising' the curriculum in Africa. It sets out two contrasting views from the literature on the nature of epistemic justice in education. The first, which draws on a long tradition of anti-colonial struggle, argues for an overhaul of the Eurocentric basis of the existing curriculum, whilst the second, drawing on the philosophy of social realism, argues that epistemic justice implies facilitating access for disadvantaged groups to powerful knowledge represented by the disciplines. The chapter argues for a *rapprochement* between these two positions. Realising curriculum transformation in the interests of decolonisation, it will be suggested, requires a systemic approach. On the one hand, it involves reorienting and democratising the process of research in higher education to make it more relevant and meaningful for facing the challenges of sustainable development in Africa. This involves a role for researchers in promoting inter- and trans-disciplinary research and drawing on indigenous as well as Western knowledge systems to facilitate social learning in the community. On the other hand, it involves democratising the processes by which specialised knowledge becomes codified in the school curriculum and translated into classroom practice. The chapter will use the case of the secondary school science curriculum in Africa to highlight the challenges and possibilities involved.

Chapter 9 then goes on to consider some of the pedagogical implications for developing transformative agency in learners so that they are equipped to tackle problems of unsustainable development in their communities. The chapter sets out contrasting view of pedagogy in Africa based on progressive and formalistic frames. Drawing on insights from complexity theory as it has been applied to theories of learning, the chapter argues the need to transcend the unhelpful binary between these two approaches. Drawing on recent scholarship that has sought to situate an understanding of pedagogy at the intersections of various complex systems encompassing the home and community background of the learner, the classroom, school, and wider education system, including the national curriculum frameworks, assessment system, and teacher training, the chapter will argue for the need for coherence at a system level in terms of the overarching moral purpose of education and between the curriculum, assessment, and teacher training but most especially at the 'pedagogical core'. This demands a focus on the specific activities facilitated by the teacher that enable the learner to engage with the content of the lesson and how these are evaluated. It will also be suggested that pedagogy needs to take account of the operation of various intersecting regimes of inequality in the classroom and wider system that limit the opportunities for learning available to different groups. This in turn involves a systemic response including investment in the professional capabilities of educators and drawing on relevant, contextualised research in African classrooms.

The final chapter focuses on the need for transformation at a system level. Rather than providing hard and fast 'solutions' (which would run counter to the underlying view of complex systems informing the book), the chapter brings together evidence from earlier chapters and from the wider literature to articulate an overall approach towards system change. The first part of the chapter makes the case for the development of a counter-hegemonic movement organised around a vision of a transformative ESD. Such a movement must include not only policy makers and practitioners in the state but organisations based in civil society, including social movements, NGOs, religious organisations, and the private sector that despite representing different interests can nonetheless be mobilised around a common, transformative vision. Both traditional and organic intellectuals based in social movements have a key role to play in articulating a counter-hegemonic vision. Drawing on a critical reading of the international literature on system change, the second part of the chapter argues that education and training systems must themselves be made sustainable if they are to support transformative change. This, it will be suggested, involves placing an ontology of learning at the centre of system reform that takes account of the capabilities of different groups to learn; developing systemic rather than fragmented responses to the learning crisis; facilitating system leadership at all levels of the education and training system and in civil society as a *sin qua non* for realising change; investing in educators as agents of transformative change; democratising the governance of education to include historically marginalised interests in the change process; creating learning systems that can act on a range of context-relevant evidence to tackle the learning crisis; and moving out of the dependency trap which has for so long acted as a break on African-led development.

Conclusion

In this chapter, a case has been made for the importance of focusing on ESD in the African context given the challenges facing the continent in relation to achieving SD and the central role afforded to education in meeting these challenges. The chapter has also provided some detail as to the nature of the SDGs, including the education SDG, and of *Agenda 2063* and CESA as a basis for more critical engagement with global and regional agendas in subsequent chapters of the book. Finally, the chapter has provided an overview of the key aims and arguments presented in the remaining chapters which it is hoped will assist in orienting the reader to what is to follow. Having outlined the rationale, background aims, and main arguments, the next chapter will consider how an understanding of complex systems can assist in conceptualising SD and ESD.

Notes

1 The OWG, with representatives from 70 countries, had its first meeting in March 2013 and published its final draft, with its 17 suggestions, in July 2014. The draft was presented to the UN General Assembly in following September. The final wording of the goals and targets followed a period of member state negotiations, and the preamble and declaration that come with them were agreed in August 2015.

2 A more cynical view might be to suggest that the underlying reason for this was to seek to get rid of some of the more uncomfortable goals, such as those relating to the environment and to their own aid commitments.

3 *The Economist* (2015, 1) estimated at about US$2–$3 trillion per year for the next 15 years which they called 'pure fantasy'.

4 Indeed, it will be suggested in Chapter 3 that ideas about SD were implicit in pre-colonial economic and social arrangements and in the development of Pan-Africanism as a social movement. More recently, at the Rio+10 summit held in Johannesburg, Sam Nujoma, who was then President of Namibia, warned of the importance of adhering to *Agenda 21* noting that as a semi-arid country, Namibia sets a lot of store in the United Nations Convention to Combat Desertification.

5 In this regard, Africa had achieved more success in achieving the MDGs than other regions of the world, albeit from a low base. Sub-Saharan Africa scored the best record of improvement in primary education of any region since the MDGs were established. The region achieved a 20 percentage-point increase in the net enrolment rate from 2000 to 2015, compared to a gain of 8 percentage points between 1990 and 2000. Its enrolment rate grew from 52% in 1990 to 80% in 2015. In absolute numbers, the region's enrolment more than doubled between 1990 and 2012, from 62 million children to 149 million (UN 2015b).

6 *Agenda 2063* consists of three components, namely, the vision for 2063 based on the Aspirations of the African People; a transformation framework or framework document which presents detailed milestones, goals, priority areas, targets and indicative strategies; and an implementation plan. It is the *Agenda 2063: The Africa We Want Framework Document* (AUC 2015a) that has provided the major focus for this and subsequent chapters as it sets out in some detail the nature of the development challenges and opportunities facing the continent.

7 The report goes on to state that in a small number of instances, such as Rwanda and Ethiopia, increased levels of growth have been attributed to increases in agricultural production.

8 The report cites statistics, for example, that show that during the 2002–2008 period, Africa's economic growth rate averaged 5.6% per annum. There has also been an increase in per capita income which more than doubled from US$958 (2004) to US$1878 (2012), although economic growth has slowed on the continent subsequent to the publication of the report because of a fall in prices of raw materials on international markets and a slowdown in growth in emerging markets which imports raw materials from Africa (WBG 2017).

9 *Agenda 2063* notes, for example, that since 1950, Africa's population size and growth has experienced an upward trend, growing from about 229 million to

1.2 billion in 2014, representing 9.1% and 15.1% of the total world population, respectively. This proportion is projected to increase to 19.7% and 35.3%, respectively, by 2034 and 2100 (AUC 2015a, 44).

10 The proportion of people living in extreme poverty (i.e. less than US$1.25/day) fell from 56.5% in 1990 to 48.5% in 2010 (AUC 2015a, 31). Furthermore, it points out that a number of countries have reached, or are close to reaching, the MDG target of halving poverty by 2015.

11 Despite progress, the report states that Africa remains the continent with the highest concentration of poverty with the number of Africans living below the poverty line in fact increasing from 290 million in 1990 to 376 million in 1999 to 414 million in 2010.

12 The framework document notes that although infectious diseases as a cause of mortality and morbidity have declined in the rest of the world, these remain as the most frequent causes of deaths in Africa due to poor environmental management, weak water and sanitation systems, and low knowledge of basic health household practices.

13 It is noted that agricultural/rural population in Africa stands at 530 million people, and is expected to exceed 580 million by 2020. About 48% of this population relies directly on agriculture for economic and livelihood needs. It is noted that 'agricultural performance is central in driving socio-economic transformation, especially in the traditionally economically marginalized and largely rural populations' (AUC 2015a, 45).

14 The report notes improvement in domestic resource mobilisation and public administration, modest progress in tackling corruption, significant improvements in the business climate, and progress in stemming illicit capital outflows.

15 Although *Agenda 2063* notes that according to transparency international, four out of five African countries are below the world average (p. 64).

16 It points to detention without trial, arbitrary arrests, torture, forced disappearances, and extrajudicial killings which it claims are still unfortunately widespread whilst access to justice and independence of the judicial system is a major concern. The report highlights pervasive weaknesses of institutions, especially in the field of human rights at national, regional, and continental levels.

17 The document notes that work done by great African scholars and writers have contributed a lot to reexamining and restoring Africa's distorted and obscured place in the history of the world. The document also notes that despite her rich cultural heritage, Africa is poorly represented in the list of protected world cultural heritage sites and that this risks is hastening the erosion of these sites.

18 It states, for example, that 'Africa's bodies of water are endowed with abundant flora and fauna and marine ecosystems including diverse fish and other aquatic life, coral reefs; and are also sources of livelihoods to many Africans including water, food, power generation and transportation. Coastal areas and lake basins have also emerged not only as major tourist attractions but also as important sources of minerals, including oil and gas. The sector creates jobs for 7.1 million fishers (2.7 million in marine fisheries and 3.4 million in inland fisheries and 1 million in aquaculture) and over 59 per cent of these people are women' (51).

19 These include habitat loss as the major factor behind biodiversity loss and accelerating erosion of the genetic resources of agricultural plants and animals. The erosion of genetic resources leads to growing genetic uniformity of agricultural plants and animals, which means an increased risk of food loss from major epidemics.

20 Linked to these developments as well as to global warming are issues of land degradation and desertification which are believed to impact 43% of Africa's land surface with serious environmental and socio-economic consequences. Similarly, the report notes that the continent lost over 4 million hectares of forests annually

over the past two decades due to extensive agricultural practices, unregulated and unsustainable wood harvesting, and illegal commercial logging.

21 These problems, it is argued, are compounded by the aggravated effects of climate change, most notably by the rising ocean temperatures and ocean acidification that is leading to the weakening of the capacity of the ocean carbon sink and loss of fishery resources and also reduction in the size of water bodies, such as Lake Chad' (AUC 2015a, 51).

22 'Crude oil reserves estimated at over 130 billion barrels – about 9.5 per cent of world's reserves; about 8 per cent of the world's total reserves of natural gas estimated at about 15 trillion cubic metres; about 4 per cent of the world's total proven reserves (about 95 per cent of these reserves found in Southern Africa); hydropower resources potential to generate over 1,800 TWh/yr of electricity; geothermal energy potential estimated at over 15,000 MW; and huge solar and wind power potential. Because of its proximity to the Equator, Africa has also the world's highest average amount of solar radiation each year. Africa's bioenergy potential is immense, particularly given rapid advances in research that have brought new energy crops into production and second-generation lingo-cellulosic technologies within reach in less than a decade' (51).

23 The report argues that the continent faces enormous energy challenges, including low-generation capacity and efficiency, high costs, unstable and unreliable energy supplies, low access to modern energy, insufficient energy infrastructure, and lack of institutional and technical capacity to harness huge resources.

24 The region could also experience as much as one meter of sea-level rise by the end of this century under a 4 °C warming scenario.

2 Introducing complex systems

Introduction

In providing a critique of global and national agendas and in seeking to outline an alternative, transformative account of education for sustainable development, the book draws on recent scholarship in complexity theory and, in particular, work on the nature of complex systems. The aim of this chapter is to provide an introduction to the view of complex systems that informs the remainder of the book. At a deep ontological level, the understanding of complexity can be said to inform the other theoretical approaches that will be introduced in later chapters.[1] The chapter will commence with a brief overview of the nature of complexity theory and of complex systems. The second half of the chapter will reflect on some of the implications for understanding and researching education system change that arise from an appreciation of complexity and that have informed the book.

Why complexity theory?

Complexity theory has its origins in the natural sciences where it has been applied to a wide variety of disciplinary fields, including neuroscience, ecology, epidemiology, computer science, and the study of physical phenomena such as turbulent fluids, gravitational systems in space, and to the intricacies of living cells (Capra 2005; Waldrop 1992; Cairney 2012; Geyer and Cairney 2015). Complexity theory has, however, become increasingly influential within the social sciences (Byrne and Callaghan 2014; Elliot 2013). The attraction lies partly in the extent to which it draws attention to phenomena or behaviours that pertain at a system level and arise from the interaction between elements within a system. It thus seems suited to a book that is fundamentally concerned with understanding education systems. For some social scientists, the attraction also lies in the understanding of systems as being in a state of constant flux and change which has been used to challenge determinism and positivism in the social sciences (Byrne and Callaghan 2014). Given its ability to span disciplines, it seems ideally suited to the study of SD and ESD which is inherently concerned with the co-evolution of complex environmental, economic, social, and cultural systems

(Sachs 2015). In this respect, complexity theory is best considered as an overall approach rather than as a general theory of education with predictive qualities. As such it is intended to complement rather than to replace other theoretical perspectives (Snyder 2013). It provides a vocabulary and a way of conceiving at a general level, the nature of complex reality. Nonetheless, it will be argued in subsequent chapters that lessons derived from complexity theory can serve as a useful guide for action for policy makers and practitioners interested in change.

In seeking to consider the relevance of complexity theory, the book will draw in particular on recent efforts to relate complexity theory to globalisation, inequality, and to an understanding of global crises (Walby 2009, 2015); work that has sought to understand public policy from the perspective of complexity theory (Cairney 2012; Geyer and Cairney 2015); the literature relating complexity theory to theories of learning (e.g. Davis and Sumara 2006; Haggis 2008, 2009); research within the field of comparative and international education that has made use of some version of complexity theory to understand education policy and governance (Andrews, Pritchett, and Woolcock 2017; Davies 2004b; Mason 2008, 2014; Nordtveit 2007; Morrison 2002; Snyder 2013) as well as work within the more general literature on aid and development (Ramalingam 2013b) and, in the specialised literature on sustainable development (Sachs 2015; Wells 2013). Complexity theory has attracted increasing attention for understanding social policy from organisations ranging from the Organisation for Economic Cooperation and Development (OECD) (Mason 2014; Snyder 2013) to UNESCO (Morin 1999) and has been particularly influential in health systems research. It has begun to have an influence on the way that education policy and education systems are conceptualised (Mason 2008, 2014; Snyder 2013).

McLennan (2003) has, however, warned against attempts to uncritically and simplistically apply complexity theory in the social sciences and the need to specify how the underlying ideas and language – often derived from the natural sciences – are being operationalised. This is especially important given the sometimes opaque and unfamiliar language and ideas that are used to describe complex systems. In relation to this last point, the task for critical theory is to ensure that complexity theory, like all theories are made to 'go to work' for the historically marginalised and dispossessed on the continent. In relation to the focus of the book, this requires engaging at a theoretical level with inequality and the causes of inequality. It requires recognising that systems and the human agents that interact within systems do not operate on a level-playing field and that these inequalities need to be understood as part of the complexity that is being considered. There is a need to develop a critical 'take' on complexity theory in which the dynamics of education systems are seen in relation to the colonial legacy in education, the marginal position of African countries in relation to contemporary processes of globalisation, and the nature of inequalities based on class, gender, race, ethnicity, etc. These realities, it will be suggested, are part of the 'fitness landscape' in which education system dynamics emerge in Africa.

General characteristics of complex systems

Natural phenomena have often provided a source of inspiration for understanding the complex and inherently unpredictable nature of the social world. A classic example is a flock of birds swarming across the skyline. Despite the fact that no single bird leads, the behaviour of the flock appears organised and demonstrates a form of group intelligence. As the birds flock, each member of the flock adjusts its location and speed based on the proximity of others nearby. The collective produces beautiful, non-uniform swarming motions that also serve to protect members of the flock by frustrating predators that try to aim at individual birds. Another example is provided by the human brain. The firing of specific neurons affects the firing of other neurons and the result in the brain considered as a whole system can then influence the individual neurons as part of a feedback loop. This dynamic ultimately produces phenomena such as ideas, dreams, images, and metaphors that are difficult to predict. Neither swarms nor dreams are predictable directly from the behaviour of individual birds or neurons.

Not all systems are necessarily complex however. Some systems, such as an aeroplane or a car, for example, may be best described as 'complicated', in that they are composed of thousands of interrelated parts whose interactions obey precise, simple, known, and unchanging cause and effect rules (Snyder 2013). Traditional views of education systems in which they are presented in the form of an organogram, for example, portray education systems as complicated sets of institutional arrangements and processes. Alternatively, an ensemble of cars travelling down a highway represents a complex system in which drivers interact and mutually adjust their behaviour based on diverse factors such as perceptions, expectations, habits, and emotions. It is therefore important to consider what is meant by a 'complex system' in the context of the book. A system can refer to any collection of related elements. Generic terms in the social sciences include 'social system' and 'socio-technical system', while more specialised terms include 'society', 'capitalism', 'regime', 'institution', 'field', 'discourse', 'domain', and 'social formation'. A key point of reference is obviously the education system. The World Bank defines the education system as

> the full range of learning opportunities available in a country, whether they are provided or financed by the public or private sector (including religious, nonprofit, and for-profit organizations). It includes formal and non-formal programs, plus the full range of beneficiaries of and stakeholders in these programs – teachers, trainers, administrators, employees, students and their families, and employers. It also includes the rules, policies, and accountability mechanisms that bind an education system together, as well as the resources and financing mechanisms that sustain it.
>
> (World Bank 2011, 17).

Whilst providing a starting point for an holistic understanding of education systems in terms of the institutions, it will be argued in Chapter 10 that the idea of education systems needs to be more expansive still to include, for example, processes of social learning undertaken by social movements engaged in campaigns around SD and ESD. The definition is also ahistorical in that it does not take account of the wider context which in the case of this book is provided by an analysis of the postcolonial condition. It will be argued in Chapter 6 that the emergence of modern education systems since colonial times is important for understanding the current path dependency that many education systems remain locked into. Secondly, the account ignores the salience of social relationships between different actors in the system, including the effects of different kinds of inequality. Thus, whilst the World Bank definition refers to rules, policies, and relationships of 'accountability', this is a thin, technocratic understanding of what are complex sets of social relationships between actors that are framed by unequal power relationships and characterised by intersecting regimes of inequality (see the following).

The understanding of education systems offered here, therefore, includes not only the institutions, stakeholders, policies, and funding mechanisms that have emerged since colonial times, both within the formal education system and in informal setting in civil society, but also the attendant social relationships, including those based on inequality that have shaped pedagogical processes in diverse settings. The book will consider specific sub-systems of education such as the curriculum, teacher training, and assessment as well as different sub-sectors, including formal schooling, Technical and Vocational Education and Training and Higher Education. Organisations such as schools, universities, and Technical and Vocational Education and Training (TVET) centres can also be considered as systems as can collectives such as groups of learners within a pedagogical space or communities of practice amongst practitioners. Besides education systems, other complex systems will be considered in the book and examples of these are set out in Box 2.1.

Box 2.1   Examples of complex systems referred to in the book

Developmental domains. These demarcate broad areas of social reality in relation to which sustainable development and education for sustainable development can be considered to occur. In much of the literature, SD is seen to emerge through the interactions between the economic, social, and environmental domains (e.g. Sachs 2015). In subsequent chapters, discussion will focus in particular on the domains of the economy, politics, and civil society as well as those of violence, culture, and of the environment. Each domain will be described in broad terms and considered in relation to how they have co evolved in relation to education systems. In the context of globalisation, domains can operate across a number of interrelated scales from the global to the local (Walby 2009).

Regimes of governance. These will be discussed in later chapters in relation to the ways in which education governance takes place at a global and regional scale with implications for national policy agendas. Two global governance regimes are discussed in particular, namely, the 'Education for All' and the 'Education for Sustainable Development' regimes whilst *Agenda 2063* and CESA are considered as examples of regional governance regimes. The book adopts the most well-known definition of governance regimes as 'sets of implicit or explicit principles, norms, rules, and decision-making procedures around which actors' expectations converge in a given area of international relations' (Krasner 1982).[2] Understood as complex systems, regimes comprise networks of actors comprising multilateral institutions, donors, national and regional governments and organisations in global civil society including international NGOs, and religious and philanthropic organisations. These are overlain and cut across by intersecting regimes of inequality. Regimes are considered to have changed when there is change to norms and principles. 'Tipping points' that can lead to a change from one regime to another can be precipitated by crisis or brought about by the rise of a new hegemon, i.e. a new, dominant state or collection of nation states that challenge the principles and norms of existing regimes and/or introduce a new regime.

Regimes of inequality operate within and between domains and governance regimes and cut across social systems such as education and health. Walby (2009) describes different kinds of 'regimes of inequality' that can themselves be understood as self-generating/self-reproducing systems linked to the operation of different kinds of power. In Chapter 4, an effort will be made to outline the emergence of different regimes of inequality that impinge on education in Africa and that arise from the operation of different forms of structural and discursive (productive) power. These include regimes of inequality based on class, race/ethnicity, gender, and rurality. Understanding each regime as being implicated in the development of different domains allows for an appreciation of their full ontological depth. Gender inequality, for example, cannot be understood without appreciating the gendered nature of labour markets, the position of women in relation to the polity, and how gender is constructed through different Western and African cultural traditions. Neither can it be understood outside of an appreciation of gendered violence which has both a public side (e.g. sexualised violence in the context of war or as an everyday occurrence in institutions, including education) and a private side (i.e. domestic violence). Importantly, regimes of inequality are not reducible to each other. Rather, they co-evolve as systems of classification and oppression. They need to be understood in the way that they intersect and mutually constitute each other at the level of individual and group experiences and identities.

Discursive systems. Attention will be given to the role of overlapping discourses in shaping education policy concerning ESD. In the context of this book, discourses are considered as systems of signification and meaning. The book will consider the effects of global and regional policy discourses on African education and training systems. Besides policy discourses, the book will seek to understand the influence of different kinds of knowledge systems (Davis and Sumara 2006). These include the formal disciplines which operate as systems of specialised knowledge and local and indigenous knowledge systems that may not have the same degree of specialisation (see Chapter 8).

Knowing systems. The idea is taken from Davis and Sumara (2006) who contrast knowing systems with knowledge systems. As will be discussed in Chapter 9, knowing systems comprise systems and processes linked to the act of knowing and incorporate both the cognitive and situated sociocultural dimensions of learning.

Natural systems. Reference is made in the book to a range of natural systems, including environmental systems and different kinds of natural habitats and ecosystems. These comprise the environmental domain along with the social institutions, including education, that are implicated in defining the relationship between human beings and the natural world (see Chapter 4). Although not a central focus for this book, reference will also be made to the operation of biological systems including the working of the brain, but also other bodily systems that need to be sustained if learners are to learn effectively. At a practical level, this draws attention to the importance of natural phenomena such as nutrition and sleep on the ability to learn as well as the need for light to be able to study at home. It draws attention to the physical barriers to learning linked, for example, to the physical demands of having to walk many miles to school every day. It also raises often controversial questions about the complex relationship between individual's genetic make-up and processes of learning. Some of these are explored in Chapter 9 in relation to the influence of scientific racism on understandings of development. Consideration of the importance of biological systems, however, should not be confused with biological determinism. In keeping with the general view systems as co-evolving in relation to each other, the relationship between natural and social systems is considered non-linear, multi-causal, and multi-directional, and in order to be understood it needs to be informed by ethically informed empirical enquiry.[3]

Although each of the preceding systems identified are very different in terms of the aspect of social reality, they also describe in their temporal and spatial dimensions, they all nonetheless share characteristics of complex systems. Drawing in particular on Cairney's (2012) and Walby's (2009) work, these characteristics may be summarised as follows:

A complex system cannot be explained simply by breaking it down into its component parts because those parts are interdependent. Elements interact with each other, communicate and combine to produce systemic behaviour (Cairney 2012). An example from the natural sciences is how the various components that make up a human cell work together to produce cell-like behaviour. The elements that comprise a social system such as education include both institutions and sets of social relationships, including regimes of inequality (see the following). With respect to education systems, system-level phenomena such as an overall improvement in the quantity and quality of the skills and competencies produced in support of sustainable development or greater gender equity cannot be explained by focusing on individual elements of the system in isolation such as teacher training, the curriculum, assessment, educational governance, processes of teaching and learning, etc. Rather, whilst the individual nature of these elements is important to understand in its own right, it is how they combine and cohere to produce improved outcomes that is most important to grasp.

Complex systems are self-organising (i.e. they exhibit autopoiesis) and the behaviour of complex systems is difficult (or impossible) to predict. Systems exhibit 'non-linear' dynamics produced by feedback loops in which some forms of energy or action are dampened in a way that preserves equilibrium in the system (negative feedback) while others are amplified in a way that destabilises the system (positive feedback).[4] In the natural world, the process of homeostasis by which the body regulates its temperature in relation to changes in the temperature of the external environment is an example of a negative feedback loop whilst processes contributing to global warming (e.g. where warming increases the amount of water vapour in the atmosphere leading to further warming) is an example of positive feedback. Learning, whether conceived at an individual or at a group level, potentially involves negative and positive feedback loops. For example, a learner who is in the process of trying to understand a particular theory or concept may through processes of active learning/experimentation or though formative feedback from the teacher or peers find out that some of her understandings are incorrect leading her to modify some of her initial understandings (negative feedback). Subsequently, she may through the same process of feedback find positive reinforcement for her emerging understanding such that her learning develops exponentially (positive feedback).

Small actions can have large effects and large actions can have small effects. A well-known phenomenon within the natural sciences is the changes that can potentially be brought about to global weather systems through a small action such as a butterfly moving its wings in the amazon. Similarly, an apparently large action such as changes in the way that the production of greenhouse gases are regulated may end up having a minimal impact on emissions of greenhouse gases, especially if not all countries that produce large amounts of greenhouse gases sign up for the agreement. Within education, there is abundant evidence of large-scale system reform having negligible effects on learning outcomes. Conversely, the cumulative actions of educators can have a profound effect. For instance, individual teacher expectations have been shown to favour certain groups, including middle-class learners, as part of a virtuous cycle in which the confidence gained by learners on account of their teachers' higher expectations has a positive effect on aspirations and achievement which in turn feeds back positively to reinforce these high teacher expectations. Conversely, if individual teachers have low expectations of certain groups of learners, for example, in relation to the perceived poorer aptitude of girls in science and mathematics, this can have a cumulative effect on the aspirations and confidence of girls towards those subject areas which in turn limits learning outcomes and leads to having less women involved in these professions who could also potentially act as role models for future generations of girls.

Complex systems are particularly sensitive to initial conditions that produce a long-term momentum or 'path dependence'. Within economics, path dependency theory is used to illustrate how economies become locked into certain trajectories for sustained periods of time. For example, in Chapter 4, consideration will be given to how a range of factors have served to lock African economies into a development pathway of neoliberalism and dependency. Similarly, many existing features of education systems in Africa can be traced back to colonial times where they were designed to cater for elites and this orientation, as we will see, has proved very difficult to change. Similarly, as Pritchett (2013) notes, it has proved difficult to change the path dependency of education systems from one that is geared towards increasing access under the old MDG regime to one that is principally focused on improving learning outcomes as implied by SDG4.

Complex systems exhibit 'emergence' or behaviour that evolves from the interaction between elements. As is suggested below, learning emerges as a consequence of interactions between different kinds of complex systems from those that constitute the biological make-up and physical environment of an individual learner to those that govern the pedagogical context, including classroom interaction and language and those that define education policy. At the level of the education system itself, change emerges not only as consequence of the interaction of different elements within the education system but also as a consequence of interactions between the education systems and other economic social and environmental systems. Important here is the idea of co-evolution – that system properties emerge through multi-directional and multi-causal processes of interaction. In Chapter 4, it will be suggested that the emergence of modern education systems has been the consequence of complex interactions between at least six domains rather than being determined by one (e.g. the economy). Importantly, human agency is also an emergent quality that is both shaped by the constraints provided by different economic, social, and environmental factors and has the capacity to shape these in turn, for example, through forms of collective action.

Systems may contain 'strange attractors' or demonstrate extended regularities of behaviour which are liable to change radically. Biological systems, for example, are often described as exhibiting periods of 'punctuated equilibria' in which long periods of stability are interrupted by short bursts of change.[5] System change in this regard may be brought about by 'tipping points'. These might include processes of incremental change that build up to produce a dramatic change. The 2008 global financial crisis, for example, constituted a tipping point in the global financial system that led to changes in economic policy in many countries. An educational example is the observed washback effect from international assessment regimes such as PISA that can prompt processes of system reform in countries that do not perform well in these assessments.

Systems emerge and develop within a 'fitness landscape' that is provided by their interactions with other systems. The terminology of 'fitness landscape' comes originally from evolutionary biology and refers to the nature of the environment and the existence of factors that either facilitate or hinder the emergence and development of systems. Systems do not saturate their space but rather operate in an environment comprised of other systems in relation to which they co-evolve. This allows for a conceptualisation of multiple forms of social relations and the interaction of multiple regimes of inequality within systems such as education. Education systems in African countries are thus understood to co-evolve with other systems that constitute the fitness landscape in relation to which the dynamics of the education system emerge. In the context of this book, these other systems are multiple and give rise to the 'postcolonial condition' in education. A fluid conception of systems allows for systems to be positioned in relation to each other in different ways, depending on the aspect of social reality that is being considered. In Chapter 3, for example, SD will be presented as emerging from the interaction of six overlapping but non-nested domains in order to emphasise the non-deterministic nature of the interactions involved. Elsewhere systems will be presented as nested. A fluid nested understanding of social systems allows for social relations to be explored at different scales. The idea of nested systems, however, should not be taken to imply a hierarchy in terms of causality, as open social systems interpenetrate each other in complex and unpredictable ways.

Understanding and researching complex systems

It will be argued in Chapter 10 that bringing about system change requires drawing on different kinds of evidence to inform processes of iterative, adaptive problem-solving. Working from a complex systems perspective, Snowden and Boone (2007) have identified four kinds of contexts that leaders have to operate in (these same types of context might equally be encountered by other actors, including educators, learners, community members, or others). In simple contexts, cause equals effect. This is the realm of the known. In education, this might relate, for example, to dealing with relatively minor administrative irregularities through the application of known procedures. Complicated contexts are the realm of expert analysis that deals with the known unknowns. Although they are complicated, the problems are still ultimately solvable provided the right mix of expertise is at hand and the right intervention is put in place that may also be replicable. An example might be constructing new classrooms as a means to increase access to education. Complex contexts, on the other hand, are the realm of the unknown unknowns. They are spaces that fit the characteristics of aforementioned complex systems above.

Complex contexts give rise to 'wicked problems', i.e. problems that are hard to define and generally resistant to an agreed solution (Rittel and Webber 1973; Head and Alford 2015). Solving the learning crisis in African education which lies at the heart of global and regional policy agendas is a classic example of a wicked problem.[6] The role of leaders in the face of these kinds of problems is to create the conditions for new patterns to emerge, including increasing levels of communication and interaction. Expertise is useful but not essential in these contexts as much as experience of solving complex problems and patience. Finally, there are contexts of chaos characterised by tremendous turbulence with no clear cause and effect relationship, which makes searching for them fruitless. It is the realm of the unknowable. In educational terms, this might equate to education systems in countries emerging from conflict and/or other kinds of emergency and demand a more command and control approach to bring together different interests with the aim of getting the system back to a state of complexity (Snyder 2013; Davies 2004a). The implications for managing system change are discussed in more detail in Chapter 10. Here the emphasis is on the deeper epistemological questions of how we can come to know through different kinds of enquiry how systems work and the potential for different kinds of knowledge and understanding in predicting system change.

In this respect, Morin (2008) distinguishes between 'restricted' and 'general' complexity. The former relates to approaches to understanding social systems such as education as being complex but that nonetheless treat them as being complicated, i.e. they rely on 'scientific' (i.e. positivist) ways of observing and interpreting reality and assume that complex relationships can be reduced to linear causal relationships between elements (Byrne and Callaghan 2014).[7] The enormous faith on the part of major donors in the use of quasi-scientific methods and, in particular, randomised control trials (RCTs) as a means to understand education systems is an example of a restricted approach to understanding complexity. Similarly, the use of linear regression models to seek to determine the causal significance of different inputs and processes on learning outcomes assumes linear relationships between elements. Neither takes account of the dynamic and emergent nature of systems such as schools.

By way of contrast, 'general complexity' starts from an assumption of the multi-causal and non-linear nature of change and the importance of context.[8] In adopting a general complexity approach, the book is informed at a philosophical level by 'complex realism' (Byrne and Callaghan 2014). This brings together Bhaskar's understanding of critical realism[9] (see Tikly 2015, for a discussion of critical realism in relation to comparative and international education) with an understanding of the nature of complex systems. Space does not allow for a full exposition of complex realism. Key aspects that are relevant for the discussion in this book are the recognition of the existence of a reality that can exist outside of human experience of that reality. However, reality is conceived as having multiple levels. The 'empirical' refers to those aspects that are observed through different kinds of empirical enquiry, whilst the level of the 'actual' refers to the world of events and phenomena. Underlying the actual for Bhaskar are the deep causal mechanisms that give rise to observable events, which he describes as depth reality and have a more stable, intransigent quality, i.e. unlike more transient events in the actual and empirical domains, they are more regular and predictable in their nature and effects. In evolutionary theory, for example, 'natural selection' is the causal mechanism identified by Darwin as lying behind the origin of species. In Marxism, the nature of social reality and historical change is linked to the underlying mechanism of class struggle. For the anti-colonial activist, Franz Fanon, overcoming the lingering effects of colonialism, relies on a cathartic moment on the part of the oppressed in which they recognise and overcome the psychological damage caused by racism. For complex realists, it is the task of research to uncover these deeper lying causal mechanisms that can provide explanatory purchase on the world of events.

Recognising complexity also requires drawing on different disciplinary and methodological approaches. In this regard, complex realism seeks to navigate a third way between positivism and interpretivism. For positivists, reality equates to what can be rigorously and objectively observed and measured using 'gold standard', scientific techniques and increasingly, randomised control trials. For complex realists, these kinds of techniques may be valuable for understanding the linear relationships between elements in complicated systems but are less useful in understanding relationships that are likely to be non-linear such as those implied by positive and negative feedback loops. Further, however sophisticated the research design (e.g. however large the sample, or however many arms are used to account for multiple possible causal relationships), it is impossible to devise a trial to follow the 'ceaseless, self-generated, emergent change' that characterise complex systems undergoing significant flux (Pawson 2013, 233). In this respect, complex realism is consistent with interpretivism in recognising the socially constructed and fallible nature of our understanding of social reality. Complex realism is, however, also critical of the relativism implicit in some forms of interpretivism that valorising the perspectives of diverse individuals and groups denies the existence of a single reality that exists independently of the actors themselves.

For complex realists, what needs to be tested through research is the underlying theory of change within a system. This is necessarily an iterative process of theory building, identifying the various causal mechanisms implied by theories and conducting research that can prove or refute these. Given that there are often multiple theories that can explain system change, the task is to identify the explanations that have the 'best fit' to reality. Seeking to develop theoretical understanding of the underlying nature of causation and change in systems requires drawing on a range of relevant qualitative and quantitative techniques, each with their own 'gold standard'.[10] Thus, quantitative methods can provide what complex realists describe as a 'surface actuality' of associations between elements. If analysis is based on longitudinal data, then for a system with a relatively enduring path dependency such as education, quantitative data can provide a useful insight into changes in the relationships between elements over time. This is especially the case where the validity of the constructs used to develop indicators in quantitative research can be tested for their relevance for different contexts through careful qualitative research (Byrne and Callaghan 2014; Danermark 2002; Pawson 2002).

Other forms of analysis have been identified as fruitful for exploring system change. For example, forms of actor network analysis (drawing on qualitative and quantitative techniques) have often been used to identify complex relationships between actors in a system. Some of the more recent work on the development of the privatisation agenda in international education has focused on the influence of different private sector actors and advocates of marketisation in education linked to their increasingly central position in policy-making networks that also include governments and donors (Ball 2012; Olmedo 2014, 2017; Verger, Fontdevila, and Zancajo 2016).[11] Other ways of understanding the nature and extent of relationships between individuals, groups, and institutions within a system are provided by qualitative approaches, including narrative inquiry that can seek to trace unfolding relationships over time. Action research and knowledge co-production techniques are also often considered useful in investigating complex systems because they are led by actors centrally involved in implementing change at different levels of the system from the whole system down to the classroom level. As will be discussed in Chapter 10 where the focus is on system change, processes of Problem-Driven Iterative Adaptation (PDIA) hold considerable promise for engaging multiple actors with different interests in processes of change within complex systems.[12]

Also discussed in Chapter 10 is the relevance of evidence derived from different kinds of assessment data. Some African countries are already involved in international assessments, including those involved in the *Southern African Consortium for Measuring Quality in Education* (SACMEQ) and the *Programme D'analyse des Systems Educators de la Confemen* (PASEC). A small number of countries, including South Africa, Ghana, and Botswana, also participate in the *Trends in International Maths and Science Study* (TIMMS) whist plans are underway to adapt the OECD's *Programme for International Student Assessment* (PISA) for low-income countries (the so-called PISA for development initiative). These assessment regimes have provided powerful motivations for policy reform and for policy borrowing (Crossley 2014). However, it will be argued in Chapter 10 that from a complex realist perspective, the data from these assessments need to be treated with caution. This is related in the African context to the difficulties of collecting and analysing the data required for these assessments and the resultant reliability of the data. It is also linked to the need to be clear about the parameters used in comparing diverse systems.[13]

In developing its own arguments, the book will seek to draw together different kinds of evidence to shed light on complex wicked problems and propose various theoretical explanations of underlying causality that provide the 'best fit' for interpreting this evidence. Alternative theoretical explanations are offered depending on the nature of the problem being identified. These include theories concerning the nature of the postcolonial condition, the nature of curriculum and of pedagogy, theories of learning, and theories of system change. As with all attempts to reflect reality, however, the account is necessarily partial and fallible. It is hoped nonetheless that the insights generated will be useful for researchers and practitioners interested in realising complex change.

A further implication of a complex realist approach is a recognition of the role of values and emotions in the research process. Whereas positivists stress the value-free and objective nature of the research process, complex realists, like interpretivists, argue the inevitably value-laden nature of research. This is manifested, for example, in decisions about what kinds of research to fund, the way that research questions and hypotheses are defined and framed, the nature of the power relations implicit in the research process itself and the interests at stake, and in the way that research findings are taken up and used to support policy (Tikly 2015). The upshot for complex realists is that rather than try to assert the 'objective' nature of research, it is necessary to be suitably reflexive about the potential fallibility of research findings and about the role of different interests in the research process. It is also important to be explicit about the ethical basis of research and to be prepared to open this up for scrutiny. It is in this spirit that the book will make clear in Chapter 3 the view of social and environmental justice that has informed the development of the book and upon which many of the key arguments are based.

Conclusion

The chapter has provided an overview of complexity theory and ideas relating to the nature of complex systems that will both explicitly and implicitly inform the remainder of the book. It has been argued that complexity theory provides a useful lens at a deep ontological level for conceiving natural and social reality and the nature of change. It has also been argued that applying complexity theory to the African context requires a critical take on complex systems that acknowledges the workings of unequal power relationships and of regimes of inequality, themselves understood as complex and irreducible systems of oppression. Finally, the chapter has made the case for a metatheoretical understanding of complex change based on complex realism. Building on the insights of this chapter, attention will turn in Chapter 3 to a discussion of the meaning of a transformative ESD.

Notes

1 For example, in Chapter 4, the 'postcolonial condition' in Africa will be explained in terms of an understanding of complex globalisation in which Africa's position in relation to global processes from the time of colonialism to the present day will be considered in relation to the co-evolution of six domains of development that will themselves be understood as complex interacting systems. The operation of power within each domain gives rise to complex, intersecting regimes of inequality. Chapters 5–7 will consider how ESD is contested in policy through the contradictory interactions between different discourses about education and development understood as complex systems of signification and meaning. In the second part of the book, pedagogical and curricula processes will be conceived in terms of the interaction between different systems of knowing and of knowledge, respectively. Consideration of pedagogy involves an understanding of complex systems in the human brain and the environment that are implicated in cognition as well as systems of language and patterns of interaction within the sociocultural context (including the operation of regimes of inequality) in which processes of teaching and learning are situated. Similarly, contestations over the curriculum are considered in terms of sometimes competing and unequal Western and indigenous knowledge systems. In the final chapter, the education system itself will be presented in terms of interrelated sub-systems and as co-evolving in relation to other institutions such as health and each of the six domains of development. The chapter will also develop a model of a future education system as a complex learning system which is offered as an approach towards implementing education for socially and environmentally just development.

2 For our purposes, principles are factors which guide the purpose of action of governments and institutions. In the case of EFA, they comprise the underlying view of education and development, including the rationale for investment in education. Norms determine what general behaviour is legitimate in pursuing a particular regime's goals. The rules are closely related to norms and particularise the actual rights and obligations of governments and institutions in a regime. In the case of EFA, they include consideration of the specific funding mechanisms that have been used. Finally, decision-making procedures are also closely linked to norms and refer to the mechanisms within and between governments and institutions through which decisions are made. As has been pointed out, there are overlaps and it is not always easy to clearly distinguish between principles, norms, rules, and decision-making procedures (Haggard and Simmons 1987).

3 An example is in relation to debates about epigenetics which focus on the complex interactions between the way that genes are expressed across generations and the natural environment.

4 It should be noted that the terms 'positive' and 'negative' are not being used in a normative sense here to describe 'good' or 'bad' change processes but are used to indicate the type of feedback in operation in a system.

5 An example from physics is that of a pendulum that after being momentarily disrupted in its swing soon reverts to its usual rhythm.

6 It involves seeking to reconcile different understandings of how the crisis is understood in the first place (e.g. a failure of the system to produce sufficient human capital, a failure to ensure the rights of all learners to a good-quality education, and/or as a failure to develop the competencies and values that are required to support sustainable development). These in turn may be linked to differing views

and emphases concerning the moral purpose of education (e.g. education as a means to ensure economic prosperity, as basic human right, and/or as a contribution to more environmentally sustainable and socially just societies). It is also difficult to agree upon a solution to solving the crisis (e.g. introducing more accountability into the system, ensuring equality of opportunity, or attending better to the affective goals of education). This is not to say that wicked problems cannot be tackled. They can but tackling them has different implications for the way that we understand social systems.

 7 Furthermore, rather than see human agency as itself complex and multiply determined, the tendency is to reduce human interactions to a series of basic assumptions such as those that inform rational action theory in economics in which motivations are reduced to individual self-interest.

 8 The importance of context has often been emphasised in the study of international and comparative education (Crossley, Broadfoot, and Schweisfurth 2011; Crossley and Jarvis 2001).

 9 See Tikly 2015 for a discussion of critical realism in relation to comparative and international education.

10 It also involves the judicious use of mixed methods, for example, testing the validity of the constructs used to develop indicators in quantitative research for different contexts through careful qualitative research (Byrne and Callaghan 2014; Danermark 2002; Pawson 2002).

11 Whilst very useful in identifying complex interactions between actors, these forms of analysis are less good at mapping changes in networks over time that is important for understanding the nature of emergence of different system elements.

12 A promising methodology relevant for the study of ESD as an example of a global education policy is the vertical case study approach adopted by Bartlett and Vavrus (Vavrus and Bartlett 2006; Bartlett and Vavrus 2017). It adopts a nested approach in which policy enactment within and across schools is considered in relation to how policy is formulated and implemented between the global and national levels in different country contexts. It therefore also allows for horizontal comparison between country and local contexts, including a consideration of how policy making is enacted and modified at school level. It is therefore consistent with the view of policy making as enactment that will be presented later. Crucially, Bartlett and Vavrus' approach also allows for a consideration of changes in policy making over time. Although the book does not draw explicitly on studies that have used this methodology, it is indicative of an overall approach for understanding

13 In this sense, it will be argued that it makes more sense to make comparisons between African education systems facing similar challenges and undergoing similar processes of change than comparing with, say, highly industrialised countries.

3   Towards a framework for conceptualising education for sustainable development

Introduction

The aim of this chapter is to begin to set out an alternative vision of ESD that can guide discussion in the remainder of the book. The chapter will start by considering how sustainable development (SD) can be understood in broad terms. Attention will then turn to developing an ethical basis for considering the role of education in relation to sustainable development. In particular, an attempt will be made to set out a view of social and environmental justice drawing on Sen's ideas of capability and Nancy Fraser's ideas about global justice but relating these to more recent scholarship on the meaning of environmental justice. It will be suggested that considering the role of education and training in relation to the development of valued capabilities for achieving sustainable livelihoods and the barriers and affordances available to different groups in society to develop valued capabilities and functionings provides a useful starting point for reconceptualising ESD.

The meaning of 'sustainable development' in global and regional policy agendas

Space does not allow for a full account of the development of SD as a discourse which has in any case been provided elsewhere (e.g. Elliot 2013). A summary of key milestones in the development of SD as a global policy discourse from the influential Stockholm Conference in 1972 and leading up to the adoption of the SDGs is provided in Box 3.1.

Box 3.1   Key milestones in the development of SD as a global policy discourse

1   The *United Nations Conference on the Human Environment*, held in Stockholm on 5–16 June 1972, first gave visibility to the idea of a need for a 'synthesis between development and environment' (UN 1972, 45).

2   The report of the *Club of Rome*, an international think tank comprised of leading industrialists, academics, and policy makers, entitled the *Limits of Growth* and produced in the same year (Meadows et al. 1972) highlighted the ecological consequences of the Western model of development and demonstrated for the first time that there are natural limits to economic growth.

3   The *Cocoyoc Declaration* (UN 1975) arising from a UN-sponsored meeting of experts in Cocoyoc, Mexico went even further in proposing 'eco-development' as a model for development.

4   The report of the World Commission on Environment and Development, entitled *Our Common Future* (WCED 1987) and otherwise known as the *Brundtland report* after the Norwegian Prime Minister who chaired it, has arguably been most responsible for propelling ideas about SD centre stage in global debates. The report famously defined sustainable development as 'development that meets the needs of the present without compromising the ability of future generations to meet their own needs' (WCED 1987, 47).

5   General Assembly resolution 44/228 of 22 December 1989 called for a UN Conference on Environment and Development and on the acceptance of the need to take a balanced and integrated approach to environment and development questions.

6   The resulting UN conference on the environment and development in Rio in 1992 (otherwise known as the *Rio Earth Summit*) resulted in the adoption of *Agenda 21* which argued that 'integration of environment and development concerns and greater attention to them will lead to the fulfilment of basic needs, improved living standards for all, better protected and managed ecosystems and a safer, more prosperous future' (UNCED 1992, 1). An important outcome of the summit was an agreement on the *Climate Change Protocol* which in turn led to the *Kyoto Protocol* (UN 1998) and the *Paris Agreement* (UN 2015a).

7   The adoption of the Millennium Development Goals (MDGs) marked a turning point in the international development arena, where, more than ever before, agencies, institutions, corporations, and nations collaborated in a bid 'to address the deep and interconnected economic, social, and environmental challenges the world faces' (Sachs 2012, 1001).

8   A decade after the Rio Earth Summit, the *Johannesburg Summit* (otherwise known as Rio+10) adopted the *Johannesburg Declaration* which focused particularly on 'the worldwide conditions that pose severe threats to the sustainable development of our people, which include: chronic hunger; malnutrition; foreign occupation; armed conflict; illicit drug problems; organized crime; corruption; natural disasters; illicit arms trafficking; trafficking in persons; terrorism; intolerance and

incitement to racial, ethnic, religious and other hatreds; xenophobia; and endemic, communicable and chronic diseases, in particular HIV/ AIDS, malaria and tuberculosis'. (UN 2002, 1).

9 The Conference on Sustainable Development in 2012 marked the twentieth anniversary of the Rio Conference. The resulting document, *The Future We Want*, renewed participants commitment to *Agenda 21* 'and to ensuring the promotion of an economically, socially and environmentally sustainable future for our planet and for present and future generations' (UN 2012, 1). The text includes language supporting the development of Sustainable Development Goals (SDGs).

10 The adoption of the 17 Sustainable Development Goals (SDGs) by the United Nations in November 2015 and enshrined in *Transforming Our World: The 2030 Agenda for Sustainable Development* (UN 2015c).

Elliot (2013) has recently provided a review of different definitions of SD. As the author explains, there have been literally hundreds of definitions. The most prominent is that provided by the Brundtland Report (WCED 1987). Written in the dominant development language of the time, it couches sustainability in terms of balancing the needs of existing and future generations with the need to preserve the environment. As several critics have pointed out, the definition is vague and lacks specificity, for example, about the 'needs' that are required by existing and future generations and the nature of the legacy that should be left to future generations, etc. Critics of the term have also focused on the use of the term 'sustainable' in that it is not clear what is to be sustained. If treated uncritically, it is suggested, it can lead to an endorsement of the status quo when what is required is a much more radical transformation (Elliot 2013; Blewitt 2018; Sneddon, Howarth, and Norgaard 2006, for example).

Whilst the vagueness of the term may be perceived as a weakness, it can also be considered as a source of strength because of the potential for the term to unite disparate interests around a common global agenda. In this regard, SD can be conceived as a 'metafix' 'that will unite everybody from the profit-minded industrialist and risk minimising subsistence farmer to the equity-seeking social worker, the pollution concerned or wild-lifer loving First Worlder, the growth-minimising policy maker, the goal oriented bureaucrat, and therefore, the vote-counting politician' (Lélé 1991). Indeed, from the review of key milestones above, it is clear that SD has operated as something of a 'floating signifier' that has shifted in form and emphasis, depending on the wider discourse of development in which it is embedded. In the context of contemporary global and regional agendas, for example, SD is articulated with sometimes contradictory discourses centred around environmental protection, the idea of inclusive growth (see Chapter 7 for a discussion of this concept), realising human rights and, in the context of *Agenda*

2063, with pan-Africanism. It is this ubiquitous quality of the term that has been important for the recent rise to hegemonic status of SD as a policy discourse. It is also the contested nature of the term that makes it necessary to clarify how SD and ESD are understood in the context of the book (see the following). In addition to the aforementioned criticisms, it will also be suggested in subsequent pages that dominant versions of SD are often reductionist in their understanding of development. This includes in the way that domains of development are conceived but also in failure to incorporate fully an understanding of the nature of power and inequality in development. It will also be suggested that although SD is most often couched in terms of a rights-based framework, it is insufficient in terms of specifying the ethical basis on which the idea of SD is based.

The meaning of education for sustainable development

Once again, a full account of the history of ESD is beyond the scope of this chapter, although readers are referred to the wider literature (see, for example, Fien, Mclean, and Park 2009; Wals and Kieft 2010; Tikly 2013). Key moments in the development of ESD are captured in Box 3.2.

Box 3.2   Key milestones in the emergence of ESD as a policy discourse

- The report of the *UN Stockholm Conference* in 1972 states that 'for the purpose of attaining freedom in the world of nature, man must use knowledge to build, in collaboration with nature, a better environment' (UN 1972, 3) and as such environmental education was promoted, though there was disagreement as to how this should be implemented.

- Education features strongly in the *Cocoyoc Declaration* of 1974 as a means for promoting eco-development. Education is identified as not only a basic need but also as necessary for providing a critical understanding and practical knowledge of the ecosystem and its relationship with social and economic structures (UN 1975).

- The UN organises its first intergovernmental conference on environmental education in Tbilisi, Georgia, USSR in 1977. The *Tbilisi Declaration* recommended the adoption of criteria that would help to guide efforts to develop environmental education at national, regional, and global levels (UNESCO 1977).

- Education is cited in the 1987 *Brundtland Report* as integral to sustainable development. Gender parity and making literacy universal are set as goals and expanding education beyond primary school is deemed necessary for 'improv[ing] skills necessary for pursuing sustainable

---

development' (WCED 1987, 96). Quality education is characterised as practical, flexible, community-based, and comprehensive with environmental education integrated into all aspects of the curriculum.

- The 1990 *Jomtien Declaration* (Unesco 1990) arising from the UN World Conference on Education for All in Jomtien, Thailand sets out principles aimed at providing access to all to a good-quality education from pre-primary, primary, secondary, tertiary, vocational, and adult basic education.

- The *Rio Earth Summit Declaration on Environment and Development* cites education as 'critical for promoting sustainable development and improving the capacity of the people to address environment and development issues. . . . It is critical for achieving environmental and ethical awareness, values and attitudes, skills and behavior consistent with sustainable development and for affective public participation in decision-making' (UNCED 1992, 3).

- The Jomtien principles were reaffirmed and developed into a *Framework for Action* (Unesco 2000) at the Dakar World Conference on Education for All in Senegal a decade later.

- The education *Millennium Development Goals*, also in 2000, emphasise a more reductionist education agenda focusing on access to primary education and gender parity at levels of education and training.

- The *Johannesburg Summit* in 2002 adopted a resolution to start the *UN Decade for Education and Sustainable Development* (DESD) from January 2005. The purpose of the decade was to create a world 'where everybody has the opportunity to benefit from education and learn the values, behaviour and lifestyles required for a sustainable future and for positive societal transformation' (UN 2002, 3).

- The decade resulted in the adoption in 2013 of the *Global Action Programme on ESD* which was launched at the *UNESCO World Congress on ESD* in 2014 (UNESCO 2017a).

- The outcomes of these conferences fed into the inclusion of ESD as a target in the *Muscat Agreement on Education for All* (and subsequently adopted by the *World Education Forum* for EFA) (UNESCO 2014a).

- In identifying priorities, the *Incheon Declaration and Framework for Action* (UNESCO 2015a) prefigures the goals of the education SDG. It blends the emphasis in the EFA movement on access to a good-quality education with an explicit reference to ESD.

As is the case with SD, ESD has also operated as something of a floating signifier in policy discourse since the 1970s and the idea of ESD has historically been articulate with a variety of concerns. Chief amongst these have been a concern to promote environmental education. Although much of this literature relates to the global North, there have been efforts to develop environmental education in Africa, although these have been more limited (Chapter 7). ESD has also been closely articulated with what Jickling (1992) has described as 'adjectival educations' ranging from education for peace, diversity, global citizenship, gender equality, etc. In relation to the development of the Education for All regime (Chapter 6), ESD has most closely been associated with the idea of lifelong learning and with a rights-based approach. In the context of contemporary global and regional agendas, it can be seen to knit together a concern with the quality of education and the focus on learning with some of these historical concerns. As with SD, there is a need to clarify how ESD is conceptualised in the present book. As with the attempt to clarify the use of SD, however, this will involve taking account of the ethical basis of SD as well as the operation of regimes of inequality that limit the capability to learn for different groups of disadvantaged learners.

The meaning of social and environmental justice

It will be recalled from Chapter 1 that the SDGs are underpinned by the five principles of people, planet, prosperity, peace, and partnership. These principles can be seen to be grounded in a rights-based approach in that they take as a point of reference inalienable human rights. Whilst providing a useful rallying call for support for the SDGs, the principles do not in themselves establish the ethical basis for the rights they seek to promote and in a way that can assist in understanding how the principles themselves arise and the processes by which they are interpreted and reinterpreted in different geographical and cultural contexts. The danger is that they are seen as essentialised categories, imposed in a top-down way and lacking in contextual meaning and significance.

A starting point for considering the ethical basis for sustainable development comes from the capability approach of Sen and Nussbaum. Described as a 'species of the rights-based approach',[1] it sees human development principally in terms of the development of human capabilities (opportunity freedoms) that enable individuals and groups to achieve valued functionings (beings and doings) that they have reason to value and that will contribute to well-being and human flourishing. In the context of the shift to SD as the dominant development paradigm, Sen (2013) has recently argued for an expansion of this idea to take account of the capabilities of future generations and the extent to which this necessitates a concern with environmental protection as inseparable and integral to the realisation of capabilities, both now and in the future. This goes beyond the concern with poverty alleviation as the meeting of basic needs as set out, for example, in the influential Brundtland Report (WCED 1987) to a concern with providing the opportunities and freedoms that enable individuals and groups to convert resources – now and in the future – in a way that supports human well-being and conserves the environment.

Sen argues forcefully that issues of freedom and of sustainability are inextricably linked and that sustainability can only be achieved through the realisation of human freedom. Whilst Sen is correct regarding the links between human freedom and sustainability, it is important to add some caveats. Firstly, to note that Sen himself sees the concept of human capability as a property of both individuals and groups (Sen 2009).[2] This is to understand that regimes of inequality represent sets of historically contingent social relationships based on unequal distribution of material and discursive power between groups and it is at a group level that many of the institutional and other barriers to realising human freedom become apparent and form the basis for group solidarity and action.

It is also important to recognise that Sen's is an anthropocentric view of capability, i.e. a view of capability as applying only to human beings. Nussbaum has begun to articulate a view of other species having capabilities linked to their inherent dignity. She goes on to explain:

> Each form of life is worthy of respect and it is a problem of justice when a creature does not have the opportunity to unfold its (valuable) power, to flourish in its own way and to lead a life with dignity.
>
> (Nussbaum 2006, 7).[3]

Extending this view, Schlosberg (2007, 142) argues that all 'individual animals, human and non-human – need not just some others of their own species, but a full environment, including non-sentient life and ecosystem relations, as part of their capability set in order to flourish' and that 'it is simply not possible to talk about the flourishing of individual animals without reference to the environment in which this flourishing is to occur' (ibid). Schlosberg argues that systems themselves have capabilities and functionings and might be considered 'agents for the work they do in providing the various capacities for their parts to function – i.e., purifying water, contributing oxygen, providing nutrition, sustaining temperature.[4] By focusing on the capabilities of living systems it is also possible to take account of the potentially harmful relationship between, for example, individual species of viruses and other species including human beings and the fight against deadly disease albeit within a recognition of the need to preserve the integrity of ecosystems as a whole.

At the heart of Sen's approach towards SD is that determining the capabilities and needs of existing and future generations requires processes of advocacy and informed public dialogue in which the interests of different groups are made transparent and open to public scrutiny. As has previously been argued (Tikly and Barrett 2013), Sen's ideas provide an important evaluative 'space' in this case for considering SD as a process of balancing the capabilities of existing and future generations and indeed of environmental systems. However, on their own, Sen's ideas about justice do not provide a means for considering the wider structural and discursive barriers that prevent some individuals and groups and indeed environmental systems from having their interests recognised in public policy. Here, it is argued that Fraser's understanding of global justice provides a multidimensional way of conceiving the barriers to social and environmental justice. Fraser defines justice as 'parity of participation.' She explains:

> According to this radical-democratic interpretation of the principle of equal moral worth, justice requires social arrangements that permit all to participate as peers in social life. Overcoming injustice means dismantling

institutionalized obstacles that prevent some people from participating on a par with others as full partners in social interaction.

(Fraser 2008, 16)

By institutionalised obstacles, Fraser is here referring to economic structures that deny access to resources that people need in order to interact with others as peers, institutionalised hierarchies of cultural value that may deny them the requisite standing, and exclusion from the community that is entitled to make justice claims on one another and the procedures that structure public processes of contestation.[5] Recognising issues of environmental justice also requires extending the view of parity of participation to include a consideration of the rights and capabilities of other species and of environmental systems (Schlosberg 2001, 2004, 2007).

Fraser draws attention to three dimensions of social justice, each related to one of the aforementioned institutional barriers. The first, redistribution, relates to access to different kinds of material resources or to services such as education and health. From the point of view of SD, distributive justice would also need to take account of the way that environmental benefits (in the form of access to natural resources) as well as risks (in the form of the effects of global warming, droughts, famines, pollution etc.) are distributed. As suggested in Chapter 4, it is an aspect of the postcolonial condition in Africa as elsewhere that disproportionate environmental risk often accrues to the most disadvantaged sections of society. In this sense, environmental inequalities cut across and reinforce other inequalities, including those based on class, race/ethnicity, gender, and disability.

The second of Fraser's dimensions, recognition, means first identifying and then acknowledging the claims of historically marginalised groups in the African context, including, for example, women, rural dwellers, victims of HIV/AIDS orphans, and vulnerable children, refugees, cultural, linguistic, religious, racial, and sexual minorities and indigenous groups. In the context of a transformative SD and ESD, this also means recognising the integrity and the right to flourish of other species and ecosystems, a view that is in keeping with many indigenous knowledge systems in Africa that have posited a more organic, symbiotic, and custodial relationship between human beings and the natural world (Maware and Mubaye 2016).[6] Closely related to recognitional justice is the idea of epistemic justice which is explored in the Chapter 8. Epistemic justice relates to the nature of the relationship between hegemonic, Western knowledge systems, and indigenous and local knowledge systems. It also draws attention to debates about what counts as 'legitimate' knowledge as well as which groups have access to different kinds of knowledge.

Participatory justice includes the rights of individuals and groups to have their voices heard in debates about social justice and injustice and to actively participate in decision-making. Importantly, for Fraser, this is a prerequisite for realising issues of redistribution and recognition. It also ties in with Sen's insistence on public participation and informed public dialogue as the basis for adjudication between justice claims. In relation to participatory justice, Fraser identifies two forms of misrepresentation. The first is related to issues of 'ordinary-political representation'. It is concerned with the nature of political rules and processes within nation states that deny some citizens the chance to participate fully in decision-making. The second form of misrepresentation is related to globalisation and has increasing significance for education in low-income countries because of the influence over national policy of global and regional agendas and frameworks. Fraser describes this as 're-framing'. Here, the injustice arises when the community's boundaries are drawn in such a way as to wrongly exclude some people from the chance to participate at all in its authorised contests over justice.

Schlosberg (2007) has considered how Fraser's and indeed Sen's views about the importance of participation might be extended to incorporate environmental and ecological concerns. Noting the obvious point that other species or natural systems do not have the same reasoning or communicative capacities to participate in processes of democratic deliberation, he nonetheless argues that the capabilities and flourishing of other species and natural systems can and ought to be the subject of public deliberation.[7] Such a view has important implications for education systems in creating a space for this understanding of the capabilities and needs of other species and of environmental systems. Nussbaum (Nussbaum 2006), for example, talks about the importance of imagination and storytelling in accessing the capabilities of other animals. All of the disciplines spanning the natural and social sciences, arts, and humanities have a positive role to play in this respect.

Drawing together the above discussion, it is useful to summarise what is meant by social and environmental justice in the context of this book.[8] At the most general level, and extending Fraser's earlier definition, social and environmental justice can be understood as putting in place social arrangements that permit existing and future generations to participate as peers in social life and that recognises the integrity of other species and of natural systems. Overcoming injustice means dismantling institutionalised obstacles that prevent some people from participating on a par with others as full partners in social interaction as well as barriers that prevent the well-being and flourishing of other species and of natural systems.

Defining transformative SD and ESD

From the preceding discussion and with reference to the discussion of the capability approach, it is now possible to define sustainable development as *socially and environmentally just development that supports the capabilities (i.e. opportunity freedoms) of existing and future generations and of natural systems to flourish.* Education for sustainable development is defined as *socially and environmentally just education that facilitates the capabilities of existing and future generations and of natural systems to flourish.* The implications of this view of ESD are set out in the chapters that follow.

Reconceptualising a transformative ESD

In much of the literature, SD is represented as involving the interaction of three domains of development, namely, the economic, the social, and the environmental (Elliot 2013). In the scholarly literature and in keeping with the discussion of the previous chapter, these have been represented in terms of complex, co-evolving systems (see, for example, Sachs 2015; Wells 2013). From the perspective of the present book, whilst a useful starting point, the understanding is considered to be overly simplistic. For example, the characterisation of 'social development' as a discrete domain elides the extent to which all development in which human beings are implicated is by its very nature social. It will be argued particularly in Chapter 7, for example, that the economic domain needs to be conceptualised as involving processes of production and exchange that are premised on (unequal) social relations of production. Similarly, the environmental domain is concerned not only with natural systems but also with how human beings interact with these systems and with how the relationship between human beings and the natural world is governed. The idea of social development in the literature also often bundles together domains that need to be considered in their own right such as the domain of the polity and of civil society as well as the domains of violence and of culture. In Chapter 4, unsustainable development will be understood as having arisen from the nature of the postcolonial condition in Africa and specifically as a consequence of the operation across six developmental domains, including those of the economy, polity, civil society, violence, culture, and the environment. These domains, it will be argued, are cut across by intersecting regimes of inequality, including those based on class, gender, race, ethnicity, and rurality. It is the operation of these regimes of inequality that in Fraser's terms limit the possibilities for different groups to realise distributive, recognitional, and representational justice. Concomitantly, the possibilities for transformative SD and for realising social and environmental justice will be seen to emerge as a consequence of policy enacted across these domains. For policy to be genuinely transformative, however, it must address the structural and discursive barriers inherent in the nature of the postcolonial condition and that give rise to unsustainable development. This understating of SD as emergent from the co-evolution of the various domains is captured in Figure 3.1.

Education and training as an example of a social institution can be seen to co-evolve with each of the aforementioned development domains. Given the understanding of the nature of co-evolution of complex open systems outlined in the previous chapter, and in contrast to dominant views of education in relation to development, the relationship between education and each domain is understood as multi-causal and multi-directional. A key argument developed in the book is that education and training cannot be seen in idealistic terms as a panacea for development as is often the case in modernisation and human capital inspired theories of development. Rather, the possibilities for a transformative ESD lie in the extent to which education and training policy can articulate with policy enacted across other domains as a whole so as to produce transformative

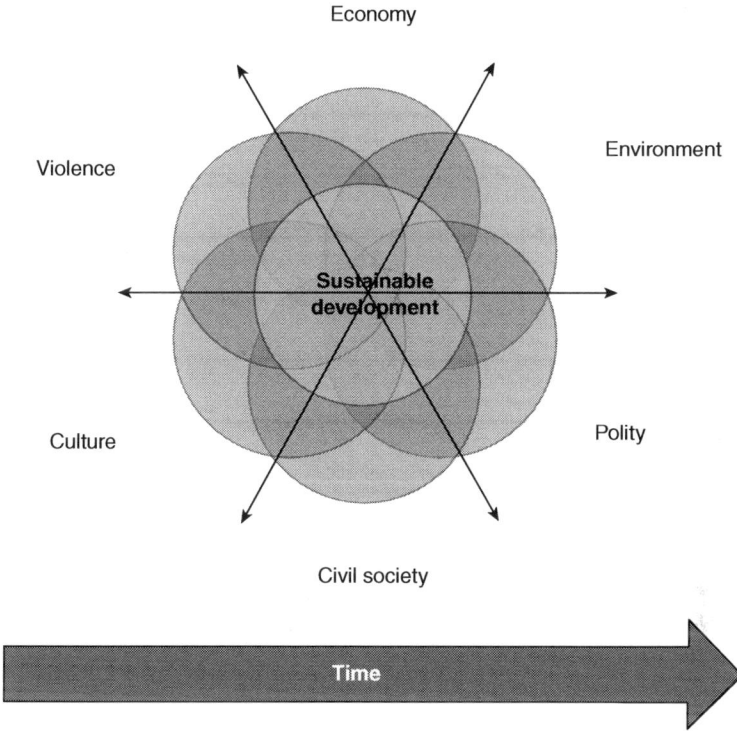

Figure 3.1 Domains of development showing cross-cutting, intersecting regimes of inequality.

sustainable development as understood in the previous section. This is necessarily a complex task and in the remainder of the book, attention will turn to a consideration of the conditions under which such an articulation might become possible.

Conclusion

The chapter has sought to develop an approach towards conceptualising a transformative ESD that is relevant for Africa. A critique of existing understandings of SD and ESD was provided focusing on the reductionist nature of mainstream accounts in terms of the underlying view of development, the extent to which issues of power and inequality are elided, and the lack of a clearly articulated ethical basis to guide transformative action. The second part of the chapter then set out such an ethical basis drawing on Sen's idea of capability and Fraser's understanding of global social justice. These were, however, also critiqued from an environmentalist perspective, drawing in particular on Schlosberg's work. The chapter concluded by setting out a what is intended to be a non-reductionist account of SD and ESD that takes account of Africa's position in the world, is sensitive to the variety of contexts represented by the African continent, and engages with issues of power and inequality. In the remainder of the book, an effort will be made to flesh out the conceptual framework provided in this chapter through a consideration of the implications of a transformative ESD for different areas of policy and practice.

Notes

1 As we have argued elsewhere, the capability approach is best seen as a 'species of the rights based approach' but with a stronger emphasis on establishing the ethical basis for rights through processes of informed public dialogue, mobilisation and advocacy rather than through the imposition of top-down rights-based agendas (Tikly and Barrett 2013).

2 This is significant in the context of this chapter because whilst it is important from an evaluative perspective to consider human capability at the level of the individual and in the context of the impact of intersecting regimes of inequality on individual freedom, it is also important to understand how regimes of inequalities impact the capabilities (agency freedoms) of different oppressed groups, including those based on class, race/ethnicity, indigeneity, gender, disability, etc.

3 Whilst it is important to take account of the rights of other species to flourish, Nussbaum's ideas have been critiqued from within the environmental tradition because by invoking animal dignity, she appears to be favouring only sentient beings (Schlosberg 2007). She has also been criticised for focusing on the rights of individual animals rather than on the integrity and flourishing of species as a whole and of ecosystems.

4 In this case, the central issue of ecological justice would be 'the interruption of the capabilities and functioning of a larger living system – what keeps it from transforming primary goods into capabilities, functioning, and the flourishing of the whole system' (p. 13). This view of environmental systems themselves having capabilities raises important considerations for educators and these are discussed further later.

5 Important to add here, however, is that an exclusive focus on institutional arrangements can detract from some of the other barriers that may prevent equal participation in social life. For example, besides institutions, discourses can have their own constitutive effects on what can and cannot be said, who can speak and with what authority, how our understanding of concepts such as education and development are shaped, and how individual and group identities are defined (see Chapter 3). Unterhalter (2007) also draws attention to the more informal, interactive networks and associations at the local, national, and global level that criss-cross institutional structures and processes but yet are often important in determining justice claims. Understanding the workings of different kinds of institutional and discursive power at different levels from the macro to the micro is important for the conceptualisation of regimes of inequality.

6 For Schlosberg (2007), it is this aspect of recognitional justice that sets his view of environmental justice apart for that of Nussbaum's in that the focus is on the flourishing of whole ecosystems rather than on the rights of individual animals. This also leads to a non-romanticised view of environmental flourishing in that, for example, being food for other living beings might form part of essence of functioning for some living things.

7 He argues that in 'applying a capabilities approach to nature, we do not need to have a particular animal or ecosystem express a desire for a particular functioning;

rather, we need to recognise a different type of agency – a potential, a process, or form of life illustrated by its history, ecology, integrity, and non-reason-based forms of communication' (Schlosberg 2007, 152).

8 Schlosberg (2007), following Sen, makes the point that definitions of concepts such as justice or capability are necessarily contextually bound and that it is in fact important to embrace the possibility of a plurality of definitions and understanding as to which aspects of social and environmental justice and which capabilities are particularly relevant across different contexts. Developing a pluralistic and context sensitive view of the meaning of social and environmental justice is important, for example, in the context of bringing together different kinds of social and environmental movements in struggles against injustice.

4 Globalisation and the postcolonial condition

Introduction

The aim of this chapter is to develop understanding of the nature of the postcolonial condition in Africa in relation to an account of complex globalisation. It is this understanding of the nature of Africa's changing relationship with global flows and networks since colonial times that provides a context for the remainder of the book. The chapter will commence by setting out in broad terms what is meant by the postcolonial condition and by complex globalisation. This will involve consideration of the nature of development itself in terms of the co-evolution of six overlapping domains of development. It will also involve consideration of different forms of power and the effects of intersecting regimes of inequality on limiting the possibilities for social and environmental justice. The second part of the chapter will then trace the arc of Africa's relationship to the global economy and the natural environment as well as the influence of the global polity, civil society, violence, and the cultural domain on processes of global governance since colonial times. Discussion will focus on the development of governance regimes in the context of contemporary globalisation as well as the emergence of developmental regionalism as a way of promoting African-led development and on the nature of the postcolonial state which circumscribes the possibilities for transformative change at a national level.

The nature of complex globalisation

Recent work by Sylvia Walby (2009, 2015) that draws on insights from complexity theory to develop an understanding of contemporary globalisation provides a useful starting point for considering the postcolonial condition in Africa. Like much existing scholarship on globalisation, however, the account is written from a Eurocentric perspective with little, if any, consideration given to the implications for the African continent. Here, insights have been reinterpreted to make them relevant for a discussion of Africa and synthesised with ideas from recent work on the political economy of Africa (e.g. Hoogvelt 1997; Ferguson 2006b; Mohan 2013; Ayers 2013).

The basic definition of globalisation referred to by Walby is taken from the seminal work of (Held et al. 1999) who define globalisation as

> a process (or set of processes) which embodies a transformation in the spatial organisation of social relations and transactions – assessed in terms of their extensity, intensity, velocity, and impact – generating transcontinental or interregional flows and networks of activity, interaction, and the exercise of power.
>
> (16)

Usefully for our purposes, Held *et al.* point out that forms of globalisation have occurred before and that colonialism can be interpreted as a previous form of globalisation that has been significant in giving rise to contemporary forms.[1] Held *et al.* (1999) understand contemporary globalisation which they interpret as coinciding with the end of the Second World War and the advent of the so-called development era, as historically unprecedented in terms of its extensity, intensity, velocity, and impact.[2]

Developing Held *et al.*'s argument, Walby (2009) argues that globalisation consists of uneven global flows of capital, trade, and people, an uneven development of global institutions, networks, and hegemons, and global civil societal waves – not a single uniform or linear process. In the language of complexity theory, this is to acknowledge more than one 'path dependency' in the way that globalisation has developed leading to different development trajectories, varieties of capitalism (see also Peck and Theodore 2007), forms of the state, and versions of modernity itself. In Walby's work, for example, she distinguishes between neoliberal and more social democratic versions of capitalism. In subsequent chapters, reference will be made to various development pathways in different eras, including differences, for example, between colonialism under the French and British colonisers, different development trajectories undertaken by nations in the post-independence phase, and differences in how development and modernity are conceived within pan-Africanism itself, including in *Agenda 2063*.

Walby (2009) following Held *et al.* (1999) argues that contemporary globalisation essentially involves the *deterritorialisation* and *reterritorialisation* of space. That is to say, rather than the nation states or the regions becoming 'irrelevant' as is suggested in some 'hyperglobalist' views of globalisation, they have been reconfigured in relation to the global scale.[3] As we will see, key moments in the de/reterritorialisation of space that are of relevance for Africa include the development of a diaspora as a consequence of slavery and migration, the advent of the so-called 'development era', the rise of pan-Africanism in the context of anti-colonial struggles, the 'hollowing out' of the state under neoliberalism, the emergence of regional developmentalism with the formation of first the OAU and then the AU, and the impact of climate change on the natural environment.

As Walby (2009) points out, contemporary globalisation is characterised by contesting global hegemons, especially the United States and the rising powers, as well as the emergence of global institutions, including the Bretton Woods financial institutions and the UN system. The period since the end of the Second World War has been marked by the emergence in Gramsci's (Gramsci 1992) terms of a dominant 'historical bloc'.[4] Taking up and adapting this concept, Hoogvelt (1997) describes sub-Saharan Africa as constituting a distinctive 'post-colonial formation', i.e. a distinctive mixture of economic, political, and cultural dynamics linked to Africa's position in the world and to the nature of regional responses to globalisation.

The current historical bloc has been described as representing a contradictory fusion of the politics of states and empire, that is, the United States and its allies and the interests of dominant factions of capital, including transnational corporations and finance capital (Harvey 2003). World order is, however, increasingly contested. Of particular relevance for Africa, for instance, is the emergence of the so-called rising powers that includes South Africa as one of the BRICS economies.[5] Also, relevant here are attempts to develop the African Union as a means for projecting African interests globally. As will be discussed below, however, an aspect of the postcolonial condition in Africa is the continued marginal position of African governments in relation to the global economy and processes of global governance.

Domains of development

Following Walby, it is argued that the development of flows, institutions, and waves involves the co-evolution of different domains. There is no assumption of a base-superstructure model as in classic Marxism or of a simple one-way impact of the economic on the rest. Walby draws attention to the multi-directional nature of change and the importance of considering how different domains 'co-evolve' rather than assume that change is unidirectional in nature.

It will be recalled from Chapter 2 that education systems can be said to 'co-evolve' with each domain in sometimes contradictory ways. Here the concept of 'articulation' (Hall 1985; Clarke 2015) is helpful for understanding the nature of the relationship between systems. In this respect, the education system and each of the six domains of development (also conceived as systems) can be said to 'articulate', i.e. to form a relatively stable correspondence over time, whether that be positive, negative, or critical. The nature of the correspondence is also contingent in that systems can disarticulate and rearticulate to form new relationships of correspondence. The target for analysis is to better understand the nature of these evolving relationships. The question of 'determination' at any point in time thus becomes an analytical one.

The upshot is that 'development' cannot be 'read off' in a simple way from any one domain such as the economic and the importance of different domains at any point in determining the direction of development pathways might shift depending on the specific conjuncture of events. Similarly, when systems reach a 'tipping point', for example, in the wake of the 2008 financial crisis, the causes of the crisis are themselves multifaceted.[6] The choice of which domains to focus on is in some sense an arbitrary one and depends on the nature of the reality being described. In this book, consideration is given in particular to education's changing relationship to six domains, including those of the economy, the polity, civil society, and violence as well as the cultural and the environmental domains.[7] The understanding of each domain is outlined in Box 4.1. All of the domains are characterised as social systems in that they comprise simultaneously both different kinds of social institutions and sets of social relations, including regimes of inequality, and operate at multiple scales from the local to the national to the regional and the global. The environmental domain is distinctive in also comprising relations between social and natural systems and between human beings and other species.

Box 4.1   Domains of development

Walby (2009) conceives of the *economic domain* as a system of relations, institutions, and processes concerned with the production, consumption, distribution, and circulation of goods and services. It is deeply implicated in the reproduction of multiple regimes of inequality, including those based on class, gender, ethnicity, rurality, etc. The conventional understanding of the economy is expanded therefore to include not only marketised activities but also domestic labour, state welfare, and predominantly 'social' institutions like education.

The *domain of the polity* according to Walby 'is an entity which has authority over a specific social group or territory or set of institutions, which in turn has some degree of internal coherence, some degree of centralised control, some rules, the ability to typically enforce sanctions against those members who break the rules, the ability to command deference from other polities in specific arenas over which it claims jurisdiction, and which in turn has authority over a broad and significant range of social institutions and domains' (Walby 2009, 157). There are different kinds of power of polities, including coercion, economic, legal, and symbolic power. Examples of polities extend beyond the state and potentially include nations, regional polities (such as the AU), some organised religions (e.g. Catholicism, Islam), empires (e.g. the British empire), hegemons (e.g. the US and its Western allies), and, in the Africa context, traditional authority structures such as clans and chieftainships. As with the economic domain, it is important to see the polity as operating at a number of interrelated scales taking into account how processes of global, regional, and national governance relate to each other and have been repositioned since colonial times.

Also deeply implicated in processes of global governance is the *domain of civil society*. This domain is taken to encompass organisations and individuals that represent distinct economic, political, and religious/cultural interests that in the African context include religious organisations, the media, the private sector, and NGOs. Civil society has a contradictory relationship with the state, sometimes being included in processes of governance and sometimes in direct antagonism with the aims of government. The idea of civil society develops Gramsci's (1992) conception in which civil society is perceived as a site for the contestation over politics and ideas and the development of hegemony, i.e. the ability of dominant groups to define what counts as 'common sense' in the identification of the causes of crises and their possible solutions. It is also the site for the development of counter-hegemony on the part of opponents of dominant interests. It is possible to conceive of various civil society 'projects' of which neoliberalism is an example (see the following). However, whereas Gramsci was concerned principally with civil society as a site for class struggle, this conception can be extended to include ideological battles between different interests, including those based around gender, 'race', ethnicity, etc. In the context of globalisation and the postcolonial condition, it is also important to conceive of civil society as operating at a number of scales from the global to the regional and the local as is discussed in the following.

A fourth domain implicated in global governance since colonial times is the *domain of violence*. According to Walby (2009), the importance of the domain of violence for people's well-being, for regimes of inequality, and for other institutional domains is much underestimated in social theory and is frequently rendered invisible. This is despite the regulation and deployment of violence 'being part of the constitution of social order, complex inequalities and globalisation' (Walby 2009, 190). Walby argues that violence needs to be understood in its full ontological depth, i.e. as an institutional domain and social system in its own right. Violence operates at different scales. It cannot be reduced to personal psychological aspects as is commonly the case in criminology, for example. Rather, it also needs to be seen as discursively constituted and a social practice that is itself constitutive of power and regimes of inequality. In this regard, violence may be perpetrated by states, individuals, or groups.

The *cultural domain* is concerned primarily with institutions that are responsible for producing and reproducing systems of signification and meaning, including those of language, religion/morality, and knowledge itself, including Western and indigenous forms of knowledge. These include organisations in civil society, including the mass media, religious organisations, museums, and traditional authorities.[8] Taken together, cultural systems are constitutive of individual and group identities.

The *environmental domain* is also not considered as a distinct domain by Walby, although it is a domain commonly referred to in the wider literature on SD (e.g.Elliot 2013; Sachs 2015). The environmental domain comprises different kinds of natural systems at different scales from the workings of sub-atomic particles to the functioning of cells, organisms, ecosystems, and the Earth's biosphere. Given that human beings are organisms, the environmental domain also comprises social relationships between human beings but also between human beings, natural systems, and other species and is concerned with the social implications of environmental crisis, including the impact of climate change. In this respect, it is, like the other domains, also a social domain in which institutions such as education are deeply implicated.

Power in global governance

Key to understanding the postcolonial condition, however, is an appreciation of the operation of different kinds of power that have the effect of maintaining the marginal position of African governments and populations with respect to processes of globalisation. Here Barnett and Duvall's (Barnett and Duvall 2005, 3), work on the nature of power in international relations is considered a useful supplement to Walby's ideas. The authors define power as 'the production, in and through social relations, of effects that shape the capacities of actors to determine their own circumstances and fate'. They distinguish between different kinds of power that can help to explain change within global and regional regimes of governance. The authors define *compulsory power* as comprising the relations of interaction that allow one actor to have direct control over another. In the context of the focus of this book, the conditionalities imposed by donors on recipients of aid can be seen as an example of this kind of power as can the inability of low- and middle-income countries to hold donor countries to account for the amount of aid provided for the nature of the aid relationship.

A second type of power is *institutional power* in which states design international institutions in ways that work to their long-term advantage and to the disadvantage of others. This kind of power is manifest in the historical dominance of the interests of powerful, Western nations and private sector interests in the governance structures of global financial institutions such as the World Bank (Jones 2007; Mundy et al. 2017; Tikly 2017). The third type, *structural power*, concerns the constitution of social capacities and interests of actors in direct relation to one another. One expression of this form of power is the working of the global capitalist economy in producing unequal social relations of production between capital and labour in Africa as elsewhere. Finally, *productive power* is the socially diffused production of subjectivity in systems of meaning and signification, including the way that 'development' itself is defined and understood. Here again, as will be suggested below, it is often Western definitions of SD and ESD that predominate in global, regional, and national agendas.

As was discussed in Chapter 2, Walby (2009) describes different kinds of 'regimes of inequality' that can themselves be understood as self-generating/

self-reproducing systems linked to the socially constitutive effects of different forms of power. It will be recalled that regimes of inequality are composed of relations of inequality that cut across institutions (such as education, health, and social welfare) and across domains. They include but are not confined to inequalities based on class, gender, race/ethnicity, rurality, disability, age, etc. Understanding each regime as being implicated in the development of different domains allows for an appreciation of their full ontological depth. Importantly, regimes of inequality are not reducible to each other. Rather, they co-evolve as systems of classification and oppression. They need to be understood in the way that they intersect and mutually constitute each other at the level of individual and group experiences and identities. Some examples of regimes of inequality that will be referred to in this book are summarised in Box 4.2.[9]

Box 4.2   Examples of regimes of inequality

Class. Class at the most fundamental level is a relational term that refers to the position of groups with respect to the dominant mode of economic production in society. Class inequalities have been a feature of pre-colonial, colonial, and postcolonial social relationships in Africa. The nature of class inequalities has, however, changed as a consequence of changing modes of production. In the colonial system, class relations were very much rooted in the realities of empire. Colonialism itself was intertwined with the emergence of a mercantilist class in Europe who benefited from imperialist policies. Africans were expected to play a menial role in producing primary commodities. In South Africa and other parts of the continent, the advent of industrialisation created new, urban working class that was also important in the development of resistance to apartheid. Under colonialism, a small elite of Africans was created who could serve in the colonial administration. They were often provided with a superior education. This also served as a source of contradiction as many of the leaders of anti-colonial movements were drawn from this educated class. Colonial education played an important role in the development of colonial and postcolonial elites. Propped up by different sides in the Cold War and in the context of structural adjustment programmes during the 1980s, these elites used access to state power to reinforce their elite status and to bring material benefits to their own kinship networks. The position of some African elites has been further reinforced under globalisation through their inclusion on the boards of multinational corporations and global financial institutions.

Race. The history of colonialism in Africa is inseparable from the history of race as a concept. European colonisation of the continent

was premised on ideas of the biological as well as the cultural superiority of white 'races'. Although discredited as a meaningful scientific means of explaining difference between human beings, the long
shadow of biological racism is evident in relatively recent phenomena, including racial segregation in schooling in South Africa and
the 1994 genocide in Rwanda. Biological racism was also used as a
divide and rule strategy in many colonial contexts.[10] European forms
of biological racism have been resisted and deconstructed by Africans. Senghor's ideas about 'negritude' and Fanon's psychoanalytical
thinking which inspired black consciousness on the continent can
be seen as a reversal or form of 'answering back' to racist European
ideas. Although in Africa as elsewhere, biological accounts of difference have largely been superseded by accounts based on cultural
difference and 'ethnicity'.

Ethnicity. Ideas about the superiority of European culture were also
used as a basis for segregation in education as in other spheres and
can be traced back to the supposed 'civilising mission' of the European missionaries on the continent. In Chapter 7, attention will turn
to the Eurocentric basis for much development discourse on the continent which has often equated modernisation with Westernisation.
African cultures and knowledge systems continue to be marginalised,
although movements like the *#Rhodes Must Fall* movement continue
to challenge Eurocentricism in education. African languages were
also devalued as a consequence of colonial rule and continue to be
treated as secondary to European languages, especially English in
the context of globalisation. The postcolonial state has often been
used to institutionalise ethnic inequalities in the postcolonial context
(see the preceding text). However, African cultural traditions have
also provided a source of strength and inspiration for anti-colonial
activists and the basis for pan-Africanism and the idea of an African
Renaissance.

Gender. The colonial economic order was premised on a gendered division of labour. It often relied on women undertaking the majority
of agricultural work as well as assuming the bulk of domestic labour.
Gendered norms based on Christian belief systems inculcated during schooling reinforced the position of women in the economy and
in the home. African cultures as elsewhere in the world have been
contradictory in their attitudes to women at times reinforcing their
inferior position in society, the economy and in the home, and at
other times assigning them a custodial role that has also served as a
source of power. The gendered division of labour introduced under
colonialism has persisted as an aspect of the postcolonial condition
and the burden on women exacerbated through the introduction

of neoliberal policies that have required them to 'take up the slack' caused by reductions in public expenditure. An aspect of globalisation is that women have increased access to the service sector and other areas of manufacturing but this is often linked to insecure, low-paid labour (Tikly et al. 2003). Women and girls continue to have unequal access to state power in many African countries. Girls remain disproportionately excluded from access to a good-quality education (Aikman and Unterhalter 2005) and are subject to institutionalised forms of gendered violence, including sexualised violence in education as in other spheres.

Rurality. Processes of urbanisation started under colonialism have gathered a pace as an aspect of the postcolonial condition. Socio-economic disadvantage and unemployment are most deep rooted in rural settings as is access to the state and to services such as education. Environmental catastrophes, including drought and flooding, often affect rural livelihoods the most as does access to sustainable sources of energy. People in rural areas are also more likely to be subject to traditional forms of governance, including more conservative cultural norms and values, which has implications for the access of some groups to their rights as citizens (Mamdani 1996).

Africa and the global economy

Whilst *Agenda 2063* provides an overview of opportunities and challenges in the economic domain, it does not go far enough in outlining the underlying causes of these or indeed the implications for society and for the environment. For example, it is important to recognise that the current path dependency of African economies on the extraction of raw materials is deeply entrenched and linked to economic interests that can be traced back to colonial times. European colonialism from the sixteenth century onwards was based largely on the extraction of raw materials, including agricultural products and minerals from the global South which were then converted into commodities in the global North and sold back to the global South often at a profit (see, for example, Rodney 1973; Hoogvelt 1997; Akyeampong et al. 2014). A key motive for European colonisation of Africa was economic and political competition between the European powers and became known as the 'scramble for Africa'.[11] The colonial economy was also based on the extraction of an estimated 12–15 million Africans in the form of the transatlantic slave trade. Whilst the slave trade benefited development in the Americas, it led to a huge loss of people and skills and played a significant role in holding back development on the African continent (Akyeampong et al. 2014; Eltis and Richardson 2008).

The roots of rural poverty and the position of rural women also need to be understood historically. The introduction of mining and the migratory system under colonialism resulted in long periods of absence for African men. This in turn had the effect of disrupting family and kinship arrangements, diminishing men's roles in resource management and increasing the workload of African women. It is in relation to the effects of colonial practices on rural poverty and social relations that the salience of the 'land question' in pan-Africanist thought emerged as a basis for grass roots political mobilisation and demands for recognitional justice (Moyo 2015). It is also the case that the vast majority of rural workers are women and are often amongst the poorest. The undermining of African rural livelihoods also contributed to urbanisation with all of the environmental and social problems that ensued. There is also an unaddressed tension in the links made in *Agenda 2063* between population growth and poverty. Whilst there are clearly challenges involved in dealing with social consequences of large population growth, there is a need to treat such links with caution. There is a long history in development discourse of locating the causes of poverty in Africa to population growth rather than in the unequal nature of the economy and polity.[12]

Even after independence, as (Nkrumah 1966) pointed out in his seminal account of neocolonialism, economic relationships between Africa and the countries of the former metropole continued to be based on the extraction of raw materials to support industrialisation in the global North. Informed by dependency theory (discussed later), many newly independent countries adopted import substitution industrialisation policies as a way of breaking dependency.[13] African countries adopted radically different growth paths however in the post-independence period with some such as Kenya pursuing an unapologetically capitalist route and others such as Tanzania and Zambia pursuing versions of African socialism. Both capitalist and socialist growth paths were, however, limited by the prices of raw materials on international markets and a failure to industrialise compounded by growing levels of debt.

The mounting debt crisis prompted the introduction of the Stabilisation and Structural Adjustment Polices (SAPs) (Robertson et al. 2007).[14] These included a range of measures related to fiscal austerity, deregulating the economy, and opening it up to international competition, rolling back the ambit of the state in financing public services and encouraging privatisation. This new policy orthodoxy became known as the 'Washington Consensus'. The policy measures were linked, through conditionality clauses with low-income debtor nations, to loan agreements issued by the IMF in agreement with the World Bank. In Barnett and Duvall's (2005) terms, they are mechanisms of conditional power. Conditionality clauses thus became the key mechanism through which neoliberal economic policies became globalised and spread throughout low-income countries (Hoogvelt 1997) and by which Africa could service global financial flows through its position as a debtor continent in an extractive global system of debt peonage.

The impact of SAPs were devastating in terms of human development and led to the so-called lost decades of development. The call for 'adjustment with a human face' (Robertson et al. 2007) represented a challenge to the international financial institutions whose policies had pushed many low-income countries (as well as those in the 'north') into prioritising debt repayments over social spending. Added to this, there was also criticism over the failure of SAPs to either reduce poverty and inequality or to achieve sustained economic growth in low-income countries. In the context of SAPs, women also had to 'take up the slack' of cuts in services such as health and education as feminist critiques of SAPs have illustrated (see, for example, Sparr 1994).

As Harvey (2011) has argued, the development of neoliberalism since the 1970s was a consequence of capitalist overaccumulation in the global North and the need to restore the profitability of capital. The major political transformations in the former Soviet Union and in China also served to release hitherto unavailable assets into the global economy as has unprecedented growth in South East Asia in the wake of the 2008 shock. These developments are associated with changes in the locus of power and influence within the global economy. Overaccumulation of capital has contributed to a 'revitalisation of primitive accumulation' (Harvey 2003) (accumulation that is based on the extraction of primary commodities and on cheap labour) as a way of increasing the profitability of capital.

It is this turn to primitive accumulation together with concerns about energy and food security in China, the United States, and elsewhere that lies behind the 'new scramble for Africa' (Ayers 2013; Mohan 2013). This has involved investing Western based capital and to a lesser extent capital linked to China and the other rising powers in extractive mining industries and agriculture. Thus, although the new scramble for Africa has coincided with a period of economic growth especially following the 2008 financial crisis, it has not led to sizeable gains for ordinary Africans because, as Ferguson (2006) has pointed out, the vast majority of this growth has been through foreign investment, has occurred in enclaves, and has remained shut off from local communities who have not benefited directly. It has also happened in the form of land grabs in which vast areas of land have been effectively privatised and sold off to foreign interests (see also Ayers 2013), which has had dire consequences for human and environmental development. China has also exported large numbers of labourers to work on agricultural and infrastructure projects in Africa such that in many cases, new projects have often not led to increased opportunities for the employment of Africans themselves (Mohan 2013).

The postcolonial condition and the environment

Issues to do with the environment are often absent in discussions about postcolonialism and the postcolonial condition. This is despite the enormous disruption caused by the colonial encounter to indigenous livelihoods and the centrality of environmental issues such as the land question in struggles against colonialism and in the campaigns of indigenous groups. As will be discussed in Chapter 8, the environmental impact of colonialism has also had implications for indigenous knowledge and belief systems which are rooted in pre-colonial relationships between human beings and the natural world. As was seen in Chapter 1, *Agenda 2063* provides an overview of the opportunities and challenges facing the continent with respect to the environment (albeit with some omissions such as the effects of climate change). It will be recalled that *Agenda 2063* identifies Africa's natural resources as playing a critical role for vast segments of Africa's population who depend on the continent's biodiversity, forests, and land for their livelihoods directly or indirectly but that the continent's biodiversity, land, and forests are facing increasing challenges. It is helpful once again to consider the environmental domain in historical perspective. The devastating social and environmental consequences of extractive economic practices noted in *Agenda 2063* can also be traced back to colonial times. As economic historians have argued (see, for example, Akyeampong et al. 2014; Ghai 1992) changes in the economy brought about by colonialism had a significant impact on environmental degradation and disrupted the long-established systems of resource management which had relied on shifting cultivation and nomadic pastoralism. The annexation and centralisation of sovereignty over forests, farm lands, and lakes and rivers also laid the foundations for environmental degradation as colonial administrations, unlike traditional authorities, often lacked the capacity to exercise effective control over resource management. The search for profits often undermined traditional agricultural practices such as crop rotation which had protected the soil and the introduction of foreign crops such as groundnuts and cotton further reduced soil fertility. It also served to confine indigenous populations to areas with least agricultural potential. Different methods involving various degrees of coercion were used to secure labour on European farms, plantations, and mines (Ghai 1992). *Agenda 2063* goes some way towards identifying the historical impact of extractive practices both on social relations and on the environment. The report highlights, for example, unequal distribution of land, exacerbated by the recent 'scramble for Africa's land' by big investors as a major risk to environmental protection and sustainable economic development. As will be discussed in Chapter 7, global and regional agendas propose the idea of 'inclusive growth' based on a more equitable distribution of resources and the adaptation of productive processes to make them more friendly. However, it will be suggested that the idea of inclusive growth is contradictory in that it continues to be underpinned by an emphasis on neoliberal market-led approaches. Neither does the report go far enough in providing an alternative basis for growth which would involve a more fundamental challenge to global and national interests that are currently invested in existing growth paths.

Changing patterns of global governance

Global governance and colonialism

The governance of African societies under colonialism was characterised by forms of direct and indirect rule. French colonial powers were more likely to favour direct rule in accordance with their assimilationist policies, a system Mamdani (1996) has described as 'centralised despotism'. The British, on the other hand, often favoured forms of indirect rule in which areas of policy were decentralised to local, traditional power structures, a system that Mamdani has described as 'decentralised despotism'. In both cases, Africans were denied the right to vote with very few exceptions. However, as Mamdani explains, under indirect rule, urban elites enjoyed many of the trappings of being treated as 'citizens' whilst in the rural areas they were treated as 'subjects' of traditional authorities. This created a bifurcation between citizens and subjects that is still evident in many formerly colonised countries today (Mamdani 1996). This bifurcation also lies at the heart of the double misrepresentation in Fraser's terms of rural communities in relation to issues of governance in that they are misrepresented both at a national and at a regional/ global level. Colonialism was also premised on the use of violence: whether it was the violent acquisition of territories, the forced removal of communities from their lands and livelihoods, the violence of slavery and of indentured servitude, the violent suppression of rebellion, or the psychological trauma caused by the effects of institutionalised racism.

At a discursive level, a key rationale for colonialism was in terms of the so-called 'civilising mission' of the white man (sic). Underpinning this view however lay different explanations. Some of these were founded on a reading of the Bible and particularly the Old Testament in which Africans are portrayed as heathens and as 'hewers of wood and drawers of water'. This particular reading of the Old Testament was influential, for example, in legitimising apartheid in South Africa (Tikly 1994). Also influential were changing discourses around race, nation, and culture that assumed the biological and cultural inferiority of the non-European 'other'.[15] As Williams and Young (2009) have argued, in the lead up to independence, the civilising mission of whites was increasingly articulated with a modernist view of progress in which educated, African elites were seen as indigenous agents of modernity.

This modernist, universalistic view of progress provided a source of contradiction with the virulent forms of religious, racial, and cultural racism with which it co-evolved. As Franz Fanon, along with many other anti-colonial activists and advocates of Pan-Africanism has pointed out, this has had a long-lasting, negative effect on the African psyche, leading to a situation where Africans have at times rejected their own cultural values in favour of European ones and, so it is argued, have been made complicit in their own subjugation (see, for example, Fanon 1961, 1986).

As will be discussed in later chapters, colonial education was complicit in these wider processes of governance through providing legitimisation for the colonial project. In general, economic terms, colonial education was important for rendering the colonised 'economically useful and politically docile' (Rodney 1973). Through legitimising social relations of production under colonialism, education also tacitly contributed to processes of environmental degradation (see Chapter 7). In political terms, colonial education also facilitated processes of elite formation (although this has contradictory implications in the context of struggles for national liberation as these were often led by Western educated indigenous elites). Colonial education played a crucial role in processes of political socialisation as well as acting as sites for the reproduction of forms of violence. In relation to the cultural domain, education was instrumental in embedding a Western *episteme* (ground base of knowledge) as the basis for the curriculum and for projecting sometimes competing views of modernity. In this way, it contributed to the marginalisation of African religions, cultures, and languages. It is also from the colonial era that many of the characteristics of modern education systems, including their highly centralised, bureaucratic, and authoritarian nature, can be traced.

Global governance in the era of 'development'

The end of empire and the advent of the 'development era' can be seen as a very conscious effort at deterritorialisation and reterritorialisation of the polity at the global, regional, and national scales. Key moments in the birth of the development era were the formation of the Bretton Woods financial institutions in 1944, including the World Bank and the IMF and the General Agreement on Tariffs and Trade, which were aimed predominantly at post–Second World War reconstruction in Europe. Another key moment was the establishment of the UN under Article 55 of the UN charter in 1945 which enjoyed the support of the United States and its Western allies.[16] However, it was President Truman's inaugural address in 1949 in which he referred to 'underdeveloped areas' and identified poverty as a threat to prosperity and peace that is often cited as the point at which the 'development era' officially commenced.[17] The advent of the Cold War in the post–Second World War period also provided a political rationale for the West to embark on a development mission as a means of keeping the newly labelled 'developing world' out of the orbit of the Soviet Union and its allies. The Cold War–fermented state sponsored violence through its role in propping up corrupt and often ethnically exclusive regimes promoting interethnic conflict over land and resources.

Discourses about 'race' were also central to emerging ideas about 'development' (Sriprakash, Tikly, and Walker 2019). Commentators have argued that what Truman's speech represented was a break or disjuncture in the way that 'development' was understood but one that continued to provide continuity on development under colonialism. Whereas development had in the past been a 'natural' phenomenon, in the emerging hegemonic worldview, development became something that could be performed by one actor or region over another actor or region. Further, whereas colonisers and colonised had previously belonged to two different universes, separated by a gulf of biological and cultural difference, the new binary represented a step in the reinvention of the 'Third World' as part of a continuity with the West (Escobar 1995). Furthermore, whereas classical colonialism was premised on the view that although the 'natives' could be 'civilised' to some degree, they could never achieve equality with the West; in 'development' discourse, it became possible for underdeveloped regions and populations to evolve into developed ones. This did not mean, however, that the previously colonised were now seen as cultural 'equals' with the West, at least until they had become more 'westernised' (Rist 1997).

The influence of global civil society on global governance

Walby conceives of global civil society in terms of global social movements of intellectual and moral energy that transverse traditional institutions and geographical borders. In the context of globalisation and the postcolonial condition, it is also important to conceive of civil society as operating at a number of scales from the global to the regional and the local as is discussed in the following. Pan-Africanism, anti-colonialism, neoliberalism, socialism, human rights, feminism, environmentalism, and religious fundamentalisms are examples of civil society waves that have impacted on Africa. They are seen to originate as projects in civil society and then to spread. The development of the Education for All (EFA) movement will be presented in Chapter 5 as an example of a civil society wave that has been significant in shaping global education policy since the early 1990s. An important civil society wave was provided by modernisation theory. Developed by Rostow in the 1950s and 1960s, it posited a view of development as a series of linear progressions from traditional, pre-modern societies to high–mass consumption, capitalist societies. It was championed by John F. Kennedy as an alternative development model to that of communism and had an important influence on US foreign aid during the 1960s. Like human capital theory, it was highly influential in shaping emerging conceptions of the role of education in relation to economic development. Both of these theories are discussed in greater depth in Chapter 7. For now, attention will turn to consider civil society waves that have been particularly influential in shaping the way that 'development' is perceived in Africa.

Neoliberalism

The emergence of neoliberalism as a global wave from the late 1970s had a major reterritorialising effect on Africa's relations with the global economy as we have already seen in relation to the discussion of the economic domain. As a way of thinking about the economy, it fed into the development of the so-called Washington consensus' and the introduction of structural adjustment policies. Based on a view of the importance of markets and the need to reduce barriers to the free market and roll back the power of the state, neoliberalism is a project that has its origins in the domestic politics of Thatcherism and Reaganism but then developed into a global wave. The way that neoliberal thinking has been incorporated into development thinking has also changed over time as is evident, for example, in the switch from the Washington to the post-Washington consensus. In this regard, Walby points out that although neoliberalism is a powerful global project that has become embedded in some governmental programmes and social formations, it is not the same as globalisation, nor is it fully hegemonic. As De Jaeghere (2017) has recently argued, it is better to think of global education policy, for example, as being shaped by different 'neo/liberal' projects that in the African context as elsewhere has involved the interplay between neoliberal ideas with other political projects and global civil society waves. In the context of

Agenda 2063, for example, neoliberal ideas are articulated to discourses around pan-Africanism.

In relation to the political domain, the introduction of neoliberal orthodoxy has been accompanied by the 'good governance' agenda which emerged in the context of the 1990s, as both an explanation of and a solution to the deficiencies of the Washington Consensus. Broadly, the concept of 'good governance' embraces the idea of an efficient public service; respect for human rights; an independent judiciary and legal framework; economic liberalism; protection of private property; political pluralism; participation, administrative accountability; transparency and respect for the law (Robertson et al. 2007). Like neoliberal prescriptions for the economy, the good governance agenda continues to play a major role in shaping how Western governments and multilateral organisations 'do business' with Africa and it is therefore not surprising given the enormous conditional and institutional power held by these organisations that the good governance agenda features so prominently in *Agenda 2063*.[18]

Pan-Africanism

It is important to recognise pan-Africanism as a global discourse with its roots in the African diaspora as well as on the continent of Africa. The term pan-Africanism was first used in 1900 by Henry Sylvester Williams, a Trinidadian lawyer who was based in London. Williams called for a conference to 'protest stealing of lands in the colonies, racial discrimination and deal with other issues of interests to blacks' (in Ackah 1999, xiii). However, it was W.E.B Du Bois who called it first in an ongoing series of pan-African congresses. That first congress was held in Paris and it ended with a call for the rights of Africans to own land and mineral resources of Africa, for an end to slave labour and forced labour and for Africans to be governed by consent rather than by force. The second congress, held in London, Paris, and Brussels in 1921 resulted in the production of a manifesto. Entitled *A Declaration to the World*, it had been authored by Marcus Garvey in 1920. The third, fourth, and fifth congresses took place in London in 1923, in New York in 1927, and in Manchester in 1945, respectively, after colonial regimes frustrated attempts to hold the congresses in Africa. The 1945 conference was significant for repeating the peaceful demands for African self-determination but added, unlike the earlier congresses, that Africans are ready to use force if necessary, to resist a forceful colonisation of Africa. The Congress adopted Kwame Nkrumah's *Declaration to the Colonised Peoples of the World* which called for the struggle for self-determination 'by any means necessary'. This was followed by the independence of a number of African countries in the next three decades. The sixth Congress was held in Tanzania in 1974 with the participation of many liberation movements and focused on issues of how to make Africa self-reliant.[19]

In the African context, the idea of pan-Africanism provided impetus for the formation of the Organisation of African Unity (OAU) in 1963 as a counterpoint to the consolidation of the US-led historical bloc.[20] It later transformed into the African Union. Similarly, the creation of the non-aligned movement as a consequence of the Havana Declaration of 1979 was an effort to create a forum to represent the views of members on the international stage.[21] An important influence for governments such as those of Ghana and Tanzania that wished to break free from these global relationships was the development of dependency theory by Andre Gunder Frank (1970) and the dependency school. Dependency theory also informed the ideas of anti-colonial activists such as Walter Rodney whose influential book *How Europe Underdeveloped Africa* was a classic text for those fighting against the vestiges of colonialism and neocolonialism. Overall, dependency theory provided a compelling argument about the negative consequences of economic dependency of low-income countries at the periphery of the global economy to countries of the former colonial metropole.

More recently, the discourse of the African Renaissance has built on the pan-African vision. For many commentators, the origins of the term lie in the idea of pan-Africanism as it developed in Africa, America, and the Caribbean at the turn of the nineteenth century (Mamdani 1996; Ajulu 2001). In the context of national liberation struggles, the idea of a 'renaissance' was evident in Consciencism (Ghana), African humanism (Zambia), Authenticism (Zaire), Ujaama (Tanzania), and Black Consciousness in South Africa (Ntuli 1998; Ajulu 2001). In each case, however, the implicit idea was embedded within a different political project. Extending Vale and Maseko's (1998) analysis, it is possible to trace through history two elements that have underpinned the idea of the African Renaissance, namely, a 'modernist' element, (i.e. one that understands the idea of an African Renaissance principally in terms of charting a path of economic growth and political development) and a 'cultural' element (i.e. one that is more concerned with rediscovering an essential 'essence' to African history and cultures as a basis for reasserting a common African identity in Africa and the diaspora). Both of these elements are present in contemporary discourses. Recent usage of the term can be dated back to Nelson Mandela's 1994 speech to the OAU summit in Tunis in which he spoke of the vision of an African Renaissance following on the liberation of South Africa (Mandela cited in Cornwall 1998, 9). It is Thabo Mbeki, however, who is most credited with articulating and developing the concept in the form of a call to action for Africans at the turn of the new millennium. The concept has informed the New Partnership for Africa's Development (NEPAD) which was adopted by African heads of state in October 2001 as well as *Agenda 2063*.[22]

OTHER REGIONAL CIVIL SOCIETY WAVES

Other civil society waves have also become increasingly influential in global governance terms. For example, recent decades have seen the rise of Islamic and other forms of religious fundamentalisms which have influenced ongoing violence in the horn of Africa through the actions of *Al-Shabaab*, in Northern Nigeria with *Boko Harem*, and in Northern Uganda with the *Lords Resistance Army*. Discourses about the so-called 'war on terror' with its origins in conservative politics in the United States, UK, and other Western countries evolved in the wake of the 9/11 attacks in New York and continue to shape the responses of the West to Africa, e.g. through the diversion of aid to the Middle East and other regions that are perceived to pose a threat to Western interests and values (Novelli 2010).[23] Finally, environmentalism has become an increasingly significant civil society wave in the context of the SDGs. Although it has its origins in civil society movements in the West, it also has had a presence on the continent, although one that has been until recently more muted compared to other development discourses (Obi 2005).[24]

Regimes of global governance

These will be discussed in Chapters 5 and 6 in relation to the ways in which education governance takes place at a global and regional scale with implications for national policy agendas. The analysis draws on recent work published elsewhere (Tikly 2017). Governance regimes are defined as 'sets of implicit or explicit principles, norms, rules, and decision-making procedures around which actors' expectations converge in a given area of international relations' (Krasner 1982)185; see also; Orsini, Morin, and Young 2013).[25] In applying regime theory, the book brings together a liberal institutionalist concern with the role of regimes in developing consensus around a common set of principles, norms, rules, and decision-making procedures in a particular issue area with a more critical understanding of the operation of power dynamics within regimes. As Jones (2007) has suggested, one way of achieving such a *rapprochement* is to conceive of regimes and regime complexes in Gramscian terms, i.e. as global institutions that are fundamentally concerned with achieving consent for the institutions and laws of global governance as a basis for maintaining hegemony within an anarchic world order. Central to this way of thinking is the issue of the legitimacy of global regimes in relation to the institutions and networks that are part of the regime and that are affected by the regime.[26] Maintaining the legitimacy of governance within a particular issue area such as education and development in the face of tension and contradictions within and between regimes provides a key motive for powerful actors in shaping regimes and a basis for regime change.

Understood as complex systems, regimes comprise networks of actors comprising multilateral institutions, donors, and national and regional governments and organisations in global civil society, including international NGOs and religious and philanthropic organisations. These are overlain and cut across by intersecting regimes of inequality. Regimes are considered to have changed when there is change to norms and principles underlying regimes. 'Tipping points' that can lead to a change from one regime to another can be precipitated by crisis or brought about by the rise of a new hegemon, i.e. a new, dominant state or collection of nation states that challenge the principles and norms of existing regimes and/or introduce a new regime.

Two global governance regimes are discussed in particular as having had an influence on the development of education policy in Africa, namely, the 'Education for All' and the more recent 'Education for Sustainable Development' regimes. *Agenda 2063* and CESA are considered as examples of regional governance regimes. As several commentators have observed, however, global governance in education as in other areas has become more 'dense' as the number of regimes impinging on different issue areas has increased (Orsini, Morin, and Young 2013). In this respect, the number of regimes that have impinged on education and development has multiplied over time to the point where EFA can be said to exist within a 'regime complex'[27] (see Chapter 5). It will be suggested that other governance regimes that have been particularly influential include the aid and human rights regimes as well as regimes concerned with trade and security. It will be suggested that the increasing complexity of global governance has implications for the role of regional and national bodies in responding to sometimes conflicting demands.

Africa and developmental regionalism

Processes of global governance do not simply operate at a global level however. They need to also be understood in the way they are taken up and mediated by regional and national policy agendas. This requires an understanding of the changing nature of regionalism in the African context. Space does not allow for a full discussion here (see Tikly and Dachi 2008) for a fuller account of regionalism in African education policy). Within the broad literature, 'regionalism' is defined as 'the body of ideas, values and concrete objectives that are aimed at transforming a geographical area into a clearly identified regional social space' whilst the related process of 'regionalisation' implies a dynamic element, the 'creation of a regional system or network in a specific geographical area or regional social space, either issue specific or more general in scope'(Grant and Söderbaum 2003):7). Regionalism and the process of regionalisation are characterised as having taken place in two main waves. The 'first wave' reached its apotheosis in the period following the Second World War and focused principally on greater economic integration.[28] The rapid development of regions, including the European Union (EU), NAFTA, APEC, and ASEAN, during the 1980s is often characterised as a 'second wave' of regionalism or 'new regionalism'.[29] Although this second wave is primarily concerned with developing frameworks to facilitate free trade and commerce, it is also concerned with identity formation and takes on a more overt sociopolitical dimension compared to the first wave.[30]

In Africa, the Southern African Development Community (SADC), the Economic Community of West African States (ECOWAS), the Common Market for East and Southern Africa (COMESA), along with the newly fledged African Union (AU), have been overtly modelled along lines similar to that of the EU and are concerned with projecting new macro- and sub-regional identities as well as encouraging economic integration and development. Like its counterparts elsewhere, the new regionalism in Africa includes informal as well as formal regional networks, including those between NGOs and the private sector, and these have grown in number and influence in recent years, as we will see in relation to education. Unlike examples of the old regionalism, the new structures and networks also operate at a range of scales.[31] War zones and regional conflicts have also proliferated and represent a darker side of the phenomenon on the continent.[32] Although there are clearly differences between the old and new regionalisms in Africa, there is also continuity and overlap. For example, just as the old regions were primarily concerned with economic integration, the new regions have also prioritised economic over sociopolitical and cultural goals (Robertson et al 2007; Vale and Maseko 1998).

Transformative regionalism

The development of the AU, NEPAD, and now *Agenda 2063* organised around a concept of an African Renaissance has also been characterised as a special case of new regionalism, i.e. as an example of 'developmental regionalism' (Tikly and Dachi 2008) which is an attempt to project a regional identity and to develop political projects at a regional level in order to advance development. These may also be considered as emerging regimes of regional governance characterised by distinctive principles, norms, rules, and decision-making procedure, though these have changed over time (see Chapter 6). Indeed, some commentators argue that regional initiatives ought to be principally focused on pre-emptive national and regional development strategies and economic policy co-ordination amongst African countries (Mazrui 1999; Adedeji 1998; Mayer 1998).[33] In this view, Africa's successful integration into global markets lies in the extent to which African economies can diversify their industrial base and export markets and hence become less dependent upon domestic markets and foreign imports through participation in regional and sub-regional trading blocs. These are seen as important both for attracting foreign investors and for intervening in the market in the interest of the poor. In this regard, regional bodies such as the AU, the various regional development communities, or, in the field of education, regional bodies such as the Association for the Development of Education in Africa (ADEA) play a role in translating global policy into regional priorities and concerns (Tikly and Dachi 2008).

Just as with the new regionalism elsewhere, however, critics have questioned whether the new regionalism in Africa reflects the hegemony of neoliberal economic models that are designed to simply slot Africa into the global market (Simon 2003; Mittelman 2000). These commentators argue that regional initiatives such as the New Economic Partnership for African Development (NEPAD) and *Agenda 2063* see Africa principally as a vast and as yet underexploited marketplace and that stronger economies, such as South Africa, are more disposed to acting as the agents of globalisation, leading other African economies into the global market and providing a 'way in' for non-African, particularly US interests into Africa (Bond 2001).[34] Questions have also been raised about the nature and extent of the democratic process in the new regional structures (Simon 2003). Many commentators have questioned the credentials of some of the leaders and regimes associated with the new regions. Through providing a legal framework protecting the sovereign authority of postcolonial states, the AU and other regional bodies, it is sometimes argued, are complicit in the whole process.

Other commentators have attempted to chart a third, critical but supportive position in relation to regionalism in Africa (Cheru 2002; Scholte 2006; Khor 2002). These authors argue that whatever one may think of globalisation and regionalism, it is unavoidable and that the task for African economies is to max-imise the advantages it brings whilst minimising the risks (Ajulu 2001, for exam-ple). For these commentators, there is a significant role for national, regional, and global regulation and intervention in markets in order to achieve the objec-tives of ending poverty and underdevelopment. The assumption is that instead of globalisation being seen simply as serving the interests of the richer nations and global elites, it can also be made to work to some degree at least in the interests of the world's poor. This view accords with what Held *et al.* (1999) describe as a 'transformationalist' view of global flows and networks[35] and with Mittelman's (2000) concept of 'transformative regionalism' which refers to the alternative and bottom-up forms of cultural identity and regional self-organisation and self-protection, such as pro-democracy forces, women's movements, environmen-talists, and other civil society movements. Cornwall (1998, 14), for example, argues that the greater accountability of African leaders ought to involve 'the creation of voluntary neighbourhood governments and rural grass roots move-ments that produce alternative institutions of decision making, drawing on cus-tomary notions of justice, fairness and political obligation'. In a similar vein, Ake (Ake 1988, 35) suggests that involving the vast majority of Africans who live in rural areas in democratic decision-making should include 'allowing rural people to build on whatever they consider important in their lives; whatever they regard as an authentic expression of themselves'.

The postcolonial state in Africa

Global and regional governance is also mediated at a state level which in areas such as education is significant because of the role of national governments in determining education policy, albeit under global and regional influences. *Agenda 2063* points to increases in the number of democracies on the continent and in multiparty elections. It also points out that most elections are now vio-lence-free. The report highlights some improvements in economic governance[36], including success in tackling corruption[37] which it considers has a bearing on the sustainability of economic performance of African countries. However, it notes that policy making and service delivery remain compromised due to poor pub-lic institutions and administration at central, municipal, and local levels, leaving many citizens poorly served by their governments (AUC 2015a, 62). The report argues that the quality of democracy remains a challenge with huge variability in the extent to which democratic norms are internalised and implemented.[38]

Again, it is useful to consider the analysis provided by *Agenda 2063* in historical perspective which allows for an understanding of the deep-rooted nature of the issues involved. Global discourses relating to politics and good governance often assume a Westphalian model of the state which has predominated in the Western world. This fails to take account of the relative newness of African states and their difficult birth as part of the 'scramble for Africa'. At a political level, European colonialism resulted in the introduction of highly centralised and authoritarian state structures which were intended to serve the interests of the colonisers and did not acknowledge some of the complexities of incorporating into one territory diverse ethnic groups and in some instances the challenges involved in governing vast, sparsely populated swathes of land given the limited governmental capacities (Herbst 2000). Indigenous elites were assimilated into these existing structures. As Mamdani (1996) has cogently argued, this led to an increasing bifurcation between urban elites subject to the power of the colonial state and rural dwellers who were still subject to traditional forms of authority – a bifurcation that is still evident in the postcolonial era between 'citizens' of the modern state and 'subjects' of more traditional forms of authority. The difficulties in instituting democratic rule and the use of the state to advance the interests of some ethnic groups at the expense of others can, according to Mamdani, be traced back to this dynamic.

Unlike in the Westphalian model which has predominated in the Western world, the mode of rule in postcolonial states has variously been described as 'personal rule', 'elite accommodation', and 'belly politics' and as a 'shadow' or 'neo-patrimonial state' (Boas and McNeill 2004). These alternative models are relevant for a consideration of the 'good governance' agenda in Africa. In the model of the neo-patrimonial state, for example, bureaucratic and patrimonial norms coexist. The state is able to extract and redistribute resources but this process, unlike in the Westphalian state model, is privatised. 'In redressing the colonial legacy of racially inherited privilege, the independent states create a specific patrimonial path of re-distribution which divides the indigenous majority along regional, religious, ethnic and at times, family lines' (Boas and McNeill 2004, 33). The resulting phenomenon of weak states but strong regimes provides a source of contradiction within the African state system, though it remains resilient.

In the context of the Cold War, state building became implicated in global politics with both Western and Eastern powers propping up sometimes corrupt and authoritarian regimes in support of their own global ambitions and economic interests. This, according to (Bayart 2009), led to the formation of two 'ideal types' of postcolonial state based on projects of 'conservative modernisation', on the one hand, and 'social revolution' on the other.[39] Both represented different underlying views of modernity. A major implication of neoliberal inspired reform, however, has been a convergence of development paths. Neoliberalism has also been associated with the so-called 'hollowing out' (Ferguson 2006) of the state in Africa. As Ferguson explains:

> In fact, the picture that seems to emerge from the recent scholarly literature is of two quite different kinds of governance, applied to the two different Africas that French colonialism once distinguished as 'Afrique utile' and 'Afrique

inutile' – or 'usable/useful Africa' and 'unusable/useless Africa'. . . . Usable Africa gets secure enclaves – noncontiguous 'useful' bits that are secured, policed, and, in a minimal sense, governed through private or semiprivate means. These enclaves are increasingly linked up, not in a national grid, but in transnational networks that connect economically valued spaces dispersed around the world in a point-to-point fashion. The rest – the vast terrain of 'unusable Africa' – gets increasingly nongovernmental states, and an array of extra-state forms of control and (often styled 'traditional') to open banditry and warlordism. This state of affairs is often violent and disorderly, but it should not be understood simply as an absence of government. . . . [E]ven banditry has its own intricate forms of social and moral order, and its forms of 'regulation' often find points of attachment with the interests of both state officials and variously militarized illegal traffickers (for whom the 'inutile' areas that are of little interest to foreign investors may turn out to be quite 'utile' indeed). At the same time, areas in which states no longer project bureaucratic control are often effectively 'governed' in a transnational humanitarian or developmental mode, as a hodgepodge of transnational private voluntary organizations carryout the day-to-day work of providing rudimentary governmental and social services, especially in regions of crisis and conflict.

(Ferguson 2006, 15–16)

That is to say that whereas states in the post-independence era were seen as the main vehicles for development and were often characterised by assertive Africa-led leadership, this has been increasingly challenged under neoliberalism. Rather, cut backs in government expenditure and the streamlining of state bureaucracies have had the perverse effect of increasing dependency as the capacity to govern has decreased further. This process of hollowing out has also exacerbated rather than eased the problems of so-called 'failed states' in which warlords and bandits often assumed the role of governing hard to govern areas (Herbst 2000).

Conclusion

The chapter has sought to set out in broad terms how the postcolonial condition can be understood in Africa. This has involved consideration of Africa's changing relationship with six domains of development since colonial times. 'Development' in the analysis presented here has been presented as multi-causal and multi-directional in relation to each of the six domains and overlain by the effects of different kinds of power and of intersecting regimes of inequality. Africa's relationship with the economic domain has largely revolved around the role of Africa as a supplier of natural resources with often damaging consequences for the natural environment. Whilst these dynamics are recognised in *Agenda 2063*, less obvious is an acknowledgement of the role of indigenous interests in the post-independence era who have benefited from the status quo. The chapter also sought to trace the changing position of the continent with processes of global governance that have been shaped by the emergence of regimes of global and regional governance and the postcolonial state. The implications for the analysis of changing patterns of global, regional, and national governance for education and training policy are considered in more detail in Chapters 5 and 6.

Notes

1 Held *et al.* (1999) provide a historical periodisation of different forms of globalisation, in the pre-modern, early modern, modern, and contemporary periods. They argue that international and global interconnectedness is by no means a novel phenomenon and seeks to advance understanding by providing a framework for assessing the qualitative and quantitative differences between the forms taken by globalisation in different eras. Of particular relevance here is their analysis of the global flows and networks associated with modern globalisation (1859–1945). Here the focus is on the enormous expansion of global, political, and military relations associated with Western global empires and the soaring of global trade and investment during this period.

2 The authors explain that by 'flows' they refer to 'the movements of physical artefacts, people, symbols, tokens and information across space and time', whilst 'networks' is used to refer to 'regularized or patterned interactions between independent agents, nodes of activity, or sites of power' (p. 16).

3 Here the term 'scale' is used in preference to that of 'level' as the former sees space as the mutable product of social relations and struggle in which the global, regional, and national 'levels' are mutually implicated (Verger, Altinyelken, and Novelli 2018).

4 At a general level, this signifies the complex relationships between different actors in any historical era, including those of states, multilateral organisations, different factions of capital, and global civil society.

5 The BRICS economics comprise Brazil, Russia, India, China, and South Africa.

6 This is similar to Gramsci's conception of organic crisis as involving the coming together of economic, political, and cultural factors to create what might be described in popular parlance a 'perfect storm'. Thus, the advent of neoliberal policies can be seen in economic terms as a response to the debt crisis in the wake of the 1973 oil shock, in political terms as a response to Mexico's decision to default on its debt, and at a cultural level as a consequence of the development of neoliberal ideas from the 1950s. Similarly, the 2008 global crisis involved the interaction of factors within the housing market as well as related to global financial regulation.

7 Walby actually refers to the domains of economy, polity, civil society, violence, and ethnicity. In the African context and in the context of a discussion about SD and ESD, it was decided to organise a discussion around what seem more relevant domains.

8 Walby (2009) conflates the cultural domain with that of civil society. However, given the centrality of cultural issues in discourses about SD in Africa and their importance in relation to education, it has been decided to treat the cultural domain as a distinct domain for the purposes of this book.

9 The discussion of different regimes of inequality is necessarily incomplete and partial. In a book of this nature, it is impossible to give all forms of inequality the attention they are due. Thus, for example, issues to do with disability and sexuality are not explicitly addressed in the book, although they are clearly important for an understanding of the effects of education policy.

10 It was argued in Rwanda, for instance, that Tutsi's were biologically more similar to Europeans which provided a justification for Belgian colonisers to privilege

them in educational and other terms, a contributing factor to the 1994 genocide of mainly Tutsis.

11   In what has been termed the 'Scramble for Africa', 14 European nations met – without African representation – at the West Berlin Africa Conference of 1884– 1885, 'wishing to regulate in a spirit of good mutual understanding the conditions most favourable to the development of commerce and of civilization in certain regions of Africa . . .; desirous on the other hand to prevent misunderstandings and contentions to which the taking of new possessions on the coast of Africa may in the future give rise, and at the same time preoccupied with the means of increasing the moral and material well-being of the indigenous populations' (General Act of the Conference of Berlin Concerning the Congo 1909, 7). The subsequent partition of the 'magnificent cake' – Africa – has been described as transforming Africa 'into a conceptual terra nullius' through an ideology of colonial rule or 'doctrine of trusteeship' (Cowen and Shenton in Okolie 2003, 33) under which 'developed' societies subordinated native claims to sovereignty and determined how 'primitive' societies would develop.

12   In development discourse, this has also been linked to ideas about 'race' and about controlling black women's' fertility (Wilson 2013).

13   The theory was critiqued for offering too pessimistic an analysis of the prospects of low-income countries in the face of dependency and the failure to address macroeconomic policies within low-income countries themselves. Nonetheless, traces of the underlying sentiment informing dependency theory, i.e. the fundamental need for African-led development, are evident in the FD. It provides a source of tension and contradiction with the reality of the new primitive accumulation on the continent led by FDI (see the following) and the continued dependency of many African countries on large amounts of foreign assistance, including in areas such as education which has the effect of increasing dependency and fragmenting the possibilities for autonomous development through the need to respond to sometimes contradictory donor agendas (e.g. between the Chinese and Western powers).

14   The Mexican debt crisis led to a dramatic shift in the policies of the World Bank and the IMF during the late 1970s and early 1980s. These institutions developed a set of neoliberal policies that served to ensure that debtor countries were able to service their debts.

15   These terms can be understood as floating signifiers with fluid boundaries between the way that they were deployed and what they were intended to signify (i.e. so-called 'races' were also often considered to have distinct cultures and to belong to different 'nations' – the Zulu, Shona, Khosa, Tswana nations, etc.). In the context of the growth of the Eugenics movement in the late nineteenth century, the inferiority of Africans was underpinned by a virulent scientific racism that posited a hierarchy between the races with white, aristocratic Europeans at the top, and Africans at the bottom of the hierarchy (Gould 1996; Loomba 2005).

16   The founding charter set out the aims of the UN as creating worldwide peace, well-being, and stability. Envisioning 'higher standards of living, full employment, and conditions of economic and social progress and development; solutions of international economic, social, health and related problems; and universal respect for and observance of human rights and fundamental freedoms for all without distinction as to race, sex, language or religion' (UN 1945), the Charter goals 'created moral pressure for institutional and policy change' (Koehler 2015, 734) as did the adoption of Universal Declaration of Human Rights in 1948.

17   President Truman set out a vision of the future for the world's low-income countries and coined the term 'development' to refer to processes of economic and social progress in colonial and postcolonial states: 'We must embark on a bold

new program for making the benefits of our scientific advances and industrial progress available for the improvement and growth of the underdeveloped areas. . . . I believe that we should make available to peace-loving peoples the benefits of our store of technical knowledge in order to help them realise their aspirations for a better life. . . . The old imperialism – exploitation for foreign profit – has no place in our plans. What we envisage is a program of development based on the concepts of democratic fair dealing' (Truman, 1949, Point Four).

18 However, as was the case during the Cold War, extractive industries have often grown just as quickly in territories that exhibit 'good governance' as they have in so-called failed states which has led to foreign governments being prepared to turn a blind eye to human rights abuses (Ayers 2013).

19 The Seventh pan-African Congress took place in 1994 in Lagos where a group of cultural nationalist tried to follow past practices of getting governments of African states to play dominant role in Congress and concluded by calling for Africans to be paid reparations for the crimes of slavery and of colonialism. The Kampala held later in the same year established a permanent secretariat and also established a pan-African women's organisation at the initiative of the women's delegates (Ackah 1999).

20 Constituting 'a crucial moment in the process of norm socialization on the continent' (Williams 2007, 263), the Organisation of African Unity (OAU) was established in 1963 at Addis Ababa, with the intention of promoting inter-African cooperation and eradicating all forms of colonialism. During negotiations, two major competing groups of African states became visible – the Casablanca bloc and the Monrovia bloc, each of which had differing visions of pan-African unity, the former based on the idea of a supranational pan-African government similar to a United States of Africa and the latter committed to a looser federation of independent states. The formation of the OAU which later transformed into the African Union can be seen as a compromise between these positions.

21 The aims of the non-aligned movement was to ensure 'the national independence, sovereignty, territorial integrity and security of non-aligned countries' in their 'struggle against imperialism, colonialism, neo-colonialism, racism, and all forms of foreign aggression, occupation, domination, interference or hegemony as well as against great power and bloc politics', by Fidel Castro in the Havana Declaration of 1979. Significantly, all the countries of Africa despite being aligned with either the Western or Soviet blocs also became members of the non-aligned movement which has more recently taken on more of a co-ordinating role in representing the voices of low-income countries around the world.

22 Subsequently, the term has become a point of reference for politicians in Africa, has spawned a number of conferences, and led to the establishment of the African Renaissance Institute in Tshwana (formerly Pretoria).

23 The war on terror, for example, was given impetus from the political response to the 9/11 attacks in the United States whilst the spread of Islamic fundamentalism can be seen to be rooted in forms of local resistance to perceived Westernisation and demands for a caliphate in parts of the Arab World as well in the horns of Africa and Northern Nigeria. Trump's virulent anti-globalisation and reassertion of protectionist policies coupled with the anti-globalisation rhetoric associated with the leave campaign in the UK may well transform into a new anti-globalisation, global wave.

24 Obi argues that environmental movements in Africa have tended to operate within a transformative logic in which struggles for power over environmental resources connect broader popular social struggles for empowerment and democracy.

25 For our purposes, principles are factors which guide the purpose of action of governments and institutions. In the case of EFA, they comprise the underlying

view of education and development, including the rationale for investment in education. Norms determine what general behaviour is legitimate in pursuing a particular regime's goals. The rules are closely related to norms and particularise the actual rights and obligations of governments and institutions in a regime. In the case of EFA, they include consideration of the specific funding mechanisms that have been used. Finally, decision-making procedures are also closely linked to norms and refer to the mechanisms within and between governments and institutions through which decisions are made. As has been pointed out, there are overlaps and it is not always easy to clearly distinguish between principles, norms, rules, and decision-making procedures (Haggard and Simmons 1987).

26 Here the book draws on Keohane's (Keohane 2011) understanding of the legitimacy of international regimes as residing in their moral acceptability, inclusiveness, epistemic quality (by which he means integrity and transparency, accountability, compatibility with governance norms at a national level, and be of perceived comparative benefit for actors, e.g. through reducing the transaction costs associated with bilateral arrangements).

27 Here a regime complex is defined as 'a network of three or more international regimes that relate to a common subject matter; exhibit overlapping membership; and generate substantive, normative, or operative interactions recognised as potentially problematic whether or not they are managed effectively' (Orsini, Morin, and Young 2013, 29).

28 In the African context, the fledgling regions in the postcolonial era such as the East African Community (EAC), which subsequently collapsed, and the Southern African Development Coordination Conference (SADCC), which transformed itself into the Southern African Development Community (SADC), can be seen as examples of the old regionalism as can the now defunct Organisation for African Unity (OAU) insofar as the key underlying principle was to bolster the sovereignty of the participating nation states through developing stronger economic ties.

29 Whereas the approach of the old regionalism was characterised as 'state-centric', with a focus on forms of co-operation between nation states, the main emphasis of the new regionalism is on the development of regions themselves as an aspect of globalisation. The new regionalism must be understood in historical context and in relation to the new division of power in the world, new forms of global integration, the erosion of the Westphalian nation-state system, and the dominance of neoliberal economic models (Hettne and Soderbaum 2000).

30 The EU, for example, which is often held up as a model for other regions, represents not only an economic space but has also emerged out of a project of identity construction which goes hand in hand with economic and political integration (Robertson et al. 2007). Crucially, the new regionalism is not confined to formal associations between nation states but includes informal networks and associations between actors in civil society operating at a number of different scales.

31 The AU is perhaps more accurately described as 'macro-regional' in scope, on a par with other macro-regions such as the EU, NAFTA, and ASEAN. SADC and COMESA are variously portrayed as either 'macro-regions' in their own right or as 'sub-regions' when considered in relation to the AU, NEPAD, and other initiatives. An interesting but unexplored dimension would be to consider the implications for education of the proliferation of 'micro-regions' on the continent, i.e. regions that operate within or across national boundaries but at a scale that is between the national and the local. Examples here include conservation areas and spatial development initiatives such as the Maputo corridor (see (Simon 2003) for a discussion of these initiatives).

32 Given the large scope of regionalism in Africa, the analysis that follows will focus on formal (state centred), informal (civil society based), and mixed (state and civil society based) examples of educational regionalism.

33 The South African President, Thabo Mbeki, for example, draws on the idea of 'developmental regionalism' as a means of securing African interests.

34 See also Vale and Maseko's (1998) critique of the African Renaissance project which preceded NEPAD and provided much of the intellectual roots for the programme.

35 This kind of view also falls within the grain of more recent calls for instituting new forms of democratic governance and accountability at the global level, including reform of the World Trade Organization (WTO) and a stronger voice for Africa and other low-income countries within the World Bank and other multilateral organisations (Khor 2002).

36 The report notes improvement in domestic resource mobilisation and public administration, modest progress in tackling corruption, significant improvements in the business climate, and progress in stemming illicit capital outflows.

37 Although the FD also notes that according to transparency international, four out of five African countries are below the world average (p. 64).

38 It points to detention without trial, arbitrary arrests, torture, forced disappearances, and extrajudicial killings which it claims are still unfortunately widespread whilst access to justice and independence of the judicial system is a major concern. The report highlights pervasive weaknesses of institutions, especially in the field of human rights at national, regional, and continental levels.

39 Each of these projects can be seen to have articulated with both 'capitalist' and 'socialist' growth paths and with single and multi-party systems. The former emerged where already established elites had maintained their power (such as in Senegal, Cameroon, Botswana, and Burundi) and the latter involved the rise of at least a section of the subordinate groups (e.g. Angola, Mozambique, Kenya, and Tanzania). Both projects had at their centre concepts of 'development' and of 'nation building', although they have differed in their specific character (see also(Mkandawire 1996). Where hegemony has been maintained in both cases, it has involved the 'reciprocal assimilation of elites', i.e. a process of ameliorating emerging or existing elites through granting limited access to status and wealth.

5 Africa and the global governance of education

Introduction

Having set out the broad nature of global governance in the context of the postcolonial condition in the previous chapter, the focus of the present chapter is on the development of the global governance of education in the context of contemporary globalisation.[1] As discussed in Chapter 4, global governance is usefully conceived in terms of the operation of different 'regimes of global governance', which are characterised as complex networks of different kinds of actors that cohere around sets of implicit or explicit principles, norms, rules, and decision-making procedures but that are overlain by the operation of different forms of power and of regimes of inequality. The chapter will commence by discussing the implications of the analysis in Chapter 4 for how education policy can be understood. Attention will then turn to a consideration of the Education for All regime of governance as it has evolved in the issue area of education and development. It will be argued, however, that it is in the process of being superseded by a new regime of governance organised around the principles of ESD and encapsulated in SDG 4.

Conceptualising global and regional education policy

At a broad level, 'education governance' relates to processes of control and contestation in the design, implementation, and enactment of education policy. It is therefore useful to outline the underlying view of what is meant by global and regional education policy. In developing understanding, the chapter builds on recent work within the critical tradition (Mundy et al. 2017; Verger, Altinyelken, and Novelli 2018) but will develop insights from this work in relation to the analysis of complex globalisation provided in Chapter 2. It was argued earlier that global governance is best conceived as the 'articulation' of processes of governance at different scales from that of the global to the regional and the local. At a global scale, consideration of policy involves drawing attention to 'meta-discourses' that shape what can be thought, or in Carney's (Carney 2008) terms, 'policyscapes' that help to frame regional agendas. In the context of this book, policyscapes are seen to emerge from the co-evolution of complex regimes of global governance. In this respect as mentioned, a key point of reference for *Agenda 2063* and CESA is the adoption of the Sustainable Development Goals (SDGs). Regional policy agendas then serve to mediate and reinterpret global policy in relation to regional interests and priorities which are in turn mediated and reinterpreted at a national level. This is not a straightforward process, however. At the regional level for example, global agendas become articulated in complex and contradictory ways with regional priorities by the operation of different kinds of structural and productive power and the relative capacity of different interest groups to shape emerging policy agendas.

At a national level, the take-up or otherwise of global and regional agendas is mediated by nationally defined development priorities but also in the context of the nature of the postcolonial state to the capacity of the state and the relative ability of governments to resist and/or modify the demands of donors. It is important to nonetheless recognise that countries are in different positions in relation to the influence of multilateral organisations and global policy agendas. Countries such as South Africa, for example, are less financially dependent on aid and have greater technical capacity which enables them to more effectively set their own education agendas. Polities also differ in the relative capacity of different interests within the state and civil society to shape policy, including, for example, the media, organised religions, grass roots indigenous movements, identifiable social groupings such as the youth and women, NGOs, teachers' unions, and professional associations. This degree of influence will vary depending on the extent to which the state is open or closed to these diverse external voices and interests.

Further, as Unterhalter and North (2017) have shown through careful ethnographic analysis of policy implementation, global agendas such as EFA and gender equality become more diluted at more localised levels as global agendas seem more remote. In this sense, it will be suggested in later chapters that education policy also needs to be interpreted in terms of the nature of the curriculum and pedagogical practices that get implemented and enacted at organisational level as well as whatever is formally instantiated in global, regional, and national policy texts. This understanding draws attention to the gap between policy rhetoric, on the one hand, and what actually goes on at the level of practice on the other. It also underlines the importance of the agency of policy makers and practitioners at different scales in enacting policy and the extent to which policy simultaneously shapes and is shaped by social relations, including those based on class, race, ethnicity, and gender. This observation draws attention to Ball, Maguire and Braun's (2011) understanding of the need to focus on policy as enactment, i.e. as what actually gets implemented in terms of policy and practice at different scales and the influence of processes of contestation and mediation.

The emergence of education for all as global regime of education governance

Governance in education as in other spheres has been reterritorialised in the global era (see Chapter 4). This has involved the insertion of national education systems into changing regimes of global governance (Tikly 2017). These have had profound implications for the development of regional and national policy agendas as is discussed in the following. It is important therefore to understand the changing nature of regimes of global governance as they have emerged since the end of the Second World War. Prior to 1990, education and development had been dominated by the funding modalities linked to World Bank structural adjustment lending and by forms of bilateral funding that had their origins in the Cold War period. These were so disparate that it is difficult to describe them as a 'regime' and indeed it was partly as a response to the uncoordinated nature of development assistance within the issue area of education and development that Education for All (EFA) emerged.

The principles governing EFA have remained fairly consistent over the past quarter of a century. They have centred on a commitment to education as a human right and as an investment in human capital, but this has had contradictory implications for the way that EFA has been conceptualised, including the scope of EFA, the relative weight attached to issues of access versus quality, which groups EFA has been targeted at, and the role of states and markets in the provision of education. They are rooted in turn in wider discourses of development from the Washington to the post-Washington consensus and more recently to sustainable development. The norms associated with EFA are encapsulated in the various targets set out in key declarations and frameworks, including the Jomtien Declaration, the *Dakar Framework for Action*, and, more recently, the *Muscat Agreement*. These are summarised in Box 5.1 in relation to key topic areas within EFA. It is evident that there has been much continuity at the level of norms between Jomtien in 1990 and Muscat in 2015. It can also be seen, however, that when it comes to the 2015 *Incheon Declaration and Framework for Action* (IDFA), there has been a subtle shift at the level of norms with a greater emphasis on the IDFA compared to previous documents on attitudes, skills, and dispositions linked to sustainable development (although many of these have also been evident to some extent since Jomtien). There has also been a greater emphasis over the period as a whole on secondary, vocational, and higher education and on learning (as compared to access) with the exception of higher education where the emphasis in the IDFA lies in expanding access, including through scholarships.[2] These changes in the level of norms are suggestive of regime change. That is, what is beginning to emerge is a new regime in the issue area of education and development organised around the principles and norms of ESD and the SDGs.

Box 5.1 Jomtien, Dakar, Muscat, and Incheon compared

Topic area addressed	1990–2000: Jomtien	2000–2015: Dakar	2015–2030: Muscat	2015–2030: Incheon
Early childhood education	1. Expansion of early childhood care and development activities, including family and community interventions, especially for poor, disadvantaged and disabled children	1. Expanding and improving comprehensive early childhood care and education, especially for the most vulnerable and disadvantaged children	1. By 2030, at least x% of girls and boys are ready for primary school through participation in quality early childhood care and education, including at least one year of free and compulsory pre-primary education, with particular attention to gender equality and the most marginalised	4.2 By 2030, ensure that all girls and boys have access to quality early childhood development, care, and pre-primary education so that they are ready for primary education
Access to basic, formal education	2. Universal access to, and completion of, primary education (or whatever higher level of education is considered as 'basic') by the year 2000	2. Ensuring that by 2015 all children, particularly girls, children in difficult circumstances, and those belonging to ethnic minorities, have access to and complete free and compulsory primary education of good quality	2. By 2030, all girls and boys complete free and compulsory quality basic education of at least nine years and achieve relevant learning outcomes, with particular attention to gender equality and the most marginalised	4.1 By 2030, ensure that all girls and boys complete free, equitable, and quality primary and secondary education leading to relevant and effective learning outcomes

(Continued)

(Continued)

Topic area addressed	1990–2000: Jomtien	2000–2015: Dakar	2015–2030: Muscat	2015–2030: Incheon
Improving education quality and learning outcomes	3. Improvement in learning achievement such that an agreed percentage of an appropriate age cohort (e.g. 80% 14 year olds) attains or surpasses a defined level of necessary learning achievement	6. Improving all aspects of the quality of education and ensuring excellence of all so that recognised and measurable learning outcomes are achieved by all, especially in literacy, numeracy, and essential life skills		
Increasing basic literacy/numeracy	4. Reduction in the adult illiteracy rate (the appropriate age cohort to be determined in each country) to, say, one-half its 1990 level by the year 2000, with sufficient emphasis on female literacy to significantly reduce the current disparity between the male and female illiteracy rates	4. Achieving a 50% improvement in levels of adult literacy by 2015, especially for women, and equitable access to basic and continuing education for all adults	3. By 2030, all youth and at least x% of adults reach a proficiency level in literacy and numeracy sufficient to fully participate in society, with particular attention to girls and women and the most marginalised	4.6 By 2030, ensure that all youth and a substantial proportion of adults, both men and women, achieve literacy and numeracy
Gender equity		5. Eliminating gender disparities in primary and secondary education by 2015,		4.5 By 2030, eliminate gender disparities in education and ensure equal access to all levels

Topic area addressed	1990–2000: Jomtien	2000–2015: Dakar	2015–2030: Muscat	2015–2030: Incheon
		with a focus on ensuring girls' full and equal access to and achievement in basic education of good quality		of education and vocational training for the vulnerable, including persons with disabilities, indigenous peoples, and children in vulnerable situations
Inclusion/reaching the most marginalised				4.a Build and upgrade education facilities that are child-, disability-, and gender-sensitive and provide safe, non-violent, inclusive, and effective learning environments for all
Access to TVET/ HE	5. Expansion of provision of basic education and training in other essential skills required by youth and adults, with programme effectiveness assessed in terms of behavioural changes and impacts on health, employment, and productivity		4. By 2030, at least x% of youth and y% of adults have the knowledge and skills for decent work and life through technical and vocational, upper secondary and tertiary education and training, with particular attention to gender equality and the most marginalised	4.3 By 2030, ensure equal access for all women and men to affordable and quality technical, vocational, and tertiary education, including university 4.b By 2020, substantially expand globally the number of scholarships available to developing countries, in

(Continued)

(Continued)

Topic area addressed	1990–2000: Jomtien	2000–2015: Dakar	2015–2030: Muscat	2015–2030: Incheon
				particular least-developed countries, small island developing states, and African countries, for enrolment in higher education, including vocational training and information and communications technology, technical, engineering and scientific programmes, in developed countries and other developing countries
				4.4 By 2030, substantially increase the number of youth and adults who have relevant skills, including technical and vocational skills, for employment, decent jobs, and entrepreneurship
Life skills/ sustainable development	6. Increased acquisition by individuals and families of the knowledge, skills, and values required for better living and sound and sustainable development, made available through all educational channels, including the mass media, other forms of modern and traditional	3. Ensuring that the learning needs of all young people and adults are met through equitable access to appropriate learning and life skills programmes	5. By 2030, all learners acquire knowledge, skills, values, and attitudes to establish sustainable and peaceful societies, including through global citizenship education and education for sustainable development	

Topic area addressed	1990–2000: Jomtien	2000–2015: Dakar	2015–2030: Muscat	2015–2030: Incheon
	communication, and social action, with effectiveness assessed in terms of behavioural change			4.7 By 2030, ensure that all learners acquire the knowledge and skills needed to promote sustainable development, including, among others, through education for sustainable development and sustainable lifestyles, human rights, gender equality, promotion of a culture of peace and non-violence, global citizenship and appreciation of cultural diversity and of culture's contribution to sustainable development
Teachers			6. By 2030, all governments ensure that all learners are taught by qualified, professionally trained, motivated, and well-supported teachers.	4.c By 2030, substantially increase the supply of qualified teachers, including through international cooperation for teacher

(Continued)

(Continued)

Topic area addressed	1990–2000: Jomtien	2000–2015: Dakar	2015–2030: Muscat	2015–2030: Incheon
				training in developing countries, especially least-developed countries and small island developing states
Financial allocation			7. By 2030, all countries allocate at least 4–6% of their gross domestic product (GDP) or at least 15–20% of their public expenditure to education, prioritising groups most in need; and strengthen financial cooperation for education, prioritising countries most in need	

The emergence of a distinct regime organised around the principles and norms of EFA was associated with a wider shift from the Washington to the post-Washington consensus (Mundy 2007; Mundy and Manion 2015b). As is widely documented, several multilateral organisations were instrumental in shaping EFA from inception, including the World Bank, UNESCO, UNICEF (where the EFA idea originated), and the UNDP. The early days of EFA in the lead up and aftermath of both the Jomtien Conference in 1990 (at which the first *Declaration on Education for All* was agreed) and the Dakar Conference in 2000 (that adopted the EFA *Framework for Action*) were marked by infighting between these organisations with the World Bank ultimately proving dominant (King 2007). Global NGOs, including the influential Global Campaign for Education, were also influential in advocating a more rights-based vision of EFA (Mundy and Murphy 2001; Mundy and Manion 2015b; Verger, Altinyelken, and Novelli 2018; Verger and Novelli 2012). EFA has also been shaped by the actions and demands of key donors, for example, in the establishment and development of the Fast Track Initiative (FTI) as a means of channelling bilateral funding for education in support of EFA (Bermingham 2011; Bermingham 2010). In 2012, the FTI itself transformed into the Global Partnership for Education (GPE) with its own charter and governance structures.[3]

There have also been changes in the decision-making procedures over the years within the EFA regime linked to its changing organisational form. EFA originally evolved as a networked movement mobilised around a common set of principles and norms enshrined in the Jomtien Declaration and Dakar Framework for Action. At its centre was a secretariat and high-level panel situated within UNESCO. Also significant was the development of an epistemic community around the Global Monitoring Report (GMR) (recently transformed into the Global Education Monitoring Report or GEMR) that draws on expertise from the UNESCO Institute for Statistics.[4] The development of the EFA Fast Track Initiative in 2002 as a vertical fund within the World Bank with its own decision-making processes added another layer of organisational complexity but did not fundamentally alter its networked nature (Bermingham 2010, 2011). The development of the FTI into the GPE as the main institution for delivering EFA with its own Board of Directors in 2012 has provided an alternative locus of power away from UNESCO. The FTI/GPE has also been the central focus for rules within the regime, although these have had contradictory implications for donors, on the one hand, and for recipients of aid on the other (discussed in the following).

The increasing complexity of global and regional governance of education

As several commentators have observed, global governance in education as in other areas has become more 'dense' as the number of regimes impinging on different issue areas has increased (Orsini, Morin, and Young 2013). In this respect, the number of regimes that have impinged on education and development has multiplied over time to the point where EFA can be said to exist within a 'regime complex'.[5]

The aid regime

The aid regime along with changing discourses concerning aid effectiveness has provided a consistent theme in the development of EFA. The aid regime has been described elsewhere (Hook and Rumsey 2015; Barnett and Walker 2015). The key institution in this regime is the OECD and specifically the Development Assistance Committee (DAC), which has often determined the nature and direction of policy within the aid regime. The World Bank has also been a powerful institution in the regime in its role as the major channel through which development assistance has been provided to low-income countries in the form of loans and grants. The model of conditional lending has remained a consistent feature of the World Bank lending in education as in other areas of development, in the context of both the Washington and Post-Washington consensus (Bonal 2011).[6] The World Bank has also evolved an extremely powerful epistemic community of its own that has played a significant role in shaping the principles and norms governing EFA (discussed in the following).

There have, however, been major shifts in the aid regime since its inception in the post–Second World War period, including the move from project to programme funding (i.e. support for discrete development projects to budgetary support). Changes in policy such as the introduction of time-bound targets were influential in the development of targets that informed the Millennium Development Goals (MDGs) (Robertson et al. 2007; King 2007). Similarly, the changing discourse of aid effectiveness has provided a consistent theme in the development of aid to education and other areas of social development.[7] For example, the *Paris Declaration on Aid Effectiveness* and the *Accra Agenda for Action* have stressed the need for greater efficiency and accountability in the use of aid. Indeed, attempts were made to align the FTI from inception with the principles of aid effectiveness and donor harmonisation that were emerging from high-level donor meetings in Rome (OECD 2003).[8] The emphasis on 'accountability' has provided a catalyst for the development of new aid modalities, including results-based aid.[9] Elsewhere it has been argued that these modalities can be seen as an application of new forms of managerialism that are themselves an aspect of neoliberal governmentality (Tikly 2017). The OECD has also developed its own very powerful epistemic community that has exercised considerable productive power in the setting of global agendas. This includes the OECDs increasingly prominent role as a broker of education policy and linked to this the administration of the PISA international assessment regime.[10]

The changes in world order linked to the changing dynamics of power in global governance have also impacted on the aid regime. Until recently, the regime has been dominated by Western interests. As is well documented, however, Chinese economic investment in Africa has been accompanied by new forms of development assistance based on the provision of infrastructure in exchange for favourable access to natural resources and land (Mohan 2013). In education, it has also involved the exercise of soft power through the role of Confucius institutes on the continent and making available large numbers of scholarships in China for African students (King 2013). A characteristic of Chinese engagement with Africa is that it has been based on strict adherence to the principles of non-interference, a key touchstone of the so-called 'Beijing consensus' (Ayers 2013). This has led some Western powers and institutions such as the World Bank to raise concerns about how Chinese development assistance is 'undermining' Western reform efforts in African economies.[11] The implication for many African countries is the need to deal with an increasingly complex and fragmented development assistance architecture that not only comprises different kinds of models of 'partnership' but also engages with different underlying conceptions of modernity and development, in this case Chinese and Western.

It is in this context that Africa's marginal position and relative weakness in relation to processes of global governance becomes apparent. As *Agenda 2063* points out,

> global governance matters a great deal for Africa as decisions made in global institutions and forums have a direct impact on the wellbeing of Africans and their continent. Yet Africa has to date been a marginal player in the governance of global institutions. This is particularly so with respect to international peace and security, economics, environment, and trade issues, and in other areas.
>
> (AUC 2015a, 74–75)[12]

From the perspective of this chapter, the aid regime has been subject to considerable criticism from its development in the post–Second World War era albeit from different perspectives. The neoliberal economist, Milton Friedman, for example, argued that by strengthening government through aid, there would be less incentive to maintain an environment conducive to business. Other critics have often focused on the extent to which aid creates dependence and merely serves to prop up vested interests within the state. Brautigam and Knack (2004) have defined aid dependence as 'a situation in which a government is unable to perform many of the core functions of government, such as the maintenance of existing infrastructure or the delivery of basic public services, without foreign aid funding and expertise (provided in the form of technical assistance or projects). This characterises many countries in Africa today, where . . . 'many governments have developed a cosy accommodation with dependency' (257).

There continue to be harsh critics of the aid regime. Moyo (2009), taking up earlier discourses around dependency, argues that aid has failed in increasing growth and reducing poverty in Africa and through its role in creating perverse incentives has become 'the disease of which it pretends to be the cure' (12). The implication for Moyo is to do away with the current system of aid altogether. Other scholars of aid such as Riddell (2007) argue that whilst aid has often not succeeded in the achievement of self-sustaining development, donors should not stop providing aid as this would have catastrophic consequences for the poor. Rather, for Riddell, the aid architecture needs to be reformed. Ramalingam (2013b), using a complex systems approach, proposes a 'transformational' perspective on aid in which the role of aid in development shifts from one of 'external push' in filling gaps in a predictable and linear fashion to one of internal catalyst that would 'identify, expand and sustain the space for change', thus providing a basis for challenging the status quo (p. 361). The idea of transformative aid which is in important respects consistent with the approach of this book is taken up in Chapter 10.

The human rights regime

A further key influence on development discourse has been from the human rights regime which emerged in the period following the Second World War and the formation of the UN. The mandates for both UNESCO and UNICEF arise from their roles in advancing human rights in education and other spheres. The *Proclamation of the Universal Declaration of Human Rights* and subsequent legally binding covenants and conventions have sought to create a framework intended to guarantee a dignified life for all human beings regardless of race, culture, or gender. Rights-based approaches, which became influential in development work from the 1990s, recast the inhabitants of impoverished parts of the globe as rights-holders entitled to justice rather than beneficiaries of the charity of the privileged (McCowan 2015). The basic needs approach emerged as a variant of human rights and this informed the understanding of human development that underpinned the Brundtland Report *Our Common Future*, which was a key milestone in the emergence of sustainable development (detailed in subsequent pages). From inception, a key influence on EFA has been from the human rights regime. Human rights have provided a consistent point of reference in the development of the principles of EFA as have been the various UN conventions on human rights and especially on the rights of the child. These are also referenced quite clearly in the Incheon Declaration and Framework for Action (IDFA).

Whilst providing an alternative liberal egalitarian view of development to that posited by modernisation theory and neoliberalism, the human rights regime has also been subject to criticism. For example, human rights frameworks have been described as an example of a universalising Western discourse and have, as a consequence, operated as source of hypocrisy and contradiction (de Sousa Santos 2002).[13] They have also been criticised for being top-down in their application and often removed from indigenous and local discourses about ethics with which they are seldom brought into conversation. In Chapter 3, it was suggested that the capability approach, which is often considered a 'species' of the rights-based approach, offers a useful development on the idea of human rights through its insistence on the importance of informed public dialogue as a basis for determining rights and capabilities.

Trade and security regimes

The world trade regime has also provided an increasingly influential (if complex and contradictory) regulatory framework, including, for example, the General Agreement in Trade in Services (GATS), the more recent Trade in International Services Agreement (TiSA), and various Regional Trade Agreements (RTAs) that are all aimed at liberalising cross-border trade in services, including education. Careful analysis has shown (Verger 2009; Verger and Robertson 2012) that the effect of these agreements is to create a regulatory and policy environment at national level that is conducive to the further privatisation and marketisation of education.[14] Connected to this broader shift in development thinking has been the growing influence of large philanthropic private sector organisations in their capacity as increasingly significant funders of education in global governance, including, for example, on the board of the GPE. Finally, the global security regime has impacted on EFA through influencing efforts on the part of some donors to link funding for areas of development, including education to the so-called 'war on terror'. This has effectively reduced the amount of aid money for education in some of the poorest regions of the world, including Africa (Novelli 2010). More recently, the UN Secretary General's own *Global Education First Initiative* has specifically linked the issue of access to a good-quality education to peace building, including an emphasis on citizenship education.[15]

The MDG regime

As indicated in Chapter 2, the development of the MDG regime under the auspices of the UN has also had significant implications for the development and future of EFA.[16] The process that led to the drafting and adoption of the MDGs did not centrally include UNESCO as the lead organisation in EFA, although UNICEF was involved as was the World Bank. The implication was the adoption of a narrower agenda than that represented by the Dakar Framework to reflect the World Bank's historic emphasis on primary education and UINICEF's concern with girls' education. The implications of this narrower agenda have often been perceived as problematic by those committed to EFA (Mundy and Manion 2015a). The two MDGs relating to education were as follows:

MDG 2: ensure that, by 2015, children everywhere, boys and girls alike, will be able to complete a full course of primary schooling.
MDG 3: eliminate gender disparity in primary and secondary education, preferably by 2005, and in all levels of education no later than 2015.

In summary to this section and as several commentators have pointed out, regime complexity can have its own causal effects. For example, some regimes have the power to demand greater compliance over governments than others. In Barnett and Duvall's terms, that is to say that they exercise greater compulsory power. Trade agreements linked to the trade regime, for example, once signed often become binding on governments. The development aid regime, on the other hand, does not force governments to comply in the same way. Although donor governments are encouraged to commit a certain proportion of their GDP to aid, they are not compelled to do so unless they adopt their own legislation to this effect. Neither are the governments compelled by legally binding agreements to commit funding to a specific area of international development or to comply with aid effectiveness principles. By way of contrast, low-income countries are often compelled to accept the conditions attached to conditional loans from the World Bank or to comply with the rules for receiving aid from vertical funds channelled through the World Bank such as the funds managed by the FTI/GPE. The great imbalance in compulsory power provides the basis for dependency and the major source of tension/contradiction within EFA and the aid regime more broadly, as will be discussed in the following.[17]

The emergence of the SDG regime

Several commentators (Wals 2010; Blewitt 2018; Elliot 2013; Sachs 2012) have provided a detailed overview of the origins of the SDG regime. A summary of the genealogy of policy relating to SD was provided in Chapter 3. The adoption of the 17 Sustainable Development Goals (SDGs) by the United Nations in November 2015 and enshrined in *Transforming our World: The 2030 Agenda for Sustainable Development* (UN 2015c) has ushered in a new era of global development thinking and propelled the idea of SD to hegemonic status within global policy agendas concerned with development. The process leading up to the adoption of the goals has been described as the largest consultation programme in the history of the UN and stands in contrast to the MDGs, which it has been suggested 'were drawn up by a group of men in the basement of the UN headquarters' (Guardian 2015). Originally proposed by the Colombian government, it was the 2010 High-level Plenary Meeting of the UN General Assembly that first muted the goals. It was at the *UN Conference on Sustainable Development* (Rio+20) that the intergovernmental process to define the SDGs was launched, including the establishment of an open working group (OWG).[18] In July 2012, Secretary-General Ban Ki-moon also announced the 27 members of a High-Level Panel of eminent persons to advise on the global development framework beyond 2015, the target date for the MDGs.[19] The report of the panel (UN 2013) also fed into the wider consultation process. The Secretary General of the UN was charged with producing a synthesis report drawing together the various consultations together with other inputs such as that from the Intergovernmental Committee of Experts on Sustainable Development Financing (UN 2015c). The report presented at the 2015 UN Summit in New York formed the basis for the *Transforming Our World* document.

The SDGs are the culmination of a long history of global debate and advocacy about SD. These were summarised in Chapter 3. Progress towards achieving the goals is the responsibility of the High-Level Political Forum on Sustainable Development convened under the auspices of the Economic and Social Council of the UN. The panel produces an annual report based on an agreed framework of indicators. The most recent report at the time of publishing (UN 2017) provides data on progress towards each of the 17 goals. Reading the report draws attention to the inherently political nature of the process of identifying goals, targets, and indicators. In this respect, the SDGs 'quilt together' a range of sometimes contradictory economic and political interests and this is reflected in the contested nature of the goals and targets (Sayed 2019).

The sometimes-contradictory nature of the goals needs to be understood in the context of how they were developed. Thus, according to Sayed, and despite being described as the largest consultation process ever undertaken by the UN, the process was dominated by elites, including representatives of governments, key multilateral organisations, and international non-governmental organisations with a more muted voice for global civil society. Further, as King and Palmer (2013) have also argued, the process was Northern led. In this respect, however, although it is the case that Northern governments and interests have predominated in global agendas about development including the SDGs, African governments have played a role in advocating for sustainable development (see Chapter 1). As with the MDGs before, the adoption of the SDGs also represented a struggle for hegemony between different multilateral organisations, including the UN, UNICEF, and the World Bank. These organisations propose sometimes competing ideas about how to achieve the SDGs (see Chapter 6). For the World Bank for instance, the issue is one of 'inclusive growth' in which wealth creation will lead to a reduction in absolute poverty through a trickle-down effect, whereas UNESCO has historically championed the idea of sustainable development and UNICEF has advocated for the rights of the child and gender equity. The upshot then can be described as something of a 'meta-fix' (Lélé 1991).

Emergence of the ESD regime

As we have seen in Chapter 1, the education SDG (SDG 4) aims to ensure inclusive and equitable quality education and to promote lifelong learning opportunities for all. As already indicated, the targets associated with SDG 4 were fully incorporated into the IDFA, as illustrated in Box 4.1.[20] This, it was suggested, is indicative of regime change in the area of international education development. That is, what we are currently witnessing is a shift from the EFA regime to a new regime organised around the norms and principles of ESD and encapsulated in the goals and targets associated with SDG4.

Conclusion

The chapter has reviewed changing patterns in the global governance of African education since colonial times. Discussion has centred on the emergence and development of EFA which has provided a focal point for the development of global education policy. It has been argued, however, that EFA has given way to a new global regime represented by the SDGs and SDG 4 in particular and organised around the principles and norms of ESD, at least as it is articulated in mainstream development discourse. The issue area of education and development has, however, also become more complex with the emergence of different regimes relating to aid, the MDGs, and trade amongst others. These have added to the phenomenon of regime complexity with implications for global and regional education policy. Some of these implications are considered in more detail in Chapter 6 where attention will turn to the governance of education at the regional and national scales.

Notes

1 In keeping with the understanding of the postcolonial condition set out in Chapter 3, colonial education policy can also be seen as a previous form of global governance. Given that the colonial legacy is experienced most profoundly in the context of national systems of education and training, discussion of colonial education policy is reserved for discussion in the next chapter on global and national governance.

2 There is also a more explicit concern with the inclusion of different marginalized groups as well as the historical concern (since Dakar at least) with gender equity. The Dakar framework was unique in specifying a target relating to financial allocations, although these are covered in other SDGs relating to global partnerships.

3 Given that the majority of funding for EFA is now channelled through the GPE, it has become a central player in the EFA architecture. This is reflected in the involvement of the GPE in the 2015 World Education Forum. Institutional involvement in the EFA regime has also broadened since Jomtien and Dakar with other new actors, including the OECD, more centrally involved.

4 The GMR was established after Dakar as a means of monitoring progress towards the EFA goals enshrined in the Dakar Framework of Action. This has provided a powerful source of advocacy for advancing the EFA agenda and an alternative locus for conceptualising education developments to the epistemic community associated with the World Bank.

5 Here a regime complex is defined as 'a network of three or more international regimes that relate to a common subject matter; exhibit overlapping membership; and generate substantive, normative, or operative interactions recognised as potentially problematic whether or not they are managed effectively' (Orsini, Morin, and Young 2013, 29).

6 More recently, World Bank lending for basic education for the poorest low-income countries including those of sub-Saharan Africa has been superseded by the GPE with the Bank's lending increasingly channelled towards supporting secondary and tertiary education in middle-income countries (Mundy and Verger 2015). The strategy of drawing in a wider range of institutions and global networks in the development of the EFA agenda can be seen as part of a wider move to achieve legitimacy for its policies in the context of the post-Washington consensus and following the success of the earlier Health for All initiative (Coleman and Jones 2004).

7 Major conferences, protocols, and agreements relating to aid effectiveness include the Paris declaration and Busan agreement. The principles relating to aid effectiveness may be summarized as country ownership of development plans; alignment between aid and national development plans and capacities; harmonization between donors; managing for results; mutual accountability for outcomes linked to aid.

8 Key documents associated with the FTI and now GPE also reference the major conferences, protocols, and agreements relating to aid effectiveness, including the Paris declaration and the Busan agreement.

9 Some donors including the World Bank and the UK's Department for International Development are increasingly seeking to link funding to the achievement of specific outcomes in education and other areas. This system of 'results based aid' (RBA) aimed at making aid more effective and accountable has often been difficult to implement because of the limited capacity for governments to meet donor implementing and reporting requirements and the complexities involved in linking funding to tangible improvements in learner outcomes.

10 Most recently, this has led to the development of the PISA for Development initiative as a means of drawing low-income countries into the same framework

of international assessments that is already inhabited by many high- and middle-income countries (see www.oecd.org/pisa/aboutpisa/pisa-for-development-background.htm).

11 As commentators such as Ayers and Mohan point out, however, such concerns smack of hypocrisy in that Chinese investments in Africa fall far short of Western interests and that raising such concerns elides the role of the West since colonial times in supporting undemocratic practices on the continent. In this regard, as Ferguson notes, a perverse effect of neoliberal policies has been that economic growth has often occurred in enclaves within highly dysfunctional states.

12 The report particularly highlights Africa's lack of representation in the United Nations Security Council, pointing out that although half of the resolutions passed in 2011 related to Africa but Africa is not among the permanent members and African members have no veto power. Similarly, Africa is not represented on the Bretton Woods global financial institutions despite the inordinate amount of influence the World Bank and IMF have had over Africa's affairs. Finally, the report points out that whereas the EU represents 27 European countries in the World Trade negotiation, the AU is not a member of the WTO which weaken the collective voice of Africa over global trade.

13 Santos contends that 'as long as human rights are conceived of as universal, they will operate as a globalized localism, a form of globalization from above' (de Sousa Santos 2002, 44). This matters because arguably human rights policies have for the most part been at the service of the economic and geopolitical interests of the hegemonic capitalist states, the same states that have legitimated 'unspeakable atrocities' revealing 'revolting double standards' (p. 45). The distinctive Western liberal mark in human rights discourses was established in the universal declaration of 1948, 'which was drafted without the participation of the majority of the peoples of the world; in the exclusive recognition of individual rights, with the only exception of the collective right to self-determination which, however, was restricted to the peoples subjected to European colonialism; in the priority given to civil and political rights over economic, social and cultural rights; and in the recognition of the right to property as the first and, for many years, the sole economic right' (p. 45).

14 The trade agreements have worked within the grain of the idea of public–private partnerships that has been promoted by the World Bank in the context of the Washington and post-Washington consensus. These effects are also contested by those working within a rights-based framework and this has in turn affected the extent to which governments have included education as a service to be traded. The net effect, however, of these external and internal pressures for privatization has been to provide a supportive regulatory and policy environment for a growth in the number of private firms operating in low-income countries in the sphere of education, including the establishment of chains of low-fee private schools as well as privately run tertiary institutions.

15 www.globaleducationfirst.org. The initiative also serves to underline the efforts by the Secretary General to highlight the important role of education within the overall aid regime.

16 Here the analysis departs from the traditional view of EFA as a movement. Rather than the education MDGs and the education SDG being seen as integral to EFA, they are seen as belonging to separate albeit related regimes governed by different principles, norms, rules, and decision-making processes.

17 Regime complexity and the degree of compulsory power linked to different regimes allow donor governments latitude to link development assistance more closely to their own economic and political interests. For example, in the context of austerity politics in the wake of the 2008 financial crash, many governments

can still choose to limit the amount of development assistance. They can also choose to channel aid to areas where there is greater evidence of value for money to appease internal critics of aid and to use aid strategically to support national security or with respect to recent developments to seek to address the migration crisis facing European countries at source. UK, whilst protecting its overall aid budget, is a good example of a country that is using aid strategically to serve wider purposes and this has been made explicit recently by the Chancellor of the Exchequer (see www.theguardian.com/world/2015/sep/06/osborne-uk-aid-budget-national-interest-refugee-crisis-syrians). On the other hand, low-income countries are in a weaker position to make decisions that will potentially benefit their own economic and social development, reflecting their weaker position in relation to structural power within the global political economy. Given their structural position, it is hard for them to resist the conditionalities associated with development assistance loans or grants from vertical funds such as the GPE.

18   The 30-member OWG was established in January 2013 and included representatives nominated by Members States from the five UN regional groups. The OWG assisted by an interagency technical support team published its final report outlining its suggestions for the 17 goals in July 2014. Alongside the OWG, the UN conducted a series of 'global conversations' that included 11 thematic and 83 national consultations, door-to-door and online surveys. The results of the consultations fed into the OWG.

19   The Panel was co-chaired by President Susilo Bambang Yudhoyono of Indonesia, President Ellen Johnson Sirleaf of Liberia, and Prime Minister David Cameron of UK and also included leaders from civil society, private sector, and government drawn from the global North and the global South.

20   Of particular interest for our purposes was the effort on the UN's part to achieve harmony between the IDFA, on the one hand, and the SDGs on the other. A key motive has been to avoid the same kind of differences in scope and focus between the IDFA and the SDGs as existed between the Dakar Framework and the education MDGs. Ensuring a common language between the IDFA and the education SDG demonstrates, on the one hand, the greater extent of interagency dialogue and co-ordination on the other, which can be seen as a response to a growing recognition by institutions themselves of the reality of regime complexity (Orsini, Morin, and Young 2013). It can also be seen as evidence of increasing efforts at interinstitutional co-ordination by a growing cadre of professionals linked to these institutions (Mundy and Manion 2015). It also serves, however, to underline the direction of power and influence within the regime complex. Just as the education targets within the MDGs proved more influential than those within EFA, it was the wording of the education SDG rather than that of the Muscat agreement that had preceded Incheon (and developed under the auspices of EFA) that is included in the declaration. Indeed, the title of the IDFA takes a cue from the wording of the education SDG goal (already detailed), i.e. Education 2013: Towards Inclusive and Equitable Quality Education and Lifelong Learning for All.

6 The regional and national governance of education

Introduction

Whereas the previous chapter has identified changing patterns in the global governance of education, this chapter considers education governance at the regional and national scales. The chapter starts with an overview of CESA as a regional regime of 'governance-in-the making', that is, as an emerging system of principles, norms, rules, and decision-making procedures at a regional level. The second part of the chapter focuses on understanding the implications of regional policy for processes of governance at the national scale. Here education governance will be conceptualised against an understanding of the changing nature of the postcolonial state and civil society since colonial times and in relation to developments within the domain of violence. Consideration will also be given to the impact of neoliberalism as a global wave on the increasing privatisation of education and training.

Developmental regionalism and education policy in Africa

CESA needs to be considered in relation to *Agenda 2063* and other regional initiatives. It was suggested in Chapter 4 that the emergence of the AU, NEPAD, and now *Agenda 2063* organised around a concept of an African Renaissance can be characterised as an example of 'developmental regionalism' (Tikly and Dachi 2008), i.e. as an attempt to project a regional identity and to develop political projects at a regional level in order to advance development. The origin of *Agenda 2063* lies in the Golden Jubilee of the Organisation of African Unity (OAU), now the African Union (AU).[1] The document is also based on an analysis of previous development experiences and initiatives. In this respect, it locates itself within the history of pan-Africanism on the continent and as part of a continuum on previous African-led development initiatives, including the formation of the OAU, its subsequent transformation to the AU, the *Monrovia Declaration*, and the *Lagos Plan of Action*.[2] A particular point of reference is to the *New Partnership for Africa's Development* (NEPAD) which was adopted by African

Heads of State in October 2001 as an integrated development plan with the goals of achieving sustainable economic growth, eradicating poverty, and ending Africa's marginalisation from the globalisation process (NEPAD 2001). It was conceived as a commitment on the part of Africa's leaders to their people and as a framework of partnership between Africa and the rest of the world. The NEPAD programme outlines a programme of action for tackling Africa's marginalisation from the globalisation process and contains many antecedents to the commitments laid out in *Agenda 2063* (Tikly 2003).[3]

The emergence of CESA as part of a regional regime of governance-in-the-making

Education has been an important focus for the wider project of developmental regionalism in Africa. It is perhaps premature to describe education policy making at a regional level as part of a fully fledged governance regime given the fragmented nature of education governance at that level in Africa. Rather taking account of the aspirational nature of CESA as a continent-wide initiative of the AU, it is perhaps more accurate to describe it as evidence of a governance 'regime-in-the-making'. It is, nonetheless, instructive to consider the nature of the emerging governance regime as a means for understanding patterns of governance at a regional scale. At the level of norms and principles, as has been discussed in Chapter 1, CESA has been strongly influenced by *Agenda 2063*. As was the case with *Agenda 2063*, CESA also provides continuity on NEPAD in the area of education and training.[4] The influence of regional agendas is reflected both in the references to pan-Africanism and in the emphasis on STEM-related subjects as a means of driving a modernist, developmental agenda. (It will be recalled from Chapter 4 that the idea of an African Renaissance is underpinned by both culturalist and modernist elements.) CESA also reflects global educational agendas, to the extent to which they have shaped thinking in *Agenda 2063* but also in educational terms in the influence of EFA discourses and of SDG4 in particular. (In Chapter 7, attention will focus on the tensions inherent in these contradictory discourses as they impact on discourses about skills for development).

In terms of decision-making processes at a regional level, it is instructive to consider the nature of the various initiatives and actors who are involved in shaping policy. Mention has been made of the origins and nature of the AU which forms the polity at a regional scale. It is possible to identify a nascent civil society at a regional level. Initiatives include the Forum for African Women Educationalists (FAWE) created in 1992 as a response to the slow pace of implementation of Education for All goals in sub-Saharan Africa.[5] The overall aim is to increase access and retention as well as improve the quality of education for all girls within the school system and for women in higher education institutions. The Association for the Development of Education in Africa (ADEA) was established at the initiative of the World Bank in 1981. Then called Donors to African Education (DAE), its objective was to foster collaboration and coordination between development agencies in support of education in Africa. ADEA now focuses on developing partnerships between Ministers of Education and funding agencies in order to promote effective education policies based on African leadership and ownership. To this end, it has recently established several inter-country quality nodes in key areas of education and training as a means to share successful practice between countries[6] as well as several technical working groups that are intended to engage regional and international expertise in developing policy. The Association of African Universities (AAU) and the Inter-University Council for East Africa (IUCEA) are regional bodies representing higher education interests on the continent[7] whilst the Southern and East African Consortium for Monitoring Education Quality (SACMEQ) developed out of a programme of research collaboration between the International Institute for Educational Planning (IIEP) and a number of Ministries of Education in Southern Africa. The focus of SACMEQ has been on establishing long-term strategies for building the capacity of educational planners to monitor and evaluate basic education systems.[8] The Programme d'analyse des systèmes éducatifs de la Confemen (PASEC) performs a similar function across Francophone Africa. There are also several fledgling initiatives at educational co-operation at a sub-regional level.[9]

There are three key points worth making about these initiatives that are important for understanding the nature of the emerging regional regime of educational governance. One is that the initiatives are dependent on donor funding and influenced by donor agendas. In this sense, the regional level provides an alternative 'way in' to influencing education policy on the continent and provides a mechanism at a regional level for global agendas to influence emerging regional and national policies. Secondly, whilst there is a nascent regional civil society space at a regional level, it is sparsely populated. Thirdly, the initiatives are state led in that they all include at the most senior-level representatives of national ministries of education. This is not surprising given that education and training are primarily state responsibilities and that the object of regional policy is largely to influence national policy agendas. This does, however, together with the lack of civil society voice, limit the potential for more radical forms of civil society engagement at a regional level.

Figure 6.1 which is taken from the introduction to the CESA document itself shows the pathways of influence in the development of CESA.

The diagram shows the significance of *Agenda 2063* and of the development of the *Common African Position* (CAP) on education post-2015 at the Kigali meeting in 2015 in shaping the document and indicates the importance of the wider context of the SDGs and IDFA. It is also notable that although there was some consultation in the process, particularly in defining the CAP on regional priorities in the education sphere, for the most part the process appears as being top-down and expert driven. In relation to the view of complex systems underpinning this book, the diagram typifies a linear rather than a complex approach to thinking about change in terms of unidirectional processes of cause and effect. This point will be returned to in Chapter 10 where an altogether different approach to managing change will be proposed.

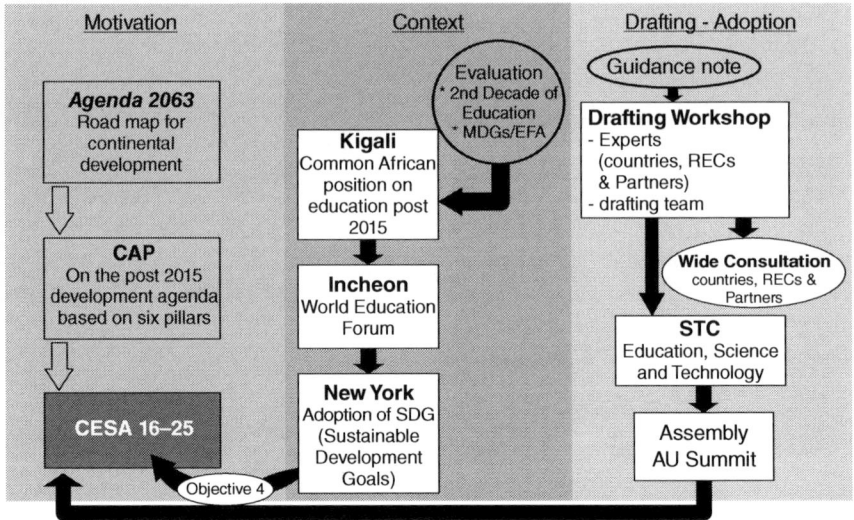

Figure 6.1 Pathways of influence in the development of CESA.
Source: AU (2015b: 2)

In conclusion to this section, it is worth reflecting on the relative influence of regional as compared to global agendas on national policy. As will be discussed in the following, global agendas achieve influence at a national level by virtue of the institutional and productive power of multilateral organisations and of aid agencies linked to economically powerful nations and the use of conditional lending increasingly tied to forms of results-based aid. As was argued in Chapter 4, investment in education and especially infrastructure by China can also be seen in terms of the exercise of soft power in shaping wider economic relationships between Africa and China. Regional agendas, on the other hand, do not have the same degree of influence. As the CESA document makes clear, there is an expectation that regionally determined priorities get integrated into sub-regional and national development agendas but this is not mandatory. Enforcing regional priorities is not linked to funding in the way that foreign development assistance is. Despite commitments in CESA to ongoing monitoring and evaluation of priorities, implementation of regional agendas continues to lie largely at the discretion of national governments. This is not to devalue the significance of regional agendas in articulating a shared vision of education in relation to regional development priorities. It does serve to illustrate, however, the imbalance between regional and global agendas in their ability to influence national policy linked to the operation of different kinds of power and wider dynamics of inequity in Africa's relationship to world order (see Chapter 4).

CESA and changing patterns of governance at a national level

Having reflected on the policy-making process at a regional level, attention will now turn to the implications of regional policy for processes of governance at a national scale. In particular, the remainder of the chapter will provide an analysis and a critique of CESA in relation to a historical understanding of the changing nature of the postcolonial state in education. In developing this understanding, however, it will be argued that it is important not to present a homogenous view of the postcolonial state and to understand differences in the nature of the political settlements and policy-making processes in each as well as differences in capacity both to implement policy and to resist and modify global and regional agendas. Attention will also be given to the role of civil society in the determination of education and training policy. The chapter will consider the historical role of education systems in relation to reproducing dominant political interests in society and in reproducing forms of violence but also as a potential site for citizenship and peace education. A key focus for the discussion, however, will be the increasing emphasis in regional agendas on the idea of public–private partnerships and on the privatisation of education and training.

Changing patterns of control over the governance of education

Like wider aspects of colonial rule, education policy making was the preserve of the external governing power, although there were differences in the way the colonising powers governed. Some of these differences were linked in Foucault's terms to differences in colonial *governmentality* (i.e. in the art and practice of colonial government)[10] with a tendency towards greater centralisation in the French compared with the English systems and with implications for relationships between the colonial state and religious bodies in civil society (discussed in the following). Despite differences, some key features in the way that education systems are currently governed can be traced back to colonial times. Firstly, it was under colonialism that the predominance of externally driven agendas emerged and became entrenched with respect to the role of both the colonising powers in shaping policy and religious organisations in advancing their proselytising aims. Secondly, it is during the colonial period that the top-down, bureaucratic, and undemocratic nature of decision-making within education systems emerged as the preferred technology of colonial government in education as in other spheres.

Thirdly, it is during the colonial period, that the dual system of educational provision between the state on the one hand and religious organisations on the other also became entrenched and provided the conditions of emergence for the current, contradictory relationship between the state and civil society in the governance of education. The churches played a significant role in education, health, and other areas under colonial rule, although their role differed depending on the colonising power.[11] These differences were also reflected in attitudes to pre-colonial Islamic schools in West and Eastern Africa which were well established dating back to the tenth century and earlier waves of globalisation from the Arab world.[12] Different religious bodies represented different interests within the state and civil society. They played a powerful role in spreading Christian and Islamic beliefs, often operating in antagonism with indigenous belief systems. Islamic and Christian-run schools also operated quite different forms of pedagogy and at a cultural level projected alternative views of modernity (Launey 2016). Religious organisations have had a contradictory relationship with the state. They can be considered to have played a legitimatory for the colonial project through tacit support for colonial regimes. Religious organisations, however, also played a prominent role in anti-colonial struggles in South Africa and elsewhere on the continent.

Education governance after independence

The insertion of national education systems into global and regional regimes of governance has had contradictory effects. In the context of the 'hollowing out' (Ferguson 2006a) of the state under SAPS, donors have often been highly influential in shaping policy through the mechanism of conditional lending. Samoff's work conducted over more than two decades in Tanzania and other African countries (Samoff 1992; Samoff 1996; Samoff 2007), for example, has shown the impact of the 'intellectual-financial complex' (by which he draws attention to the role of organisations such as the World Bank and IMF along with their related epistemic communities of experts and consultants) and has exerted a strong influence over policy for low-income African countries. The rules for receiving donor funding in the context of new global governance regimes involve new, more subtle forms of conditionality in which governments are expected to produce robust plans for the education sector in exchange for aid. Whilst it was argued in Chapter 4 that African governments have different abilities to mediate global agendas, they are often, nonetheless, limited in their capacity to mediate global agendas and are often reliant on external experts to assist in drawing up such plans thus reinforcing dependency (Tikly 2017).

It is, however, important not to homogenise the nature of the postcolonial state in education. Recent research carried out across four African countries into the politics of educational reform is useful for identifying differences in education governance within and between African countries linked to the nature of the 'political settlement' in each (i.e. the nature of the dominant coalition of interests represented within the state)[13] and the dynamics of the education policy process, including the capacity of the state and of scales below the state such as regions to implement policy (Hickey and Hossain 2019). The team sought to specifically consider the effects of different political dynamics on the ability of countries to implement reforms aimed at raising learner outcomes in the context of emerging global and regional policy agendas. Crucially this involved

> moving beyond the focus on formal institutions [as in the so-called 'good governance' agenda], to capture the significance of informal power relations and practices; the ways in which material aspects of a nation's political economy

shape the capacity of different groups to make demands; the particular forms of political agency (e.g. leadership coalitions) required to navigate these structural conditions at multiple levels; and the role of governance arrangements and relationships within the state, as well as between the state and citizens.

(Hicky, Hassain, and Jackman 2019, 173)

A common finding is that elites are more likely to commit to the expansion of access to education which has tangible results, is easier to achieve, and can thus play a legitimatory role in relation to the wider political project being pursued. Expanding access is also easier in relation to the legacy of top-down, centralised systems than improving the quality of education and training which according to the authors requires more transactional tasks of improving front-line service delivery. Shifting to an emphasis on quality requires a paradigmatic shift in the central message of government which is problematic, given the historic emphasis on expanding access as a means to secure the legitimacy of governing elites. Furthermore, it is argued that the coalitions in civil society, including NGOs, the private sector, parents, and community organisations etc. are either too complicit in existing coalitions or are weak in their ability to put quality rather than simply issues of access on the agenda or to hold institutions to account for service delivery. It will be suggested in Chapter 10 that one implication of this finding is to focus more on the politics of education (i.e. a focus on the nature of the political settlement, of power relationships, and interests at stake within the state and civil society) rather than on the common focus of the good governance agenda, including decentralisation and the development of strong vertical accountability mechanisms between central government and institutions. It will be argued that this has implications for understanding the role of civil society in education governance.

Civil society, the state, and education governance

Despite the significance of civil society in relation to development on the continent, *Agenda 2063* is relatively quiet on the role of civil society in national governance. It draws attention to the fact that 'civil society participation and contributions to democracy is frequently handicapped by their capacity and resources' (AUC 2015a, 62) but it does not delve more deeply into the issues involved. CESA appears ambivalent on the role of civil society in education governance. Thus, limited mention is made of key actors in civil society that have historically played a significant role in education governance, including the churches, NGOs, and social movements. The exception is in advocating for greater involvement of the private sector in education governance, including the use of public–private partnerships in the provision of education.

Religious organisations

As has been discussed, churches played a contradictory role in relation to the colonial project. This contradictory role has persisted into the post-independence era. In the period following independence, churches were often allowed to maintain their position as a provider of education and managed a significant proportion of state-aided and independent secondary and primary schools in many African countries. In the context of nation-building, a favoured pathway for the state following independence was to take legal ownership of church-owned schools. In countries such as Kenya, churches often maintained a role as 'sponsors' of education contributing to the costs of schooling but with the state subsidising teacher salaries. Whilst there were often efforts to secularise the curriculum, churches continued to be permitted to offer spiritual and moral guidance through their role as sponsors and had a limited say in policy making through processes of consultation. They thus played a legitimatory role through acting as mediators between civil society and post-independence regimes. This role shifted, however, to one of opposition under Daniel Arap Moi. The Church moved from being a somewhat ambiguous and ambivalent meditative agent to being a vocal and active opposition to the state's tyranny (Sabar 2001). Churches have often continued to run fee-paying private schools and have thus played a role in processes of elite formation. By way of contrast, as will be discussed below, religious fundamentalist organisations have also specifically targeted educational institutions as part of their ongoing battles with the state.

NGOs

Manji and O'Coill (2002, 568) have argued that 'NGOs today form a prominent part of the "development machine", a vast institutional and disciplinary nexus of official agencies, practitioners, consultants, scholars and other miscellaneous experts producing and consuming knowledge about the "developing world" '.[14] In the immediate post-independence period, official development agencies remained unenthusiastic about the work of NGOs preferring to channel aid through the state. The work of NGOs in education as in other spheres was marginal and limited to project work. The rise of neoliberalism and the good governance agenda, however, saw a change in attitude towards NGOs in which NGOs and other civil society organisations were often co-opted by international development agencies to a repackaged programme of welfare provision.[15] This provided a safety net that served to legitimise the neoliberal state in which economic policies focused on austerity were increasingly determined by international financial institutions. This period saw a mushrooming of NGOs in Africa. According to Pinkney (2009), NGOs nowadays are concerned either with service delivery or with 'advocacy'.

This dual function is evident in education. A key feature of the changing educational landscape in Africa and other parts of the postcolonial world has been the emergence of NGOs as a major player in education and other areas of development. NGOs are increasingly expected to make up the shortfall in educational provision. At the same time, NGOs such as UWEZO[16] in East Africa enjoy significant donor support in holding governments to account for the quality of education. This places many NGOs as was the case with religious organisations, in a contradictory relationship with the state: on the one hand, playing a legitimatory role through seeking to enhance state provision and, on the other hand, seeking to hold the state to account and often benefit from donor funding in the process.

Teacher unions

Teacher unions, like NGOs, have played a contradictory role in relation to the postcolonial state. During the colonial era, only unions or professional associations that were considered as not being a threat to the colonial regime were allowed to function if at all. Some key leaders of liberation movements, including, for example, Julius Nyerere in Tanzania and Robert Mugabe in Zimbabwe, had previously been teachers. Following independence, teachers' unions have advocated for better pay and conditions for teachers and opposed the worst excesses of state reform. Along with other trade unions, teachers unions have played a role in the democratisation process, including struggles for multiparty reform and against structural adjustment (Kraus 2007). Conversely, teachers' unions have often also been perceived as a brake on education reform through opposing, for example, efforts to make teachers and schools more accountable to the public (Moe and Wiborg 2017). It is for this reason that proponents of the good governance agenda in education have often argued for a decentralised approach with more robust processes of vertical accountability between the government and individual institutions. Rather, as Hickey *et al.* have argued, their analysis

> questions the extent to which teacher unions should be the central focus for the political economy analysis of education in that unions are a powerful obstacle to promoting learning in developing countries because the evidence that unions are a powerful obstacle to promoting learning seems to rest on a specific handful of country cases. Instead we find in our country cases that teacher unions play positive as well as negative roles in advancing learning reforms, and that focusing exclusively on unions risks overlooking the highly significant roles played by other key player, particularly politicos, bureaucrats, and other politically salient stakeholders, such as aid donors and teachers' associations, in shaping educational reforms.
>
> (Hicky, Hassain, and Jackman 2019, 175)

South Africa provides an interesting example that serves to illustrate Hickey *et al.*'s arguments. On the one hand, teachers' unions in South Africa as elsewhere have often been accused of obstructing reforms aimed at improving quality through, for example, opposing efforts to introduce quality control and performance management techniques in schools that would have held schools and teachers more accountable for learner outcomes. On the face of it, this would seem to reflect the dominant narrative about the role of teachers in quality-related reforms. The picture is, however, much more complex. The South African Democratic Teachers Union (SADTU) played a central role in educational struggles to overthrow apartheid. As Chisholm's longitudinal study shows, whilst part of the dominant ANC-led alliance in the post-1994 government, SADTU (by far the largest teachers union in South Africa), has had a contradictory relationship with the state in which they have sought to alter relations of authority and the nature of their work within schools, and how these have interacted with new managerial and state initiatives (Chisholm 1999). For example, SADTU played a progressive role in processes of curriculum reform following the demise of outcomes-based education in the early 2000s, both supporting and challenging the government-led reform agenda as it impacted on teachers' work (Chisholm 2005). In support of Hickey *et al.*'s aforementioned assertion, this role needs to be seen in relation to the broader politics of the reform process at the time, including the role of different factions of the ruling ANC and the role of academics and other stakeholders involved in the reform. This kind of analysis warns against a simplistic uptake of the good governance agenda and encourages a more critical and holistic view of the political interests at stake in the reform process. Some of the implications of this understanding are discussed in Chapter 10.

Social movements

Africa has a rich history of social movements aimed at advancing the interests of groups within civil society, although these often receive less scholarly attention than social movements elsewhere. It is also the case that categorisations and analyses of social movements in Africa do not conform readily to categorisations of social movements in Europe and North America (Ellis and Kessel 2009; Aidi 2018). It is possible to identify three waves of social movements on the continent. The first coincides with the struggles for national liberation from colonial rule. From the 1950s, liberation movements emerged from within civil society as a direct political and military challenge to European colonialism. In some instances, they had an explicit educational agenda. The African National Congress and Black Consciousness movements in South Africa along with the South West African People's Organisation (SWAPO), for instance, had strong educational agendas (Tikly 1994). The ANC, for instance, organised its own school on land donated by the Tanzanian government in the early 1980s based on a vision of an alternative to Bantu education whilst Steve Biko as a figurehead of the Black Consciousness movement wrote extensively about education as a means to liberate the black mind from the effects of apartheid and racism (Biko 1978). The Tanzania African National Union (later Chama Cha Mapinduzi) in Tanzania launched an ambitious adult literacy programme at independence linked to a vision of *Ujaama* (African socialism) that was highly successful in eradicating illiteracy in the early years following independence. For the most part, however, once national liberation was achieved, the education systems often reverted back to the path dependency of elitist models of education established under colonialism. Expanding opportunities for adult literacy is a priority in CESA. However, in contrast to Nyerere's vision of literacy as a form of community empowerment, the emphasis in CESA is more on the instrumental value of literacy in supporting development based on technological innovation.[17]

In recent years, anti-colonial and postcolonial scholarship have found expression in debates about decolonising the curriculum. As with previous eras of anti-colonial struggle, these debates are rooted in grass-roots protests such as those instigated by students at the University of Cape Town in 2015. At the heart of these movements are related issues of the prohibitive costs of higher education for students from disadvantaged backgrounds (encapsulated in the #Fees Must Fall movement) and issues of epistemic justice and the hegemony of Western knowledge in curricula (encapsulated in the #Rhodes Must Fall movement). Demands to 'decolonise the curriculum' have been given intellectual impetus through the work of scholars such as Santos (e.g. Santos 2002, 2007, 2012; Santos 2017), Mbembe (e.g. Mbembe 2016), Dei (e.g. Dei 2017; Dei and Kempf 2006) and Connell (e.g. Connell 2007, 2012, 2014). These issues and movements are discussed further in Chapter 8.

The second wave of social movements emerged during the 1980s and 1990s in the context of structural adjustment to challenge the single-party state in many countries from Zambia to Mali. As multiparty systems were introduced, many of these social movements became NGOs or development agencies, part of a process of 'NGO-ification' of the opposition, and these NGOs tended to get caught up in the contradictory relationship with the postcolonial state already mentioned (see also Aidi 2018). A third wave is associated with continuing austerity in the 2000s and the broadening of social protest to encompass a plurality of concerns. Habib and O'poku-Mensah (2009) have provided an overview of social movements in Africa. These include campaigns for access to basic services such as water and electricity and have, for example, anti-privatisation campaigns in South Africa, Ghana, Zambia, and Zimbabwe; campaigns against eviction and for land rights such as the Landless People's Movement in South Africa, the Kenyan Land Alliance as well as the struggles of the San to have their claims to land recognised in Botswana; forms of social movement unionism focused on securing workers' rights, including women working in the informal sector and vulnerable groups of workers such as those working in export processing zones, oil workers, and those working on flower farms; environmental campaigns such as Environmental Justice Networking Forum in South Africa, Kenya's Green Belt Movement founded in 2004 by the Nobel Peace Prize winner Wangari Maathai, and the environmental movements in the Niger delta; campaigns to advance the rights of oppressed minorities, including refugees, women, sexual minorities; campaigns around HIV/AIDS, including campaigns highlighting prejudice against those with HIV/AIDS and demanding access to anti-retroviral drugs; and movements opposed to multilateral organisations and transnational corporations linked to broader global movements like the Jubilee Campaign, the Third World Network (TWN), the Zimbabwe Coalition on Debt and Development (ZIMCODD), the Uganda Debt Network, the Third World Forum, the West African Social Forum, the Forum of African Alternatives, and the Senegal-based Environment and Development Action-Third World (ENDA). It will be argued in Chapter 10 that a key focus for counter-hegemonic struggles in education must involve the mobilisation of these social movements around a transformative vision of ESD.

The private sector

Another key actor within civil society that has significantly impacted education and training systems since colonial times is the private sector. Foundations such as the Phelps-Stokes Foundation played a significant role in influencing colonial education policy on the continent in the early part of the twentieth century. More recently and driven by diverse philanthropic and ideological motives, Foundations including the Hewlett Foundation, the Bill and Melinda Gates Foundation, and Mastercard Foundation have played an increasingly prominent role in not only seeking to influence policy at the global scale (Chapter 5) but at a national level through supporting various initiatives. In this respect, the private sector has played an increasingly significant role not only in shaping policy but in providing educational services (discussed in the following). This also serves a legitimatory function through filling perceived gaps in state provision but, it will be argued later, is also a source of contradiction and incoherence with regard to the development of policy contributing to the increasing fragmentation of education and training systems and perpetuating regimes of inequality.

The privatisation of education and training in Africa

Closely linked to the emphasis in global and regional agendas on the importance of nurturing public–private partnerships and with considerable significance for the governance of education and for the realisation of distributive justice has been the increasing trend towards the privatisation of education and training on the continent. It is important, however, to put these developments into historical context. Non-state actors have had a history of providing education since colonial times (see also Kitaev 1999). Schooling was provided, often on a fee-paying basis by the churches and mosques. Elite private schools served the children of European settlers and indigenous elites. They were often allowed to flourish in the postcolonial era, providing a key institution for the reproduction of the class privilege enjoyed by indigenous elites. (An infamous example was Kamuzu School, built by Malawi's infamous dictator, Hastings Banda. A homage to British schooling, it consumed almost all of the country's education budget.)[18] In the post-independence period, different polices were pursued with respect to non-state actors. In most countries, church schools were either subsidised (e.g. through paying teacher salaries) or allowed to continue on a private basis alongside a growing government school sector. Community schools (which also had precedents in colonial Africa) were established by parents, often desperate for their children to get education and filling the many gaps in state provision, particularly at secondary level. These included the *Harambee* (self-help) school movement in Kenya. In many cases, these schools also gained state subsidy over time but continue to charge user fees. In many African countries, unregulated 'fly by night' schools have also flourished in the post-independence period. Established for profit, they are the precursors to low-fee private schools (discussed in the following) in so far as they were intended to cater for low-income learners not able to access mainstream government or other kinds of school (Kitaev 1999).

During the 1980s, economists associated with the World Bank developed rates of return (ROR) analysis which sought to calculate the rate of return to investment to different levels and stages of education. It was partly on the basis of ROR analysis that the World Bank and other financial institutions came to prioritise basic education in the context of the MDGs as this was considered to have the highest rate of return to social investment in terms of promoting economic growth. The private rate of return to individuals in terms of estimates of future wages was used as a basis for arguing the introduction of user fees at primary level during the imposition of SAPS but particularly at higher stages of education and training. It was also used to justify a growing trend in the privatisation of schooling. As Ilon (1994) points out, the introduction of user fees led to middleclass 'flight' from the system which in turn led to an increasing reluctance on the part of this group to pay taxes to support state schools. The consequence was a decline in the quality of government schools which in turn impacted negatively on enrolments. The imposition of fees in primary education in particular was seen to have contributed to the deepening of poverty and inequality during the 1980s under SAPs. This, however, reinforced the emphasis on primary education in the context of the MDGs (Robertson et al. 2007).

It is worth clarifying at this point what is meant here by the term 'privatisation'. Following Ball and Youdell (2008) (see also Verger, Fontdevila and Zancajo 2016), privatisation can be understood as comprising two interrelated elements, both of which are linked to the spread of neoliberal-inspired policies in education and other areas of social spending since the 1980s. The first is *exogenous privatisation* which involves the opening up of public education services to private sector participation including on a profit-making basis such that the private sector is invited to design, manage, or deliver aspects of education. In the African context, it involves harnessing resources from the private sector in the provision of schooling but also increased private (i.e. household) contributions to education at all levels, though tuition fees were of different kinds as well as increasing household expenditure on essential materials such as textbooks and payments in kind.[19]

In relation to exogenous privatisation, in many sub-Saharan countries such as Ghana, Kenya, Malawi, and Nigeria, there has been a rapid growth in the numbers of for-profit low-fee private schools (LFPS). These have often proved popular with parents, especially where government schools are unavailable or are of a poor quality. Many are run by international chains such as Omega and Bridge Academies and have enjoyed the support of donors such as DfID and the World Bank and philanthropic organisations such as Bill and Melinda Gates Foundation and the Zukerberg Foundation as well as some African governments (Verger, Fontdevila and Zancajo 2016; Olmedo 2014). Liberia has recently outsourced 98 of its primary schools to be run by seven different LFPS providers.[20] LFPS are highly controversial. Advocates of LFPS argue that they are affordable for the poor and offer a better quality of education compared to government schools. This, however, is contested in the literature. With respect to affordability, LFPS often operate a pay as you learn policy because they are aware that poor parents often get paid on daily rather than on a weekly or a monthly basis. Nonetheless, evidence suggests that LFPS are not affordable by the very poorest. Thus, these schools might attract poor families, but they tend to attract those families amongst the poor that have a higher level of education and higher expectations/ aspirations for their children's education (Verger, Fontdevila, and Zancajo 2016).

The evidence is also inconclusive as to whether learning outcomes are better for LFPS compared to government schools (Ashley et al. 2014; Verger, Fontdevila, and Zancajo 2016). In some cases, learning outcomes have been improved compared to government schools but this needs to be offset against the social class profile of the intake to these schools and against the tendency of private schools to 'play the system' with regard to learning outcomes.[21] Further, LFPS often rely on unqualified teachers and adopt highly scripted pedagogies that allow little room for differentiation to the abilities of individual learners. There is often a narrow focus on teaching to the test which means memorisation of facts and a neglect of the affective and moral dimensions of education. Furthermore, there is a lack of regulation of LFPS which means that what is taught is not necessarily coherent with government policy, including the skills and competencies advocated by national curricula. In many African countries, private schools remain largely unregulated and therefore outside of the ambit of national education policy (Ashley et al. 2014). Indeed, Bridge Academies were recently ordered to shut down their schools by the Ugandan government due to many not being properly licensed and concerns about safety and quality (Brehm and Silova 2019).

The second related form is privatisation *in* public education which the authors term *endogenous privatisation*. This involves changes in the very nature and culture of education systems themselves through seeking to import techniques and practices from the private sector in order to make use of public resources more effective and efficient. It might take many forms, including the introduction of performance management techniques including performance by results as well as attempts to decentralise budgets to the point of service delivery to increase accountability in education. Endogenous privatisation has been evident in Africa education since the 1980s. It is manifested, for example, in the increasing use of contract teachers and in the use of performance management and payment by results. Performance-related pay is often promoted as a means to increase teacher accountability and several studies have found that individual teacher performance pay can have a large and significant impact on student outcomes. For example, a study of a programme in Kenya (Glewwe and Kremer 2010), where teachers received financial incentives on the basis of student examination scores, found that the programme led to significant increases in examination scores. The mechanism through which performance pay worked, however, was unclear since there was no observable impact on teachers' attendance or teaching practices, except that teachers did conduct more examination preparation sessions, i.e. focused more on 'teaching to the test'. Improvement in student outcomes also did not last beyond the life of the intervention. Performance-related pay could also be difficult to implement as it can undermine teachers' morale and become the subject of opposition by unions (Robertson, Mundy, and Verger 2012). A recent review of the available evidence suggests that teacher motivation and improved quality emerge from the interaction of a number of factors including but not confined to levels of subject and subject-specific pedagogical knowledge, pay and conditions of service, status in the wider society and community, and the quality of supervision over teachers work in schools (Bainton, Barrett, and Tikly 2016).

CESA, privatization, and the future funding of education and training

Before considering the approach taken by CESA to privatisation, it is worth providing some contextual information about the resource implications of meeting the ambitious targets identified in CESA. It will be recalled from Chapter 1 that the document argues for an expansion of access at all levels of schooling, including those for historically marginalised groups such as rural dwellers and girls as a means for providing the skills required for development and tackling poverty and inequality. In line with global policy agendas, CESA argues for an increase in the basic education cycle from six to nine years so as to encompass lower secondary school.[22] As we have seen, a revitalised TVET sector is seen as important as is an expansion of adult literacy. The focus on expanding *all* areas of the education and training system in CESA marks a decisive break with the MDG era when the emphasis was on basic education. The scale of the expansion envisaged to different sub-sectors has major implications for the funding of education and training. For example, UNESCO estimates that an additional 17 million teachers will need to be recruited across the continent by 2030 to meet the expansion in learner numbers. There is a need also to focus on the professional development of teachers and the provision of teaching and learning materials, including textbooks all of which require significant increases in recurrent expenditure. Expanding education will further involve a large investment in capital expenditure, including building tens of thousands of additional classrooms and investing in sanitary facilities and providing safe drinking water (UNESCO 2017b).[23] A key priority in CESA is the greater use of ICT to support learning in schools. However, the majority of schools in the region report no access to electricity with more than 95% of schools not having access in many countries. Unsurprisingly, this limits the possibilities for using ICTs in education except for in the most advantaged state and private schools[24] (UNESCO 2017b). Further, with regard to the emphasis on STEM, there is a shortage of basic lab equipment for the teaching of science in secondary schools (see Chapter 7).

Although the objectives for CESA have not been costed, UNESCO's costing estimates and spending projections to 2030 for the achievement of education targets suggest that, on average, countries will need to have increased spending on pre-primary, primary, and secondary education from 3.5% to 6.3% of GDP between 2012 and 2030 (UNESCO 2015). In the majority of countries in SSA, the costs will need to triple as a percentage of GDP in order to expand access of education to all, including the most marginalised groups. This means that funding the proposals in CESA is likely to remain heavily dependent on donors.[25] The dependence of African governments on donor funding, however, is itself a source of contradiction and generates relationships of dependency, as was discussed in Chapter 5. Further, UNESCO (2017b) has estimated that donor financing for basic and secondary education will need to increase sevenfold in order to fill the funding gap left by shortfalls in government expenditure. At present, however, donors are often failing to meet their existing commitments under international protocols.

Against this background, CESA calls for increased mobilisation of national resources that reflect the following principles:

1   Diversification and increasing of funding sources owing to new partnerships, south–south cooperation, private investments, foreign direct investments, diaspora, foundations, and other champions.
2   Cost sharing with different stakeholders, including tuition fees at all levels.
3   Strengthening effective and efficient management resource systems in public institutions.
4   Expansion of private education and training providers (CESA REF: 33).

It also calls for mobilisation of finance through a range of public–private partnerships.[26] Here, CESA is clearly committed to the continuing privatisation of education. For example, in relation to Ball and Youdell's typology of privatisation, exogenous privatisation is evident in points '1', '2', and '4', whilst endogenous privatisation is evident in point '3'. As we have seen, exogenous privatisation is increasingly evident in the school system. It is also linked to the proliferation of government subsidies and private schools within the schooling sector.

This kind of privatisation, however, seen in historical context has contributed to the development of class inequality. Writing in the early 1990s, Lynn Ilon, an economist of education, painted a future scenario involving a growing gulf in educational opportunities between emerging global elites and the rest of the population in the low-income postcolonial world. According to Ilon, 'a national system of schooling is likely to give way to local systems for the poor and global systems for the rich' (p. 99). Within this highly differentiated environment, a top tier will benefit from a private education that will make them globally competitive; a middle tier will receive a 'good' but not 'world class' education, whilst the majority, third tier, will have a local, state education that will make them 'marginally competitive for low-skill jobs' (p. 102). In very large measure, Ilon's predictions have been realised, although with the caveats that state provision for the poorest is itself being privatised under current agendas leading to even greater inequality and fragmentation. Millions of children on the African continent still have no access to any form of education at all. It can be argued that this educational scenario, whilst having a negative correspondence with the vision of inclusive growth contained in *Agenda 2063*, actually enjoys a positive correspondence with the existing system of global capitalism in which African elites have limited access to economic opportunities and resources but the majority can expect a lifetime of poverty in the rural and urban areas with limited opportunities on the margins of the economy.

There are, however, alternatives to privatisation, although these are not discussed in CESA. For example, as Lewin (2018) has argued, one alternative is financing schooling through progressive forms of taxation. This remains one of the surest ways to ensure access to a good-quality education in highly unequal societies (although this in turn relies on reforms to the tax system and improvements in the efficiency of tax collection). There are also other areas of the budget such as military spending which has increased in many African countries over the past ten years. A reduction in military spending and a subsequent increase in educational spending could be seen in terms of a peace dividend and could make a significant contribution to educational finance if governments chose to deploy resources in this way. Similarly, the cost for donors to meet their obligations for funding SDG4 whilst appearing large overall is equal to just eight days of annual global military expenditure, which totalled US$1.75 trillion in 2013 (UNESCO 2019).

The state and political socialisation

An important aspect of the relationship between education and the political domain is the historical role of educational institutions in legitimising dominant political interests in society through forms of political socialisation (Harber 1988). Colonial education acted as a mechanism for the political socialisation of indigenous populations with the aim of rendering the colonised economically useful and politically docile (Rodney 1973). The education of indigenous urban elites in the language and culture of the colonisers was central to the process of elite formation[27] and contributed to the bifurcation between urban citizens and rural subjects that persisted into the post-independence era (Mamdani 1996). In countries that experienced settler colonialism such as South Africa and colonial Rhodesia, racially and ethnically segregated education systems also served a socialisation function through reinforcing racialised divisions within wider society. Scholarship has also identified the role of colonial education systems in reproducing gendered identities and a gendered division of labour (Gaitskell 1988). Conversely, the limited opportunities afforded to indigenous groups to participate in secondary and tertiary education also had the unintended consequence of developing a cadre of Africans some of whom would go on to lead national struggles for independence (Chafer 2007).

In the immediate post-independence period, control over education became more closely tied to the interests of indigenous elites and education systems became vehicles for processes of class formation. For example, as already discussed, private schools, often established under colonialism, flourished in the postcolonial era, providing a key institution for the reproduction of class privilege. As Harber (1988) has shown, educational institutions were often explicitly used as a means to promote political socialisation on the part of post-independence regimes through the curriculum and textbooks in countries such as Kenya and

Tanzania, albeit linked to different political projects (see also Koff and Von der Muhll 1967). Schools have also remained since colonial times undemocratic and authoritarian institutions characterised by the prevalence of formalistic, teacher-centred approaches to delivering the curriculum, the widespread use of corporal punishment, and the lack of opportunity for community, teacher, and student voice in the governance of organisations (Davies 2008).

Global citizenship education

It is against this historical backdrop that UNESCO has been promoting global citizenship education (GCE) in Africa and elsewhere [28] as a means to develop democratic agency, respect for the rule of law, and peace building. To date, however, take-up of GCE has been limited on the African continent (see, for example, Keevy and Matlala 2016). Although CESA does not explicitly reference citizenship education, it is referenced in the CAP (refer to preceding text) and is a key component of SDG goal 4.7. Recent scholarship has attempted to identify the challenges of implementing citizenship education in autocratic (Waghid et al. 2018) and unequal (Vally and Spren 2012) contexts on the continent and the tensions between Western conceptions of democratic citizenship and African philosophical traditions (e.g. Enslin and Horsthemke 2004). For some commentators, there is a danger that GCE can play a legitimatory role in reproducing wider inequalities through presenting GCE as a panacea for creating more just societies, thereby letting governments off the hook for addressing the roots of inequality and injustice which lie outside of the school in wider structural inequalities (Vally and Spren 2012). For these reasons, and in the context of the current book, the idea of GCE needs to be seen in relation to efforts to decolonise the curriculum (Chapter 8) as well as in efforts to democratise processes of educational governance and to wider struggles for participatory justice. These issues are explored in more depth in Chapter 10.

Education, the state, and violence

As indicated in Chapter 1, armed conflict is widespread across the Africa continent. It will be recalled that *Agenda 2063* goes some way towards recognising the ontological depth of violence, the multiple scales at which it operates, and it also tacitly acknowledges the implication of violence for inequalities, including those based on rurality, class, gender, and ethnicity. Violence is however first and foremost identified as arising from inequalities within communities. The document identifies poor management of Africa's diversity – ethnic, religious, cultural – as being a source of conflict on the continent. It also identifies religious extremism, including Boko Haram in Northern Nigeria and the Lord's Resistance Army (LRA) in Uganda as examples of what can happen on account of this mismanagement. It is in this context that *Agenda 2063* proposes a stronger role for the state in dealing with violence. However, this role is, in accordance with the good governance agenda, seen principally in terms of managing community-based conflict through sound institutional frameworks.[29] The role of education in peace and conflict resolution is highlighted by CESA. Education is identified in regional agendas as a key institution for promoting peace education and conflict resolution in order to develop better community relations.

It is important to unpack some of the assumptions underlying this view of the causes of violence and the potential role for schools in ameliorating these. Firstly, and with reference to the depiction of the postcolonial condition in Chapter 4, the causes of violence are structural in nature. They are linked to the operation of wider power relationships and to regimes of inequality. *Agenda 2063* does not address the fundamentally political nature of violence and the extent to which in the postcolonial world violence is embedded in the nature of the state and linked to interests within the state and civil society.

As several authors have argued, education has a Janus face with respect to violence in that besides being implicated in the propagation of violence, educational systems also hold out the possibility of supporting forms of peace education in pre-and post-conflict settings (Bush and Salterelli 2000; Davies 2004a; Smith 2010). In relation to the first 'face' of education, attention needs to be given to how processes of education governance can fuel conflict (Smith 2010; UNESCO 2011a; Paulson 2011). For example, the unequal distribution of educational resources between different groups defined in racial, ethnic, religious, or linguistic terms has often in itself been a cause of resentment fuelling conflict in many countries. Educational institutions can also be targeted in conflict in a wider context where there has been an increase in civilian involvement in war in Africa as elsewhere. In the case of fundamentalist religious groups, this is because education is perceived as bound up in religious identity and therefore part of the wider struggle for hearts and minds with the state and/or other opposition groups. The targeting of secular schools and the kidnap of girls in Chiboc in Northern Nigeria by *Boko Harem* fighters can be seen as a recent instance of this as can the abduction and recruitment of thousands of children into the *Lords Resistance Army* in Northern Uganda. In both cases, attacks have been along gendered lines with girls in particular being targeted for abduction by Boko Harem and forced into marriage. In Uganda, the experience of sexualised violence perpetrated against girls in the context of conflict provided a barrier to them returning to school (Murphy et al. 2011). The recent rise in political tension between Anglophone and Francophone regions of Cameroon has its roots in part in the segregation and differences in identity through immersion in parallel systems of Anglophone and Francophone schools dating back to colonial times (Kuchah 2016). Neither does *Agenda 2063* or CESA acknowledge the role of institutions such as the education system in perpetuating violence. As discussed in relation to the role of education systems in political socialisation, schools are often authoritarian institutions characterised by the widespread use of corporal punishment. Educational institutions in Africa are also often sites for the perpetration of gender based and sexualised violence (Leach 2004).

The complex nature of the relationship between education and violence has implications for the potential role of education in conflict resolution and peace building. CESA outlines several priorities, including the formulation national policies for peace education involving relevant ministries as well as representatives of civil societies and groups grounded in African values and mechanisms of conflict prevention and resolution; training teachers, social workers, security forces, representatives of religious organisations, and civil societies as peace actors and mediators; developing and disseminating teaching and learning materials on peace education; capitalising on ongoing innovative peace-building experiences in various African countries; and, reinforcing the initiatives and activities of the inter-country quality node on peace education which is a community of practice and a platform for policy dialogue and exchange of experiences.

Other global agendas go further than CESA in outlining a role for education and training in post-conflict reconstruction. The 2011 Global Monitoring Report on Conflict (UNESCO 2011b), for example, identifies a range of short-term measures for getting education systems back on track following conflict, including withdrawing user fees, building on existing community initiatives to provide education in conflict torn regions, rehabilitating schools and classrooms, recognising prior attainment of those returning to education following conflict, supporting accelerated learning programmes, providing skills training, and psychosocial support and recruiting teachers. The report also calls for a restructuring of aid to better target conflict-affected areas as a basis for building long-term recovery and identifies a number of priorities for peace building. These include reviewing key aspects of the governance of education including, for example, language of instruction policies and curriculum reform (focusing on specific areas of the curriculum such as history and religious education as well as introducing dedicated peace education programmes). Crucially, the report highlights the need to transform schools into non-violent institutions outlawing corporal punishment, gendered violence, and other forms of bullying. Recent research has also highlighted the critical role for teachers in facilitating peace building (Sayed and Novelli 2016).

What emerges from the literature and in keeping with complexity theory is the need for systemic responses at different scales if education is to contribute to peace building. At a system level, it points towards all aspects of education policy from the governance and funding of education in post-conflict societies to curriculum reform and reform to initial and continuing teacher education. At an organisational level, as research in Sierra Leone has illustrated, a systemic response would also need to focus holistically on the role of leaders, curriculum and pedagogy, psycho-social support for learners, community engagement, and opportunities for staff development (Bretherton, Weston, and Zbar 2003). There are other silences too in CESA such as the need to focus on provision for refugees, including internally displaced refugees. As with the discussion of GCE above, however, there is a danger that education is seen as a panacea for preventing conflicts that have their roots in wider dynamics in the economy and society. If education is to play a role in transitioning societies towards peace and reconciliation, then it needs to be clearly articulated with wider processes of peace building (Smith 2010; Sayed and Novelli 2016).

Conclusion

The chapter has reviewed changing patterns of education governance at the regional and national scales. It has been argued that much of the path dependency in the way that education and training are governed can be traced back to colonial times. It has also been suggested that proposals to privatise education and training as a means to provide for the expansion of the system public–private partnerships do not provide a sustainable basis for expansion in the longer term and contribute to inequality. Finally, it has been argued that whilst education systems can play a role in peace building and in developing citizenship as global and regional agendas imply, education cannot be considered as a means for realising peace on its own and education reform needs to linked to wider processes of peace building and democratisation in society as well as within the education system itself.

Notes

1 The AU summit tasked the African Union Commission (AUC), supported by the New Partnership for Africa's Development (NEPAD), the Planning and Coordinating Agency (NPCA), the African Development Bank (AfDB), and the UN Economic Commission for Africa (UNECA), to prepare a 50-year continental agenda. This was to be achieved through an extensive consultative process involving a series of meetings across the continent with stakeholders spanning many areas of African society, including youth, women, civil society organisations, the diaspora, African think tanks and research institutes, planners, the private sector, religious organisations, the Forum for Former African Heads of State, and others. This gave rise to the Aspirations of the African People, the driver of *Agenda 2063*.

2 *Agenda 2063* also refers to externally driven development agendas. Prominent amongst these are the structural adjustment programmes (SAPS) introduced under the auspices of the World Bank during the 1980s as well as the Millennium Development Goals (MDGs) and the Sustainable Development Goals (SDGs). An important point of reference are the 'success stories' of the South East Asian 'tiger' economies to which several references are made.

3 The specific goals were to achieve economic growth of 7% per annum for the next 15 years and to meet the international development targets agreed on by the United Nations in 2001. The programme of action outlines initiatives that will provide the necessary conditions for achieving these objectives in the areas of peace, security, democracy, political and economic governance, and developing regional co-operation. NEPAD goes on to identify a range of sectoral priorities that are organised around specific themes. The first is to bridge the infrastructure gap in transport, energy, ICT, water, and sanitation. The second is to develop human resources through poverty reduction, bridging the education gap, reversing the brain drain, and developing health services. Other themes include strategies to develop agriculture, sustain the environment, and develop African culture and indigenous science and technology programmes. The NEPAD document sets out a series of measures for mobilising resources to support the overall programme, including tax reform, debt relief, an increase in external aid, and measures to increase private capital flows. It also outlines a range of initiatives for increasing market access for African countries, including diversification of production, developing mining, manufacturing, tourism and services, promoting the private sector and exports, and removing trade barriers.

4 In NEPAD, education has a role in agricultural development through agricultural extension initiatives, in health education and measures to reduce population growth, in bridging the digital divide, and developing science and technology. The NEPAD Secretariat has produced four key documents in the area of education and training covering reversing the brain drain; bridging the education gap; skills development; and on integrating higher education (Tikly 2003c).

5 FAWE was registered in Kenya as a pan-African NGO in 1993 with a Secretariat in Nairobi. Since then, it has grown into a network of 33 national chapters with a wide range of Membership that includes women policy makers and male ministers of education who are associate members. For more details about FAWE, see www.fawe.org.

6 The inter-country quality nodes (ICQNs) are intended to reflect regional priorities and have been established in the areas of early childhood development, literacy and national languages, mathematics and science education, peace education, teaching and learning, books and learning materials, and technical and vocational skills development.

7 The AAU, whose headquarters is in Accra, Ghana, was formed in November 1967 at a founding conference in Rabat, Morocco, attended by representatives of 34 universities who adopted the constitution of the Association. The AAU is the apex organization and principal forum for consultation, exchange of information, and cooperation among the universities in Africa. The Secretary General of IUCEA has also emphasised the resolve to move the council to the centre position in co-coordinating and enhancing academic undertakings of both private and public universities in East Africa.

8 The network works closely with the International Institute for Educational Planning (IIEP) to co-ordinate the delivery of intensive training programs focused on the requirements of the research and also to facilitate access to advanced technical knowledge and computer-based techniques. The SACMEQ network has completed two major cross-national studies of the quality of education in Southern and Eastern Africa. The SACMEQ I Project (1995–1999) was completed by seven Ministries of Education (Kenya, Malawi, Mauritius, Namibia, Tanzania (Zanzibar), Zambia, and Zimbabwe). The SACMEQ II Project (2000–2003) was completed by 14 Ministries of Education (Botswana, Kenya, Lesotho, Malawi, Mauritius, Mozambique, Namibia, Seychelles, South Africa, Swaziland, Tanzania (Mainland), Tanzania (Zanzibar), Uganda, and Zambia) whilst the more recent SAQMEQ III project involved 16 countries.

9 This includes, for example, the ratification of various protocols on education and training by the Southern African Development Community largely aimed at facilitating cross-border mobility of skills and qualifications. The Great Lakes Initiative, on the other hand, is a recent intergovernmental response to civil strife, political instability, and health calamities (like Ebola and the HIV/AIDS pandemic) in the Great Lakes Region. Even though education is touched upon only perfunctorily in the founding declaration, the members did make some commitments, including a pledge to meet the Millennium Development Goals (MDGs); to develop and promote comprehensive curricula on the culture of peace in their educational systems; and to promote the use of Kiswahili as a working language in the Great Lakes Region.

10 See Tikly (2003a) for a discussion of the application of Foucault's ideas about governmentality to colonial and postcolonial contexts.

11 Within the more centralized French system, for example, mission schools for the most part were absorbed within the system of government schools. More decentralized education systems introduced under the English, on the other hand, experienced less direct control from the British Colonial Office and allowed for

greater autonomy for missionary bodies in the running of schools, mirroring the more voluntarist nature of the English education system (Whitehead 2003).

12 Although treated with suspicion by both the British and the French, they were more likely to be tolerated within the British colonial system than the more secular French system (Launey 2016). The legacy of some of these differences have become implicated in present-day conflicts such as that between Boko Harem and the state in Northern Nigeria (discussed later).

13 For example, Rwanda is characterised by a highly dominant political elite, although one committed to impersonality and the 'good governance' agenda in education; Uganda, on the other hand, has a weakly dominant elite coalition but one that is highly personalised in relation to policy (exemplified by Museveni's personal leadership style); Ghana also demonstrates the personalised nature of elite bargains and competitive clientelism within the state (i.e. the education system is highly politicised and open to rent seeking and other kinds of activities); South Africa, on the other hand, has more impersonalised elite bargains and greater institutional complexity with political power within the education system contested at national, regional, and local levels.

14 The authors explain that the emerging discourse of development in the period following the Second World War provided a rationale for the emergence of two distinct types of NGOs. The first group consisted of overseas missionary societies and charitable bodies that were present in the colonies prior to independence. Christian aid evolved out of an amalgam of such charities. The second group is typified by organisations such as Oxfam, Save the Children, and Plan International that had no direct involvement in the colonies but rather emerged as 'war charities'. Each group had different motivations for adopting the development mantle.

15 Increasing amounts of development assistance were channelled through NGOs. In the early 1970s, less than 2% of NGO income came from official donors. By the mid-1990s, this figure had risen to 30% (Manji and O'Coill 2002).

16 UWEZO means 'capability' in Kiswahili. It aims to improve literacy and numeracy among children in the basic education cycle through what it claims are citizen-driven approaches to accountability. UWEZO produces the results of a literacy and numeracy test that it administers annually so as to draw attention to poor learning outcomes in schools (see www.uwezo.net/). UWEZO often operates in an antagonistic relationship with Ministries of Education in the countries concerned.

17 Illiteracy is identified by CESA as a major challenge to the adoption of scientific and technological innovations geared towards improvement in health, agriculture, and livelihoods. The document argues that with one of the fastest growing population growth rates, if the rise in illiteracy is not stemmed, illiteracy may jeopardize economic and social progress on the continent.

18 See www.theguardian.com/education/2002/nov/25/schools.uk

19 It is estimated that across SSA, households currently contribute 33% of total domestic public spending on education at primary and 68% at the lower secondary level which is a major part of the average household budget.

20 The schools were not allowed to screen for intake or to charge fees. Rather the government gave each school $100 per learner (compared to an average of $50 per learner in government-run schools).

21 For example, the recent evaluation of the first year of the privatisation programme in Liberia reports that after one year, 'public schools managed by private contractors in Liberia raised student learning by 60 percent, compared to standard public schools. But costs were high, performance varied across contractors, and contracts authorized the largest contractor to push excess pupils and under-performing

teachers onto other government schools' (Romero, Sandefur, and Sandholtz 2017).

22 Only a third of countries in sub-Saharan Africa currently guarantee this compared to 64% of countries globally. Currently, 21% of primary school age children, 36% of lower secondary school age adolescents, and 57% of upper secondary school age youth in Africa are not enrolled (UNESCO 2017b).

23 In many cases, girls have to share toilets with boys, which has implications for the safety, health, and dignity of girls, especially after the onset of puberty and is one cause of girls dropping out from schools (UNESCO 2016).

24 This includes computers but also older ICTs such as radios and televisions. The vast majority of schools are also without reliable Internet connectivity, specially at primary school level and in the rural areas.

25 Approximately 20% of total public expenditure on education came from donors, although there has been a decline in donor funding, particularly for primary education (Brookings 2015).

26 Specifically, this will involve the private sector in providing direct financial support to public institutions, granting scholarships, providing mentorship and internship opportunities, and supporting the management of levies to support education and training. As we will see in the following, the encouragement of public–private partnerships is also a feature of new initiatives by donors to support education and training in Africa (CESA REF: 33).

27 In Francophone Africa from the turn of the twentieth century up to independence, the French colonisers pursued a policy of 'association' aimed explicitly at developing modern African elites who could assume leadership roles albeit in the French image.

28 See https://en.unesco.org/themes/gced

29 It is in this context and with an eye on East Asian countries such as Singapore that have prospered under globalisation that *Agenda 2063* posits the notion of the 'developmental state' as a possible way forward for improving governance and driving development (in this respect, the term shares similarities with that of 'developmental regionalism').

7 From colonial education to the SDGs

Changing discourses on skills for development

Introduction

The first aim of this chapter is to consider the changing nature of debates about skills for development since colonial times. This involves taking account of the shifting view of 'development' along with the underlying views of 'modernity' and considering the implications these changing meta-discourses have had for debates about education and training. In terms of the six development domains identified in Chapter 4, the main focus is on the relationship between education and the economic domain. This reflects the emphasis on economic concerns in global and regional agendas. However, given that views of modernity are also cultural discourses, the chapter will engage with the cultural domain in so far as it has shaped the skills debate. Further, as discussed in Chapter 4, economic development has wrought environmental catastrophe on the continent and education continues to be complicit in these processes as well. The chapter will therefore also consider the changing relationship between education and the environment.

The chapter will explore the possibility, held out by global and regional agendas, that education and training are in the process of being repositioned in their relationship with the economic and environmental domains. In other words, that education and training systems are being decoupled from processes of unequal growth based on extractive economic practices and repositioned so that the outcomes of education and training support the development of knowledge economies and environmental sustainability. It will be argued in this respect that the nature of the path dependency built between education and training and the economic domain since colonial times has proved remarkably resilient. Further, it will be suggested that what is likely to emerge under current proposals is a continuation of the old correspondence between education and unsustainable development on the continent.

In developing the arguments in the chapter, the book draws on the critical tradition for considering the skills for development debate. Rather than see the relationship between education and training in linear, functionalist terms as is often the case in human capital theory, the relationship is understood in terms of processes of 'skills formation' (Brown 1999; Tikly 2003b). The term skills formation is defined as the 'social capacity for learning, innovation and productivity' (Brown 1999, 233). Use of the term draws attention to the wider cultural political economy within which debates about skills take place in different settings. Skills themselves are considered to be more than just the acquisition of narrow technical competencies but are also considered to have a social basis linked to the inherently social nature of learning.

The second aim of the chapter is to begin to set out an alternative basis for considering skills formation compared to dominant approaches. This will involve considering alternative ways of conceptualising economic development that takes account of social needs on the one hand and planetary boundaries on the other. Closely linked to this is the idea of sustainable work which has been posited by the International Labour Organisation (ILO) as an alternative to conventional views of labour markets in mainstream economics. In exploring the relationship between education, training, and sustainable work, the chapter will further develop the idea that skills are fundamentally social in nature through considering the relationship between skills, competencies, and capabilities. The chapter will conclude by reconceptualising three of the priorities set out in CESA, namely, the emphasis on literacy and numeracy, on the one hand, and on science, mathematics, engineering and mathematics (STEM) education on the other in the light of the new understanding of SD and of social and environmental justice.

Skills for economic development: changing priorities

As will be discussed here, CESA prioritises specific skills and competencies in its discussion of the contribution of education to development in Africa. Although grounded in contemporary discourses about knowledge economies and twenty-first-century skills (discussed later), they also bear the hallmarks of older discourses evident since colonial times. In order to fully understand contemporary discourses, it is therefore important to undertake some genealogical investigation into their origins and to consider how ideas about the relationship between education and the economy have emerged over time.

Skills formation under colonialism

In his classic text *How Europe Underdeveloped Africa*, Walter Rodney (1973) describes the following features of pre-colonial African education as 'outstanding':

> its close links with social life, both in a material and spiritual sense; its collective nature; its many sidedness; and its progressive development in conformity with the successive stages of physical, emotional and mental

development of the child. There was no separation of education and productive activity or any division between manual and intellectual education. Altogether, through mainly informal means, pre-colonial education matched the realities of pre-colonial African society and produced well-rounded personalities to fit into that society.

(Rodney 1973, 262)

Rodney's account is useful in that it helps to place pre-colonial approaches to skills formation into a broader historical and material context[1] and because it serves to demonstrate the possibility for a positive correspondence between education and sustainable livelihoods, a possibility that will be explored in the next chapter. Whilst there are dangers in both homogenising and romanticising education and training before the arrival of the Europeans, this general account of pre-colonial education and training in Africa nonetheless stands in stark contrast to the development of education policy since colonial times.

Colonial education policy on the African continent was driven by a complex mixture of differing interests and motives, as historians have made clear (see, for example, Mangan 1988; Kallaway 1984, 1994; Altbach and Kelly 1978). The first attempts to introduce European models of education in Africa were made by the missionaries dating back to the sixteenth century. In South Africa, missionary education was introduced following the arrival of the Dutch in 1652. In many parts of the continent, however, missionary education preceded formal colonial rule. Evangelical missions, predominantly from Protestant churches in Europe, taught literacy and manual skills, while the Anglican and Catholic missions (the latter predominating in French and Portuguese colonies) generally had a more academic focus (Cowan, O'Connell, and Scanlon 1965, p. 4).

As noted in Chapter 5, it is also important to take account of differences between the colonial powers in the way that colonial education was conceived in relation to the broader 'civilising mission' (White 1996) including the ways in which education was governed by different colonial powers in relation to different forms of colonial governmentality. In all cases, access to education was not universal and was for most learners limited to a few years of basic education with very limited access indeed to secondary education. Access was particularly limited for girls, although greater emphasis was placed on the education of girls within the British system. Here, however, as historians have argued, this was linked to efforts to socialise girls into the roles expected of them in the home and in the labour market (Gaitskell 1988; White 1996).

There were also differences in the form and content of education introduced by the different colonial powers. The French approach was more assimilationist in orientation. In the eyes of the coloniser, the policy of assimilation was based on a very real need:

> The black races of Africa have not attained a complete and coherent civilization of their own, nor do they possess the necessary foundations on which to build up a real system of education. The great contribution that we can make lies precisely in the interweaving and blending of primitive civilizations with our own universally applicable civilization, which will have to justify its position of superiority and authority by the manner in which it acquits itself of the responsibility it has assumed.
>
> (Charlton, in White 1996, 15)

At the heart of the idea of assimilation was the use of French as the medium of instruction at all levels of the education system. As White (1996) explains, the use of French was explicitly justified by the French colonialists at the time with reference to the underlying view of the technical inferiority of African languages and in order to make Africans more employable. Whilst there was an emphasis on a curriculum more suited to the rural areas at primary level, there existed a stronger emphasis on the 'formation' of African elites into French culture through secondary and latterly tertiary education (from the turn of the twentieth century up to independence, this policy became one of 'association' aimed explicitly at developing modern African elites who could assume leadership roles albeit in the French image). The British by way of contrast explicitly pursued a policy of 'adapted education'. This meant teaching in the mother tongue at primary level and a curriculum 'adapted to the mentality, aptitudes, occupations and traditions of the various peoples' and particularly focused on developing agricultural and other skills suited to life in the rural areas (White 1996; Bude 1983). The view of adapted education was based on notions of cultural relativism in contrast to the cultural universalism of the French. In this view, African cultures could at times be valorised. In keeping with the French view however, it was also premised on a paternalistic view of the exotic and ultimately inferior 'other'.[2] Unlike the French tradition, the British also instituted technical and vocational education and training, although this was always much debated and this continued to be the case in the post-colonial period.

There were also differences between the French and British as the two major colonising powers about how the outcomes of colonial education might be evaluated. For the French, whilst there was a need to account for expenditure, the 'success' of colonial education lay largely in the success or otherwise of its assimilationist project and 'quality' was very much equated with exposure of learners to the academic rigour of the French curriculum. By way of contrast, the quality of education in the English system was more likely to be equated with efficiency and the need to avoid wastage of money and human material (White 1996). One can arguably see in modern-day emphases on the efficiency and effectiveness of education systems echoes of this more technicist anglophone approach.

Skills formation and 'modernisation'

The path dependency developed by colonial education systems persisted into the post-independence period. Indeed, education systems have until relatively recently been characterised by low levels of access for the poorest, outmoded, academically oriented, content-driven curricula and assessment systems that are both cognitively and linguistically demanding and operate principally as a filtering mechanism to limit access to higher levels of education and training. This is despite considerable reform efforts in the immediate post-independence period, including attempts to vocationalise the curriculum in order to create a stronger correspondence between education and changing economic needs. Foster (1965) famously described these efforts as part of the 'vocational schools fallacy' in that they ignored the lack of availability of jobs within the formal economy requiring vocational skills which reinforced within the popular consciousness the perception of the superiority of academic qualifications. This antipathy towards vocational education pathways is apparent today despite global and regional efforts to develop vocational education (AU 2007; AUC 2015b; UNESCO 2015b).

With regard to the post-independence period and the advent of contemporary globalisation, two discourses have been particularly influential at a global level in defining the wider 'policyscape' (Carney 2008) within which regional and national policies have emerged. The first of these was modernisation theory developed by Rostow (1960).[3] Drawing on ideas about the nature of modernity and progress going back to Durkheim and Weber, it is based on an idea of development as comprising discrete stages from the traditional to the high-mass consumption society. The stages are summarised in Figure 7.1.

In the context of US aid policy in the 1960s, the role of development agencies was to focus assistance on supporting the 'pre-conditions for take off' stage. Education is deeply implicated in this stage and in the project of modernisation more broadly through its role in inculcating the skills, attitudes, and dispositions

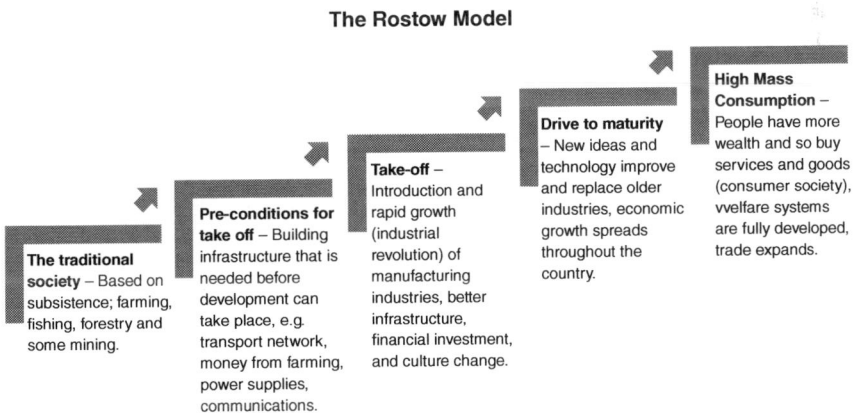

The Rostow Model

The traditional society – Based on subsistence; farming, fishing, forestry and some mining.

Pre-conditions for take off – Building infrastructure that is needed before development can take place, e.g. transport network, money from farming, power supplies, communications.

Take-off – Introduction and rapid growth (industrial revolution) of manufacturing industries, better infrastructure, financial investment, and culture change.

Drive to maturity – New ideas and technology improve and replace older industries, economic growth spreads throughout the country.

High Mass Consumption – People have more wealth and so buy services and goods (consumer society), welfare systems are fully developed, trade expands.

Figure 7.1 The Rostow model of development.

required to produce 'modern' citizens. As was discussed in Chapter 3, modernisation theory was heavily critiqued by dependency theorists such as Gunder Frank for not taking into account the unequal nature of the relationship between countries at the core and periphery of the global capitalist system and the inherent contradictions and crisis tendencies of the capitalist system. It was also critiqued for positing only one view of modernity that is presented as synonymous with Western consumer societies. Many of the assumptions underlying modernisation theory, however, have proved remarkably persistent, including the assumption of a linear view of progress and the equation of modernity with mass consumption, consumer societies. These assumptions can be said to underpin *Agenda 2063* and CESA by the emphasis placed on economic growth as the indicator of development and the emphasis on inculcating in the population through exposure to education and training modern, 'scientific' ways of thinking.

The rise and rise of human capital theory

The other major discourse to have shaped education policy in Africa in the postwar years that has also proved remarkably enduring is that of human capital theory originally developed by Thoedore Schultz (1961).[4] Human capital theory (HCT) has however changed in form and emphasis over the years (Robertson et al. 2007). During the 1960s and 1970s, it was associated with modernisation theory through positing the link between education, human capital formation, and capitalist growth. This belief, although still very popular amongst mainstream economists and policy makers, has been subject to sustained criticism.

Firstly, the idea of positing 'growth' as the ultimate goal of development has been critiqued from a number of directions. For economists such as Raworth (2017), for example, the obsession on the part of governments with economic growth at any cost ignores the need to live within planetary boundaries and to meet basic needs of people living in poverty (see the following). For Sen, the end goal of development is human and planetary flourishing and well-being and that in this sense, growth is only a means for achieving these wider goals (Sen 1999, 2013). The emphasis on economic growth also leads to a narrow set of priorities put forward in CESA regarding the kinds of skills and competencies that education needs to develop, a point that is also taken up in the following. A further critique of HCT is that it is based on an idealised view of the role of education as a means for achieving economic development (Tikly 2004; Vally and Motala 2014). In particular, HCT assumes a linear relationship between the development of skills and economic growth. This fails to take account of the effects of economic crises in shaping the ability of education systems to provide the skills actually required by economies or to tackle issues of poverty and inequality. It will be recalled, for example, that the effects of economic crisis in the 1980s was an overall reduction in government investment in social institutions such as education with the effect of rendering them less effective in providing access to even the most basic skills (Ilon 1994; Samoff 1994).

Skills formation, knowledge economies, and twenty-first-century skills

Closely linked to HCT in dominant global discourses is the idea that education can contribute to the development of 'knowledge economies'. The idea of the knowledge economy has been advocated by the World Bank since the 1990s (Robertson et al. 2007). Resting on the four pillars of education and training, the development of an information infrastructure provides an economic and institutional regime to support knowledge flows and innovation systems. Policies linked to the idea of the knowledge economy have for a while now found prominent expression in the education and training policies of several African countries, including, for instance, Rwanda and Tanzania (Tikly et al. 2003). It has provided an impetus for the recent shift towards competency-based curricula in many African countries. Emerging out of discourses of the knowledge economy has been an emphasis on the so-called twenty-first-century skills. This emphasis is also evident in CESA. A recent, influential World Economic Forum publication (Forum 2015) grouped these skills into three categories: foundational literacies, competencies, and character qualities (see Table 7.1). These have proved influential in shaping approaches towards competency-based curricula in Africa as elsewhere.

Like the master narratives of HCT and modernisation theory, the idea of the knowledge economy has also been subject to sustained critique (e.g. Robertson et al. 2007). The concept emerged in relation to Western industrialised nations and other countries at the centre of the global economy, including the countries of the Pacific Rim. Whilst twenty-first-century skills may have purchase in Africa as elsewhere as a means of supporting economic and social innovation, the emphasis on these types of skills in global and regional policy agendas stands in stark contrast to the nature of labour markets in low- and many middle-income countries which continue to be characterised by poorly paid, insecure employment in the formal and informal sectors. Thus, whilst the idea of a knowledge economy and of twenty-first-century skills might be intuitively appealing to

Table 7.1 Twenty-first-century skills.

Foundational literacies *How students apply core skills to everyday tasks*	*Competencies* *How students approach complex challenges*	*Character qualities* *How students approach their changing environment*
Literacy	Critical thinking/	Curiosity
Numeracy	problem-solving	Initiative
Scientific literacy	Creativity	Persistence/grit
ICT literacy	Communication	Adaptability
Financial literacy	Collaboration	Leadership
Cultural and civic literacy		Social and cultural awareness

Source: World Economic Forum (2015).

policy makers, it can often operate more as a rhetorical device removed from the realities of low- and middle-income economies. Like HCT, it can be perceived as idealistic in positing the development of twenty-first-century skills as a 'solution' in and of itself for the problems of unsustainable development whilst the need for more profound changes in the economy and labour market in order to create a demand for these skills in the first place is not taken into account.

Skills formation and lifelong learning

A parallel narrative to that of knowledge economies and twenty-first-century skills, however, emerged out of the Education for All (EFA) movement in the 1980s and 1990s (Chapter 4). In this discursive context, the concept of 'life skills' has been used in different but overlapping ways by various international organisations working within a rights-based framework. Within the EFA Movement, life skills was a catch-all term for 'skills for sustainable livelihoods' which has historically formed part of UNESCO's wider ESD discourse (Maclean and Wilson 2011). Closely linked to the idea of life skills is that of lifelong learning which is seen as essential for developing relevant life skills in rapidly changing societies and economies across the life span. The idea of lifelong learning has a long pedigree on the African continent. It was used by Nyerere, for example, to encapsulate his view of education in relation to self-reliance (Nyerere 1967). Within a rights-based framework, the idea of lifelong learning has been central to evolving discourses of EFA (Chapter 4). The Dakar Framework for Action adopted at the World Education Forum (WEF) states:

> All young people and adults must be given the opportunity to gain the knowledge and develop the values, attitudes and skills that will enable them to develop their capacities to work, to participate fully in their society, to take control of their own lives and to continue learning.
>
> (UNESCO 2000, 16)

The ideas of life skills and lifelong learning resonate more closely with the realities of the development challenges facing Africa and other parts of the low-income, postcolonial world than does the list of twenty-first-century skills. The idea of life skills has also been subject to critique. One criticism, for example, has centred on the extent to which it presents a top-down 'one size fits all' approach to skills development and pay insufficient attention to the processes by which skills and competencies are identified in policy at different levels of the system (Tikly 2013). (A similar critique is made of the way that twenty-first-century skills are portrayed.) In this respect and in relation to the capability approach, it is important to define skills and competencies in relation to the capabilities and functionings that communities, governments, and other stakeholders have reason to value. This point is taken up in the following section.

Skills formation and regional agendas

In this section, attention will turn to how debates about skills for development are reflected in regional agendas. Before turning to a consideration of CESA, it is important to understand how economic development is portrayed in *Agenda 2063* as it is in relation to this broader understanding and the contradictions inherent within it that the understanding of skills for development is framed.

Framing regional skills agendas: *agenda 2063* and 'inclusive growth'

A key point of reference in *Agenda 2063* is the notion of 'inclusive growth'. The idea of inclusive growth has been popularised through sometimes contradictory discourses emanating from key multilateral organisations, including the World Bank (2008), the OECD (2014), the United Nations Development Programme (2017), and the African Development Bank (2014). Although there are differences in emphasis in the way that inclusive growth is defined,[5] at the most basic level it is premised on a view of broad-based growth across sectors. Growth can be made more inclusive largely through the creation of job opportunities arising from the removal of regulatory constraints and through creating a climate conducive to investment. Inclusive growth is also 'green growth' in the sense that growth should be compatible with environmental protection through processes of adaptation and the use of green technologies. *Agenda 2063* defines the idea of inclusive growth in the following terms:

> ending poverty, inequalities of income and opportunity; job creation; addressing the challenges of rapid urbanization, improvement of habitats and access to basic necessities of life; providing social security and protection; developing Africa's human and social capital (through an education and skills revolution emphasizing science and technology and expanding access to quality health care services, particularly for women and girls); transforming Africa's economies through beneficiation from Africa's natural resources, manufacturing, industrialization and value addition, as well as raising productivity and competitiveness; radically transforming African agriculture to enable the continent to feed itself and be a major player as a net food exporter; exploiting the vast potential of Africa's blue/ocean economy; and finally putting in place measures to sustainably manage the continent's rich biodiversity, forests, land and waters and using mainly adaptive measures to address Climate change risks.
>
> (AUC 2015a): v)

It can be seen that the definition links together key elements of global discourses, including a concern with economic growth as a driver of prosperity, with concerns about the environment and human development. These elements are, however, contradictory in nature. For example, for advocates of the ideas of 'degrowth' (Latouche 2007), 'prosperity without growth' (Jackson 2016), or 'post-growth' (Blewitt and Cunningham 2014; Blewitt 2018), the very idea of 'growth' is antithetical to the idea of a sustainable environment given that natural resources are limited and the damage that growth under capitalism has historically wrought on natural systems. The emphasis on the use of 'adaptive measures' (an idea that is implicit in the concept of inclusive growth) has been criticised in the environmental literature as being based on the assumption that climate change and environmental degradation can be dealt with primarily through processes of technological innovation. Rather, for environmentalists such as Blewitt (2018), these solutions alone are insufficient for tackling the root causes of climate change which lie in patterns of production and consumption as they have developed under capitalism and particularly in the global North. Further, there is a contradiction between the idea of inclusive growth, current patterns of growth on the continent which are highly unequal and based on the extraction of natural resources in order to maximise profit and the prevalence in regional agendas of neoliberal, market-led solutions to achieving growth. It was argued in Chapter 4 that the path dependency of many Africa economies on growth based on neoliberal principles is linked to Africa's position in relation to globalisation and to dominant global and national interests. These interests are largely unacknowledged and unchallenged in *Agenda 2063*.

Skills formation and CESA

As will be recalled from Chapter 1, CESA prioritises several areas of skills that are specifically related to economic development. These include basic literacy and numeracy, STEM-related skills, as well as vocational skills and adult literacy. At a general level, it is possible to see the influences of several discourses linking education to development. For example, as already suggested, the continued influence of modernisation theory is evident in the underlying assumptions concerning the nature of progress and what it is to be 'modern'. It is also evident in the emphasis given to inculcating in youth 'scientific' ways of thinking. It is also possible to see the influence of rights-based discourses. They are reflected, for example, in the references to lifelong learning in the document and in priorities that emphasise the expansion of all levels of education and training. It is HCT and ideas of the knowledge economy and twenty-first-century skills, however, that predominate in CESA. Objective one, for example, specifically references both human capital and the knowledge economy. These contradictory discourses are nonetheless successfully 'knitted together' in the document in providing a rationale for the development of specific skills. As will be discussed later, however, they also provide a source of tension in the document. Some of these tensions, it will be suggested, reflect larger tensions implicit in the concept of inclusive growth.

CESA and basic literacy and numeracy

At this point, it is worth critically discussing some of the specific areas of skill identified in the document in relation to the view of social and environmental justice outlined in Chapter 3. As we have seen, a key priority for regional agendas in the primary phase is the development of literacy and numeracy skills. On the one hand an emphasis on basic literacy and numeracy can be seen to accord with an HCT approach in that these skills are considered foundational for the development of higher-order twenty-first-century skills. Literacy skills, including adult literacy, are however also critical from a rights-based perspective. For example, literacy and numeracy are important for making accessible information about disease prevention and child nutrition. The development of literacy and numeracy can contribute to women's empowerment (e.g. through increasing women's finical independence and enabling greater control on the part of women over their own fertility). Literacy and numeracy are also important as a means of empowering communities to understand and take steps to mitigate environmental risk (Lotz-Sisitka et al. 2017). It is the fundamental contribution of literacy and numeracy to capability development that has led Sen to describe these skills as 'basic capabilities'.

The priority afforded to basic literacy and numeracy in CESA is further justified from an analysis of the results of regional assessment regimes. In Francophone countries, the *Programme d'analyse des systèmes éducatifs de la Confemen* assesses competency in mathematics for end-of primary students against a 'sufficiency threshold'. In 2015, across the entire SSA Francophone region, 59% tested below this threshold, with Côte d'Ivoire at 73.1% and Senegal at 41.2% below the threshold (PASEC 2015). Similarly, the Southern African Consortium for Monitoring Education Quality which has measured changes in numeracy and literacy levels from 2000 to 2007 in ten Anglophone Southern and Eastern African countries provides an equally bleak picture, although with significant variations within and between countries (Hungi 2011).[6] Where global regional agendas fall short, however, is in recognising the nature of systemic inequalities in education systems, including those based on class, gender, race and ethnicity, and disability that limit the capabilities of disadvantaged groups. This, it will be suggested in subsequent section, requires taking account of evidence of the barriers and facilitators that can hinder or improve literacy and numeracy development for the most disadvantaged groups.[7]

CESA and STEM-related skills

Besides basic literacy and numeracy, regional agendas also place a high premium on science, technology, engineering, and mathematics (STEM) education. The high priority afforded to STEM-related subjects can be linked to the continuing influence of modernisation theory and HCT in regional agendas. Access to STEM-related skills is also justified in relation to rights-based concerns through an emphasis on increasing access to scientific knowledge for all groups of learners. From the perspective of social and environmental justice and as elaborated on in the following section, there is potential for a more comprehensive view of STEM-related skills than that offered in CESA to make a contribution to the more expansive view of labour markets that takes account of the social as well as the environmental nature of labour markets. The emphasis in CESA, however, is the role of STEM-related skills in promoting economic growth through techno-logical innovation.[8] As with basic literacy and numeracy skills, the report is also limited in not recognising the nature of the barriers impacting on the capabilities of different groups of learners to participate in STEM subjects, a point that is also developed in the following section.

Technical and vocational education and training

Finally, CESA places emphasis on the development of vocational skills as a means to support sustainable livelihoods and to tackle youth unemployment in urban and rural areas. In this regard, the recommendations in CESA also need to be considered alongside the *Continental Strategy for Technical and Vocational Education and Training* (AUC 2015b) which fed into the development of CESA as well as global discourses about the future of TVET (UNESCO 2015b). These documents define TVET broadly to include technical and vocational skills acquired through basic schooling and participation in formal secondary and tertiary TVET provision and work-based training, as well as informal processes of skills development acquired though participation in the informal economy, voluntary work, etc.

The policy texts correctly identify a range of challenges facing TVET in Africa. These include a mismatch between the supply and the demand for skills with provision largely supply driven; a highly fragmented TVET system and a lack of clearly articulated pathways for developing skills across the life span; the predominance of informal skills training with limited opportunities for updating skills or developing associated skills such as literacy necessary for progressing to higher order skills; limited and unequal access to more specialised skills training at secondary or tertiary level, either within the private sector or within TVET colleges; the high costs of provision of formal TVET; the absence of common qualifications frameworks that would enable the recognition of prior skills and facilitate the transfer of skills across national borders; inequalities related to social class that limit access for the poorest who cannot afford to pay fees; inequalities linked to gender, including, for example, in access to STEM-related TVET opportunities; and inequalities linked to rurality in that most TVET centres are located in urban rather than rural areas.

In addressing these challenges, however, there are a number of tensions and contradictions in global and regional agendas. Firstly, there is a tension between objectives aimed at expanding TVET provision and proposals to further privatise provision which will have the effect of exacerbating regimes of inequality and in the absence of strong regulatory frameworks, it is likely to contribute to the further fragmentation of TVET systems. Secondly, global and regional agendas increasingly emphasise the importance of entrepreneurial skills as a means for ameliorating youth unemployment. Here, however, as with other areas of skills formation, there is a tension between developing entrepreneurial skills and the creation of opportunities for entrepreneurs in the labour market. This tension has been recognised, for example, in Tanzania (DeJaeghere and Baxter 2013; De Jaeghere 2017).

There are also important policy decisions that are not dealt with in global and regional agendas concerning TVET. For example, there are an increasing number of vocational streams in secondary education in Africa but questions to do with the balance between academic and vocational education and the point at which learners specialise in either vocational or academic subjects are not addressed. In this respect, it is important to take account of previous attempts to vocationalise the curriculum. In particular and with reference to the earlier discussion of the vocational schools fallacy (Foster 1965), there is a need to link an increase in the supply of vocational skills on the one hand to initiatives within the economic domain that will lead to an increase in a demand for these skills on the other. This is important if long-held public perceptions, dating back to colonial times about the superiority of academic education, are to be altered.

CESA and the cultural basis of skills formation

As has been already intimated above, debates about skills for development have a strong cultural influence since colonial times. As the *Agenda 2063* Framework Document notes, education has historically been a key institution for the imposition of Western cultural hegemony and the underlying view of skills for development reflects this. Thus, colonial curricula introduced a Western *episteme* (ground base of knowledge) which differed considerably from indigenous knowledge systems but also from other forms of education in Africa such as Qur'anic education (Launey 2016). Similarly, in relation to assessment, the introduction of competitive examinations in the context of a highly selective education systems stood in contrast to the role of assessment in traditional African education which focused on demonstrating relevant knowledge and skills on the job to one's seniors and peers (Rodney 1973). As has been discussed, modernisation theory as a master narrative of development has often been equated being modern with Western industrialised economies which has reinforced the idea that skills for development should imitate policies and underlying view of skills borrowed from the West.

This is reflected, for example, in the valorisation of STEM-related skills without recognising the cultural nature of these skills. In Chapter 8, it will be argued that providing access to STEM-related skills is extremely important in the African context but that this needs to go hand in hand with a transformation of what is understood by STEM-related skills to take account of indigenous as well as Western forms of knowledge. There is also a more fundamental need to transform the nature of STEM-related disciplines through reorienting STEM-related research on the continent to address the challenges of sustainable development. Closely linked to this, it will be suggested in Chapter 9, is the need to promote indigenous languages as a means to access local and indigenous knowledge systems and to make cognitively demanding STEM disciplines more accessible to disadvantaged groups of learners. Similarly, and in relation to entrepreneurial education, recent longitudinal research into entrepreneurial education programmes in Tanzania has highlighted a tension between Western, individualised conceptions of entrepreneurialism and the more communal approach to economic activity that has characterised many African societies (evident, for example, in the legacy of *Ujaama* in Tanzania) (DeJaeghere and Baxter 2013; De Jaeghere 2017). That is to say, that like the area of STEM, there is a need to reorient entrepreneurial education along with other skills for development to the African context.

As will be discussed in Chapter 8, a key omission from CESA is in relation to the language question. The pattern of early exit from the mother tongue (i.e. a subtractive bilingual approach) is very widespread on the continent. It reflects the view amongst many policy makers and parents that a good-quality education means learning in a European language and the association particularly between competence in English and access to elite jobs (Trudell 2009). These attitudes towards indigenous languages, as we have seen, have their roots in colonial education systems and in the influence of modernisation theory. This is despite the evidence that learning in the mother tongue for at least eight years and learning a global language as a second language (i.e. an additive bilingual model) is far more effective for conceptual and linguistic development, particularly for learners from disadvantaged backgrounds (Heugh 2005). Crucially, as will be argued in Chapter 8, the ability to learn literacy skills in mother tongue is important for the development of literacy. A key effect of the omission of language considerations form CESA is to reinforce a separation between predominantly Western oriented elites, fluent in European languages who reside largely in the urban areas and the urban and rural poor who have not been 'Westernised' to the same extent.

CESA, skills, and the environment

Education has had a contradictory relationship with the history of environmental degradation on the continent. There has been an emphasis on the teaching of agriculture as part of 'adapted education' and then in the post-independence period as a school subject. Agricultural Education and Training is also a recognised part of the TVET and Higher Education sectors, although there are often concerns about its quality and relevance which has affected the status of these subjects (AU 2007). There is also a history of environmental education in Africa. This was given impetus by the Decade for Education for Sustainable Development, although the overall reach of environmental education initiatives remains limited (Lotz-Sisitka et al. 2017). It is therefore unfortunate that CESA makes little mention of these subjects or indeed of a broader conception of ESD that would embrace environmental, economic, and social dimensions of the challenges facing the continent. This suggests that enormous challenges lie ahead in Africa as elsewhere to ensure a holistic conception of ESD gets instituted in the curriculum.

There has, however, been an increasing emphasis in global agendas related to TVET on the idea of 'green skills' as a means to 'green' the economy (Maclean and Wilson 2011; McGrath and Powell 2016). Although these find only a faint echo in regional agendas (both CESA and the Continental Strategy for TVET make hardly any reference to green skills), the idea is likely to gain increasing purchase in the context of the SDGs. In this respect, there is a danger that the idea of green skills as with twenty-first-century skills can be seen as a quick fix for achieving sustainable development. Rather, as was argued in relation to the objective to expand vocational training opportunities, simply producing graduates with skills in environmentally sustainable production techniques is meaningless unless there is a concomitant effort to transform production processes themselves to make them more environmentally sustainable (McGrath and Powell 2016).

Towards a sustainable approach to skills formation

To summarise, the account of skills for development in CESA is contradictory. Some of these tensions reflect those implicit in the idea of inclusive growth. In this respect, inclusive growth seeks to balance a neoliberal concern with the salience of markets as the driver of economic growth with concerns about human development and the environment, although, as already suggested, it is often the market-driven concerns that predominate. This tension is writ small in CESA where the emphasis is given primarily to human capital concerns over rights-based and environmental concerns in the identification of skills for development. There is also a lack of attention in CESA to the cultural basis of skills and a failure to sufficiently engage with the effects of regimes of inequality in limiting the opportunity freedoms available to disadvantaged groups of learners. Having provided a critique of skills for development discourses as they appear in global and regional agendas, the remainder of the chapter will now seek to outline an alternative approach to skills formation that, it is argued, is more consistent with a transformative SD and ESD.

Beyond 'inclusive growth'

A starting point for offering an alternative vision is in seeking an alternative to the idea of inclusive growth as a basis for conceiving skills for development. In this respect, Raworth (2017) drawing on complex systems thinking in economics has proposed the need for a more radical transformation of the economy than that envisaged in *Agenda 2063*. In her conception, policy makers must strike a balance between meeting basic needs such as education and health and operating within planetary boundaries. This involves not only moving away from a linear model of growth as the basis for thinking about economic development but also putting in place redistributive mechanisms to more equitably distribute wealth which in her view will lead to more sustainable economies. Raworth's understanding builds on a long lineage of thinking about the economy in relation to sustainable development going back to the Club of Rome (Chapter 3).[9] At the heart of the understanding is a view of the purpose of economic development as meeting social needs on the one hand and operating within ecological boundaries on the other. These ideas are encapsulated in Figure 7.2. For Raworth, the aim of economic policy is to achieve a dynamic equilibrium in the 'sweet spot' between the social foundation and the environmental ceiling of economic activity (hence the term 'doughnut economics' which Raworth applies to her model).

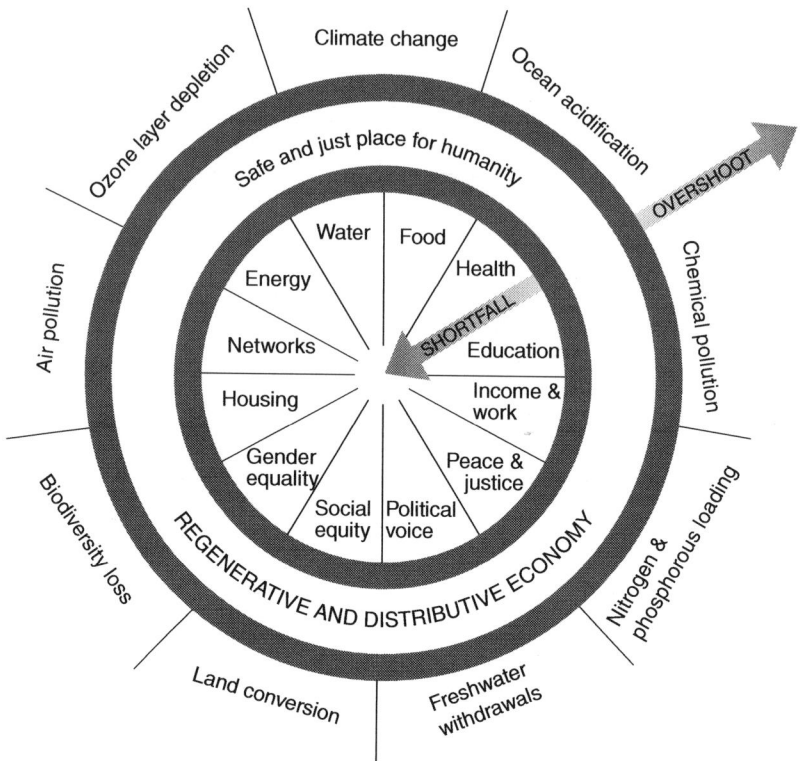

Figure 7.2 The model of 'Doughnut economics'.
Source: Adapted from Raworth (2017)

There are several advantages of Raworth's model for an understanding of SD in the context of the current book.[10] Firstly, in relation to the critique of the idea of inclusive growth, the model provides a useful guide for action for policy makers in conceptualising the purposes and limits of growth. Secondly, in keeping with Walby's (2009, 2015) understanding, the model offers an expansive view of the economic domain as inclusive of the social and environmental dimensions of production and consumption. This seems particularly pertinent for the African continent where the main scourges of SD are related to the existence of deep-rooted poverty and to the ever-increasing threats caused by climate change and other environmental risks. Secondly, the model explicitly takes account of the SDGs in that all of the elements that comprise the 'social foundation' along with the environmental risks identified in the outer ring are addressed in the SDGs. In relation to the conception of ESD in particular, the model encourages an overall approach to skills formation that takes account of the social nature of skills, including the role of skills in meeting basic needs and supporting environmentally sustainable production. Thirdly, through emphasising the role of the economy in meeting basic needs, the model accords with Fraser's redistributive principle of social justice. It provides an alternative model to the neoliberal emphasis on markets and instead suggests a more redistributive approach to the finance of education and training in keeping, for example, with the arguments developed in Chapter 6.

Skills, competencies, and capabilities for sustainable development

It has already been suggested that regional agendas do not adequately take account of the differences in opportunity facing different groups in developing skills or indeed the importance of relating skills and competencies to the livelihoods and aspirations of communities. Here it is helpful to clarify the relationship between the idea of skills and competencies as they are often portrayed in global and regional agendas and that of capabilities discussed in Chapter 3. Much of the language about education's relationship to development is in terms of 'skills' and 'competencies' and so it is important to distinguish what we mean by these and the relationship between these concepts and the idea of capabilities that informs the book. Within the mainstream literature, 'skills' are often defined as the ability to perform tasks and to solve problems. A 'competence', on the other hand, includes the ability to apply theory, concepts, or tacit knowledge to solve real-world problems alongside interpersonal attributes (e.g. social or organisational skills) and ethical values (e.g. CEDefop 2014; Rychen and Salganik 2003). Rychen and Saganik make the following distinction between skills and competencies:

> A competence is more than just knowledge or skills. It involves the ability to meet complex demands, by drawing on and mobilising psychosocial resources (including skills and attitudes) in a particular context. For example, the ability to communicate effectively is a competence that may draw on an individual's knowledge of language, practical IT skills and attitudes towards those with whom he or she is communicating.
>
> (Rychen and Salganik 2003)

These definitions are in some respects consistent with the view of complex learning that will be discussed in Chapter 9. For example, they draw attention to the importance of both the cognitive and the more contextually situated scales at which learning emerges (Davis and Sumara 2006). However, the definitions are also limiting. For instance, the emphasis on the acquisition of skills and competencies is at an individual rather than at a group level, thereby limiting consideration of the sociocultural dimensions of learning and indeed of the systems of wider social relations within which processes of skills formation are embedded. Conceptions of skills and competencies are also often cast in a technicist language that ignores the highly politicised nature of the processes by which skills and competencies are determined, the effects of different kinds of power in the process of defining skills and competencies, and of effects of intersecting regimes of inequality on the ability of different individuals and groups to access skills and competencies and convert these into valued functionings that can support well-being.

Here the capability approach provides a starting point for thinking about how one might evaluate the opportunity freedoms available to different individuals and groups. One way of conceiving skills and competencies in relation to the capability approach is to think of them as comprising part of the 'capability set' that learners need to pursue higher levels of education and training and/or to achieve sustainable livelihoods once they have left formal education and training. In this respect, for our purposes and in relation to the priorities set out in global and regional agendas, skills and competencies such as literacy and numeracy can be seen as 'basic capabilities' (Sen 2002) that are fundamental if learners are to function effectively either at higher levels of the education and training system or outside of the school in the wider economy and society. The development of other kinds of skills and competencies acquired during secondary education can also be seen as a basis for expanding opportunities, for example, for entry into higher education and/or areas of the labour market that require them.

Relevant to the discussion is the idea of 'conversion factors'. Robeyn's work (Robeyns 2005); 2017) identifies various conversion factors that are used to describe the ability of different individuals and groups to convert various inputs, including material and other kinds of resources into capabilities and functionings. Robeyns identifies three types of conversion factors:

> First, personal conversion factors (e.g. metabolism, physical condition, sex, reading skills, intelligence) influence how a person can convert the characteristics of the commodity into a functioning. . . . Second, social conversion factors (e.g. public policies, social norms, discriminating practices, gender roles, societal hierarchies, power relations) and, third, environmental conversion factors (e.g. climate, geographical location) play a role in the conversion from characteristics of the good to the individual functioning.
>
> (99)

The idea of conversion factors are important for the discussion in the book because they provide a useful starting point for identifying how personal and environmental factors interact with social and institutional arrangements, including the operation of intersecting regimes of inequality, and with wider factors such as exposure to environmental risk in shaping the opportunities that different individuals and groups have to develop skills and competencies by the end of schooling.

Here it is important to acknowledge scholarship within international and comparative education that has sought to apply the capability approach to better understand the relational nature of capabilities and the effects of different conversion factors in determining outcomes for different individuals and groups. In many instances, this scholarship involves the development of 'hybrid' theories that combine an interest in capability with an analysis of wider structural and discursive affordances and constraints that impinge on the opportunity freedoms available to different groups (Robeyns 2017). In their study of the development of entrepreneurial skills in Tanzania, DeJaeghere and Baxter (2013) make use of Bourdieu's ideas about habitus and field to understand how the presence or absence of different forms of social and cultural capital impact on the capability sets of different individuals and groups. Walker's (Walker 2019) recent work, on the other hand, focusing on higher education highlights the impact of the absence of epistemic justice in denying the opportunities of women and people of colour from accessing the curriculum and having their voices heard. Similarly, Unterhalter's work has shown how the absence of gender justice impacts on the capabilities of girls and women to achieve in the education system (Unterhalter 2007).

Complex capabilities

Extending these arguments, it is also useful to consider the capability approach including the ideas of conversion factors, capability sets, and functionings, in relation to the understanding of complexity theory that informs this book. Taking account of complexity draws attention to how skills and competencies as well as the opportunities to develop these emerge as a consequence of the interaction between systems at different scales. These include biological systems that constitute the human body in their interaction with the natural environment as well as with systems operating within and between institutions such as schools, the family, the church, the mosque, etc. These in turn emerge in relation to the wider economic, social, and cultural domains that extend beyond local to national, regional, and global scales. These social systems (institutions and domains) are cut across by regimes of inequality that operate in specific ways to facilitate or inhibit the development of capabilities.

Conceiving capabilities through a complexity lens, however, has implications for the way in which the relationship between different kinds of inputs, capabilities, and functionings are conceived in relation to human well-being. Quite often these relationships are portrayed in terms of a linear progression in which inputs are converted into capabilities and then potentially into valued functionings. Applying a complexity lens implies a messier relationship in which capabilities and functionings (and indeed human agency more generally) emerge as a consequence of the non-linear articulation of elements across different institutions and domains. This point is illustrated in the following discussion in relation to the development of the capability to read. Another example of the non-linearity of the relationships between capabilities and functioning is that functionings can themselves be considered as the basis for other capabilities. For example, in the following section, the functioning of achieving basic levels of literacy and numeracy becomes part of the capability set in the context of developing higher-order skills and competencies, including those relating to STEM.

It is also helpful to conceive of capabilities in relation to the understanding of policy developed in the first part of the book in which policy was presented in terms of complex systems operating at different scales. For example, Unterhalter and North (2017) have recently shown how the translation of global policy agendas relating to gender equality into policy enactments by various governmental and non-governmental institutions and agencies (e.g. donors, NGOs, professional associations, trade unions, etc.) in the so-called 'middle space' between global, regional, national, and local policy agendas has the effect of reproducing gender inequalities and limiting the capabilities of girls through a disarticulation between the way that gender equality is represented in policy and its enactment in practice. In the language of complex systems, this is to acknowledge the lack of coherence between systems responsible for implementing gender equality at different scales contributing to the reproduction of a gendered regime of inequality in education.

Considering skills and competencies in relation to the capability approach highlights key considerations for policy makers. Firstly, it raises questions about which skills and competencies are valued in the curriculum. This in turn raises questions about which specific skills and competencies and subsequent outcomes from schooling are 'valued', by whom, and the interests that are served in the process. This is considered further in Chapter 8 in the context of a discussion of the challenges of decolonising the curriculum. For now, it can be assumed, that whilst foundational skills and competencies such as literacy and numeracy are easy to justify in that they are essential components of the capability set required to develop higher-order skills and competencies, this assumption becomes more problematic in relation to other skills and competencies.[11] Secondly, it raises questions, as suggested earlier, about the affordances and barriers that impact on the capabilities of different groups of disadvantaged learners to develop valued skills and competencies.

Thirdly, considering skills and competencies in relation to the capability approach raises questions about how capabilities can be evaluated and measured. This has also been the subject of considerable debate within the capability approach (Unterhalter 2017).[12] It draws attention to the extent to which existing processes of formative and summative assessment are able to capture the distribution of valued skills and competencies. In this respect, the current high stakes, largely content-driven assessment regimes that predominate in Africa, will require substantial reform if they are to succeed in this respect. It also draws attention to the extent to which assessment data are able to serve as a basis for evaluating complex policy interventions, including changes to the curriculum, the introduction of new resources, and improvements in teacher professional development. Here it will be suggested in Chapter 10 that existing assessment regimes are often limited in relation to the indicators that are used and the cross-sectional rather than longitudinal nature of data which make it difficult to capture complex change over time.

However, whilst it is possible to conceive of how skills and competencies can be measured through processes of assessment, this does not capture fully the idea of how one measures and evaluates other aspects of capability, i.e. the opportunities that an individual has to develop skills and competencies or the conversion factors involved in converting resource inputs into opportunities. This is especially the case given the highly contextual and sometimes tacit information that is required to understand the institutional processes and discursive practices that facilitate or constrain the development of capabilities (Unterhalter 2017).

Addressing this issue requires drawing together a range of quantitative and qualitative evidence. In the section that follows, two 'worked examples' will be provided of how the capability approach can provide a guide for policy makers in beginning to identify the affordances and barriers in the way of different groups in realising their capability to master different kinds of skills and competencies. The two examples relate to key regional priorities, namely, the development of basic literacy and numeracy and of STEM-related skills. In the case of STEM-related skills, consideration is also given to how an expanded view of sustainable work might inform decisions about what kinds of STEM-related skills to include in the curriculum. (This is based on the assumption that unlike literacy and numeracy skills which are considered basic capabilities, the inclusion of STEM-related skills in the curriculum requires a more careful and contested process of selection on the part of policy makers.)

Primary schooling and the development of basic capabilities

As we have seen, a key priority for regional agendas in the primary phase is the development of literacy and numeracy skills. In Chapter 6, it was argued that these basic skills or capabilities are important in relation to both the development of human capital and rights-based and environmentalist concerns. The issue of a lack of proficiency in literacy and numeracy based on the results of regional assessments was also discussed. School effectiveness studies based on an analysis of SACMEQ data have also revealed considerable variation in literacy scores within countries. In general, these studies have found that the most important pupil background characteristics which can be attributed to explaining differences in attainment for primary school learners in formal education are socio-economic background, gender, whether they live in an urban or rural environment (e.g. Smith and Barrett 2011), and exposure to language of instruction outside of school (Yu and Thomas 2008).

These data on their own, however, say little about causality and the conversion factors associated with the development of the capability to read and to perform basic mathematical functions. Of relevance here is (Smith and Barrett 2011) own analysis of the SACMEQ data using multi-level modelling techniques.[13] Smith and Barrett describe basic resource inputs, including books, table, lighting, and electricity as well as meals eaten in the day. They also identify for the data and wider literature a series of conversion factors. These include personal conversion factors (gender, age, history of repetition, and absenteeism); social conversion factors (gendered norms, parental education, and peer group influence); and environmental factors (rural/ urban location and weather). From these, they infer a number of capabilities, including freedom from hunger (i.e. having more than two meals per day); the opportunities that parents have to meet the financial costs of primary education; freedom from the need for learners to be self-reliant either economically (i.e. not being obliged to work outside of school) or emotionally and practically (e.g. on account of having to live away from their parents); and relatedly being able to pursue primary education whilst living with close family; the opportunity to use language of instruction outside of the school or the opportunity to be schooled in the langue used in the pupil's community; and the opportunity to read and to write at home.

Extending their analysis, it is possible to begin to see how different regimes of inequality operate within and between different country contexts to shape the development of the capability set. Thus, the effects of basic capabilities that, it can be argued, are most associated with social class, including, for example, the ability for parents to afford the costs of schooling or to provide a basic place to study are significant in countries that are relatively poorer overall, including Tanzania, Zambia, Mozambique, Uganda, and Zimbabwe. It is also in these countries that learners most often report having being absent on account of having to undertake paid work outside of the home. Similarly, in relation to gender, boys generally outperform girls in rural areas in these poorer countries whilst in relatively wealthier countries, such as Botswana, rural girls outperform their male counterparts. In some rural contexts such as those based on pastoralist economies in countries such as Lesotho, boys may be disadvantaged from having the additional responsibilities of looking after cattle. In general, girls living in large cities tend to achieve better than boys in all of the countries covered by SACMEQ. One explanation offered by the authors is that girls are more likely to be impacted by negative gendered norms and expectations and by levels of parental education than is the case for girls living in urban contexts.

For policy makers, the aforementioned analysis shows the importance of understanding the range of localised conditions that impact on the capabilities of learners and of working across sectors to address the range of poverty-related issues that limit the opportunities for children to learn basic skills, including issues of child nutrition and living conditions.[14] For practitioners, it also draws attention to the importance of being aware of the challenging home backgrounds and forms of inequality and injustice facing different groups of disadvantaged learners. Indeed, there is evidence that successful primary school principals spend considerable time engaging with parents and the wider community to ensure that learners have the opportunity to study outside of the school and that parents are aware of the nutritional needs of children if they are to learn effectively. In some instances, this might involve developing the literacy skills of parents (Ngcobo and Tikly 2010).

Whilst the analysis provided by Smith and Barrett focuses on the out-of-school factors associated with the capability to read, it is also important to take account of in-school factors. Mention has already been made, for example, to the importance of being able to access textbooks and other learning materials that are written at a cognitive and linguistic level that are appropriate for learners and that reflect learners cultural backgrounds and contexts (Milligan et al. 2017, 2018). In particular, it is important to invest in the professional development of educators.

Work by *Westbrook et al.* (2013) into teacher preparation and professional development in the area of reading and numeracy across six African countries has identified the large gap that often exists between the skills and competencies that are acquired by African teachers and the highly complex task of developing reading and numeracy skills amongst diverse learners in difficult delivery contexts. Teaching reading and numeracy requires that teachers are able to draw on a range of pedagogical techniques and to apply them creatively in different settings to meet diverse needs. This complexity provides a powerful argument against the increasing use of un- or under-qualified teachers and the use of scripted pedagogies, including for example, those used in many low-fee private schools.

In relation to initial teacher education, Westbrook *et al.* identify the often-outmoded teacher education curricula developed in higher education institutions, the disjuncture between the experience and expertise of teacher educators and the realities of African classrooms, and the limited opportunities to develop relevant pedagogical skills during practicum. Linked to these issues is the reliance on theories of learning and related approaches to the teaching of reading and numeracy imported from outside of Africa (see Chapter 9). The issues have been amplified by high enrolments and overcrowding in teacher education programmes that put additional pressures on already stretched teacher educators and the introduction of fast track, minimal training that does not give trainee teachers sufficient background knowledge.[15] The upshot is that teachers often resort to using outmoded techniques that were used to teach them rather than up-to-date approaches grounded in the realities of African classrooms.

Reconceptualising STEM-related skills

Unlike the basic capabilities of literacy and numeracy, decisions about which kinds of higher-order skills, including STEM-related skills, to include in the curriculum is more complex and contested. Here, recent developments in conceptualising the nature of work can, it is suggested, usefully guide informed public debate and policy making. It has already been suggested that whilst the prioritisation of STEM-related speak to a traditional view of the economy, they do not sufficiently take account of the more expansive view of the economy offered by Walby (2009). Here the idea of 'sustainable work', put forward by the United Nations Development Programme (UNDP 2015), is more helpful. The notion of 'sustainable work' encourages a break with a purely instrumental view of work as being solely for financial gain or profit and recognises the many forms of work that are not paid, as well as informal work that is for profit but nonetheless makes a valued contribution to society and/or the natural environment (see Figure 7.2). Figure 7.3 expands HDR2015's categories of work to identify the forms of STEM knowledge demanded by each.

It can be seen that some jobs require a higher degree of STEM specialisation than others. These include but are not limited to jobs in research and design (R&D); manufacturing and productivity, including in agriculture, engineering, and mining; training, education, and communication; and environmental

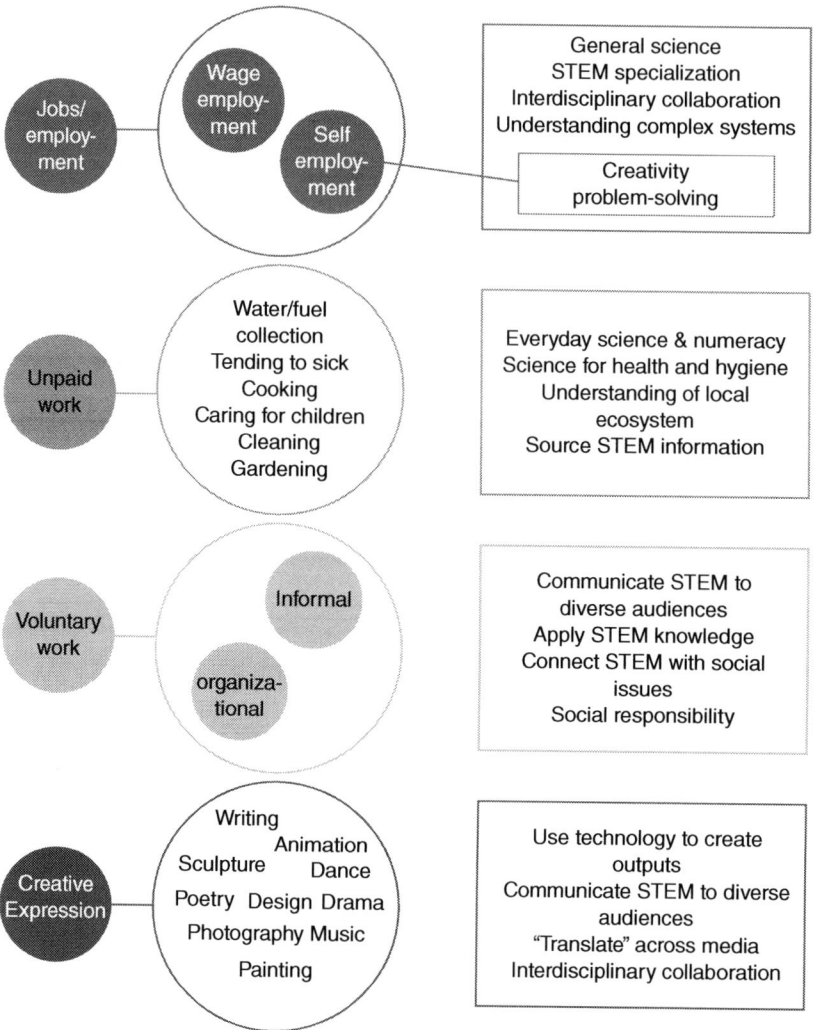

Figure 7.3 The contribution of school STEM education to sustainable work.
Source: (Tikly et al. 2018, 19).

protection and social care and development. Other kinds of jobs require more general, integrated understanding of scientific principles and the use of technologies. Interdisciplinary approaches to teaching STEM and ICT allow for the practical application of scientific theory and knowledge and as such serve as a pathway to understanding the relevance of, as well as improving the equity of access to, secondary STEM and ICT education.[16] What this suggests is the need for a more expansive but also nuanced understanding of the relationship between

STEM-related education and the demands of the economic domain. Importantly, such an understanding needs to take account of domestic work as a key component of the economy. In this respect, gender issues are not confined to access on the part of girls to specialised STEM subjects but also access by boys to the skills and competencies required for conducting domestic work.

Also evident from Figure 7.4 is the potential role of the creative arts and humanities as well as science and mathematics and technology education in contributing to the economy. It is this realisation that has prompted some governments such as the Western Cape Department of Education in South Africa to integrate Arts and Humanities subjects with STEM and ICT in the secondary school curriculum as a means of promoting versatility, creativity, and innovation

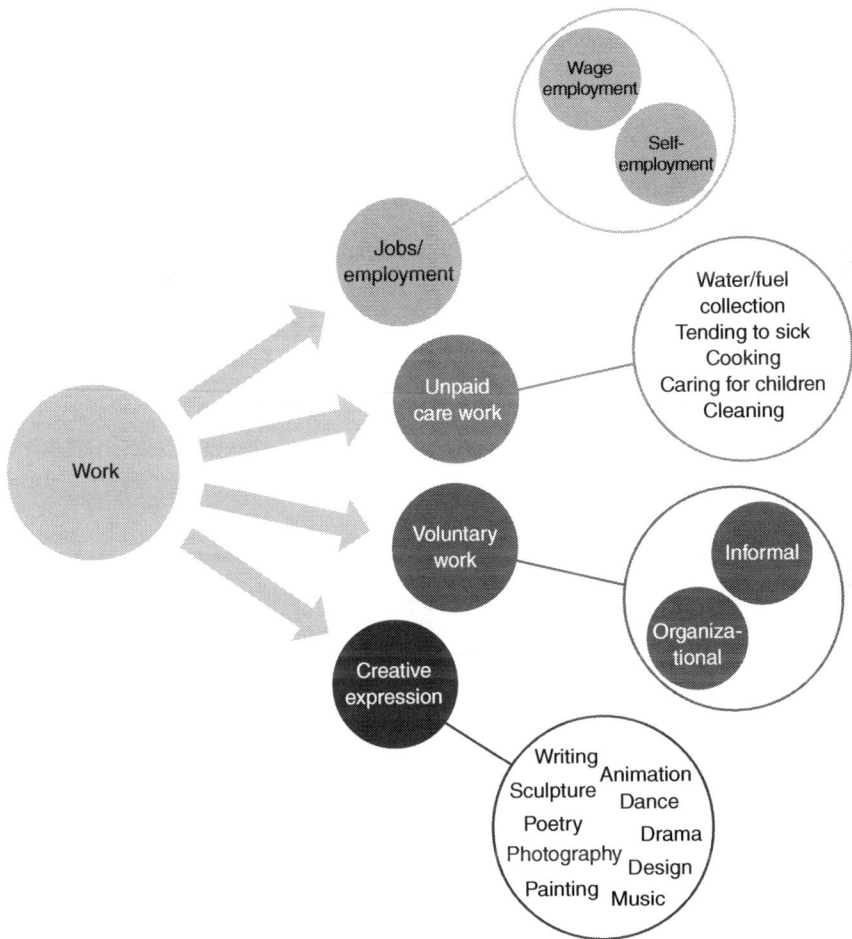

Figure 7.4 Sustainable work is more than jobs.

Source: UNDP 2015, 31

in the field. It is thought that STEAM (Science, Technology, Engineering, Arts, and Mathematics), rather than traditional STEM, allows students to execute both the convergent and divergent skills necessary for innovation (Land 2013). Further, if innovation is to be put to the service of sustainable development, then it is also important to develop appreciation of the political, cultural, environmental, and ethical issues involved.

As was the case with a consideration of basic literacy and numeracy, it is also important for policy makers to engage with the barriers that prevent some groups of disadvantaged learners from accessing STEM-related skills. These have been discussed at length elsewhere (Tikly et al. 2018; Gardner et al. 2018). For example, girls are often discouraged from pursuing STEM-related skills on account of the prevalence of sexist gendered norms and values. The literature also points to the enormous practical barriers in the way of increasing access to a good-quality STEM education. These include a lack of suitably qualified teachers who have sufficient subject and pedagogical content knowledge to deliver demanding curricula, large class sizes, a lack of resources, including textbooks and science equipment that militate against hands-on practical work and outdated, overloaded, and linguistically demanding curricula, and heavily content-driven, high-stakes examinations that continue to overdetermine what is actually taught in schools. Problems are compounded where basic laboratory equipment is lacking as learners then need to rely on teachers limited content knowledge to impart more theoretical explanations. These factors militate to ensure that good-quality STEM education (both subject-based and more integrated) is limited to a minority of well-resourced schools. Governments such as the governments of Malawi and South Africa have tried to ameliorate this situation through programmatic interventions that have involved the professional development of teachers in STEM-related areas, the distribution of cheap science kits and more learner-friendly workbooks but these initiatives have had mixed results given the degree of the problems involved. Evaluation has identified not only practical difficulties but also a lack of political will to address the underlying problems (Tikly et al. 2018).

Conclusion

The chapter has sought to trace changing discourses relating to skills for development since colonial times. It has been suggested that global and regional agendas still bear the imprint of earlier ways of conceiving skills for development. These include the continued influence of modernisation theory with its Eurocentric bias in the way that skills are conceptualised and the dominance of human capital theory which promotes a narrow, instrumental view of skills for economic growth. These predominance of human capital concerns provides a source of contradiction in relation to human rights and environmental concerns that are also reflected in global and regional agendas, albeit to a more limited degree. The second part of the chapter has attempted to articulate an approach to skills for development that draws on the capability approach. It was argued that the approach is more consistent with new ways of thinking about the economic domain in relation to meeting human needs and protecting the environment and can direct policy makers to pay greater attention to the opportunity freedoms available to different groups of learners to develop valued skills and competencies.

Notes

1 In particular, Rodney links the development of more formal specialisation in pre-colonial skills formation (iron-making, cloth manufacture, pottery moulding, professional training as well as religious, medicinal, and military instruction) to shifts in the mode of production (pre-Feudal to Feudal) before the Europeans arrived.
2 At a more instrumental level, part of the rationale for adapted education, as Whitehead explains, was to circumvent a situation similar to the one in India in which there were limited employment opportunities for Western educated Indians leading to resentment and rebellion.
3 Although principally an economic model, modernisation theory was developed in the sociological literature by authors such as Inkeles and Smith (1974) and in the psychological literature by authors such as McClelland (1961).
4 This can, like modernisation theory, also be characterised as arising as part of a civil society 'wave' in that it has been championed by individuals, think tanks, and foundations that have formed part of the wider 'epistemic community' (Haas 1989) that has been influential in shaping the policies of the World Bank, IMF, and other global financial institutions, including the African Development Bank.
5 Whilst for the World Bank growth is defined principally in terms of GDP, for the OECD it is defined in terms of improvements to overall measures of well-being (OECD 2014). It is also defined in terms of a reduction of poverty and inequality through the provision of basic welfare. In this sense, the idea can be seen to provide continuity on earlier discourses associated with the post-Washington consensus (Robertson *et al.*, 2007).
6 Six SACMEQ countries (Botswana, Kenya, Mauritius, Seychelles, Swaziland, and Tanzania) showed high levels of achievement because they were substantially above the SACMEQ average for both reading and mathematics in both 2000 and 2007. On the other hand, the red figures showed that three SACMEQ countries (Lesotho, Malawi, and Zambia) had much lower levels of achievement because they were substantially below the SACMEQ average for both reading and mathematics in both 2000 and 2007. The other six SACMEQ countries had 'mixed performance levels'. For example, Mozambique performed well in reading and mathematics during 2000 but poorly in these areas during 2007.
7 Thus, whilst analysis of SACMEQ data, for example, have found that the most important pupil background characteristics associated with differences in attainment for primary school learners in formal education are socio-economic background, gender, whether they live in an urban or rural environment (e.g. Smith and Barrett 2011), and exposure to language of instruction outside of school (Yu and Thomas 2008), more information is needed about the impact of these various intersecting regimes of inequality on the learning of basic skills.
8 The vision of inclusive growth contained in *Agenda 2063* identifies key areas of economic development that STEM-related skills and competencies developed during schooling can contribute towards manufacturing, agriculture, and the blue-ocean economy.
9 Indeed, Raworth is herself a member of the Club of Rome.
10 Some caveats are necessary, however, in interpreting the model. Firstly, the model is first and foremost an economic model. As already suggested, SD requires co-ordinated action across the six domains of development if it is to be achieved.

Secondly, whilst it is useful for heuristic reasons for Rowarth to present SD in terms of nested systems, this is not intended to imply a hierarchy between elements in the diagram. A further caveat is that Raworth's original model does not acknowledge the role of culture in SD, perhaps reflecting its origins in the discipline of economics. As has been discussed in Chapter 3, the cultural domain has impinged since colonial times on economic development in Africa as elsewhere in the postcolonial world. For this reason, the 'social foundation' which appears in Raworth's original model has been recast as the 'socio-cultural' foundation. Finally, whilst Raworth conceives economic development in relation to a notion of justice, she does not fully explain what she means by justice. Here work within the capability approach is more helpful.

11 Unterhalter (2017) argues that the attempt to capture this complexity in itself amounts to a negative capability because it involves an attempt to 'measure the unmeasurable'.

12 Unterhalter's own recent work has focused on seeking a rapprochement between attempts to capture 'what works' and 'what matters' in measuring gender equality, for example, through linking quantitative indicators of female participation and learning gains to indicators aimed at capturing processes.

13 They make use of the capability approach to thematically develop from the data and from a wider engagement with the quantitative and qualitative literature, an interpretive framework for considering the capability set for learning to read at school (it is possible to develop a similar model to explain the capability to be numerate). From a complexity perspective, the model developed by Smith and Barrett highlights the potential for using advanced quantitative techniques to consider the complex interaction of factors that give rise to capabilities in different settings. It has the advantage of being based on a large data set that gives a snapshot in time of the relationship between different variables. However, SACMEQ like PASEC assessments rely on cross-sectional rather than on longitudinal data and so are less effective at capturing trends over time. From a complexity perspective, this is problematic given the emphasis on emergence. The lack of availability of good-quality, longitudinal assessment data on which to develop understanding of the factors involved in the development of literacy and numeracy necessarily limits the extent to which robust analyses on which to base policy are possible.

14 The data on which the analyses are based are necessarily constrained by the countries covered. In this respect, they do not include countries involved in conflict or those that have just merged from conflict. Neither do they relate specifically to the needs of refugees displaced by poverty and conflict and some of these issues are discussed in Chapter 8. For many of the continents millions of displaced young people, the issue is having the opportunity to access any kind of basic education at all but it is also about being able to access teachers and learning materials that are able to engage with and reflect the cultural backgrounds and experiences of refugees. The data are also limited by the indicators used. In this regard, the data do not deal in much detail with issues of disability. Here the wider literature indicates the need to overcome deep-rooted stigmas against people with disabilities, to make building and materials accessible, and to develop the pedagogical skills and capabilities of teachers in dealing with diverse learning needs.

15 The authors also highlight the potential for continuing professional development to develop the professional capabilities of educators but the limited professional development opportunities available to primary school teachers in many countries.

16 One area in which interdisciplinary approaches to STEM and ICT have already been introduced and are, thus, already being practised in sub-Saharan Africa through vocational education pathways, which are often non-compulsory and not

universally available. However, the teaching of 'everyday science' has been written into various mainstream academic pathways in the region. In Namibia, for example, the Life Science curriculum combines 'biology (emphasis on human physiology), agriculture (emphasis on animal husbandry) and environmental education' (Ottevanger et al. 2007, 14) and thus makes 'natural sciences more accessible to learners at [the secondary] level and opens up curriculum space for exploring the interconnections between natural and human systems' (Barrett 2017, 972).

8 Decolonising the curriculum

Education for an African cultural renaissance

Introduction

The aim of this chapter is to explore in more depth the cultural dimensions of education and training. The discussion will focus on two issues that, it is suggested, lie at the heart of an African cultural renaissance. In the first part of the chapter, attention will focus on better understanding the complexities involved in contemporary debates about decolonising the curriculum. Recall from Chapter 1 that *Agenda 2063* has identified the Eurocentric nature of the curriculum as a major impediment to realising African culture and values through education and training although these concerns are not realised in CESA. Issues of decolonising the curriculum have recently been highlighted by students protesting against the Eurocentric nature of the curriculum in South Africa, and there is a growing literature focusing on this issue that draws for inspiration on previous eras of anti-colonial struggle. The issues relating to decolonising the curriculum are, however, complex and involve negotiating different understandings of epistemic justice. These complexities will be explored in the chapter using the secondary school science curriculum as an example.

The second part of the chapter will focus on the burning language question in African education through an exploration of contemporary language in education policy. Language has featured strongly in pan-Africanist discourse over many decades. The importance of developing indigenous languages as an affirmation of African identities and as a means of overcoming regimes of inequality based on ethnicity and social class have been made by many eminent scholars and activists. As Sen[1] has recently pointed out, developing capability in more than one language is a key enabling factor in accessing goods and services as well as labour market opportunities within an increasingly globalised economy. It is also crucial for converting these into valued outcomes that can contribute to well-being and the fight against poverty (see also Mohanty 2009). The promotion of multilingualism also serves as an important basis for national and regional unity and for promoting democracy. In relation to education, being proficient in both the mother tongue[2] and a global language is not only an important outcome in its own right but is also critical for achieving other learning outcomes. There is a large body of evidence, however, to suggest that medium of instruction policies often impact negatively on the development of linguistic capabilities for disadvantaged groups and that this in turn has a negative impact on other learning outcomes, including basic literacy and numeracy. The chapter will aim to critically engage with this evidence as a basis for better understanding how language in education policy might work in the interests of disadvantaged African learners.

Decolonising the curriculum

As indicated earlier, debates about decolonising the curriculum are hardly new on the African continent and have featured in previous eras of anti-colonial struggle. They have been given impetus in recent years, however, by student protests at the University of Cape Town in 2015. Although initially targeted at the continued presence of a statue in memory of the imperialist Cecil Rhodes, the protests soon escalated into a wider critique of the Eurocentric nature of the curriculum. The *#Rhodes Must Fall* protests spawned similar campaigns at universities in South Africa, the UK, the United States, and elsewhere under the theme of *# Why Is My Curriculum White?* The protests ran parallel to a sister campaign entitled *#Fees Must Fall*.[3]

The chapter will commence by setting out some of the theoretical background to the decolonising the curriculum debate. It will focus on two broad approaches to epistemic justice. In the context of this book, epistemic justice is concerned with issues of the representation of different disadvantaged groups in the curriculum and pedagogy, the extent to which the curriculum is accessible to different disadvantaged groups and enhances their capabilities for understanding the natural world and responding to the risks posed by unsustainable development. (It thus can be seen as a special case of Fraser's understanding of representation justice) (see Chapter 7). The first has evolved out of anti-colonial and more recently postcolonial and decolonial scholarship. It emphasises the need to reflect a plurality of epistemologies in the curriculum, including 'epistemologies of the South' (de Sousa Santos 2012; Santos 2017). The latter position has been adopted by academics and practitioners who subscribe to a social realist perspective in which issues of epistemic justice are framed in terms of ensuring the access of disadvantaged groups to the powerful knowledge represented by the disciplines and codified in the formal curriculum. It will be suggested that whilst both forms of epistemic justice are important, and despite the fact that they have different bases in sociology of knowledge, when seen through the prism of complex systems presented in this book, they are not mutually exclusive.

Nonetheless, reconciling these two broad approaches to epistemic justice is not straightforward. The tensions will be explored in the second part of the chapter, where the focus will be on the secondary school science curriculum. Here the focus will be on the challenges of decolonising the science curriculum through the integration of indigenous and local knowledge systems on the one hand and ensuring access to the powerful knowledge represented by existing curricula. Resolving the tension requires taking account of the nature of Western and indigenous knowledge (IK) systems and the nature of the existing relationship between the science curriculum and these different knowledge systems. It also involves consideration of the relationship between different forms of pedagogy used in science education as well as wider understanding of the relationship between the school and the community in Africa. The main argument advanced is that decolonising the science curriculum requires a systemic response that includes not only the selection of relevant content for the secondary school science curriculum but also the transformation of the wider system of knowledge production. It also involves developing the role of educators as mediators between the forms of local and IK represented by the learners' home backgrounds and the disciplinary knowledge contained in the curriculum. This in turn requires actively breaking down the barriers between schools and the local community.

Decolonising the curriculum and the sociology of knowledge

Education is identified as a key institution in relation to the pan-Africanist vision. On the one hand it is seen as the basis for reproducing dominant Western cultural forms. For example, *Agenda 2063* notes the effects of cultural domination during the slave trade and colonial era, which it is claimed 'led to the depersonalization on the part of African peoples, falsified their history, systematically disparaged and combatted African values and tried to replace progressively and officially their languages by that of the colonized' (AUC 2015a, 68).[4] Education is singled out as having accelerated Africa's integration into a Western, global culture along with news media, music, and art. The report argues that while Western influences can enrich the African cultural heritage, 'they can also be a source of erosion and ultimately can supplant and replace African values and ethics'. Aspiration five of the document calls for an Africa with a strong cultural identity, common heritage, values, and ethics in which 'the common history, destiny, identity, heritage, respect for religious diversity and consciousness of African people's and her diaspora's will be entrenched' (AUC 2015a, 7). *Agenda 2063* highlights the role of education in promoting IK and languages. Indeed, it makes the bold claim that at least 80% of content on educational curriculum is on indigenous African culture, values, and language targeting primary and secondary schools by 2030.

As already indicated, however, these insights are not addressed in education policy. Indeed, the only mention of indigenous culture in CESA is in relation to strategic objective seven which includes a clause on promoting indigenous scientific knowledge and culture. Rather than promoting IK as having a role in the curriculum, however, the emphasis is on inculcating Western scientific thinking in indigenous cultures. It will be suggested later that this provides continuity on the role of the curriculum since colonial times in undermining and marginalising African IK. Rather than seeing IK as a potential resource, it is seen as a brake on progress. Here the influence of modernisation and human capital inspired thinking is evident (see Chapter 7).

Before turning to explore some of the practical issues and challenges involved in considering the role of IK in the curriculum, it is worth placing regional agendas in the context of contemporary debates about decolonising the curriculum.

In this respect, the critique of the Eurocentric nature of the curriculum and the racialised nature of identities in colonial and postcolonial societies, which finds limited expression in *Agenda 2063*, provides continuity on decades of anti-colonial thought and activism. Here the theoretical reference point is social constructionism,[5] which is concerned with the socially constructed nature of knowledge, versions of social reality and views of human nature, and how these articulate with different interests and the operation of power. Social constructionism has its roots in phenomenology as well as in psychoanalysis.

Within the Marxist tradition, ideas about the socially constructed nature of reality have been used to demonstrate how the dominant ideas within class societies are those of the ruling class. Marxist sociologists of education argue that the education system has been a key institution in the perpetuation of the ideology or, in Gramsci's (1992) terms, the 'hegemony' (intellectual and moral leadership) of the ruling class. Much Marxist-inspired scholarship has explored the often-subtle modalities through which the education system serves to legitimise the class system but also its potential as a site to develop counter-hegemonic views of reality that can assist in the radical transformation of society. As discussed in Chapter 4, in the African context, Marxists have used a class analysis to explain the role of education systems in maintaining class and race privilege in colonial settings as well as the role that education systems have played in perpetuating the class advantages enjoyed by indigenous elites in the postcolonial period (Rodney 1973; Nkrumah 1966). Marxist literature on the apartheid education system developed quite sophisticated analyses of the complex relationship between Bantu education and the needs of a changing racial capitalist order in South Africa (Kallaway 1984; Wolpe 1988; RESA 1988).

The question of what knowledge ought to be transmitted through formal education as a means to challenge the power of the ruling classes is, however, contested within the Marxist tradition. The debate can be seen to polarise between two extremes. On the one hand, following on from Freire, education is sometimes seen as a site for encouraging the questioning of the taken for granted nature of class society and to counterpose bourgeois knowledge through raising an awareness through the curriculum of working-class knowledge, histories, and identities. On the other hand, the role of education in countering the dominance of the ruling class is seen as fundamentally developing organic intellectuals of the working class. This finds echoes in recent work within social realism, which although not a 'Marxist' theory of knowledge as such is fundamentally concerned with the issue of how to ensure epistemic access for working class and other disadvantaged learners to 'powerful knowledge'. By this they mean knowledge that is codified in the disciplines as they have developed since the European enlightenment and with potentially more formalistic implications for pedagogy.[6]

The idea that knowledge is socially constructed and hence relative has also been given an impetus by the development of postmodernism and poststructuralism. Lyotard's (1986) famous mistrust of 'grand narratives' can be seen as a questioning of the certainties of modern thought underpinned by an unwavering belief in the truth of Western science which lies at the heart of Western culture.

Foucault's work has been especially influential in critiquing the Western *episteme* (ground base of knowledge). His archaeological approach outlined in *Order of Things* (Foucault 1989) and used in his analysis of the history of madness and the birth of the clinic drew attention to the emergence of the disciplines and their role in constituting versions of social reality and identity through the rules that govern what can and cannot be said, by whom and under what circumstances. His genealogical studies sought to demonstrate the historically contingent nature of knowledge and the links between the development of detailed knowledge of populations through the disciplines and the exercise of modern forms of power and control. For Foucault, the dominance of certain disciplines, including for example neoclassical economics, help to constitute a 'regime of truth' that lies at the heart of neoliberal governmentality (understood here as the art and practice of modern governments under neoliberalism). Forms of 'disciplinary' or 'productive' power, it has been argued, are key to understanding the nature of control of populations in the low-income, postcolonial world during the so-called development era as well as the long shadow of colonial discourses on 'race' (Escobar 1995; Wilson 2013; Tikly 2004, 2003a; De Jaeghere 2017).

Questioning the so-called universality, objectivity and 'truth' of Western knowledge has also been a key feature of anti-colonial struggles past and present. As we have seen in Chapter 4, anti-colonial activists from Nyerere and Walter Rodney to Steve Biko have provided a trenchant critique of the role of colonial education in legitimising Western rule through the valorisation of Western forms of knowledge and the systematic undermining of African knowledge systems, languages, and cultural values. The negritude movement in the 1930s under the influence of thinkers such as Aime Cesaire and Leopold Senghor drew attention to the racialising effects of Western colonial discourse and sought to challenge this through the projection of positive conceptions of black identities. Bringing into conversation with each other's ideas from psychoanalysis, phenomenology, and Marxism, the Martinique psychoanalyst and revolutionary Frantz Fanon drew attention to the damaging consequences on the Black psyche that arise as a consequence of internalising racialised identities transmitted through Western language and culture (Fanon 1961, 1986). Fanon's work was in turn influential on the thinking of Steve Biko and other leaders of the Black Consciousness movement in South Africa (Biko 1978). A key figure whose ideas continue to resonate in debates about decolonising the curriculum is the Kenyan writer and dramatist Ngũgĩ wa Thiong'o. As we have seen, Thiong'o challenged the role of Western languages in African higher education and emphasised the potential of African languages as a means for countering hegemonic Western ways of knowing the world (see, for example, Thiong'o 1986).

More recently, postcolonial thought has provided a major impetus for challenging the hegemony of Western knowledge. Drawing on poststructuralist as well as Marxist ideas and providing continuity on the work of earlier anti-colonial intellectuals, postcolonial scholarship has drawn attention to the role of Western knowledge in perpetuating the dominance of the West through knowledge of the non-Western 'other' as an aspect of the postcolonial condition (Said 1978).

It also draws attention to the contingent and contested nature of postcolonial identities with clear echoes of Fanon's thought. In recent years, anti-colonial and postcolonial scholarship has found expression in debates about decolonising the curriculum. As with previous eras of anti-colonial struggle, these debates are rooted in grass-roots protests such as those instigated by students at the University of Cape Town in 2015.

At the heart of these movements are issues of epistemic justice (Santos 2017). In the case of the *#Rhodes Must Fall* and *Why Is My Curriculum White?* movements, the issues are to do with the hegemony of Western knowledge in curricula. Demands to decolonise the curriculum have been given intellectual impetus through the work of scholars such as Santos (e.g. Santos 2017; Santos 2012, 2007, 2002), Mbembe (Mbembe 2016; Mbembe and Posel 2005), Dei (Dei 2017; Dei and Kempf 2006) Maldonado-Torres (2007), Ndlovu-Gatsheni (e.g. 2013, 2015), Comoroff and Comoroff (2011), Connell (e.g.Connell 2014, 2012, 2007) and others. In the case of Santos and Mbembe, the emphasis has focused on a critique of the assumption at the heart of Western knowledge and Western science, in particular, that it represents a universalising truth. For these authors, despite its claims to objectivity, Western science since the European enlightenment has been linked to particular interests and in particular to those of European colonialism and the development of global markets. They also link the dominance of Western knowledge to the marketisation of education and the commodification of knowledge, which they argue detracts from the role of the university in promoting critical, independent thought (Santos 2017; Mbembe 2016). This has led, in Santos' terms, to the 'epistemicide' of non-Western cultures. For Santos, decolonising the curriculum entails bringing the disciplines as enshrined in the university curriculum into conversation through forms of knowledge production with grass-roots movements and with IK.

For Santos, the aim is to develop a 'pluriversity' based on a recognition of multiple ways of 'knowing' the world that can benefit social and environmental justice. For Mbembe, a key goal must be to challenge the very basis of Western humanism itself, which he claims lies in the separation of subject from object, nature from culture, and human beings from other species. Rather, education should aim to develop 'a new understanding of ontology, epistemology, ethics and politics has to be achieved. It can only be achieved by overcoming anthropocentrism and humanism, the split between nature and culture' (42). For both Santos and Mbembe, this involves a more fundamental shift in the way that the role of the university is perceived. For Santos, it involves protecting the idea of the university as a public good. For Mbembe and Dei, it means developing diasporic intellectual networks that can transform the curriculum to reflect the experiences of Africans in Africa and in the diaspora. It also means engaging with and challenging new configurations of racism and in particular 'to explore the emerging nexus between biology, genes, technologies and their articulations with new forms of human destitution' (44).

For Maldonado-Torres and Ndlovu-Gatsheni, decolonising the curriculum is part of a wider project of 'decoloniality', which implies 'the dismantling of relations of power and conceptions of knowledge that foment the reproduction of racial, gender, and geo-political hierarchies that came into being or found new and more powerful forms of expression in the modern/colonial world' (117). Connell's decolonisation is linked to the recovery of Southern theory, i.e. a renewed focus on the scholarly works of non-Western scholars. In her book *Southern Theory* (Connell 2007), she draws attention to the depth and breadth of non-Western scholarship that she claims has been subsumed by the hegemony of Western knowledge.[7] In a more recent publication, Connell (Connell 2012) has linked ideas about decolonising the curriculum to a wider concept of a 'just curriculum'. She argues that curricula justice entails

> *a curriculum organized around the experience, culture and needs of the least advantaged members of the society – rather than the most advantaged, as things stand now. Socially just curriculum will draw extensively on indigenous knowledge, working-class experience, women's experience, immigrant cultures, multiple languages, and so on; aiming for richness rather than testability.*
>
> (682)

It is this appeal to the importance of 'bringing in' other epistemologies and ways of knowing the world that is the subject of trenchant critique by social realists (Young 2013a, 2013b, 2014; Young and Muller 2013; Young 2008; Moore and Young 2001; Barrett, Hoadley, and Morgan 2018). The social realist approach has been particularly influential in South Africa through the work of sociologists of education who have used a social realist position to provide a critique of the progressivism implicit in outcomes-based education (Muller 2009; Barrett, Hoadley, and Morgan 2018). Social realists take issue with the assumption in the earlier accounts of the socially constructed nature of knowledge. In particular, social realists take issue with the relativism implicit in social constructionism in which the status of truth is seen as relative to the subject position of the knower. Social realists counterpose this relativism with an insistence on the 'objectivity' of truth claims arrived at through the work of knowledge specialists working within the disciplines. For social realists, whilst knowledge is socially produced by knowledge specialists and has a historicity in this respect, the nature of specialised knowledge has its own implications for the curriculum that is independent of wider power relationships in society. It is this 'sociality' of knowledge that social realists are interested in understanding and that it is argued, progressivists elide.

Social realists are concerned with the extent to which disadvantaged learners have access to 'powerful knowledge', which is defined as follows:

> Powerful knowledge is specialized knowledge. It is knowledge that draws on the work of communities of specialists that we describe as disciplines which are primarily forms of social organization for producing new knowledge . . . . [D]isciplinary specialists have worked with school teachers who have themselves studied one or more disciplines and in their preparation to be teachers become subject specialists. They draw on their knowledge of how

children learn and of the capacities of pupils levels to create school subjects which set out the possibilities for students to progress in their learning.

(Young 2013a, 1)

It is through granting epistemic access to learners from disadvantaged backgrounds that 'powerful knowledge', as encoded in the disciplines, ceases to simply be solely the 'knowledge of the powerful'. As was discussed in Chapter 8, a key point of reference for social realists is Bernstein's work on language codes. Realist ideas about knowledge have in the past also found expression in literature on environmental education. For example, Jickling (Jickling 1992) has argued against a focus on inculcating the affective skills associated with different kinds of 'adjectival educations' – a term he used rather pejoratively at the time to refer to a range of areas historically linked to ESD, including for instance peace, citizenship, and diversity education. In a similar vein to social realists, Jickling argues that formal education ought to remain largely 'disinterested' with respect to these affective goals, focusing instead on the development of lower- and higher-level content and procedural skills learned through mastery of the disciplines, in this case environmental science. The idea that some knowledge is powerful is also implicit in CESA. For example, there is an emphasis on what are perceived to be 'powerful' subject areas such as STEM-related subjects.

Reference will be made in the next chapter to the work of Basil Bernstein on language codes, which has provided a source of inspiration for social realists. A further point of reference for social realists derived from Bernstein's work is his idea of the 'pedagogic device' (Bernstein 2000, 1990). He developed the idea of the device to explain the relationship between the macro- and micro-societal conditions and institutional contexts of reproduction and the way that the 'grammar' of the disciplines gets translated (re-contextualised) in stages. The first process of re-contextualisation is when specialised knowledge, produced through research in the disciplines, is translated into curriculum knowledge by curriculum experts. This involves a necessary selection of what counts as 'relevant' knowledge for the curriculum and the process can be more or less top-down/bottom-up and restricted or democratic in nature. The second stage is when the curriculum becomes re-contextualised once again through the process of enactment in the classroom. For many social realists, a more formalistic approach is one in which the underlying structure of school subjects remains strongly framed and is not weakened or obfuscated during these processes of translation, e.g. through an overemphasis on cross-curricula themes, integrated subjects (like integrated science for instance), or through bringing in localised knowledge.[8]

However, this critique does not sufficiently take account of either the rapidly changing wider context or of pedagogical considerations. In relation to the former, it was argued in Chapter 4 that existing curricula and assessment systems in Africa have historically emerged along academic lines and have served largely as a filtering device for access to higher levels of education and training and to the labour market. This was linked under colonialism to the role of secondary education in preparing a small elite of indigenous workers to serve in the colonial administration. Subsequently, the highly academic bias of the curriculum has ensured a continued elitist bias and the limiting of opportunities to progress to tertiary education. As the *Agenda 2063* and CESA documents make clear, there is a need to urgently address the outdated, academically biased nature of the curriculum in many African countries. For example, there is an increasing recognition of the need for practical/vocational skills, particularly amongst youth, and this has formed part of the impetus to vocationalise the upper secondary curriculum in some African countries such as Zambia and Tanzania (Gardner et al. 2018; Tikly et al. 2018).

Related to the previous point are the changing nature of the disciplines themselves. In the language of complexity theory, this is to acknowledge that disciplines are themselves best considered as adaptive systems that are subject to change due to forces internal and external to themselves even if the pace of change may be relatively slow (see Chapter 8 for a discussion of the mathematics curriculum through a complexity lens). Processes of internal change include the incremental, day to day development of disciplinary understanding through iterative processes of research, design, and diffusion, but also the effects of more profound paradigm shifts that affect the basic axions on which the disciplines are founded (Kuhn 1962). Disciplines are also subject to external change forces. For example, all disciplines increasingly involve both 'applied' and 'pure' (theoretical) elements. This relates to STEM-related subjects but also to arts, social science, and humanities disciplines. For critics such as Santos (2017) and Mbembe (2016), these changes are a consequence of the broader instrumentalisation of the curriculum in higher education in the context of neoliberal globalisation.

It was also argued in Chapter 2, however, that addressing issues of sustainable development requires not only applying disciplinary knowledge in its own right but also increasingly developing interdisciplinary understanding in order to address the 'wicked problems' posed by human development and environmental protection (Byrne and Callaghan 2014; Bhaskar et al. 2010). For this reason, scholars working in the area of sustainability pedagogy in higher education have increasingly emphasised the importance of transgressing disciplinary boundaries as a means to facilitate critical awareness of transformative practice (Lotz-Sisitka et al. 2016). This suggests that the Bernsteinian distinction between strong and weak framing is increasingly too simplistic and unhelpful as an analytical aid to understanding the curriculum with implications for the role of so-called performance and competence pedagogies (Chapter 8). What is increasingly needed are both strong subject knowledge in its own right and a basis for engaging in interdisciplinary inquiry. The tendency towards interdisciplinarity increases further up the education and training system and applies to both academic and vocational subjects. (It is reflected, for example, in subjects ranging from health to engineering to education, which are often better described as fields of inquiry rather than as disciplines.)

Further, the conservative approach towards knowledge implicit in much of the social realist literature can also be critiqued from a decolonising perspective which has provided an analysis of the historically Eurocentric nature of the curriculum in African education (Rudolph, Sriprakash, and Gerrard 2018). For example, there is little recognition from social realists as to the historical role of the disciplines in legitimising the colonial project. In Chapter 4, for instance, reference was made to the role of eugenics during the nineteenth and early twentieth centuries in providing a justification for colonialism through a theory of hierarchies in intelligence between different so-called 'races'. As Wilson (2013) has argued, eugenicist understandings of 'race' continue to cast a long shadow on contemporary discourses about issues ranging from population control to HIV/AIDs. Mbembe (2016) has also drawn attention to the potential of more recent developments in understanding of genetics and of the human genome to feed into new projects of racial classification and domination as has been discussed. He argues, for instance, that

> Race has once again re-entered the domain of biological truth, viewed now through a molecular gaze. A new molecular deployment of race has emerged out of genomic thinking. . . . Worldwide, we witness a renewed interest in the identification of biological differences. Genomics, for instance, has produced new complexity into the figure of humanity. And yet the core racial typology of the 19th century still provides a dominant mould through which this new genetic knowledge of human difference is taking shape and entering medical and lay conceptions of human variation.
>
> (Mbembe 2016, 43)

Understanding the relationship between science and popular understandings of 'race' draws attention to two inter-related issues. The first is the contested nature of the sciences themselves. Historical analysis has shown that even though the weight of scientific evidence and opinion since the end of the Second World War provides support for the view that 'race' is a not a scientifically meaningful way for explaining or classifying human difference, efforts persist within the academic community to argue for differences between so-called 'races', for example in relation to intelligence (see, for example, Omi and Winant 2015; Gould 1996). A separate but related point is the misuse that is often made of science in political and popular discourses about race, including the persistence of eugenicist thinking in popular discourse alluded to by Wilson. A similar point can be made in relation to debates about climate change in which climate change deniers make spurious claims based on a selective reading of scientific evidence to question the reality of human-induced climate change despite the weight of scientific evidence over several decades, clearly indicating a positive relationship between human activity and changes in the Earth's temperature.

On the one hand, a consideration of the contested nature of scientific knowledge and the potential for scientific evidence to be misrepresented in political and popular discourse can be seen as providing strong support for a social realist insistence on focusing on the procedural understanding of the disciplines. Such an understanding would support, for example the development of the capability for autonomous evaluation of different sources of evidence in order to arrive at an informed, rational understanding of the issues involved. However, in seeking to champion the role of formal, procedural knowledge in determining objective truth, social realists are in danger of underplaying both the contested nature of truth claims within the disciplines and the ultimate fallibility of all knowledge, including knowledge linked to so-called 'hard sciences'. Social realists also elide the ethical basis of knowledge claims and the importance in its own right of drawing attention to the ethical uses to which knowledge is put in society. From a complex realist perspective such as that outlined in Chapter 2, all knowledge claims are ultimately fallible even if they are supported by the best available evidence.[4] In this respect, complex realism is consistent with a social realist position in insisting on procedural/methodological rigour in research underpinned by an understanding of the strengths and weaknesses of different kinds of evidence obtained through different procedural/methodological practices. Where it diverges is in relation to the emphasis that is placed on the politics and ethics of knowledge production.

Of relevance here once again is the idea of Bernstein's pedagogic device alluded to earlier. Social realists make much of the idea of the device but as a means for arguing for a greater degree of coherence between the processes by which the formal knowledge of the disciplines is translated first into curricula and then into pedagogical approaches in the classroom. Missing from much of the literature is an understanding of the political economy of knowledge production within the academy where the disciplines are developed (this is despite explicit recognition by Young and others of the historicity of the processes of knowledge production). Such an understanding would draw attention amongst other things to a consideration of the way that research is funded, the uses that research is put to, and which interests are served in the process. In a recent article, Melber (2018) has argued forcibly that the decolonisation debate needs to be seen in relation to inequalities in access to the intellectual means of production between the Northern and Southern hemisphere – an inequality that is particularly pronounced in the African context. This includes control over access to publishing in international peer-reviewed journals (including issues of language) to research funding and the fact that control over the 'rules of the game' for what counts as 'excellent' research also resides in Northern institutions.

Part of the context for this inequality are the continuing effects of years of sustained underfunding for higher education in Africa in the context of SAPs (Chapters 5 and 6). Many academics not only experience low levels of pay and poor conditions of service but must also meet the demands of increasing teaching loads which limit time for research. There is also the effect of the growing marketisation of higher education. The charging of fees has rendered higher education inaccessible to the majority of disadvantaged learners. The increasing trend towards privatisation has also shifted the purpose of the university away from a public good to one that is oriented towards meeting market needs often defined in narrow instrumentalist terms. An aspect of marketisation and of the dominance of epistemic communities linked to the aid industry is involvement of academics in whatever limited time they do have away from teaching, marking, and administrative responsibilities in consultancies. As Ndlovu-Gatsheni (2013) has argued, the malaise in knowledge production in Africa needs to be seen in the wider context of the extractive nature of research in which Africa provides the 'raw materials' for producing knowledge about Africa. This takes the form of the 'brain drain' from the continent. It is also manifested in the role of Southern-based researchers in providing data for Northern based researchers, who then develop the analysis and reap the benefits in terms of publications etc. Ndlovu-Gatsheni also addresses the tendency for African researchers in whatever limited time they may have for research to get drawn into consultancy, which pays more but is also linked to extractive knowledge practices, this time linked to furnishing the epistemic communities of multilateral organisations and other aid agencies and NGOs.

All of these factors limit the possibilities for autonomous, critical scholarship and to undertake African-led research aimed at solving Africa's sustainability problems. Superimposed on the material inequalities in the processes of knowledge production is the predominance of the Western episteme and of Western-inspired theories and methods in research. The formal nature of university teaching, including teaching about research methods, has its roots in the traditional models of the university inherited from colonial times. This in turn limits the potential for less conservative, more radical approaches to knowledge production that seek to break down the traditional 'ivory tower' status of universities and provide support for forms of transformative social learning through forms of knowledge co-production with communities (Lotz-Sisitka et al. 2016).

The politics of knowledge production also draws attention, however, to the political and ethical nature of the processes of 'translation' whereby the formal knowledge of the disciplines becomes instantiated as subject knowledge in the curriculum. This is not simply a technical process of sequencing the curriculum in a way that facilitates epistemic access to the structure of the disciplines as is sometimes implied in the social realist literature. It also involves processes of selection of different kinds of evidence against which truth claims can be evaluated in disciplinary terms and it is this aspect that makes the curriculum an unavoidably political domain. More research is needed into these processes although anecdotal evidence in many African countries suggests that the processes of curriculum production are often bureaucratic and top-down and expert-driven in nature, reflecting dominant interests in the state and civil society rather than open and consultative. Recognising the politics of knowledge production also provides a way of conceptualising how the formal curriculum might serve the purposes of social and environmental justice through developing understanding of how disciplinary knowledge has been used (and misused) for different social and environmental purposes.

Decolonising the secondary school science curriculum

Whereas the target for decolonising the curriculum protests and debates has often been higher education, the focus of the second part of this chapter is on the secondary school science curriculum. The reason for focusing on the school curriculum is that although it is like the curriculum in higher education often perceived as being Eurocentric in nature, it is relatively neglected in debates about decolonisation. This is despite the fact that it is accessible to a higher number of learners than those attending higher education and provides the first point in the education cycle at which the scientific disciplines are encountered as discrete subjects. It therefore draws attention to both issues of epistemic injustice flagged in the introduction, namely, the Eurocentric nature of existing secondary school science curricula on the one hand, and the lack of access experienced by disadvantaged groups of learners to a good-quality secondary science education that would place them in good stead to proceed to university. The decision to focus on science as a subject is partly on account of the extent to which Western science, in particular, is often implicated in debates about the Eurocentric nature of the curriculum, the overlaps with environmental and sustainability education, and because of the potential (largely unrealised) to incorporate IK systems into understanding of the natural world. It will be argued that focusing on the secondary school science curriculum, however, serves to highlight both the complexities and systemic nature of the issues involved.

As we have seen, Western science is on the one hand given a big priority within regional agendas, largely for instrumental reasons to do with the use of scientific knowledge in the development of the economy as was discussed in Chapter 7. It will be argued in this section that it is also important to consider Western science as a cultural discourse, i.e. one that has emerged in relation to colonialism and the spread of Western global capitalist interests. As has been suggested, however, it is also contested as a discourse and has been used to serve a range of interests. Understanding the cultural nature of Western science is important for considering the place of IK in the science curriculum and also has implications for pedagogy. In relation to discussions about social and environmental justice, debates about decolonising the school science curriculum must also be seen in relation to issues of epistemic justice – both recognising the cultural identities of learner's home backgrounds, but also enhancing the capabilities of learners to operate within and between the world views represented by scientific and IK.

Firstly, it is important to be clear what we mean by the term 'indigenous knowledge'. The term 'indigenous' is itself contested in the Africa context.[9] Given the focus of this chapter on knowledge systems understood in relation to the postcolonial condition, the term 'indigenous' will be used here to refer to those groups that have been settled in Africa prior to the arrival of Europeans. In this understanding, 'knowledge systems that existed in numerous parts of the non-Western world before the advent of colonialism are referred to as indigenous knowledge systems (IKS)' (Hewson and Ogunniyi 2011, 680). For Hoppers, indigenous knowledge systems (IKS) 'refer to the combination of knowledge systems encompassing technology, social, economic and philosophical learning, or educational, legal and governance systems' (Hoppers 2002, 8). For Keane (2008), IKS amounts to a world view, i.e. a thought system that determines to a large extent the habitual way in which an individual copes with experience.

Expanding on this understanding, UNESCO defines local and IK in the following terms:

> Local and indigenous knowledge refers to the understandings, skills and philosophies developed by societies with long histories of interaction with their natural surroundings. For rural and indigenous peoples, local knowledge informs decision-making about fundamental aspects of day-to-day life. This knowledge is integral to a cultural complex that also encompasses language, systems of classification, resource use practices, social interactions, ritual and spirituality. These unique ways of knowing are important facets of the world's cultural diversity, and provide a foundation for locally-appropriate sustainable development.
>
> (UNESCO 2018, 2)

With respect specifically to IK of the natural/environmental domain, Orlove *et al.* (2010) in their study of knowledge of the climate by a group of people in Western Uganda use IK to mean 'the place-based knowledge that is rooted in local cultures and generally associated with long-settled communities which have strong ties to their natural environments'. This knowledge they argue tends to be the result of 'cumulative experience and observation, tested in the context of everyday life and devolved by oral communication and repetitive engagement rather than through formal instruction' (p. 224). As Otulaja, Cameron, and Msimanga (2011) point out, it is important to distinguish between IKS, which comprise an entire world view, and IK, which refers to discrete elements of localised/IK that might be included in the curriculum, including knowledge of specific cultural practices and facts/beliefs about the local environment etc. In this respect, Keane (2008) identifies three key elements:

1 *IK*. Factual knowledge, such as community histories and understandings of the environment.
2 *Culture*. Performative knowledge and values; including talents usually manifested in cultural practices.
3 *World view*. Deep, ontological/philosophical, representational knowledge; foundational presuppositions about reality.

Whilst point '1' relates to IK, IKS can be conceived as encompassing all three points. There are some important caveats in relation to the use of the term IKS. Firstly, there is the danger that IK is seen as homogenous rather than recognised in its diversity across time and space (e.g. Hoppers 2002). It is also often perceived as being 'traditional' and as something to be conserved rather than having contemporary relevance (Battiste 2009). That is, it is perceived as being somehow hermitically sealed off from Western and other knowledge systems and from the wider forces of history. Rather, and in keeping with the language of complexity theory, IKS have co-evolved not only in relation to each other but also in relation to Western Arabic, Asian, and other systems of thought over many centuries although under colonial relations the nature of this relationship has often been conflictual and imbued with unequal power relationships (Mbembe 2016; Santos 2017).

In this respect, modern African livelihoods often involve drawing on multiple cultural resources and ways of knowing the world, and this is manifested in forms of cultural hybridity. This applies not only to linguistic, musical, culinary, religious, and hybrid practices but also to other important areas of people's livelihoods, including health (where traditional medicines administered by traditional healers continue to be used sometimes alongside Western medicines), the commercialisation of indigenous crafts, and agricultural production (where traditional ways of working with the land are used alongside more contemporary agricultural practices). By way of contrast, 'western' knowledge as represented in the disciplines is often seen as synonymous with modernity itself. It is assumed to be 'universal' and therefore also lacking in historicity. That is to say that the disciplines as we currently understand them have developed ultimately from indigenous forms of knowledge over many centuries and in relation to other non-European knowledge systems. As discussed earlier, they have been deeply implicated in the development of broader economic and social interests, including the development of the capitalist system, of patriarchal relations and of colonialism itself.

There is broad consensus amongst African science educators who are interested in IKS of the value of including IK in the curriculum albeit for different reasons. Some argue for the inclusion of IK on the grounds of human rights, as a positive affirmation of African identities and as a contribution to recognitional justice (Battiste 2009; Hoppers 2002; Keane 2008; Asabere-Ameyaw, Dei, and Raheem 2012a). This is to acknowledge, for example, that Africa was rich in ways of knowing the natural world and in technological innovation before the advent of European colonialism in areas as diverse as agriculture, mathematics, astronomy, metallurgy, medicine, navigation, and architecture but also that African thought contributed to the development of the Western civilisation through its influence on Ancient Greek civilisation and as a consequence of this on European Renaissance and Enlightenment thinkers (e.g. Bernal 1989). Others make the case for including IK for cognitive and pedagogical reasons (e.g. Aikenhead 1996, 2006; Battiste 2009; Jegede 1995; Le Grange 2008; Ogunniyi 2011). Drawing on progressive views of learning, these authors argue the importance of relating the scientific curriculum to the local, IK brought to the classroom by learners. For these authors, it is the failure of school science to integrate IK that helps in explaining the cognitive dissonance, alienation, and lack of engagement of African learners with the teaching of science. Significantly, in relation to environmental justice, others make the case because of the potential for knowledge of IKS to address issues of conservation, sustainable use of biological diversity, and sustainable development given the strong emphasis on the custodial relationship between human beings and the natural environment underpinning IKS (Battiste 2009; Lotz-Sisitka et al. 2017; Moyo 2015).

Despite the consensus amongst many educators of the importance of recognising IKS and IK in the curriculum, there are very few instances where IK is included in national curriculum statements. An exception in the African context is South Africa, where curriculum statements include specific reference to IK. It is perhaps partly for this reason that much of the literature about the role of IK in science education originates for South Africa. IKS appears under the science learning area's third specific aim 'appreciating and understanding the history, importance and applications of Life Sciences in society' (DBE 2011, 16). IKS is however not defined in the new documents, but explanations given under Specific Aim 3 are very informative:

> Learners must be exposed to the history of science and indigenous knowledge from other times and cultures. . . . [I]ndigenous knowledge systems . . . have their origins in different worldviews. Learners should understand the different cultural contexts in which indigenous knowledge systems were developed. . . . Examples of indigenous knowledge that are selected for study should, as far as possible, reflect different South African cultural groupings.
>
> (DBE 2011, 16)

This view of IK is in keeping with the earlier discussion in that IK is presented as neither homogenous nor static. As will be discussed later, however, the inclusive approach towards IK creates significant practical issues for teachers.

There are also different perspectives on how IK and Western science ought to relate to each other in the curriculum. Several authors argue that it is possible to talk of 'African' or 'indigenous science' as a distinct form of enquiry that includes 'both the science of the natural/physical/biological and the science of the social'. As Asabere-Ameyaw, Dei, and Raheem (2012b) explain,

> by 'science of the social' we mean science defined broadly to include the nexus of the physical, social, natural and biological terrains of knowledge which can be taken up equally as methodological tools and ways of knowing providing a more comprehensive understanding of our worlds.
>
> (1)

Jegede (1995) contrasts indigenous with Western science. The former is characterised as 'monistic-vitalistic', by which he means that it assumes a unity and relationality/interconnectedness amongst all things, it is based on people, and it posits a metaphysical (spiritual) dimension to all life and all living things. This is in contrast to Western science, which is characterised as mechanistic, exact, and hypothesis driven, seeking empirical law, principles, generalization, and theories, whilst in the process separating subject from object and humans from nature (this relates directly to the discussion of postcolonial critiques linking Western science to the development of Western versions of modernity discussed earlier). Whilst it is claimed that Western science is often dismissive of African science as 'fuzzy' (Asabere-Ameyaw, Dei, and Raheem 2012b), African science is considered more embracing of different ways of knowing the world and alternative sources of evidence, including potentially evidence derived from practical experience gathered over time and spiritual revelation.

Asabere-Ameyaw, Dei, and Raheem (2012a) argue against a dichotomous view of Western and African science. Rather, as has been discussed, they argue for an expanded view of 'science of the social' as a subject that can embrace the more social and spiritual dimensions of IK. Such an expanded view has a place not only in the teaching of science as a subject but also across the curriculum and as basis for interdisciplinary enquiry. They see an important role for 'Western science' in the curriculum but a role that is subordinate to African science. The authors argue that Western science needs to be 'retooled' to make it more relevant for the African cultural context. This might require, for example, a reappraisal of 'Western-centric' approaches such as the teaching of 'argumentation' in science classes, which relies on the competitive counterposing of alternative hypotheses and sources of evidence to arrive at robust scientific understanding and an over-reliance on logic-deductive forms of inference which, according to the authors, run counter to the more consensual and epistemologically diverse approaches to arriving at truth characteristic of IKS.

Considered against a view of epistemic and recognitional justice, there are both strengths and weaknesses to the position discussed earlier. On the positive side, there is a strong effort to recognise the cultures, histories, and backgrounds of learners as a means for granting epistemic access to a culturally relevant notion of 'Africa science'. There is a difficulty, however, in that the idea of 'African science' precisely because of the colonial encounter cannot be considered 'powerful knowledge' in the way that 'Western' science is. Thus, whilst the quest for an African science may be a valid goal, it has yet to be realised and as such any attempt to conflate Western science with IK under the umbrella of 'African science' risks watering down the specialised knowledge that has made Western science 'powerful knowledge' (discussed earlier). By failing to grant African learners access to this powerful knowledge would therefore constitute an epistemic (and hence recognitional) injustice in that learners would be disempowered from gaining access to knowledge that can assist them in realising valued capabilities and functionings. Further, seeking to conflate IK and science would compromise the distinctiveness and value of each and would have the perverse effect of reinforcing the dominance of Western science as IK would most likely be absorbed within an overall Western scientific epistemology (Cobern and Loving 2001; El-Hani and Souza de Ferreira Bandeira 2008; Khupe 2014).

It will be recalled that Bernstein's idea of the pedagogical device considers processes of curriculum reform at different scales and is concerned with how the disciplines become instantiated in the curriculum and in classroom practice through processes of translation. The development of the disciplines in their current form has been undertaken by networks of specialists, largely based in universities and other research institutions over centuries. As was also argued, the development of specialised knowledge has been linked in complex and contradictory ways to wider social interests and purposes. On the one hand the scientific disciplines have played an instrumental role in the development of capitalism and of colonialism. In this sense, as was suggested earlier, the sciences are never purely 'objective' but are imbued with values linked to different interests in the world. This is starkly demonstrated, for example, in the development of eugenics and scientific racism. On the other hand, scientific disciplines have been instrumental in progressing many areas of human development, including the fight against poverty and disease. Evidence for science has also been used in the fight against racism and to point to the threat to the planet caused by human activities. In this sense, although not entirely value-neutral in the way they have developed as specialised systems of thought, they are relatively autonomous from wider social forces. They are also not static and have evolved in relation to internal dynamics as well as in relation to a changing external environment.

On the other hand, there are scholars who advocate maintaining a clear distinction between Western science and IK in the curriculum. There is also a recognition of the importance of granting epistemic access for all learners to 'Western' scientific approaches. A focus for much of the literature written in this vein is to provide a means for bridging the gap between the local indigenous culture brought by the students and school science whilst valuing IK. Building on Jegede's (1995) idea of an 'ecocultural paradigm', which aims at enabling learners to feel at ease in different cultures, Jegede and Aikenhead (1999) have identified several basic principles that facilitate successful 'border crossing' between world views:

1   Make border crossing explicit for pupils;
2   Facilitate these border crossings;
3   Promote discourse so pupils are (a) talking in their own cultural interpretative framework as well as in the framework of Western science without cultural violence; (b) immersed in either the pupils' indigenous life-world culture or the culture of science; and (c) cognisant about which culture they are talking in at any given time;
4   Substantiate and build on the validity of pupils' personally and culturally contracted ways of knowing; and
5   Teach the canonical content of Western science and technology in the context of science's societal roles, for instance, science's social, political, military, colonial, and economic roles.

The idea of bridging cultures or border crossings has led to the development of pedagogical approaches in the classroom and associated theories of learning. For example, Jegede (Jegede and Aikenhead 1999; Jegede 1995, 1997) has elaborated a theory of 'collateral learning' which is used to explain why many pupils, non-Western and Western, experience culturally related cognitive dissonance in their science classes. Collateral learning theory postulates a spectrum of cognitive experiences (parallel, simultaneous, dependent, and secured collateral learning) to explain cultural border crossings. Whereas meaningful learning can occur at different points in the spectrum, in order for learners to be properly 'enculturated' into Western science whilst retaining and valuing IK requires secured collateral learning in which the learner identifies a satisfactory reason for holding onto schemata from both world views (even if they appear to conflict) or where schemata from alternative world views may in fact reinforce each other leading to a 'convergence towards commonality'. The authors propose a range of specific teaching and learning strategies and activities that can assist in moving learners along the spectrum from parallel to collateral learning. These include, for example, learners being actively encouraged to compare and contrast local understanding of concepts based on IK with 'culture of science' concepts.

For writers such as Le Grange (2007), a key component of border crossing is to impart an understanding of the sociology of knowledge production which allows learners to appreciate how different knowledge systems have emerged historically and in relation to each other but also as a means for solving real-world problems. In this respect, Le Grange argues for a focus on procedural rather than representational approaches to science education in which the emphasis is on 'the act of doing science, that is science as a human and social activity that is messy, heterogeneous and situated' (2007, 587).

Building on this insight, Zazu (2017) considers the example of a curriculum innovation in Zimbabwe called the culture hut for integrating indigenous understanding of environmental issues in the curriculum. Influenced by Zimbabwe's cultural policy of 2004, the culture hut concept entails the establishment of a culture hut or village in primary schools which serves as a mini-cultural museum. Whilst according to the findings from Zazu's case study research it is currently used predominantly by teachers of social studies and of the Shona language as a learning resource, there is also potential according to Zazu for it to be used to understand how IK of the environment was integrated into the development of the huts themselves as well as into sustainable livelihoods.

Keane (2008) and Khupe (2014) offer rich ethnographic evidence based on case study research in different parts of rural Kwa-Zulu Natal. Through the use of participatory and collaborative methods they gathered data from a range of school and community stakeholders, including teachers and learners, community members, elders, and chiefs about the kinds of IK that are valued locally. In Keane's study, these included knowledge of local history, medicine, and food; an appreciation of elements central to the world view of the participants, including the importance of interconnectedness, of the cultural as well as material significance of water, of local conceptions of time, of underlying values of *ubuntu* (African humanism), of the environment, the nature of community self-identity and knowledge of associated performative cultural practices; and an awareness of taboos such as a lack of acknowledgement of the existence of HIV/AIDS and of pregnancy before marriage. Khupe (2014) also emphasises the potential for developing understanding of IK through practical application, e.g. in through the teaching of agricultural skills that are often valued highly by these communities. Both authors stress the importance of understanding isiZulu as a means to access understanding of IKS.

Both argue that through seeking better understanding of these elements of IKS and forms of collaboration with the community, it becomes possible to identify useful IK resources that can be drawn on strategically to enrich understanding of the science curriculum. Keane describes a student science fortnight and community science festival that she claims were successful in informing local understanding of the realities of HIV/AIDS. She describes these as

> constructive interventions for bringing scientific reasoning, evidence-based arguments, a search for information, and a frankness to the taboo of acknowledging the existence of AIDS. Traditional practices were balanced with this new frank acknowledgement, which for some participants would have been shocking and unacceptable.
>
> (2008, 607)

In relation to the discussion of the previous chapter, these are examples of schools working with local communities to foster processes of social learning. Underpinning processes of reciprocal learning in both studies was a relationship of trust and mutual respect established over several years. Nonetheless, tensions remained, including the relationship between some of the rights-based elements of education policy and some local practices. These included, for example, a tension between the effects of patriarchal norms and values on the experiences of women, including the sterilisation of pregnant women and the commitment to gender equality in official policy (see also Khupe 2014) and the widespread use of corporal punishment in the community despite it being officially banned. These kinds of initiatives in which the school engages in ethically based dialogue with the community has potential relevance for the role of education and training systems in combatting violence (see Chapter 5).

The burning language question in African education[10]

Central to debates about decolonisation, and indeed to pedagogy which are addressed in the next chapter, is the burning language question in African education. A leading proponent of the need to develop African languages was the anti-apartheid activist and scholar Neville Alexander who spent ten years incarcerated on Robben Island for his role in the anti-apartheid struggle. Alexander was passionate about the importance of African languages not just as a contribution to an African cultural renaissance but as a key component of ongoing class and anti-colonial struggle on the continent. Crucially, Alexander understood the importance of mother tongue education as a means for improving learning outcomes for disadvantaged groups of learners (Alexander 1989, 1997; Alexander 1999).[11] Another example is the Kenyan playwriter and novelist Ngũgĩ wa Thiong'o. Thiong'o challenged the role of Western languages in African higher education and emphasised the potential of African languages as a means for countering hegemonic Western ways of knowing the world (see, for example, Thiong'o 1986). However, whilst *Agenda 2063* states that 'language is at the heart of a people's culture and the acceleration of Africa's socio-economic transformation is impossible without harnessing in a practical manner the indigenous African languages' (AUC 2015a, 68) and that a 'major threat to African culture and heritage is the educational system which is marginalizing African languages', this realisation is not carried through in the CESA document which makes hardly any mention of language at all.

The instrumental approach

The neglect of language-in-education policy often means that narrow, instrumentalist approaches towards the medium of instruction are implemented by default. Instrumentalist approaches typically characterise the status quo in many African countries (Clegg and Simpson 2016; Trudell 2016). At their heart is a view of language as contributing to national development in a globalised world. Here, the view of 'development' is usually equated with ideas of modernity and measured in increases in gross national product (see Chapter 7). Within this approach, language-in-education policy is principally conceived as contributing to the development of human capital. As some commentators have pointed out, this is in the form of cultural, linguistic capital that can be traded in global markets (Rassool, Heugh, and Mansoor 2007). In many countries, this leads to an emphasis on the development of a global language (often English) as a target language for policy. Instrumental approaches are also often concerned, however, with the role of language as a basis for national unity. In the context of developmental regionalism, they may also often be implicated in regional integration.[12]

In many high-income countries, these twin goals of national development are achieved through the use of strong bilingual models in which the mother tongue is used as the medium of instruction at least through the primary and secondary cycle and in some instances through the tertiary cycle. Here both the mother tongue and one or more global languages are the target languages of policy. Proficiency in global languages is realised through the teaching of these languages as subjects throughout formal education.[13] In many low- and middle-income countries, including those in Africa on the other hand, mother tongue education is more often seen as a bridge to the development of global languages with global languages rather than mother tongue as the principal target language for policy (Alidou et al. 2006; Benson 2014). These weak bilingual models often involve mother tongue education in the early years with a global language taught as a subject. Early exit from mother tongue education to a global language usually takes place at some point in the basic education cycle. These 'subtractive approaches' often result in the devaluing of the mother tongue in favour of a global language. As various commentators have pointed out, instrumental approaches are often justified with reference to pragmatic concerns about the use of global languages as a *lingua franca* in multilingual societies and with reference to the resource implications involved in producing materials in multiple languages (Alidou et al. 2006).

Instrumentalist approaches are characterised by top-down, state-led approaches to policy making although they may draw on and reinforce popular ideas about the relative importance of local and global languages for national development.

In this respect, many parents and communities also often adopt an instrumentalist view of the importance of global languages for the future success of their children in the labour market. For many parents, education in English or another global language is synonymous with quality (Trudell 2007). This is evidenced by the prevalence of low-fee private schools in many low-income countries in which the medium of instruction is English (Ashley et al. 2014; Rubagumya et al. 2011; Rubagumya 2003). The perception of parents is often fuelled by the observation that the children of middle class, urban elites almost invariably send their children to schools in which a global language is the medium of instruction. There is often, however, a disjuncture between the official policy and pedagogical practice in the classroom, where many qualitative studies have revealed the widespread illicit use of 'code-switching' as a means by which the teacher makes the curriculum more accessible to disadvantaged learners who are struggling linguistically (Afitska et al. 2013; Brock-Utne and Holmarsdottir 2004; Brock-Utne 2015; Clegg and Afitska 2011).

The rights-based approach

An alternative approach towards framing language-in-education policy is provided by rights-based perspectives. Space does not allow for a full exposition of the various frameworks that give rise to linguistic rights and their policy implications (UNESCO 2003).[14] Rights-based approaches have in common a view of language-in-education policy as contributing to the achievements of linguistic rights and as a means of achieving further rights for disadvantaged and marginalised populations, including in the context of the SDGs, to sustainable livelihoods. The emphasis is on mother tongue and often a language of wider communication as target languages for policy. These are seen as complimentary rather than contradictory goals. Exponents of a rights-based approach often favour a mother tongue-based strong bilingual approach in low income contexts in which both the mother tongue and a global language are supported (Alidou et al. 2006; Phillipson et al. 2014; Phillipson 1996; Skutnabb-Kangas 2009; Rubagumya et al. 2011).

Rights-based perspectives provide a powerful normative basis from which to critique instrumental approaches where these are seen to inhibit or contravene the realisation of linguistic rights.[15] As already suggested, rights-based approaches also offer a pedagogical critique of the impact of weak bilingual approaches on classroom practice. Part of this critique is associated with the perceived importance of conceptions of learner-centeredness within a rights-based approach. In this respect, qualitative studies have revealed the extent to which weak bilingual approaches reinforce teacher-centeredness as the opportunities for more learner-centred approaches usually rely on a firmer grasp of language (Afitska et al. 2013; Brock-Utne 2015; Brock-Utne and Holmarsdottir 2004).

Rights-based approaches may also serve as a point of reference for policy makers. Trudell (2016), for example, discusses how some countries may on paper adopt a strong bilingual approach, but in reality this translates into a weak bilingual model when it is implemented, often on account of community pressure for children to learn in a global language. South Africa provides a good example of this (Desai 2016). There is also a danger that rights-based approaches may appear too homogenising in their implications for addressing the complex linguistic needs and identities of diverse groups in multilingual, postcolonial settings (Pennycook 2009; Rassool, Heugh, and Mansoor 2007; Tikly 1999) It has also been argued that they tend to elide issues of the power and status of different languages and to not adequately take account of the aspirations and views of parents and communities in these settings.[16] As several commentators writing broadly within a rights-based framework have acknowledged, strong advocacy for language rights also needs to be accompanied by informed public dialogue on language and education policy if it seeks to engage with and transform rather than to appear simply dismissive of entrenched attitudes, for instance with respect to the use of mother tongue versus a global language in the early years of schooling (Tollefson 2013; Rubagumya et al. 2011; Alidou et al. 2006). Such an approach is consistent with the view of social and environmental justice outlined in Chapter 7.

Language-in-education policy, theory, and research

Instrumentalist approaches as they are enacted in policy are rarely evidence-led. To the extent that they make reference to relevant evidence at all, this is often partial at best. Alidou *et al.* (Alidou et al. 2006) have described the processes by which evidence relating to the importance of a strong bilingual approach can become distorted in the process of policy take-up and implementation and used to justify weak, early-exit bilingual models. Proponents of a rights-based view on the other hand are able to draw on a range of international evidence relating to language acquisition and cognitive achievement. Such evidence has played a powerful role in critiquing an instrumentalist approach and in advocating for strong bilingual models. Alidou *et al.* go on to provide a useful summary of the implications of such evidence that are used to support a strong mother tongue-based bilingual approach:

- The L1 needs to be reinforced and developed for 12 years in order for successful L2 learning and academic success to take place. This means birth to 12 years, i.e. L1 medium for at least six years of formal schooling.
- The international second language acquisition (SLA) literature indicates that under optimal conditions (these do not apply in most education systems in Africa) it takes six to eight years to learn an L2 sufficiently well enough to use it as a medium of instruction.
- Language education models which remove the L1 as a primary medium of instruction before grade 5 will facilitate little success for the majority of learners.
- Language education models which retain the L1 as a primary medium of instruction for six years can succeed under very well-resourced conditions in African settings.
- Eight years of MTE may be enough under less well-resourced conditions.

Existing language-in-education policies are also explicitly or implicitly linked to theories of bilingualism/multilingualism that have implications for pedagogical practice. Although theories of bilingualism rarely explicitly inform instrumentalist approaches, they often rely at a 'common sense' level on a deficit view of bilingualism in relation to cognitive development, which is in turn based on an underlying assumption of languages as autonomous linguistic systems that are stored separately in the brain, taking up finite amounts of 'room'. This contrasts with more recent theories of language acquisition that see the development of linguistic competencies across languages as fluid, relational, and interdependent.

Cummins' model of bilingualism (see Cummins 1979, 1981) has provided a key point of reference for those working within a rights-based approach. He proposes that rather than proficiencies in two languages being stored separately in the brain, each proficiency is in fact interdependent on the other.[17] This underlying view of bilingualism is often used to support the policy implications outlined by Alidou *et al.*, i.e. that transfer is only possible once proficiency in L1 and L2 have been developed for between six and eight years.[18] Cummins' subsequent work has also led him to develop over time a pedagogical approach for supporting literacy development in multilingual classrooms that is consistent with his underlying model of language development in bilinguals (Cummins 2011).[19] In relation to the arguments of the book, the model is significant for demonstrating the links between language and literacy development. With respect to capability theory, it also serves to illustrate the conversion factors, barriers, and affordances implicated in early literacy development.

More recently, Cummins' insights have been developed by researchers working within a 'translanguaging' framework in Africa and elsewhere. Drawing on interdisciplinary insights from pyscho- and sociolinguistics, translanguaging theory emphasises a dynamic view of bilingualism. According to Garcia and Wei

> Unlike the view of two separate systems that are added (or even interdependent), a dynamic conceptualization of bilingualism goes beyond the notion of two autonomous languages, of a first language (L1) and a second language (L2), and of additive or subtractive bilingualism. Instead, dynamic bilingualism suggests that the language practices of bilinguals are complex and interrelated; they do not emerge in a linear way or function separately since there is only one linguistic system.
>
> (Garcia and Wei 2014a, 49)

Translanguaging approaches deepen Cummin's views on language, including his literacy development framework.[20] From a sociolinguistic perspective, translanguaging draws attention to the processes of language use in multilingual settings 'under social and historical conditions that both constrain and make possible the social reproduction of existing conventions and relations, as well as the production of new ones' (Heller 2007, 15). Translanguaging is, therefore, alive to issues of power and inequality in postcolonial settings. By positing integrated linguistic functions, it affirms and values linguistic diversity as a potentially positive resource for developing linguistic capability whilst recognising the power relations inherent between the language used in the home/community and in the school. In the context of classroom practice, translanguaging also provides theoretical support for the strategic use of 'code switching' in order to enable learners to make use of the diverse language resources at their disposal in order to access the formal curriculum.

The potential for translanguaging in the African context has yet to be fully explored although it has recently been investigated by researchers interested in the effectiveness of a multilingual teaching pedagogy in South African classrooms (Heugh 2015; Makalela 2015; Probyn 2015). Probyn's study, for example, reports on the potential for the systematic and purposeful use of the learner's home language described as 'pedagogical translanguaging' as opposed to the relatively brief and reactive code switching or complete avoidance of the learner's home language. Although based on a pilot study, the approach appeared to show promise in improving the learning outcomes in the teaching of science. Makalela's study, on the other hand, highlights the potential contribution of teacher education in developing the capabilities of educators in using translanguaging techniques to improve learning outcomes. There is clearly scope for further research in this area.

Creating an enabling environment to support the development of linguistic capability

The aim of this section is to outline a model that can inform policy, practice, and research aimed at developing linguistic capability across different multilingual contexts. The model will seek to draw together key themes relating to language and education policy outlined in the article, the wider literature and other contributions to the special issue. An important caveat is necessary here, however. A criticism of some interpretations of a rights-based approach is that the education system is seen as the locus for achieving wider linguistic justice. As commentators have pointed out, the education system alone cannot compensate for the broader issues of the status of different languages within the public and private spheres although a key goal of policy making would be to seek coherence between policies aimed at achieving linguistic rights and capabilities in education and policies aimed at achieving these within the wider society and the economy. In this regard, the domains draw attention to the areas that language-in-education policy can realistically hope to influence.

The domains are represented in diagrammatic form in Figure 8.1. The large circle in which the domains are pictured represents the wider sociocultural/historical and policy contexts within which they are situated. Consistent with the view of complex systems is that these contexts will invariably differ within and between countries, leading to the possible identification of different language-in-education policies and priorities across contexts. In this sense, the ideas presented and their implications for policy, practice, and research need to be (re)-interpreted/articulated in relation to different contexts. The double headed arrows between

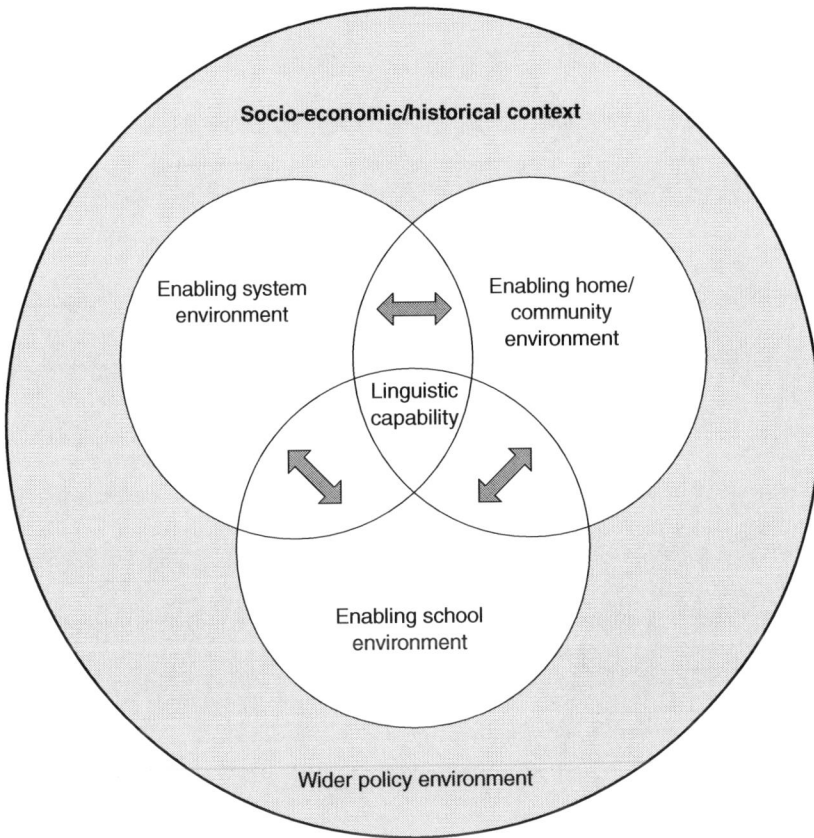

Figure 8.1 Creating an enabling environment for the development of multilingual capability.

Source: (Adapted from Tikly 2016)

each domain represent the importance of considering the relationship between domains, i.e. the importance of considering the nature of the home–school, system–school, and system–home relationships in developing linguistic capability. Each domain will be briefly considered in turn.

The school environment

A key barrier to the development of linguistic capability at a school level is the capability of teachers to implement appropriate language-supportive pedagogy. This relates both to their own multilingual capabilities and to their pedagogical knowledge of how to develop multilingual capability in learners (Clegg and Afitska 2011; Afitska et al. 2013; Brock Utne and Holmarsdottir 2004; Brock-Utne

2015). In this regard, it is suggested that models of language, literacy, and pedagogy such as those outlined earlier provide a useful point of departure for future enquiry in low-income settings. Cummin's model draws attention to processes of scaffolding and of a school ethos and leadership that is supportive of multilingualism as a positive feature of school life.

The home/community environment

A key finding from research in low-income settings is that where children, particularly those from the most socio-economically disadvantaged backgrounds and from linguistic minorities, do not speak the language of instruction in their home and community environment, they are more likely to underachieve at school in basic literacy and numeracy (Trudell 2016). Conversely, where parents are empowered to develop their own linguistic capabilities and to support the development of their children's capabilities (for example, by reading with their children), this can lead to more positive outcomes. The project for the development of Alternative Education in South Africa, for example, provides substantial evidence of the positive and empowering effect of community literacy interventions on children's learning outcomes (Bloch 2014). As Trudell (2016) argues, forms of community engagement and mobilisation on the part of governments and NGOs can prove instrumental in shifting deep-seated attitudes in support of early immersion in global languages in support of strong bilingual models.

The education system environment

The choice of policy, including whether to opt for a weak or a strong model, can have profound effects on learning outcomes for disadvantaged groups of learners. Even where strong models are officially adopted, the tendency can be for them to become diluted. There is a need for a better evidence base in low-income settings relating the choice of bilingual model with the learning outcomes of different groups as well as evidence from where policies have been more effectively implemented. Clegg and Simpson 2016) draw attention to the disjuncture that often exists between the model of bilingual education adopted and other features of the education system. For instance, they highlight the lack of preparation that teachers receive for working in multilingual environments during initial and continuing teacher training; the large gap that exists between the linguistic demands of the curriculum, textbooks, and the assessment system and the linguistic capabilities of learners. All this serves to highlight the need to place language-in-education policy at the heart of debates about education quality and education planning so as to create greater coherence between elements of the education system in support of improved learning outcomes for disadvantaged groups. As many curricula in Africa move towards a competency-based model, this would mean embedding the development of linguistic competencies/capabilities across the curriculum. It would also mean working with the publishing community to ensure that the textbook procurement process includes criteria relating to the accessibility of language and that assessment processes are designed to assess the development of linguistic capability as a central feature of learning (Milligan, Clegg, and Tikly 2016; Milligan et al. 2018).

Conclusion

The chapter has sought to illustrate both the importance and the complexities involved in decolonising the curriculum. It has considered the tension between two conceptions of epistemic justice. The first relates to the complexities of addressing the Eurocentric nature of the curriculum in Africa. Here two broad aspects were explored. Firstly, it was argued that decolonising school science is inextricably linked to the issues of decolonising research in higher education. Challenging the Eurocentric bias of the disciplines as they have developed since the European enlightenment and transforming understanding of the natural and social worlds to take account of Africa's issues of sustainable development, however, is a 'long game' and needs to be seen in relation to the wider political economy of knowledge production on the continent and the need to transform research.

Nonetheless, through a consideration of secondary school science education it was suggested that it is both possible and desirable to integrate consideration of the value of IKS alongside the so-called 'Western' science. It was argued that whilst it is important to keep knowledge systems distinctive, it is possible to impart the value of IKS through processes of pedagogical border crossing and through engaging learners in understanding of how knowledge of the natural world evolves in different social and historical contexts to serve different interests in society. Including consideration of IKS in the context of science education also relates to the second aspect of epistemic justice, namely, ensuring that disadvantaged learners have epistemic access to the powerful knowledge represented by the scientific disciplines. Here pedagogical processes that focus on border crossing can play a role in bridging the gap between local and IK and the content of the formal curriculum. These processes are enhanced by developing closer links with local communities which potentially have wider benefits in terms of fostering forms of social learning and democratic citizenship. These issues of epistemic access to powerful knowledge have implications for the capabilities that learners have to progress in their formal education. As such they also need to be seen alongside some of the wider barriers affecting disadvantaged learners in STEM-related education that were discussed in Chapter 7.

The second part of the chapter focused on the related issue of language in education policy. It was argued that current languages in education policies in many African countries adopt an instrumentalist approach consistent with both modernisation and human capital theory. Although instrumentalist approaches enjoy some popular support, the predominance of subtractive bilingual approaches and early exit from the mother tongue work to the detriment of disadvantaged learners. The chapter also discussed rights-based approaches, which it was suggested, are more closely aligned to principles of social and environmental justice.

Discussion focused on the evidence in support of additive bilingual approaches in education. Consideration was given to emerging thinking relating to language use in the classroom inspired by developments in linguistic understanding that seek to draw strategically on multiple linguistic resources as a means to develop linguistic capability. Building on the evidence presented, the chapter concluded by arguing for a systemic approach towards supporting the development of linguistic capabilities on the continent linked to wider efforts to empower African languages.

Notes

1 See YouTube video with Sen entitled "Language as Capability." Available at www. youtube.com/watch?v=V3MZvPnZW8g (Accessed 5 January 2016).
2 The term 'mother tongue is used here to refer to a local/familiar language, the language of the immediate community which is best known to the child.
3 Whilst the *Rhodes Must Fall* and *Why Is My Curriculum White?* protests focused on issues of representation in the curriculum, the *Fees Must Fall* protests rather took aim at another issue perceived by students as preventing the access of disadvantaged learners to HE, namely, the imposition of tuition fees. Critical accounts of these student protests have been provided elsewhere (e.g. Jansen 2018).
4 The document notes that work done by great African scholars and writers have contributed a lot to re-examining and restoring Africa's distorted and obscured place in the history of the world. The document also notes that despite her rich cultural heritage, Africa is poorly represented in the list of protected world cultural heritage sites and that this risks hastening the erosion of these sites.
5 Not to be confused with social constructivism (which as we have seen in Chapter 8 is concerned with the processes through which individuals and groups construct meaning at a social psychological level).
6 There are parallels between social realist concerns and the ideas of Antonio Gramsci. Gramsci, a Marxist activist and journalist in fascist Italy in the 1920s and 1930s, argued that control over hegemonic knowledge, including that enshrined in the formal curriculum, was key to how the ruling class maintained its intellectual and moral leadership and power to 'define' common sense in a way that served to legitimise their own interests. For Gramsci, it is only through developing organic intellectuals of the working class who have mastered 'bourgeois knowledge', including that enshrined in the disciplines that it becomes possible to counter the intellectual and moral leadership (hegemony) of elites in the interests of the organised working class. On this basis he argued against the fascist government's attempts to vocationalise the curriculum. In the same vein in which social realists distinguish between 'specialised' and 'everyday' knowledge, Gramsci distinguished between the 'good sense' learned through mastery of the disciplines and knowledge linked to common folklore. For Gramsci, as for social realists, schooling needed to be 'disinterested' (i.e. removed from the direct experience of the learner) and that the role of the teacher was to inculcate into children from working class and peasant backgrounds the same habits and dispositions towards study taken for granted by learners from bourgeoisie backgrounds.
7 There are echoes here of previous scholarship that has sought to trace the development of classical Western civilisations to their Afro-Asiatic roots (Bernal 1989), thereby drawing attention to the historicity of Western knowledge. Comoroff and Comoroff (2011) take up the theme arguing that theory from the South can provide a useful lens from which to view the current crisis in Western modernity.

8 It should be pointed out that the idea of weak and strong framing applies as much to vocational as to academic subjects/disciplines in social realist thought. This is significant for the African context and for CESA and *Agenda 2063* given the emphasis on vocational education and on generic skills. In discussing vocational subjects, Young (2008) invokes another concept from Bernstein's work, namely, that of 'vertical' and 'horizontal' discourses. Whereas the latter refers to the hierarchically organised knowledge developed by knowledge specialists, the latter refers to the everyday, more diffuse and context-dependent, knowledge that whilst practically useful in specific work situations is not necessarily transferrable. Accountancy or computer science are examples of hierarchically organised vocational subjects, developed by experts in 'communities of trust'. These are considered on a par in terms of their claims to objectivity as traditional disciplinary subjects. Newer vocational school subjects such as leisure and tourism or life skills would be considered more akin to horizontal discourses in that the kinds of skills imparted are linked to specific contexts (e.g. booking a flight in leisure and tourism). Young has sounded a note of caution about including the kinds of skills identified by the World Economic Forum in curricula. It is suggested later that social realist discourses are in danger of perpetuating unhelpful binaries including those between horizontal and vertical discourses.

9 At a global level it is often associated with concepts such as 'native' or 'first peoples'. In South Africa, for example, this would apply to the Koi-San peoples. However, in South Africa as elsewhere 'indigenous' is also associated with the broader notion of 'African', which includes waves of migration of peoples from other parts of the African continent over many centuries prior to the arrival of Europeans. The definition becomes more unclear when some white European groups such as Afrikaners who have been in Africa for many centuries also self-identify as indigenous.

10 This section develops earlier work on language-in-education policy (Tikly 2016; Milligan and Tikly 2016).

11 The following clip features an interview with Alexander in which he clearly articulates his views on the importance of African languages: www.youtube.com/watch?v=991CCfgPsD0

12 This is the case with respect to Rwanda's choice of English as the medium of instruction, for example, which is linked amongst other things to closer economic integration with the Southern and East African Development Community.

13 As Kedzierski shows, English Medium Instruction is now widespread throughout the higher education systems of East Asia and in other parts of the world.

14 At a general level they may be differentiated between basic Linguistic Human Rights that include, for example, access to education in the mother tongue as well as access to an official language and other linguistic rights that might include, for instance, access to a second (e.g. a global) language.

15 This relates to a view of rights to in and through education as being central to a conception of education quality and finds expression, for example, in concepts such as the child- or girl-friendly school (Tikly and Barrett 2011b).

16 For example, Freeland (2013), in her discussion of the rights-based language-in-education policies adopted by the Nicaraguan government and aimed at indigenous groups in the Caribbean Coast Region whilst well-meaning failed to address the complex linguistic needs and identities of these diverse groups exposing a disjuncture between indigenous and official interpretations of language rights and indeed of language itself.

17 Using the concept of Common Underlying Proficiency (CUP) illustrated through the image of the duel iceberg, Cummins suggests that although on the surface the structural elements of two languages might look different, there is a cognitive

interdependence that allows for the transfer of linguistic practices. The acronyms BICS and CALP refer to a distinction introduced by Cummins (see Cummins 2008) between basic interpersonal communicative skills and cognitive academic language proficiency. The distinction is intended to draw attention to the very different time periods typically required by immigrant children in Canada to acquire conversational fluency in their second language as compared to grade-appropriate academic proficiency in that language. Conversational fluency is often acquired to a functional level within about two years of initial exposure to the second language, whereas at least five years is usually required to catch up to native speakers in academic aspects of the second language (Klesmer 1994; Cummins 1981). Failure to take account of the BICS/CALP (conversational/academic) distinction has resulted in discriminatory psychological assessment of bilingual students and premature exit from language support programs (e.g. bilingual education in the United States) into mainstream classes (Cummins 1984).

18   A word of caution is needed, however, in relation to the existing evidence and theories of bilingualism. Whilst policy implications such as those outlined earlier by Alidou *et al.* and the models of bi- and multilingualism and pedagogy discussed are based on the best available evidence and therefore ought to serve as a rule of thumb for policy makers, the evidence on which they are based is derived from well-resourced North American and European settings and to a lesser extent from middle- and low-income countries. This is compounded by the historical nature of some of the evidence. More research is needed to establish the impact of different models of bi- and multilingual education on learning outcomes that take account of the different contexts across low-income countries in which learning takes place.

19   It emphasises key elements required for developing literacy in a second language. The framework posits print access/literacy engagement as a direct determinant of literacy attainment that Cummins claims is well supported by empirical evidence. The framework also specifies four broad instructional dimensions that Cummins argues are critical to enabling all students (and particularly those from socially marginalised groups) to engage actively with literacy from an early stage of their schooling. Literacy engagement will be enhanced when (a) students' ability to understand and use academic language is scaffolded through specific instructional strategies, (b) their prior experience and current knowledge are activated, (c) their linguistic and cultural identities are affirmed, and (d) their knowledge of, and control over, language is extended across the curriculum. Although the model has been developed from work with immigrant learners in Canada, Cummins (Cummins 2015) discusses the potential of elements of the model for disadvantaged learners in low-income settings in Africa.

20   As Cummins (Cummins 2015) has suggested, the dynamic bilingual model is consistent with his own views of languages as not being hermetically sealed off.

9   Towards a transformative pedagogy

Introduction

In this chapter, an attempt will be made to set out a conceptual understanding of pedagogy that is relevant for debates about ESD in Africa. The understanding of pedagogy is taken from Alexander (2008). Alexander provides an expansive notion of pedagogy that goes beyond the narrower view of 'instruction' that dominates much of the literature and that focuses on the technical processes of teaching and learning in the classroom. For Alexander, pedagogy is defined as

> the act of teaching together with its attendant discourse of educational theories, values, evidence and justifications. It is what one needs to know, and the skills one needs to command, in order to make and justify the many different kinds of decision of which teaching is constituted.
>
> (p. 47)

This more comprehensive definition places pedagogy as the central focus for schooling that encompasses other key domains, including those of teaching and learning and curriculum and assessment. In this view, the teacher engages, as a matter of necessity, with the following domains of ideas and values:

- Children: their characteristics, development, motivation, needs, and differences;
- Learning: its nature, facilitation, achievement, and assessment;
- Teaching: its planning, execution, and evaluation;
- Curriculum: the various ways of knowing, doing, creating, investigating, and making sense, which it is desirable for children to encounter, and how these are most appropriately translated and structured for teaching.

Such a view of pedagogy as comprising overlapping domains articulates with the view of complex systems outlined in Chapter 2 and with the view of complex learning set out later. Alexander points out that pedagogy also needs to be understood in relation to the nature of the school as an institution which he defines as a 'microculture', i.e. as a conveyor of popular messages; and, of policy, which defines what is taught and how. Pedagogy in Alexander's sense is also more widely 'situated' in an understanding of community (through the influence of familial and local expectations, attitudes, opportunities, and constraints that shape learners' outlooks), culture (understood as a web of values, ideas, institutions, and processes that shape and explain a society's views of education), and indeed self (understanding of what it is to be a person). For our purposes such a definition is useful because it allows for the development of a more nuanced understanding of pedagogical approaches that are potentially relevant for Africa linked to a range of contexts found within and between African countries. It also allows for an appreciation of continuities and discontinuities in the development of African pedagogy from pre-colonial times to the present.

Pedagogy understood in this sense is deeply implicated in global and regional agendas. Firstly, as we have seen in Chapter 6, regional agendas are organised around a vision of the role of education in relation to sustainable development that is articulated in contradictory ways to pan-Africanist, modernisation, human capital, rights-based, and environmental discourses. Although the implications of these discourses for understanding classroom interaction and the processes of teaching and learning are rarely made explicit in policy, African teachers are currently expected to grapple with a range of externally imposed pedagogical approaches that are often far removed from the realities of their everyday practice and for which they have been inadequately prepared. Further, despite calls to use more formative modes of assessment in CESA, teachers continue to be faced with a high stake, content-driven examination system that constrains what is possible in relation to classroom practice. In this regard, a central argument of the chapter is that there is a need to reconsider how pedagogy is represented in policy and that the quest for more relevant, African-centred approaches that speak to the realities of African classrooms should itself become a policy priority.

The chapter will consider in turn two dominant approaches that are used to describe pedagogy in Africa, namely, 'progressive' and 'formalistic' approaches. Consideration will be given to the main themes from the literature that help to define each approach with particular attention to how knowledge is understood and the implications for the curriculum as well as how processes of teaching, learning, and assessment are conceived. It will be argued that whilst each coheres at a very basic level around assumptions concerning the nature of knowledge and the respective roles of the teacher and learner in processes of teaching and learning, each also contains within it contradictory ways of positioning the various elements described in Alexander's definition. Further, each contributes to an unhelpful polarisation of pedagogy (Barrett 2007) that limits their potential for addressing either the realities of African classrooms or the needs of current policy agendas.

Building on the critique of existing approaches, the chapter will then set out an alternative 'transformative' approach that it is suggested, provides a means for reconceptualising pedagogy in a way that is relevant for the African continent. It will be suggested that a starting point is to consider pedagogy in relation to the view of complex adaptive systems set out in Chapter 2, and here the chapter will draw on recent scholarship that has sought to situate an understanding of pedagogy at the intersections of various complex systems encompassing the home and community background of the learner, the classroom, the school, and the wider education system, including the national curriculum frameworks, assessment system, and teacher training. Central to this understanding is the need for coherence at a system level in terms of the overarching moral purpose of education and between the curriculum, assessment, and teacher training but most especially at the 'pedagogical core'. This demands a focus on the specific activities facilitated by the teacher that enable the learner to engage with the content of the lesson and how these are evaluated. In this regard, however, it will also be suggested that pedagogy needs to be conceptualised in relation to the operation of various intersecting regimes of inequality that limit the opportunities for learning available to different individuals and groups and that educators must be aware of and actively engage with.

The progressive approach

The progressive approach centres on various forms of Learner-Centred Education (LCE) (Schweisfurth 2011; Schweisfurth 2013a, 2013b). It can be traced back to the diverse educational ideas of thinkers such as Rousseau and Dewey, Piaget, Bruner, Freire, and Vygotsky. It has been argued that progressive approaches have a long pedigree in pre-colonial African education systems that were focused on learning by doing (Lotz-Sisitka et al. 2017). At the heart of the approach is the idea of the active role of the learner or the 'knower' in the learning process in contrast to more formalistic teacher-centred approaches. Progressive approaches also tend to stress the constructed nature of knowledge itself, which is seen to arise as a consequence of cognitive interactions between individuals and groups. Learner-centred ideas have informed the educational policies, programmes, and initiatives of key multilateral organisations including UNESCO and the World Bank as well as of NGOs. Through this kind of international advocacy, they have found their way into the policies adopted by many African governments, including recent shifts towards a competency-based curriculum (Chapter 6).

As Schweisfurth (2013b) has pointed out, there are three main narratives that have provided a motivation for the uptake and advocacy of progressive approaches. One of these she describes as the *cognitive narrative*. These draw on constructivist theories often inspired by the work of Piaget, which focus on the cognitive processes by which learners actively create knowledge of the world through engagement with their learning environment. Knowledge of the world is considered to be an emergent property triggered by cognitive interactions between individuals. The cognitive narrative draws on evidence that increased learner control helps learners to start from their existing knowledge of the world and as a consequence to develop neural connections and meaningful patterns from which more effective and sustainable learning emerges (see, for example, Westbrook et al. 2013; Wagner 2018; Barrett et al. 2007). The intrinsic motivation that comes from learning something of significance and importance to them additionally helps to focus students on learning and this engagement is crucial to the process. As we will see in Chapter 9, similar arguments are advanced as a rationale for including reference to indigenous and local knowledge systems in the science curriculum.

Social constructivist approaches on the other hand, inspired by the writings of Vygotsky and his contemporaries, focuses attention on the social dynamics involved in learning and the creation of knowledge within specific sociocultural contexts mediated by artefacts and language which needs to be the learner's first language or at least one very familiar to them, and facilitated by drawing on examples or contexts familiar to the learners so that meaning making is prioritised. Social constructivist thinking has inspired a range of classroom approaches globally, including forms of communicative and co-operative learning exemplified by small-group, pair, and whole-class interactive work, extended dialogue with individuals, higher-order questioning, problem, and enquiry-based activities (Westbrook et al. 2013; Wagner 2018; Barrett et al. 2007). Social constructivist theories also find expression in forms of classroom-based assessment such as assessment for learning (see, for, example Berry 2008), which has been taken up albeit in a limited way by some African education systems where it stands in contrast to the predominance of high-stakes examinations (Sayed and Kanjee 2013). It stands as a measure of the influence of progressivist thought in CESA that the importance of classroom-based forms of assessment are explicitly acknowledged. Given the salience attached to issues of language and communication in the learning process, social constructivism has also been used as the basis for language-supportive approaches to teaching and learning and as a basis for literacy development in multilingual classrooms (see later).

The second narrative that Schweisfurth describes is one of *emancipation*. It draws on the ideas of Paulo Freire and John Dewey and is concerned with education's potential both to undermine and to serve the freedoms of individuals and groups. It is also concerned with how pedagogy can help learners to develop the knowledge, skills, attitudes, and behaviours which over time can transform society. As Schweisfurth points out,

> again, the emphasis on learner control is central, but made more radical with the introduction of the notion of critical pedagogy, in which learners not only have more control over what they learn and the process of learning, but are encouraged to critically question canons of received knowledge and the unequal structures of society which they support.
>
> (Schweisfurth 2013b, 2)

Developing citizenship skills that can enhance democratic societies has been a long-standing goal of the Education for All Movement (Tikly 2017) and is included in SDG goal 4.7. In the African context, this narrative has found particular resonance in the context of anti-colonial struggles as we saw in Chapter 4. The writings of Paulo Freire, for example, have long been an inspiration for anti-colonial activists in Africa, including the Black Consciousness movement

(Tikly 1994). His ideas were used to critique the highly authoritarian system of Bantu Education, which, following Freire, was equated with the 'transmission' or 'banking' model of education as well as to conceive of education's role in processes of conscientisation, i.e. of raising awareness through political activism in grass-roots movements of the nature of oppression and possible alternatives.

Progressive approaches also find strong support amongst advocates of different forms of sustainability education as it has been articulated in the African context, including those concerned with developing capabilities that will prepare learners to realise environmental and/or sustainability goals. The final report of the *UNESCO Decade of Education for Sustainable Development* (UNESCO 2014b, 86) argues that there is a 'growing recognition that effective ESD is contingent on a shift in pedagogical approaches, from traditional teacher-centred pedagogies towards teacher-facilitated and collaborative discovery and problem-solving approaches' (86). Lots-Sisitka has succinctly captured the essence of a widely shared view of ESD amongst educators as being both situated and transformative. It is therefore worth quoting in full:

> ESD brings the importance of situated learning to the fore, an approach to learning that focuses on the cultural, social and socio-material 'figured worlds' . . . in which individuals act as members of social groups and interact with material and linguistic resources that are situated in and emerge from historical and cultural contexts. . . . ESD learning processes are, within a situated learning framework, seen as active and constructive meaning-making processes in which participation in a system of distributed knowledge and practice emerges in ways that are also contextually located and situated in the real socio-material world, out of which learning praxis emerges. In this way, ESD learning processes can therefore also be described as 'adaptation' to constraints and affordances, but they are also potentially transformative of these situations.
>
> *(Lotz-Sisitka et al. 2017, 53–54)*

A point of reference for Lotz-Sisitka and her colleagues interested in implementing ESD in South African schools is O-Donohugh's active learning framework which has been adapted to reflect ESD themes. As Lotz-Sisitka *et al.* point out, the framework captures key elements of ESD learning that draw on progressive themes, theories, and ideas. As the authors state,

> This active learning framework proposes the following important ESD learning processes: mobilising learners' prior knowledge and experience; identifying possible focus, risks or concerns that need to be investigated; seeking out new information on the issues or risks; undertaking enquiries; taking action; and reporting on findings.
>
> (Lotz-Sisitka et al. 2017, 77)

Closely related to ideas of transformative pedagogy are theories of social learning. At the most general level, social learning may be defined as 'a change in understanding that goes beyond the individual to become situated within wider social units or communities of practice through social interactions between actors within social networks' (Reed et al. 2010, 3). This type of learning may take place in a number of contexts, including, for example, attempts by governments to change the behaviours of populations in areas such as drink driving or other risky behaviours to processes of organisational learning. It has, however, increasingly been implicated in a range of sustainability initiatives. These may include, for example, efforts to change the behaviour and attitudes of individuals or projects involving multiple stakeholders engaged in tackling 'wicked' problems at the nexus of a number of sustainability challenges (e.g. Wals 2007).[1]

In their uptake of social learning theory, Lotz-Sisitka *et al.* adopt what they describe as a 'transformative, transgressive' approach to pedagogy (Lotz-Sisitka et al. 2015). At the heart of such an approach is a recognition that sustainability issues are deeply implicated in the colonial legacy in Africa as elsewhere – neoliberalism, amplified forms of commodification, patriarchy, dehumanisation, nature–culture bifurcations, and social injustices. It is argued that all of these features of what has been described in this book as the 'post-colonial condition' need to be transgressed for real transformations to sustainability to emerge. In this context, transformative, transgressive learning includes the pursuit of epistemic justice, solidarity building, metaphorical meaning making, social critique, optimal disruption, creating empathy, and reclaiming knowledge(s) and cultures lost (amongst other features of such learning) (Bengtsson 2019).

Returning to Schweisfurth's typology, a third *preparation narrative* that has particular policy relevance as we have seen in Chapter 6 is the development of so-called twenty-first-century skills and competencies described as a broad set of knowledge, skills, work habits, and character traits 'that are critically important to success in today's and tomorrow's world' (Siekmann and Korbel 2016, 27). For organisations such as the World Bank and OECD, the skills developed through enquiry-based, self-regulated learning such as problem-solving, communication, teamwork, and entrepreneurship are believed to support the development of knowledge economies. Preparation narratives have not been the preserve of dominant global agendas. They have also featured in Marxist-inspired efforts to transform education and training on the continent. For example, the *education with production* approach pioneered by Patrick van Rensburg in Botswana in association with the Brigade Movement was based on the idea of combining academic and vocational education (see Chisholm and Leyendecker 2008, for example). In this way, the idea was to break down the mental manual division of labour characteristic of class divided, formerly colonised societies and to develop a situated understanding of production as part of a wider social and environmental context. The approach had a wider resonance in the region and in important respects can be seen to prefigure the more recent development of ideas around transformative and social learning (discussed earlier).

The formalist approach

The second approach, formalism, draws on two key strands in the literature. Both provide a trenchant critique of progressivism, albeit from different starting positions. The first discourse is the formalism posited by writers such as Guthrie (e.g. 2003, 2018), Tabulawa (e.g. Tabulawa 1997, 2003) and Horn (2009), and which focuses on classroom practices. Drawing on an array of empirical evidence, these authors argue that there is no evidence that the introduction of progressive reforms has improved learning outcomes either in Western countries in which they originate or particularly in African contexts. Rather, they point to the numerous examples of concerted attempts at introducing progressive education on the continent that have failed, because they fail to take account of the realities of resource-starved African classrooms, often characterised by large class sizes, a lack of resources, and where teaching and learning are driven by the realities of high-stakes examination systems.[2]

A key theme for exponents of this kind of formalism is that progressive approaches are incongruent with the 'revelatory' epistemologies of traditional African cultures in which knowledge and truth are derived from ancestors and deities rather than from enquiry and transmitted from one generation to the next, reinforcing the authority of the teacher as the importer of knowledge. For commentators such as Tabulawa (2003), the imposition of progressive methods based on an individualised view of the learner can be seen as a form of cultural imperialism that complements the introduction of neoliberalism on the continent. As will be discussed in the next chapter, progressive approaches to pedagogy are also often critiqued for focusing too much on the life world of the learner. By emphasising the background and contexts brought to the classroom by learners, it is argued that progressive approaches place insufficient emphasis on exposing learners from disadvantaged backgrounds to the powerful, specialised knowledge of the disciplines as they are codified in the curriculum.

The implication for authors such as Guthrie is that rather than revert to progressive methods, African governments would be advised to build incrementally on the existing formal frame based on a teacher-centred approaches which are more congruent with classroom realities and with African cultural traditions. Guthrie makes the case as follows:

> Even where teachers are not particularly conscious of the underlying epistemology, formalism provides a model for the classroom with assumptions that students can and do share. Teachers' and students' intuitive, culturally derived assumptions about the nature of knowledge and the ways it ought to be transmitted, as well as their perceptions of their classroom roles and of the goals of schooling, influence their teaching and learning styles. Formalistic teaching is an organised processing of fixed syllabuses and textbooks, with emphasis on memorising basic facts and principles as a building block for future learning. . . . In formalistic classrooms, the teacher's basic role is to have knowledge and transmit it; the learner's basic role is to remember that knowledge,

preferably develop an understanding of it, and later act on it in an appropriate fashion and teach others eligible to receive it. The formalistic teacher is hierarchical and didactic, but uses formalism as a path to knowledge rather than promoting obedience as such. Limited overt teacher-student and student-student interaction (such as question and answer routines and paired work) may be permitted under conditions controlled by the teacher, who will predominantly use closed questions to check student recall (whereas the progressive teacher will tend to ask open questions to check student understanding). Students generally play a passive role in whole-class teaching, but they can share formalistic values with teachers and be complicit in maintaining them in a dominant role. Good formalistic teachers are authoritative rather than authoritarian, and physical punishment is not necessarily used as negative reinforcement.

(Guthrie 2018, 262–64).

In putting forward this view, Guthrie takes aim at the pejorative view of formal pedagogies often evident in the progressive literature in which formal teacher-centred approaches are portrayed as dull and repetitive, based on rote learning, a textbook culture, and underpinned by authoritarianism and the use of corporal punishment. Rather, he presents a typology of teacher-centred approaches spanning authoritarian to more democratic approaches. Guthrie also provides an explicit critique of the use of corporal punishment as reflecting teacher incompetence and insecurity. In keeping with the formal approach, his typology is very much focused on the role of the teacher rather than on the role of the learner/knower. The typology is also practitioner-oriented rather than theoretically driven, i.e. it does not espouse preference for any one form of classroom practice or theory of learning but in fact makes a cogent case for more African-based research into effective classroom pedagogical practices as an antidote to importing Western forms.

Nonetheless, the emphasis of much of the scholarship that falls within a formalist frame is consistent with a transmission model which is the dominant model in many African classrooms (Westbrook et al. 2013). Transmission models are based on behaviourist theories of learning which emerged from the work of thinkers such as Thorndike, Pavlov, and Skinner, amongst others. Based on laws of stimulus-response and classical and operant conditioning, they were used to explain the learning process through the use of rewards and sanctions. Transmission models are associated with teacher-centred practices such as whole class chanting, lecturing, demonstration, and copying from textbooks. The transmission model is also associated with teacher-led rather than teacher-centred approaches such as 'structured' or 'direct/explicit' instruction. This may involve forms of scripted learning in which teachers follow a specific sequence as in the teaching of phonics in early grade literacy, or the inculcation of basic numeracy skills, although this may subsequently develop into more student-centred activities at later stages of the learning process (Westbrook et al. 2013; Barrett 2007; Horn 2009).

In more recent years, some of the critiques advanced by formalists have been taken up in the literature on social realism (see Chapter 8). A key point of reference for social realists is the work of the British linguist and sociologist of education, Basil Bernstein. Bernstein was interested in the role of language in reproducing inequalities between working- and middle-class learners in the UK. He distinguished between 'elaborated' and 'restricted' sociolinguistic codes, where a code refers to the principles regulating meaning systems. The former makes explicit the hidden rules governing how knowledge and assessment are organised, whereas the latter refers to the everyday, taken-for-granted 'shorthand' language used by individuals and groups who have mastered elaborated codes (Bernstein 1962a, 1962b). Bernstein was interested in the extent to which the curriculum is delivered using restricted codes that favour middle-class learners from backgrounds where they are more likely to have had some prior exposure to these codes. Bernstein understands this subtle process of differentiation as being instrumental in reproducing class-based inequalities through the operation of everyday classroom practice. The idea of language codes draws attention to the subtle ways in which exclusion can take place in the classroom and thus has relevance for the African context.

The task for educators interested in facilitating epistemic access to knowledge for disadvantaged learners is to focus on making explicit the elaborated code as part of the teaching and learning process. In this regard, Bernstein in his later work contrasted two models of classroom interaction. In the so-called 'performance model', the teacher makes explicit to the students what and how they are to learn. There is a recognizable, strong framing, and lesson structure, with expected ways of behaving and standardised outcomes. The 'competence' model on the other hand is less explicit and more weakly framed, resulting in a more informal approach where the teacher responds to individual children's needs and in which learning outcomes are less overt (Bernstein 1990). It should be pointed out that the idea of weak and strong framing applies as much to vocational as academic subjects/disciplines in social realist thought.[3]

For supporters of Bernstein's ideas in the African context (Young and Muller 2013; Barrett, Hoadley, and Morgan 2018), more formally oriented 'performance' models are advocated to the extent that they make explicit the formal grammar of the disciplines and provide learners with the basic knowledge that will enable them to access this. In the context of literacy development, for example, developing phonemic awareness and reading fluency is often seen as a means to inculcate awareness of the formal structure of words and language. A similar case is often made for the teaching of grammar. In the teaching of science, the emphasis for formalists might be on developing through carefully sequenced enquiry and understanding of the axioms, key facts, theories, and methods that comprise the natural sciences rather than say an emphasis on interdisciplinary approaches which are often used to impart understanding of environmental risk, its social causes, and consequences. Many social realists do not espouse a specific theory of learning or advocate a specific classroom approach although in contexts such as South Africa, social realist perspectives have sometimes been used to justify a shift towards more prescribed forms of teaching that have focused – in the absence of strong teacher subject knowledge – on providing scripted lesson plans, teaching and learning materials, and teacher guides that make explicit the content and procedural knowledge that children require to master the formal curriculum.

The formalistic approach has also been subject to criticism. Whilst providing a trenchant critique of the relevance of progressive approaches for Africa, formalists pay relatively little attention to the deficiencies of more traditional approaches. For example, they pay relatively little attention to issues of inclusion in the access that different groups of learners have to the medium of instruction (Barrett 2007; Shalem 2018). With respect to the take up of Bernstein's work in the Africa context, performance models are advocated but there is little indication of how these are applied (if at all) and if they are beneficial to all learners given the intersection between academic literacy and proficiency in the medium of instruction (discussed later). There is also substantial evidence that classroom interactions are gendered in that girls in particular are often given less attention by teachers in class than are boys (Westbrook et al. 2013). This in turn suggests the need to pay great attention to the diversity of learner backgrounds and to the operation of intersecting regimes of inequality at a classroom level, issues that are very hard to address within a formalist frame in which traditional norms and values are taken as a 'given'.

In this regard, as Shalem (2018) has recently pointed out, evaluations of more scripted pedagogical approaches in South Africa have revealed that they tend to favour on average more advantaged learners and that there is limited evidence that they have succeeded in closing the attainment gap between relatively advantaged and disadvantaged schools. This would seem to suggest that there is no escaping the absolute necessity in investing in teachers' pedagogical knowledge *regardless of the pedagogical approach adopted*. This is because of the need to be able to constantly adapt teaching styles and classroom activities to the needs of learners and to recognise that no two classes, or indeed learners, are the same. The apparently inescapable need to invest in teacher quality would seem to have implications for one of the supposed 'advantages' of working within a more formal framework, namely, that it is cheaper and more cost-effective and is thus more sustainable and equitable in terms of existing education budgets (Guthrie 2018). Rather, recognising the necessity to differentiate in order to meet divergent learner needs inevitably means an increased investment, especially in the skills of the teaching force (see Chapter 5).

A key argument for a more formalistic approach as discussed earlier in relation to Guthrie and Tabulawa's work is the view that formal pedagogies are more relevant for African cultural contexts which are based on revelatory epistemologies. However, by emphasising the enduring nature of traditional belief systems, these authors are in danger of reifying African culture and reinforcing a form of reductionism in which African cultures are seen as homogenous, hermetically sealed off from a rapidly globalising world and impervious to change. Thus, whereas in some rural contexts, for instance, traditional cultures appear entrenched, processes of urbanisation and the interplay of different, sometimes conflicting, visions of modernity have led to forms of cultural hybridity. Further, the critique fails to adequately engage with the extent to which formalist approaches were also externally imposed as an aspect of colonial education (see Chapter 5). Indeed, it might be argued that the formalist approach introduced by the colonisers fundamentally clashes with pre-colonial forms of skills formation as suggested in Chapter 6. In this respect, a key issue in Africa as elsewhere in the postcolonial world is the continuing predominance of externally imposed pedagogies, whether formalistic or progressive in orientation and the need to focus on and nurture indigenous models of successful pedagogical practice where these exist.

For many progressivists, behaviourist theories of learning are seen to underpin the transmission or banking model of learning with all of their authoritarian overtones that are characteristic of formal systems. It is also argued that they correspond to a reductionist form of truth in which truth is reducible to what is apprehended by the senses and mirrored through absorption by the memory (Scott 2010). As such, behaviourist approaches stand in antithesis to the development of critical capabilities that can only be achieved through learning by doing.[4] For advocates of progressivism, democracy is realised through the processes of active learning and encouraging learner voice as well as through the integration of forms of citizenship. Many of the skills of democratic citizenship are developed through encouraging processes of learner (and educator) 'voice' and eliminating undemocratic practices such as corporal punishment. These aspects of the so-called 'hidden curriculum' are barely addressed in scholarship within the formal frame.

The polarisation of pedagogies implicit in both formalist and progressivist literature is also unhelpful in terms of learning because of the accumulation of evidence that learning is enhanced if classroom activities are able to build on learners' backgrounds and prior experiences even if this is to lead them towards more formalised knowledge/understanding contained in the formal curriculum (Westbrook et al. 2013; Barrett et al. 2007). As supporters of progressive approaches have pointed out (see, for example, Schudel 2017), critics of progressivism sometimes wrongly assume that progressive minded educators are focused only on the immediate experiences of leaners and therefore neglect the necessity that they should engage learners with the 'powerful knowledge' contained within the formal curriculum. Rather, it is argued, many educators who adopt a progressive approach might in fact aim to impart powerful knowledge but will use local and/or IK as a resource for facilitating the learning process through grounding the learning journey in contexts and ways of knowing that are familiar with the learner. Defenders of progressive approaches also acknowledge the role of the teacher in 'scaffolding' the learning process through providing meaningful learning activities that can lead the learner from localised to more global/universal understanding (Barrett 2007).

Towards a transformative pedagogy for Africa

In this section, an effort will be made to begin to outline an approach towards conceptualising pedagogy in a way that is relevant for the complexities and diversity represented by Africa education systems and that can provide a reference point for subsequent chapters. This involves drawing on the strengths of existing approaches but bringing these approaches into conversation with alternative theoretical perspectives. A starting point is through complexity theory (see Chapter 2) and in particular work that has sought to link the idea of complex adaptive systems with theories of learning (Davis and Sumara 2006; Haggis 2008, 2009). This is significant for the arguments of the chapter for two reasons. Firstly, it will be contended that it is helpful to see learning as emerging from the co-evolution of different systems, including those of the learner and their home and community environments, the classroom, the school, and the wider education system. Secondly, at a deep ontological level, as has been argued in Chapter 2, learning is a necessary characteristic of all adaptive systems and complexity theory can provide pointers as to how education systems can more effectively 'learn', i.e. become learning systems. Whilst this second aspect is more the focus of Chapter 10, some general principles will be introduced in this chapter.

Complexity and learning

It is worth considering some of the characteristics of complex systems that are particularly relevant for a consideration of learning. It will be recalled that the view of complexity theory outlined in Chapter 2 relates to the idea that the world is composed of multiple open dynamic systems. Whilst not all systems are complex, complex systems are composed of multiple elements that demonstrate autopoiesis (i.e. they are self-organising) operating in a state of dynamic equilibrium. The behaviour of systems is non-linear and therefore unpredictable with interactions within systems and between systems being characterised by the operation of positive and negative feedback loops. The properties of systems are constantly emergent. The nature of a system depends on its initial conditions such that two systems that appear similar can never be considered the same. Systems also emerge in relation to other related systems that comprise the wider 'fitness landscape'.

In relation to an understanding of learning within education systems, it is possible to conceive of several interpenetrative complex, adaptive systems at different scales that emerge in relation to each other. These include (but are not necessarily confined to) neurons within the brain, the mind (which comprises consciousness, perception, thinking, judgement, language and memory, etc.), the home and community environments of the learner, the classroom, the department, the school, the education district, the curriculum, subject disciplines, national assessment regimes, teacher education, etc. The understanding of complex systems leads to a view of learning as an essential property of all complex adaptive systems in response to emergent conditions and changes in the wider 'fitness landscape'. The implication is that learning at the level of the individual needs to be understood in a non-reductionist way, not as a fixed entity but as a property of individuals that emerges in relation to other individuals, natural and social systems that exist at different scales. That is to say that learning is not just 'situated' in the sense implied by social constructivism but at a much deeper ontological level in relation to an ecosystem comprised of other dynamic systems.

Davis and Sumara (2006) present a view of learning school mathematics in terms of the interpenetration of complex systems at different scales (see Figure 9.1).

Their model raises important points about theories of pedagogy and of learning. It indicates, for instance, the potential value of constructivist and social constructivist theories of learning as each draws attention to processes of learning from the vantage point of distinct but interpenetrating scales. Thus, constructivist theories focus on processes of cognition from the vantage point of the individual learner, whilst social constructivist theories take as their starting point the situated nature of individual learning and the distributed nature of cognition within collectives shaped by sociocultural dynamics and mediated by language and artefacts (e.g. teaching and learning materials and aids, ICTs, etc.). They also draw attention to different modalities by which learners engage with the content of the curriculum.

In agreement with both Barrett (2007) and Guthrie (Guthrie 2018) (both of whom have different starting points but arrive at similar conclusions), there is a need for grounded contextualised understanding of how different pedagogical practices articulate in the classroom context and in the context of delivering syllabi for different subjects in the curriculum to support learning. In keeping with

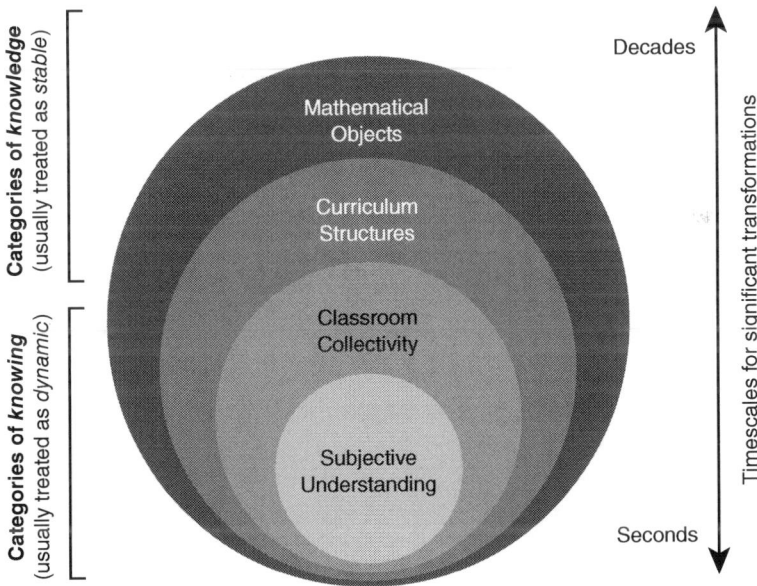

Figure 9.1 A model of learning mathematics in terms of complex, interpenetrating systems.

Source: Davis and Sumara 2006.

Barrett and unlike Guthrie, it is argued that attention needs to focus simultaneously on the active role of the teacher *and* of the learner. Here, the idea of what is termed the 'pedagogical core' is useful. The idea builds on Elmore's (2008) concept of the 'instructional core'. For the purposes of this book it has been reinterpreted in line with Alexander's more expansive view of pedagogy and to a view of classroom practice that is embedded in wider social, cultural, and environmental systems. Elmore cogently argues that there are only three ways to improve student learning at scale:

> You can raise the level of the content that students are taught. You can increase the skill and knowledge that teachers bring to the teaching of that content. And you can increase the level of students' active learning of the content. That's it. Everything else is instrumental. That is, everything that's not in the instructional core can only effect student learning and performance by, in some way, influencing what goes on inside the core. Schools don't improve through political and managerial incantation; they improve through the complex demanding work of teaching and learning.
>
> (Elmore 2008, 1)

In the language of complexity theory, learning arises from creating coherence between the systems represented by each of these elements. The concept of the pedagogical core draws attention to the active role of both the teacher and the learner in bridging the gap between the background knowledge and experience of the learner and the content of the curriculum. It therefore helps to break down the unhelpful dualism between progressive and formalist frames.

A further implication to flow from this is that any change to one element, whether in the nature of the backgrounds of learners, the content of the curriculum, or the agency of the teacher, requires commensurate changes to the other two elements if coherence is to be maintained. For Elmore, other aspects of the education system, including, for example, school leadership, the nature of the curriculum and of teacher training and assessment systems, are relevant insofar as they impact on the pedagogical core. The idea of the pedagogical core therefore focuses attention in particular on the kinds of activities that take place in classrooms that more or less effectively bridge the gap between knowledge and the knower but also on the value of an institution-wide approach to supporting coherence at the pedagogical core. For Elmore, as in other areas of professional practice such as medicine, it is the attention that is given to ongoing monitoring and evaluation of these activities by teachers and supervisors, themselves actively involved in the classroom, which leads to improved learning outcomes. In the context of disciplinary, subject-based teaching, it draws attention to the fundamental importance of subject-specific pedagogical knowledge as it is at this level that it becomes possible to drill down to the 'nitty gritty' of 'what works' in different classroom environments, for different groups of learners and in relation to specific subjects. The view of complex learning leads, therefore, to the antithesis of scripted pedagogy in which the active agency of the teacher and other educational professionals is explicitly denied.

In this respect, a challenge to the coherence of education systems is that they are often subject to competing demands and 'global pedagogies' pushed by different donors. For example, the highly formalistic phonics approach to reading favoured by the World Bank and that forms the basis for the Early Grade Reading Assessment that is widely used in Africa (Gove and Wetterberg 2011) often stands in tension with approaches that favour reading for meaning and are advocated by many donors and NGOs. Tension and difference in pedagogical approach is not necessarily a 'bad thing'; however, provided coherence can be achieved at the 'pedagogical core' as well as at the level of how the moral purpose of education is defined in education systems (Chapter 10) and in the links between various subsystems, including those relating to classroom practice, curriculum, assessment, and teacher education.

An example of the importance of coherence in pedagogical approaches is provided by Vare and Scott in their discussion of models of ESD (Vare and Scott 2007). Whilst it has been suggested earlier that the view of transformative ESD as involving situated learning finds support in the scholarly literature, Vare and Scott in fact distinguish between two broad approaches towards ESD learning in practice. Both approaches are evident in efforts across the world to implement ESD as the DESD final report suggests (UNESCO 2014b). The first, ESD 1, is described as learning *for* sustainable development. It aims to promote/facilitate changes in behaviour with respect to SD through promoting awareness of the kinds of informed and skilled behaviours and ways of thinking that are considered important for tackling SD challenges. It is suggestive of a formalistic approach to teaching and learning. ESD 2 on the other hand is described in terms of learning *as* sustainable development. It is fundamentally concerned with building capacity to think critically about (and beyond) what experts say and to test sustainability development ideas so as to explore the contradictions inherent in sustainable living. ESD 2 contains many of the characteristics of a progressive approach in that it emphasises the process of learning and is based on the active engagement of learners in activities that will develop critical thinking. Interestingly, and despite professing a bias towards ESD 2, Vare and Scott argue that both forms are potentially relevant for promoting ESD learning provided coherence can be maintained between the different approaches at the level of learning objectives and moral purpose about what it is important to learn with respect to ESD.

Returning to Davis and Sumara's model, Figure 9.1 is also interesting for flagging a temporal dimension in relation to transforming system dynamics. 'Categories of knowing' (which the authors use to refer to systems and processes linked to the act of knowing and incorporate both the cognitive and situated sociocultural dimensions of learning) are treated as relatively dynamic with relatively short timescales in terms of transformation. Curriculum structures and mathematical objects by way of contrast are treated as more stable systems with consequently longer timescales for transforming these systems. In relation to the mathematical objects, this is related to the way in which disciplines such as mathematics evolve. This has implications for debates about decolonising the curriculum and the need to think strategically about the broader system of knowledge production, distribution, and exchange in Africa and globally (see Chapter 9). In relation to the curriculum, the relatively long timespans involved in curriculum change relate to the complexities of designing and implementing curricula. In Chapter 8, it was argued that from a decolonising perspective this involves engaging with the wider politics of curriculum reform.

Missing for Davis and Sumara's schema, however, is reference to inequality and power. In this regard, Haggis's (2008) understanding is relevant. Haggis discusses how each of the systems implicated at each scale co-evolves in relation to wider, intersecting regimes of inequality. For Haggis, understanding the implications of different regimes of inequality in relation to learning can happen at different scales. She focuses in particular on the school/classroom context in which inequalities in access and outcomes to a good quality education can be seen to operate at a group level. This might involve overt or implicit forms of discrimination of some groups or favouring on the part of the teacher of other groups.

There is evidence, for instance, that some teachers have higher expectations of boys than girls in subjects such as mathematics and science and this impacts on girls' likelihood of pursuing STEM-related subjects (Tikly et al. 2018). Girls might be less likely to be included in STEM-related streams as a consequence. Other forms of discrimination of racialised or sexualised violence and bullying may impact the outcomes for some groups of learners. A key source of inequality at the classroom level is in relation to the medium of instruction and arises where learners are expected to learn in a second or third language and little provision is made for this. Importantly for Haggis, a key focus for research is the extent to which regimes of inequality intersect at a group or individual level and present multiple barriers for some individuals and groups to engaging with the curriculum. This has implications for policy relating, for example, to the medium of instruction and in supporting schools to tackle discrimination as well as for other areas such as teacher education.

Conclusion

The aim of this chapter has been to present an overall approach towards conceptualising pedagogy that has resonance for the complex and highly unequal contexts represented by African education systems. It has been argued that although formalist and progressive frames each share strengths and weaknesses in the Africa context, they in fact represent an unhelpful dualism or, as Barrett (2007) has argued, an unnecessary polarisation of pedagogy. It was also argued that the thrust of language-in-education policy in many African countries, whilst favouring indigenous elites, is detrimental to learners from disadvantaged backgrounds. In relation to both classroom pedagogy and language-of-instruction policy, the role of educators is crucial in creating coherence at the pedagogical core so as to improve learning outcomes. This view stands in antithesis to the current trend towards scripted forms of pedagogy. Supporting successful pedagogical practice also requires a coherent, systemic response whether at the level of policy or of the organisation in the support that is provided to educators and learners. Whilst the chapter has reviewed a range of evidence concerning effective pedagogical practice, it is itself an aspect of the postcolonial condition in education that there is a need for more African-based research that can seek to capture and scale up successful practice.

Notes

1 There are many examples of social learning projects in areas ranging from agriculture to health and other areas of environmental and social development. By way of illustration, Lotz-Sisitka *et al.* identify two examples in the African context. The first is a project bringing together academics, the community, local government, and civil society in the area of water and food security. The project operates at the nexus of a number of sustainability challenges, including drought conditions, climate variability and change, poverty, historical marginalization and exclusion from sustainable and viable land use, and modernization cultures influencing youth. The second example is a project located in the Chilwa Basin in Malawi which focused on the nexus between food and water security affecting agriculture, poverty, and insecure economic activity and involved a similarly diverse group of stakeholders (Lotz-Sisitka et al. 2016).

2 See Guthrie (2018) for a comprehensive account and Schweisfurth (2013a) for a more sympathetic account of the failure of progressive reform.

3 This is significant for the African context and for CESA and *Agenda 2063* given the emphasis on vocational education and on generic skills. In discussing vocational subjects, Young (2008) invokes another concept from Bernstein's work, namely, that of 'vertical' and 'horizontal' discourses. Whereas the latter refers to the hierarchically organised knowledge developed by knowledge specialists, the latter refers to the everyday, more diffuse and context-dependent, knowledge that whilst practically useful in specific work situations is not necessarily transferrable. Accountancy and computer science are examples of hierarchically organised vocational subjects developed by experts in 'communities of trust'. These are considered on a par in terms of their claims to objectivity as traditional disciplinary subjects. Newer vocational school subjects such as leisure and tourism or, in the Africa context, newer subjects such as life skills would be considered more akin to horizontal discourses in that the kinds of skills imparted are linked to specific contexts (e.g. booking a flight in leisure and tourism). In this respect, Young has sounded a note of caution about including the kinds of skills identified by the World Economic Forum. It is suggested that there is an implicit danger in social realist discourse of perpetuating unhelpful binaries including those between horizontal and vertical discourses.

4 However, it is also important to acknowledge that there may be points in the learning process where practices of rote learning have a place, especially in lower levels of schooling where there is a need to memorise basic facts (learning times tables in mathematics is a possible example here) as a basis for higher-order conceptual development (Horn 2009).

10 Towards a transformative agenda

Introduction

The aim of this concluding chapter is to seek to outline the basis for a transformative agenda in African education and training. As such the chapter also serves as a means to summarise the insights gleaned from previous chapters and to offer a way forward. In keeping with the view of complex systems that underpins the book, the chapter will not seek to offer prescriptions for reform. This would be counter to the view of the importance of context and of the role of African based policy makers, practitioners, and other stakeholders in civil society who are centrally implicated in the change process in identifying and acting on priorities. Rather, the chapter will offer suggestions about an overall approach to reform based on the analysis provided in previous chapters and the wider evidence about system-level change from the literature.

Two key arguments are developed in this chapter. The first is the importance of building a counter-hegemonic movement organised around a project of implementing a transformative ESD. This is to recognise the fundamentally political and ethical nature of transformative change. In broad terms this must include building as broad a coalition as possible both within the state and civil society and at different scales and developing an overarching rationale and vision for change. The second argument is the need for a systemic response to implementing ESD that must also focus on developing sustainable systems of education and training. That is to say, that they must be based on strong indigenous systems leadership, committed to overcoming dependency on foreign assistance in education, putting learning at the centre of reform, developing learning systems that are able to engage with complex change, and investing in educators as agents of change. In setting out the arguments, the chapter will engage with recent literature on education system change, including recent interventions by the World Bank as well as more scholarly literature written from a complexity perspective. Although it will be suggested that some of this literature offers valuable insights for transforming African education systems, much of this literature originates from North America and the Western Europe and so an effort will be made to critically consider its relevance for the African context. The chapter will commence, however, with a consideration of the politics of system reform.

In both the first and second halves of the chapter, discussion focuses on related aspects of system change. It should be pointed out that these are not intended as representing discrete steps that need to be followed in a linear fashion. Rather, and consistent with the view of complex systems, these should be seen as interconnected elements when considered as a whole are necessary for moving education and training systems towards a tipping point, away from their current path dependencies linked to unsustainable development and towards systems aligned to a vision of a transformative ESD.

Towards a counter-hegemonic movement for transformative change

A key argument advanced in the first half of the book is the fundamentally political nature of education governance at the global, regional, and local scales. As will be suggested in the following sections, this involves building a broad coalition for change, articulating the causes of unsustainable development and of the learning crisis, developing an alternative counter-hegemonic vision through critically engaging with global and regional agendas, and understanding the role of social movements and of intellectuals in supporting processes of change.

Building a broad-based coalition for change

Building a coalition in support of a vision for SD and ESD is itself both a necessary and complex task but one that is not addressed in global or regional agendas. Chapters 4 and 5 focused on the governance of education at different scales from the global to the local. The processes of policy making at each scale were presented as involving the bringing together within governance regimes of different interests and voices organised around hegemonic and counter-hegemonic projects relating to SD and ESD. Developing such a coalition requires an active effort on the part of actors within the state and civil society. It requires a process of 'articulation' (Chapter 2) in which a vision for SD and for ESD is aligned with the interests of diverse groups. These may be factions within the ruling elite, practitioners, and researchers or groups in civil society. For example, in Chapter 5, there was discussion of a range of actors in civil society with differing interests in the education system from NGOs, religious organisations, the private sector, and a multitude of social movements. These clearly represent at times conflicting interests and so developing a coalition around implementing a common vision of ESD is necessarily a complex and contested process involving in Gramsci's terms a 'war of position' fought within the 'trenches' of both the state and civil society (Gramsci 1992). Here there is a role in Gramsci's terms for both organic and traditional intellectuals in facilitating and leading change (see the following). Key to the success of any counter-hegemonic strategy is the ability to recognise competing interests and to link the emerging vision of ESD to core demands and issues faced by different groups whether these be social movements interested in environmental justice, campaigning against privatisation, the fight against HIV/AIDS, the rights of indigenous people, or women's groups campaigning for gender justice (see Chapter 6).

The operation of governance regimes, however, also needs to be seen against the backdrop of world order, developmental regionalism, and of the postcolonial state as well as in relation to the operation of different kinds of institutional, conditional, structural, and productive power that gives rise to intersecting regimes of inequality. Returning to Sen and Fraser's work, these inequalities lead to differences in the capacity and degree of voice possessed by different groups to participate in decision-making processes. These differences need to be both recognised and addressed through attention to the processes by which policy is defined and the voices of different groups included in decision-making (discussed later). In relation to Fraser's understanding of global justice, democratisation involves simultaneously a concern with strengthening the voice of African governments in processes of global governance and seeking to deepen democratic participation, particularly for the poor and marginalised in African countries themselves.

The idea that policy is contested at different scales has been a recurring theme in the book. In Chapters 4 and 5, for example, the development of global education policy was seen in relation to processes of contemporary globalisation and against the backdrop of a changing world order. Nonetheless, and in keeping with Held *et al.*'s understanding, globalisation was presented as a contradictory process, opening up the possibilities for the development of counter-hegemonic struggles in global civil society. In Chapter 5, the model of developmental regionalism, whilst supportive of the interests of regional elites, was also presented as a contested set of processes. In this respect, reference was made to the concept of transformative regionalism (Mittleman 2000). Consideration was also given to the nature of the postcolonial state and to the possibilities for organisations in civil society to contest the interests of indigenous elites and to develop counter-hegemonic social movements in support of transformative change. Understanding the nature of different postcolonial states and indeed of developmental regionalism and of contemporary globalisation is therefore a prerequisite for imagining the possibilities as well as the limitations for developing a counter-hegemonic movement in support of a transformative ESD (see the following section).

Articulate the causes of unsustainable development and of the learning crisis

A first step in building a counter-hegemonic alliance of actors committed to implementing a transformative ESD is to articulate the nature and causes of unsustainable development on the continent and of the learning crisis as a basis for a call to action for change. As noted in Chapter 1, *Agenda 2063* and CESA attempt to set out the nature of the sustainability challenges facing the continent as well as those involved in transforming education systems so that they can play a role in tackling these challenges. It was argued in Chapter 3, however, that in the case of *Agenda 2063*, the analysis does not go far enough in understanding the causes of unsustainable development which it was suggested are deeply rooted in the postcolonial condition and need to be understood in relation to the colonial legacy and Africa's position in relation to wider processes of globalisation. To the extent that regional agendas elide issues of power and inequality and in the context of the analysis of the nature of developmental regionalism and of the postcolonial state offered in Chapter 5, they can be seen to operate at a rhetorical level to support dominant interests at regional and local levels.

In this respect, it is important to acknowledge the silences in regional agendas with respect, for example, to the extent to which indigenous elites as well as foreign interests benefit from the current path dependency of African economies on extractive economic practices that have contributed to poverty, inequality, and environmental catastrophe. It is also important to point out the silences in regional agendas with respect to the role of social movements in civil society in bringing about transformative change. Here it is important, as was argued in Chapter 5, to consider the changing nature of social movement activism on the continent. There is evidence that this is undergoing further shifts. Some contemporary social movements such as the #Fees Must Fall and #Rhodes Must Fall movements in South Africa, for example, as well as the recent civil protests in Sudan tend to be more organically networked potentially signalling a shift in the nature of social movements on the continent. As Choudry and Vally (2018) have recently argued, although the nature of social movement activism has changed, there is much that contemporary social movements can learn from previous eras of social activism and change.

Of particular relevance is the need to highlight the role of education and training systems since colonial times in supporting processes of unsustainable development linked to the postcolonial condition. For example, a key theme of the book has been the role of education systems in reproducing regimes of inequality, including those based on class, race, gender, and rurality through providing highly fragmented and unequal access to a good-quality education. In this regard, as was argued in Chapter 7, there has been a positive correspondence between the way that education and training systems have evolved on the one hand and the nature of the labour market in many African societies on the other. Education systems have also largely failed to prepare learners for the challenges posed by increasing environmental risks and have also often served to reproduce violence rather than support peace building and conflict resolution. Furthermore, the effects of SAPs and continued austerity under neoliberalism have been to reduce the capacity for African-led development and to increase dependency on foreign development assistance. The continued Eurocentric nature of the curriculum and valorisation of global at the expense of local languages has served to further entrench dependency. The effects of dependency are to limit the possibilities for genuinely African-led development, a point that is taken up in the following.

Chapter 1 also set out the nature of the so-called 'learning crisis' facing education systems. The idea of a learning crisis has been popularised by the World Bank amongst other organisations as a powerful rationale for whole system change (Bank 2018). It is therefore worth critically exploring how the Bank characterises the nature of the crisis. The Bank identifies three dimensions of the crisis, namely, 'poor learning outcomes', 'schools failing learners', and 'systems failing schools'. The recommendations set out in the report seek to address these dimensions, namely, to assess learning to make it a serious goal; to act on evidence – to make schools work for learners; and to align actors – to make the whole system work for learning. However, from the point of view of this book, both the analysis offered by the Bank and the proposed solutions are partial thus limiting understanding of the nature of the crisis and calling into question the relevance of the proposed 'solutions'.

For example, the World Bank report identifies the lack of reliable assessment data as limiting the ability of education systems to track the progress of different groups of disadvantaged learners over time and as a means to support processes of teaching and learning. In Chapter 9, a case was made for the importance of assessment for learning as a means of supporting teaching and learning. Missing from the World Bank report, however, is a more critical engagement with the nature of global assessment regimes, including their effects in dictating the curriculum and pedagogy (see the following pages). The report also does not problematise the question of what ought to be assessed, i.e. the nature of the curriculum itself. In Chapter 7, a critique was provided of some of the assumptions concerning the curriculum, including the emphasis given to the development of so-called twenty-first-century skills and to the knowledge economy by the World Bank and regional agendas. Here discussion focused on the narrow, instrumental nature of these skills and competencies and their limited relevance for the African continent. In contrast to global and regional agendas, Chapter 7 argued instead for the need to link skills and competencies to the functionings that African governments and stakeholders including communities themselves have reason to value the importance of informed public debate and advocacy at different scales of governance in identifying these. Furthermore, the report does not consider the relationship between different kinds of assessment practices and their implications for pedagogy.

The report also identifies the lack of capacity at different levels of the system to make use of assessment and other relevant evidence to improve learning outcomes. The report points to the apparent abundance of evidence that education systems can draw on to ensure that schools 'work for learners'. In Chapter 2, however, a critique was advanced of the 'what works' agenda. It was suggested for example, that the reliance of the World Bank and other multilateral organisations on the results of RCTs in particular does not take account of the nature of complexity and the importance of contextually grounded research evidence, including practitioner-led research, in supporting evidence-based practice to address the learning crisis. It was argued in Chapter 9, for example, the importance of developing both the professional capabilities of educators and indigenous research capacity to facilitate the development of more grounded understandings of successful pedagogical practices for improving learning outcomes in Africa. The World Bank report (in keeping with CESA) also points to the effects of different kinds of disadvantage linked to the home background of learners and the lack of specific inputs preventing different groups of disadvantaged learners from achieving desired learning outcomes. In Chapter 7, a case was made for the importance of better understanding how different factors relating to the home backgrounds of learners and the availability of resources interact in shaping the capabilities (opportunity freedoms) of different groups of learners.

However, in addition to learner background and resource input factors, the book has identified other kinds of characteristics of education and training systems as being highly significant in understanding the capabilities of disadvantaged learners. In Chapter 5, for example, consideration was given to the prevalence of violence including corporal punishment and sexualised violence that impacts on the capabilities of learners. Consideration was also given to the effects of the privatisation of education and training in perpetuating class-based inequalities. In Chapter 8, discussion focused on the impact of highly content-driven and cognitively demanding curricula coupled with the prevalence of teacher-centred approaches in limiting the access of disadvantaged groups to the formal curriculum. Discussion also turned to the burning language question in African education and the negative implications of early exit bilingual models on learning compounded by other factors such as class and gender. Further, in Chapter 9, attention was given to the Eurocentric nature of the curriculum that limits the accessibility of learners to relevant knowledge that can assist in realising transformational change. These factors are deeply engrained in the fabric of education systems inherited since colonial times but are not addressed in the report.[1] More research is needed to understand the role of education systems themselves in perpetuating inequalities as a necessary basis for understand how education systems can be transformed so as to genuinely address the interests of disadvantaged groups.

The World Bank report identifies factors at a systemic level that militate against improved learning outcomes. The first of these are issues of coherence between, for example, the curriculum, pedagogy, assessment systems, and teacher training. The need for coherence between system elements was also argued in the book, particularly in Chapter 9 in the context of a discussion of a pedagogy for Africa. Missing from the World Bank analysis, however, is a consideration of the effects of sometimes contradictory global pedagogies and forms of assessment in contributing to incoherence in processes of teaching and learning. A second issue identified in the report is a lack of alignment between the interests of politicians, bureaucrats, the private sector, and other key stakeholders and the need to reorient education and training systems to focus on improved learning outcomes. Realigning interests around improved learning outcomes is, however, more than simply a rational-technical exercise of convincing different stakeholders of the importance of a focus on learning as is implied in the report. Rather, as already indicated, it involves processes of informed public debate, advocacy, and struggle in the state and civil society. This in turn means taking into account the undemocratic nature of regimes of governance in education at different scales and the effects of different kinds of power in privileging some voices and perspectives whilst silencing others. This is especially the case because, as argued below, it is not simply a question of reorienting education systems to focus more on learning that is at stake. At issue also are fundamental questions about the moral purpose of education and training and how this relates to competing visions of sustainable development.

Develop a counter-hegemonic vision for ESD

It is through clearly articulating the nature and causes of unsustainable development and of the learning crisis and how these play out in specific contexts that it becomes possible to begin to identify possible solutions. A key figure in the literature on education system reform, Michael Fullan, develops a concept of 'moral purpose' that goes some way towards providing a basis for conceiving the underlying ethical nature of education and training policy and as a means for guiding reform in complex, turbulent times (Fullan 1993, 1999, 2003). Moral purpose can be seen to constitute a key part of the rationale for hegemonic and counter-hegemonic projects. In keeping with the analysis provided in earlier chapters, moral purpose is never straightforward. It is always contested by different interest groups within the state and civil society. In Chapter 3, consideration was given to the often contradictory nature of discourses about both sustainable development and education for sustainable development. In this respect, both SD and ESD were considered as 'floating signifiers' that 'articulate' (i.e. discursively bring into relation to each other) different interest groups and ways of thinking about development.

A critique was offered in Chapter 7 of dominant approaches to ESD and SD, including human capital and modernisation theories which continue to exert a hegemonic influence in relation to global and regional agendas. Whilst dominant theories were subject to a range of criticisms, some common cross-cutting themes are that they tend to elide issues of power and inequality; are based on a limited idea of sustainable development as equivalent to economic growth; are Eurocentric in their assumptions about the nature of progress and of modernity itself; and are idealistic in assuming an unproblematic and linear relationship between investments in education and training and 'development'. In Chapter 3 an attempt was made to articulate an alternative vision of social and environmental justice that, it was suggested, might guide thinking about the nature of ESD or, in Fullan's terms, the basis for an alternative moral purpose. Achieving a transformative ESD was presented in terms of both increasing access to a good-quality education at all levels of the education and training system whilst simultaneously redefining what is meant by a good-quality education in a way that is consistent with the principles of social and environmental justice.

The complexities of moral purpose were also illustrated with respect to a critical engagement with specific aspects of global and regional agendas and how these relate to a transformative ESD. For example, Chapter 7 outlined alternative ways of articulating the relationship between education systems and the economy based on a more expansive view of the economy to take account of the social dimensions of production and exchange, the significance of domestic labour, and the effects of economic development on the natural environment and the need for citizenship education. It was argued in this respect the importance of moving beyond the narrow instrumentalist nature of current skills for development discourses and to think more expansively and creatively not only about the relationship of education to the economic domain but to social development and to the environment. In Chapter 8, consideration was given to the complexities of demands to decolonise the curriculum. It was argued that decolonising involves both ensuring epistemic access for historically marginalised groups to 'powerful knowledge' codified in the disciplines which remains largely 'knowledge of the powerful' whilst simultaneously seeking to transgress the current Eurocentric nature of the disciplines through reorienting knowledge production towards meeting the challenges of unsustainable development and in the interests of transformative sustainable development. Chapter 9, on the other hand, sought to critique traditional approaches to teaching and learning and to develop a conception of a transformative pedagogy that is relevant for the African context and that takes account of the burning language question. In each case, the arguments were framed in terms of a view of social and environmental justice. However, and in contrast to the World Bank discourse, all of these ideas were presented as complex and contested in nature with ethical and political implications. In this respect, and central to Sen's ideas about ethics, is their comparative nature (Sen 2011) and the importance of informed public debate, advocacy, and struggle in fleshing out valued capabilities and functionings that could underpin a vision of SD and ESD.[2]

The role of intellectuals in developing a counter-hegemonic vision

Intellectuals have a critical role to play in developing a counter-hegemonic vision of ESD. Here reference is made to Gramsci's (1992) ideas about the role of intellectuals. Gramsci had a broad conception of intellectuals as including not only academics, journalists, artists, teachers, and other 'custodians of culture' of a particular epoch but also bureaucrats, technicians, managers, politicians, and others who play a role in producing and reproducing the dominant ideas and values of the day. Gramsci distinguished between traditional and organic intellectuals. The former are linked to tradition and to past intellectuals and often see themselves as autonomous from wider processes of social struggle and change. Organic intellectuals, on the other hand, emerge through processes of class struggle and are able to exercise intellectual and moral leadership in relation to hegemonic and counter-hegemonic projects linked to specific class interests. Extending the conception somewhat and with reference to the African context, organic intellectuals can be understood to play a role in articulating multiple interests besides those based on class organised around the recognition of multiple regimes of inequality and the work of diverse social movements including indigenous groups, women's movements, landless people's organisations, campaigns against privatisation, etc. Organic intellectuals have a potentially critical role to play in identifying the nature and causes of unsustainable development and developing a coherent counter-hegemonic vision for SD and ESD.

Following Gramsci, there is also a key role for traditional intellectuals such as teachers and researchers in higher education to play a role in supporting the development of counter-hegemony through identifying with the struggles of social movements against unsustainable development and in supporting the development of organic intellectuals in civil society. In Chapter 8, for example, there was discussion of the potential role for teachers to get involved in processes of social learning in the community as a contribution to decolonising the curriculum whilst in Chapter 9 discussion focused on the potential role for researchers in higher education in facilitating forms of social learning through forms of knowledge co-production. Traditional intellectuals working within the formal education system also have a critical role to play in advocating and facilitating change within the context of system reform which is the topic of the second part of the chapter.

Realising complex change through developing sustainable education and training systems

In this second part of the chapter, attention will turn to the challenges of realising complex change. This involves understanding education and training systems as complex systems. In each of the sections that follows, consideration will be given to factors that when considered together can contribute to the development of sustainable systems of education and training which are necessary for implementing ESD. In developing the arguments, the section will draw on recent research conducted in Rwanda that sought to understand the conditions under which the Rwandan education and training system can support innovation in education (Tikly and Milligan 2017; MINEDUC 2015). As will be discussed, the research provided valuable insights into the challenges of realising system change.

Placing an ontology of learning at the heart of system reform

As we have seen, the World Bank in its recent report on the learning crisis (2018) argues for learning to be placed at the centre of education reform efforts. It was also suggested earlier, however, that the underlying view of learning is limited in World Bank discourse. For example, in describing the learning crisis, the Bank elides key aspects of the underlying causes of the crisis. It has been argued in Chapter 9 that learning needs to be understood in terms of the complex interaction of systems at different scales (see also Tikly 2015). In this respect, learning involves the complex interaction of natural/biological systems and processes with the systems of knowledge, culture, and language in which they are situated. Importantly, the capabilities of learners to learn are impacted by a range of home background and community factors as well as by the operation of regimes of inequality and these also need to be understood and made explicit as part of an ontology of learning. A full ontology of learning also needs to take account of what is to be learned, which in the context of the book is the content of a transformative ESD.

Developing systemic responses to the learning crisis

In Chapter 9, it was argued that a focus on learning means a focus on creating coherence at the 'pedagogical core' (i.e. coherence between the level of the content learners are taught, the knowledge and skills of teachers, and the level of active learning on the part of students). It was argued that facilitating this coherence is essential for promoting learning. Other parts of the education and training system, for example, the curriculum, assessment, and teacher training, are important insofar as they create coherence at the pedagogical core. The need for coherence across different sub-sectors of the education and training system as well as between education and training and other systems has also been made in relation to other areas of development identified in the book. In Chapter 6, for example, reference was made to the literature on education in post-conflict contexts which has identified the need for holistic, systemic responses in which peace education is articulated to initiatives aimed at eliminating violence from education system as well as to wider processes of peace building. Similarly, in Chapter 7, it was argued that efforts to green the economy require coherence between the development of green skills in education and training systems and wider policy shifts across the economic, environmental, and related domains. It was also argued that the development of global citizenship education needs to be clearly articulated to wider processes of democratisation at the local, regional, and global scales if it is to be meaningful rather than simply rhetorical in nature. In Chapter 8, discussion focused on how education systems as a whole might be oriented to supporting processes of decolonising the curriculum through articulating transformative practices in knowledge production in higher education with transformation in the school curriculum. Attention was also given to how a systemic response might support the development of linguistic capabilities. These examples are not exhaustive!

Facilitating system leadership

The concept of system leadership is increasingly invoked in literature on system reform as a means for enabling collective leadership in order to develop systemic responses to intractable problems.[3] Globally, the interest in system leadership is often linked to the growing interest in system improvement (e.g. Mourshed, Chijioke, and Barber 2010). System leadership is conceived as a form of leadership required in order to develop coherent approaches to change through the sharing of successful practice across diverse communities of practice, including schools, district offices, different stakeholder groups, parents, and communities (Hopkins and Higham 2007; Fullan 2005). By its nature then, system leadership has both top-down and bottom-up dimensions (i.e. it is concerned simultaneously with the work of policy makers in facilitating the conditions for change and with the development of leadership at different scales of the system as a prerequisite for realising change.

As Mason explains, system leadership is particularly important in relation to an understanding of complexity in education:

> In the complexity of the educational environment, the plethora of relevant constituent elements – agents and structures – includes teachers, students, parents, community leaders, the state and its education departments and policies, economic structures and business organisations, NGOs, agencies, and so on. Intervention to differing but sufficient extents in each of these areas is what would probably be necessary to shift a prevailing ethos in education. In other words, change and sustainable development in education, at whatever level, are not so much a consequence of effecting change in one particular factor or variable, no matter how powerful the influence of that factor. It is more a case of generating momentum in a new direction by attention, as I have argued, to as many factors as possible. . . . Such a conclusion asks a lot more of governments and their education departments, of research analysts and policy-makers, and of donors, aid agencies and development specialists, than has typically been asked in the past.
>
> (Mason 2014, 6)

At a general level, the idea of system leadership would seem to accord with the challenges faced by African governments in the move from a priority on access under the MDG regime to a focus on learning under the SDG regime and in particular to the complexities of engaging with the learning crisis.

Much of the existing literature on system leadership, however, comes out of North America, Western Europe, and other highly industrialised contexts. Much less attention has focused on low- and middle-income countries such as those on the African continent. It is, therefore, important to critically consider the relevance of the term for the African context. Firstly, the idea of system leadership needs to be seen in relation to the expanded view of education systems presented in Chapter 2, i.e. as incorporating both formal sites of learning within the state (including schools, TVET centres, universities, etc.) and informal sites in civil society (e.g. adult basic education and processes of social learning in the context of social movements). This requires paying attention to the development of leadership capability both in the state and in civil society. Secondly, the idea of system leadership needs to be seen in relation to an analysis of developmental regionalism and of the postcolonial state such as that provided in Chapter 6 as well as in relation to struggles for greater democracy – a point that is developed in the following section.

Investing in educators as agents of transformative change

The central role of educators as potential agents of transformative change has been discussed at different points in the book. In Chapter 8, the case was made for the need to develop the capacity of educators so that they are able to respond to the diverse needs of learners. In Chapters 8 and 9, there was also discussion of the potentially transformative role of educators in relation to processes of social learning to address sustainability challenges in the community. In this respect, and in relation to the discussion in the previous section, educators are integral to processes of system leadership as they are on the front line of system improvement. These concerns whilst partially recognised in CESA are inadequately addressed in regional agendas. If teachers are to play a transformative role in relation to ESD, a key focus must be the development of their own professional capabilities. There was discussion in Chapter 7 of the disjuncture between the provision of forms of initial and continuing professional development and the professional learning needs of teachers in meeting the demands of teaching increasingly diverse groups of learners often in extremely challenging delivery contexts. Regional agendas are also contradictory in their implications regarding teachers. In Chapter 6, for example, discussion focused on issues of teacher governance, including the effects of the increasing privatisation of schooling on undermining teacher autonomy and professionalism through an emphasis on scripted forms of pedagogy and the limited voice that teachers have in the policy-making process. These factors militate against a transformative agenda. Rather, it is argued that efforts to improve the quality of the teaching force require an holistic, system-wide response. For example, it requires a stronger match between teacher education, the content of the curriculum, and the demands of teaching and learning. There is also the need to approach issues of teacher motivation and quality in a systemic way that addresses simultaneously the status and pay and conditions of service of teachers with issues of teacher supervision and accountability.

Democratising the governance of education

Often in the international literature, issues of governance in education are couched in narrow, technicist terms to issues of decentralisation and accountability which are linked to the hegemony of the good governance agenda in development discourse since the 1990s. In a recent influential intervention in the debate on education governance, for example, Pritchett (2013) has argued the need for education systems to move from so-called 'spider' models of governance based on top-down centralised decision-making to 'starfish' models based on developing bottom-up system improvement through processes of vertical accountability to the centre and horizontal accountability to parents and communities. This reflects in Pritchett's view the more transactional forms of accountability required at a local level in order to promote learning as opposed to simply expanding access.

Whilst paying attention to issues of accountability is important for providing coherence within education and training systems, as Pritchett asserts, it is argued that a sole focus on accountability is insufficient for the task of transforming education systems. In relation to the previous section, for example, it has been suggested that harnessing the collective agency of stakeholders at different levels of the education and training system through developing system leadership is a sin qua non for realising complex change. Closely linked to this, however, is the need to democratise processes of governance at different levels of the system. This is important from the perspective of social and environmental justice offered in Chapter 7 which itself rests on the importance of clarifying the ethical basis for ESD through forms of public debate, advocacy, and social activism.

The idea of deepening democratic participation in education governance also finds support in the literature on system change. It is often argued in this literature that the success of interventions aimed at improving learning requires the input and ownership of agents at different levels of the education and training system and representing different interests. Ensuring that different stakeholders have 'voice' in the change process is not only important at the level of principal but is crucial for developing systemic responses to change, for example, through facilitating better understanding of what is working in the reform process and what is not and being attuned to the potential barriers to change. In Chapter 5, for example, consideration was given to the role that civil society has historically played in contesting education policy but also to the potentially positive role that teachers unions, NGOs, social movements, the private sector, and religious organisation can play in facilitating positive change.

This draws attention at a regional level to the need to reform the top-down process of education decision-making linked to the nature of developmental regionalism. At a national level, it draws attention to the contradictions inherent in many African countries between the nature of the political settlement, which in many instances remains characterised by top-down, authoritarian approaches to governance. This also involves appreciating the contradictory nature of the relationship between civil society and the state since colonial times, a point that was also discussed in Chapter 6. On the one hand, this allows for the potential for civil society to challenge the government on issues of education as organisations such as UWEZO in East Africa currently do. On the other hand, it also allows, however, for a potentially productive role for civil society in working with governments in the interests of implementing a transformative ESD. This potential is currently not sufficiently recognised in regional agendas but is crucial if the legitimacy of an emerging counter-hegemonic, transformative vision of ESD is to be realised. Recognition of the interests and contradictions involved in democratising education governance draws attention to the wider politics of transformative change discussed in the first part of the chapter and the need to clearly articulate efforts to democratise education and training with wider struggles for democracy at the local, national, regional, and global scales.

Creating learning systems

The idea of system learning is prominent in the international literature on system change. In many parts of the world, including in many African countries, however, the idea of system learning can be seen as operating an oxymoron in that education and training systems are anything but learning systems. In the African context, for example, reference was made in Chapter 5 to the effects of aid modalities exacerbated by the effects of structural adjustment policies since the 1980s on increasing the dependency of education systems on foreign rather than indigenous expertise.[4] This limits the capacity of African education systems to operate in the interests of African-led development. In this regard, reference is made here to recent research conducted in Rwanda which serves to underline the difficulties in the African context of generating genuinely learning systems.

Mason's quote draws attention to the inescapable need to develop holistic approaches towards solving the learning crisis and implementing ESD rather than relying on 'magic bullets' in the form of quick-fix solutions to complex problems. A classic example of this is the use of technological solutions such as the one laptop per child initiative which had limited impact due to a failure to appreciate the nature of the conditions in schools including the lack of infrastructure and ability to service/maintain equipment as well as the lack of preparedness of educators to make use of the new technology (Kraemer, Dedrick, and Sharma 2009). It also draws attention to the dangers of uncritical policy borrowing. Even where education systems may be considered to have shared similar trajectories since colonial times, no two systems and indeed no two educational institutions or learners are the same (Forestier and Crossley 2015; Crossley, Broadfoot, and Schweisfurth 2007; Crossley and Jarvis 2001).

In Chapter 2, consideration was given, for example, to Snowden and Boon's (2007) work on how leaders ought to approach change. It will be recalled that the authors refer to four contexts of change which are of relevance for Africa but which have different implications for system learning. According to Snowden and Boon, some aspects of system change can be classified as 'simple' in that cause equals effect and solutions are known to policy makers. Examples include correcting minor administrative errors through the application of known procedures. The construction of classrooms in order to increase access to education was discussed as an example of a 'complicated' problem in that problems are ultimately solvable with the correct mix of expertise. Here it may also be possible to replicate interventions trialled elsewhere. Education and training systems emerging from periods of protracted conflict were characterised as chaotic in nature. System leadership in this kind of context may demand a more command and control approach to bring together different interests with the aim of getting the system back to a state of complexity (Snyder 2013; Davies 2004a). Solving the learning crisis and implementing ESD, on the other hand, are best described as 'wicked problems', i.e. problems that are hard to define and generally resistant to an agreed solution (Rittel and Webber 1973; Head and Alford 2015). In Snowden and Boon's (2007) terms, the role of system leaders in the face of these kinds of problems is to create the conditions for new patterns to emerge, including increasing levels of communication and interaction. Expertise is useful but not essential in these contexts as much as experience of solving complex problems and patience.

As different authors have argued, what is more important than uncritically importing initiatives and policies from elsewhere is nurturing the roots of local innovation (Ramalingam 2013a; Tikly and Barrett 2013; Samoff, Sebatane, and Dembele 2005). Africa is often presented in the literature as a continent devoid of the ability to innovate, forever dependent on outside ideas in order to 'develop'. This view of Africa as a *tabula rasa* to be filled up with modern ideas from elsewhere has its roots in colonial times. As was discussed in earlier chapters, however, there have been many examples of African-led reform in education from Nyerere's experiment to introduce mass literacy programmes in Tanzania to people's education in South Africa to education with production initiatives in Botswana and to efforts to indigenise the curriculum. It is an aspect of the hollowed-out nature of the postcolonial state that the capacity to innovate has been reduced under neoliberalism.

It is also incorrect to assume that teachers in Africa, despite the many challenges to their professional autonomy, are unable or unwilling to innovate as is sometimes also implied in the literature. Recent research on the possibilities for transforming the Rwandan Ministry of Education (MINEDUC) into a Hub for Innovation has helped to shed light on some of the challenges involved in developing learning systems in Rwanda with potential implications for other African education and training systems (Tikly and Milligan 2017; MINEDUC 2015).[5] As part of the hub for innovation project, teachers across several districts in Rwanda were encouraged to develop innovative approaches to teaching and learning and to present these at innovation fairs. What became apparent from the work of the teachers was the tremendous creativity and potential to innovate making use of whatever limited resources were available and their willingness to share and to learn from fellow professionals as part of emerging communities of practice.[6]

At the heart of the hub for innovation project was the aim to foster innovation at different levels of the education and training system as part of the commitment on the part of MINEDUC to improve learning outcomes. The initiative can therefore be seen in the context of a wider thrust to decentralise the education and training system through, for example, placing primary schools under local government control, supporting various capacity building initiatives at a local level, and introducing new performance management contracts linking financial and other incentives to improvements in learning outcomes at a local level. Attempts to decentralise the education and training system in Rwanda have, however, proved highly challenging for a number of reasons. Part of this is to do with the nature of the political settlement in Rwanda and the continuing role of a highly dominant political elite in driving development (Hicky, Hassain, and Jackman 2019).

This provided a source of tension and contradiction in relation to the development of the system leadership required to foster innovation at different levels of the system. For example, despite the tremendous potential to innovate exemplified by the success of the innovation fairs, officials and practitioners at lower levels of the education and training system were often extremely risk averse in relation to actually imitating change. This problem was exacerbated by a lack of effective communication channels necessary to disseminate effective practice and to affect change. A major finding of this and other studies is the challenge of decentralising responsibility for innovation to district officers, school principals, and classroom teachers who are often overwhelmed by the demands of day-to-day maintenance of the existing system. In the case of teachers, this was often related to the challenges of delivering a highly content-driven curriculum to increasingly diverse student body in a wider context where teacher salaries, status, and conditions of service are generally poor.

Revealing also were the testimonies of system leaders within the Ministry itself. In face-to-face interviews and focus groups they reported the importance that they as policy makers attached to their ability to solve intractable problems through creative and innovative thinking but the practical difficulties that prevented them from behaving in this way. These related to a variety of considerations from a lack of professional development opportunities to build communities of practice amongst policy makers at a national level to the need to constantly respond in a reactive rather than in a proactive way to meeting the often-incoherent demands posed by different development partners.

As part of the same project, the team evaluated 26 larger innovation projects. The projects were initially selected by MINEDUC to fit within the aims of the Education Sector Strategic Plan (ESSP) and with the ultimate goal of scaling up successful pilots. The topics covered ranged from initiatives to introduce new ways of teaching and learning, including the use of information and communication technologies, developing the skills of teachers, creating leadership and accountability, and increasing access to good quality education for all. Although targeted at different areas, each was explicitly aimed at improving student learning outcomes. Some were also aimed at achieving a range of intermediate outcomes, including the development of skills (including green skills) and changes in behaviours and attitudes that, it was hoped, would eventually have an impact on student learning.

What became clear from the meta-analysis of the 26 projects was the importance of paying attention to conditions for implementing change. These included the degree of fit to policy priorities and central advocacy and in particular to the curriculum; local capacity to implement complex interventions; the perceived need, relevance, and practicality of the innovation; local ownership/engagement of stakeholders; and the existence of supportive infrastructure such as electricity (in the case of interventions that relied on technology) (Tikly and Milligan 2017). In a similar vein, Dembele *et al.* have written about the challenges of scaling up reform in Africa. In keeping with the findings of the Rwandan study, the authors conclude that

> rather than replicating the specific elements of the reform, what must be scaled up are the conditions that permitted the initial reform to be successful and the local roots that can sustain it. That challenge involves finding ways to generate widespread and locally rooted demand for the reform and to support an informed and inclusive locally-based deliberation over the content and form of the reform. That challenge also requires finding ways to make political space for the reform and to protect it from vested interests who perceive it as a threat and a bureaucracy whose efforts to routinize change often

smother it. At the same time, those directly involved in the reform must understand reform as a continuing process rather than a specific outcome and must structure it to embed learning at its core.

(Samoff, Sebatane, and Dembele 2005, 21)

Of relevance here is recent work, also written within a complexity frame on the importance of building state capacity to undertake reform (Andrews, Pritchett, and Woolcock 2017). Here the authors argue escaping the trap of stagnant capability requires new conceptual models that go beyond 'transplanting other countries' institutional blueprints'. Rather, they advocate a problem-based approach to solving wicked problems such as the causes of the learning crisis that they describe as problem-driven iterative adaptation (PDIA). The PDIA approach[7] argues that instead of more 'experts' selling 'best practice' solutions in the name of efficiency and the adoption of global standards, there is a need for organisations to generate, test, and refine context-specific solutions in response to locally nominated and prioritised problems. They argue for systems that tolerate failure as the necessary price of success. In a similar vein, Ramalingam (2013a) in his book *Aid on the Edge of Chaos* argues for new, more fluid and responsive approaches to development assistance that reward local innovation. He contrasts his view with results-based approaches that are currently in vogue with Western donors but are based on outmoded, linear views of cause and effects and are insensitive to local contexts and social relations.

Ramalingam as well as Andrew's *et al.* make the case for the importance of evidence in driving problem-solving. In Chapter 2, reference was made to forms of realist evaluation that rather than seeking to measure discrete outcomes based on a cause–effect assumption are more suited to evaluating complex interventions. Reference was also made to the potential of different kinds of 'gold standard' evidence in order to explore the validity of the underlying theory of change (or in other terms the 'programme ontology') on which interventions are based. A case was made for the importance of using mixed methods and inter- and transdisciplinary approaches as a means for understanding causality. There was also discussion of the importance of using longitudinal data, including assessment data (both quantitative and qualitative), in order to understand the emergent nature of change. These approaches were contrasted with quasi-experimental designs including RCTs that, it was suggested, have more limited utility in understanding causality and emergence within complex systems.[8]

A major issue facing African policy makers is the lack of appropriate evidence on which to make decisions. Very often governments rely on data from education management information systems that are antiquated and are more suited to monitoring access to education than to the challenges of evaluating learning.[9] One response has been for African governments to take part in international assessments. In Chapter 7, there was discussion of the potential for regional assessments such as PASEC and SACMEQ to provide information about the factors that impact on the capabilities of primary school children to learn (although it was also argued that these data are limited because of their cross-sectional nature). A small number of African countries take part in more globally focused assessment regimes such as PISA and TIMS, although they inevitably achieve very poorly in these raising questions about the value of their involvement in these regimes in the first place (i.e. their usefulness as a means to benchmark progress).[10] From a complexity perspective, however, participation in international assessments can have unintended consequences such as the so-called washback effect (where the results of assessments feed into processes of positive feedback within the system whereby the system adapts so as to score higher in the next round).

Of particular relevance at the national scale is the need to develop longitudinal data that can track the progress of different groups of disadvantaged learners over time, including data derived from national assessment regimes (Thomas and Salim 2011). These kinds of data are also important for evaluating the impact of different interventions aimed at improving learning outcomes. As discussed in Chapter 5, however, national assessment regimes have historically acted principally as a filtering mechanism aimed at limiting access to higher echelons of the education and training system. Efforts to reorient national assessments in a way that enables them to support teaching and learning require first taking account of this legacy. It is not just the availability of different kinds of data, however, that is important but the capacity of policy makers, practitioners, and other stakeholders to interpret and act on data as part of ongoing processes of problem-solving. A finding from our study in Rwanda, for example, was the very limited capacity of governments to make use of evidence to support policy making, contributing to a sense of dependency on external consultants (Tikly and Milligan 2017).

Much of the earlier discussion has focused on identifying processes of system learning within the ambit of the state. Whilst approaches to system change such as PDIA emphasise the importance of context and of local agency in addressing wicked problems, they largely elide analysis of the effects of power and inequality in development initiatives. Furthermore, the focus is on building state capacity when it has been argued earlier that it is also crucial to develop the leadership and voice of different groups in civil society in the change process. It was argued in Chapter 9 that processes of social learning led by communities but involving other stakeholders can also contribute to system learning about the causes and solutions to a range of sustainability challenges. It was also suggested in Chapter 8 that through getting involved in forms of knowledge co-production in the context of social learning projects, educators can directly contribute to processes of decolonising and indigenising the curriculum.

Moving out of the dependency trap

In Chapter 4, reference was made to the literature relating to the 'dependency trap' faced by many African governments linked to the nature of the aid regime which, it was argued, works principally in the interests of foreign powers including Western powers but also increasingly the so-called Rising powers including China. It is the nature of dependency and of the wider power relationships in which they are embedded that need to be challenged. Indeed, a key feature of the development of East Asian education and training systems in the post-independence era has been precisely the ability to reduce dependency in the form of foreign aid linked to externally driven reform agendas to the point where these systems are now in many respects considered world leading.

The pitfalls of the dependency trap have been discussed at different points in the book. It was suggested in Chapter 5, for example, that the predominance of externally imposed agendas has been a defining characteristic of African education systems since colonial times. In this respect, foreign aid to education provides continuity on previous eras of education governance through the effect – whether intentional on the part of foreign donors or not – of imposing externally defined agendas on African governments. It was suggested earlier that recent developments in thinking about aid informed by complexity theory provide a useful way of reconceptualising aid as supportive of processes of African-led development, although these insights are rarely realised in practice. It was also argued in Chapter 6 that seeking ways to reduce financial dependency, particularly with respect to recurrent costs of education through, for example, the greater use of progressive forms of taxation and a peace dividend on military expenditure, is important for reducing dependency. It has also been argued earlier that developing learning systems that are not dependent on external 'experts' is also crucial for reducing dependency and supporting Africa-led development in education. Discussion of dependency, however, also draws attention to the wider power relationships in which relationships of dependency are embedded. These were discussed in some detail in Chapters 4 and 5. One implication of the discussion presented in these chapters is the need to link the development of indigenous system leadership with efforts to redress unequal power relationships between African and other countries in processes of global governance in all areas from control over financial markets and terms of trade to aid itself.

Conclusion

Rather than seeking to present a set of prescriptions, the chapter has sought to set out an overall approach towards realising a transformative agenda in African education and training. It has been a central argument of this book that whilst implementing ESD is inevitably a complex and contested process, it is a necessary one if education and training are to play a role in supporting sustainable development on the continent. In this respect, it is timely to recall Nelson Mandela's famous dictum that 'education is the most powerful weapon you can use to change the world'. Whilst there is considerable truth in emphasising the importance of education, it has also been argued in the book that education on its own cannot solve the problems of unsustainable development on the continent and that education and training policy need to be articulated to wider struggles for transformative change across each of the various domains of development. Given the deep-rooted nature of unsustainable development on the continent, realising transformative change in education as in other spheres requires, in Gramsci's terms simultaneously 'a pessimism of the intellect and an optimism of the will'. That is to say, that whilst struggles for a genuinely transformative ESD must be based on a realistic appraisal of the nature of unsustainable development and of the learning crisis, change is absolutely necessary. Furthermore, we can continue to be inspired in the process by the spirit of pan-Africanism and those who have struggled over many centuries to overcome injustice, inequality, and environmental catastrophe in order to build a better future for all of our children.

Notes

1 They are also not exhaustive. For example, limited attention has been given in the book to the role of education systems in perpetuating different regimes of inequality, including those based, for example, on disability and sexuality.
2 A criticism of Fullan's work in this respect is that he plays insufficient attention to the nature of power and inequality which it has been suggested are critical for understanding postcolonial contexts and shape the ability of different groups to define the moral purpose of education and training in relation to sustainable development. Fraser's work, on the other hand, as argued in Chapter 6, draws attention to the nature of the institutional and discursive barriers that limit the opportunity freedoms of disadvantaged individuals and groups and impact on their ability to participate in decision-making.
3 In this respect, as key proponents of system leadership have recently argued, Nelson Mandela can be considered a system leader par excellence in that he was able to bring forth collective leadership within the context of transformative change in South Africa (Senge, Hamilton, and Kania 2015, 27–28)
4 Thus, whereas commentators Pritchett (2013) is critical of what he terms 'isomorphic mimicry', i.e. the process by which African education systems uncritically mimic the structure and function of Northern systems, missing from his account is consideration of what is a fundamental feature of postcolonial education systems which is their reliance on foreign expertise.
5 The Hub for Innovation project which forms the basis for discussion here aimed at developing the Ministry of Education (MINEDUC) into a hub for innovation with the ultimate aim of improving learning outcomes in the country. It was part of a larger DfID-funded initiative to support innovation in education in Rwanda which included capacity building in innovation, innovation fairs and conferences, and the introduction of an innovation award for teachers. Space does not allow for a full account here. The parts of the project that this discussion draws on mainly were a meta-evaluation of 26 innovation projects all aimed at improving learning and evidence gathered in the form of a diagnostic survey and semi-structured interviews with key policy makers and other stakeholders on the possibility of developing MINEDUC into a hub for innovation (see Tikly and Milligan 2017 for a fuller account).
6 Many innovators showcased various ideas on improving the quality of education ranging from best practice in developing teaching and learning resources using low-cost teaching resources, small income generating projects for enabling girls and boys to remain in school, scientific projects aimed at creating sources of energy from various things (such as from potatoes, charcoal), crafts and art work for teaching hands-on skills, improving school leadership, school feeding for reducing dropouts, early years modelling learning using play materials, to computerized approaches of recording school data and analysing it.
7 The PDIA approach rests on four principles, namely, local solutions for local problems (transitioning from promoting predetermined solutions to allowing the local

nomination, articulation, and prioritisation of concrete problems to be solved); pushing problem-driven positive deviance (creating and protecting environments within and across organisations that encourage experimentation and positive deviance); try, learn, iterate, adapt (promoting active experiential and experimental learning with evidence-driven feedback built into regular management that allows for real-time adaptation and scaling up change through processes of diffusion (engaging champions across sectors and organisations who ensure reforms are viable, legitimate, and relevant).

8 The reliance of economists such as Pritchett on the results of RCTs to understand causality stands in contradiction to his overall recognition of the nature of complex systems, including emergent nature of phenomena.

9 Many of these do not include indicators related to learning, for example, indicators that can measure progress towards goal 4.7 on ESD.

10 More recent initiatives such as PISA for development have sought to develop assessment regimes that are more suited to low-income country contexts.

References

Ackah, W. 1999. *Pan-Africanism: Exploring the Contradictions: Politics, Identity and Development in Afrioca and the African Diaspora.* London: Routledge.

Adedeji, A. 1998. "African Renaissance, Economic Transformation and the Role of the University." *Indicator South Africa* (Winter):64–70.

Afitska, Oksana, Y. Ankomah, John Clegg, Patrick Kiliku, Osei-Amankwah, and Casmir M. Rubagumya. 2013. "Dilemas of Language Choice in Education in Tanzania and Ghana." In, 154–67. London: Routledge.

African Development Bank. 2014. *Inclusive Growth: An imperative for African Agriculture.* Tunisia: African Development Bank.

Aidi, H. 2018. "Africa's New Social Movements: A Continental Approach." In. Rabat: OCP Policy Centre.

Aikenhead, Glen S. 1996. "Science Education: Border Crossing into the Subculture of Science." *Studies in Science Education* 27 (1):1–52. doi: 10.1080/03057269608560077.

Aikenhead, Glen S. 2006. *Science Education for Everyday Life: Evidence-based Practice.* New York: Teachers College Press.Aikman, Sheila, and Elaine Unterhalter. 2005. "Beyond Access: Developing Gender Equality in Education." In. London: Oxfam.

Ajulu, R. 2001. "Thabo Mbeki's African Renaissance in a Globalising World Economy: The Struggle for the Soul of the Continent." *Review of African Political Economy* 87:27–42.

Ake, C. 1988. "Building on the Indigenous: A Challenge for Development Cooperation in the 1990s." In. Stockholm: SIDA.

Akyeampong, E., R. Bates, N. Nunn, and J. Robinson. 2014. "Africa's Development in Historical Perspective." In. Cambridge: Cambridge University Press.

Alexander, N. 1989. *Language Policy and National Unity in South Africa/ Azania: An Essay by Neville Alexander.* Cape Town: Buchu Books.

———. 1997. "Language Policy and Planning in the New South Africa." *African Sociological Review* 1 (1):82–92.

———. 1999. "An African Renaissance without African Languages?" *Social Dynamics* 25 (1):1–12. doi: 10.1080/02533959908458658.

Alexander, R. 2008. *Essays on Pedagogy.* Abingdon: Routledge.

Alidou, H., A. Boly, B. Brock-Utne, Y.S. Diallo, and K.W. Heugh. 2006. *Optimizing Learning and Education in Africa – the Language Factor.* UNESCO Institute for

Education. http://scholar.google.com/scholar?q=related:9y5NaEabkPcJ:scholar.google.com/&hl=en&num=20&as_sdt=0,5

Altbach, P., and G. Kelly. 1978. *Education and Colonialism*. New York: Longman.

Andrews, M., L. Pritchett, and M. Woolcock. 2017. *Building State Capability: Evidence, Analysis, Action*. Oxford: Oxford University Press.

Asabere-Ameyaw, A., G. Dei, and K. Raheem. 2012a. "Contemporary Issues in African Scineces and Scinece Education." In. Rotterdam: Sense Publishers.

———. 2012b. "The Question of Indigenous Science and Sceince Education: A Look at Current Literature." In *Contemporary Issues in African Sciences and Scence Education*, edited by A. Asabere-Ameyaw, G. Dei, and K. Raheem, 15–28. Rotterdam: Sense Publishers.

Ashley, L.D., C. Mcloughlin, M. Aslam, J. Engel, J. Wales, S. Rawal, R. Batley, G. Kingdon, S. Nicolai and P. Rose (2014) *The Role and Impact of Private Schools in Developing Countries: A Rigorous Review of the Evidence*, London: Department for International Development.

AU. 2007. "Strategy to Revitalize Technical and Vocational Education and Training (TVET) in Africa." In. Addis Ababa: African Union.

———. 2015. "Continental Education Strategy for Africa." African Union. Retrieved 5th November 2019 https://edu-au.org/strategies/cesa

AUC. 2015a. "*Agenda 2063* Framework Document: The Africa We Want." Addis Ababa: African Union Commission/.

———. 2015b. "Continental Strategy for Teschnical and Vocational education and Training (TVET) To Foster Youth Employment." In. Addis Ababa: African Union Commission.

Ayers, A. 2013. "Beyond Myths, Lies and Stereotypes: The Political Economy of a 'New Scramble for Africa'." *New Political Economy* 18 (2):227–57.

Bainton, D., A. Barrett, and L. Tikly. 2016. "Improving Seocndary School Teacher Quality in Sub-Saharan Africa: Framing the Issues." In *Bristol Working Papers in Education*. Bristol: School of Education.

Ball, S., and D. Youdell. 2008. *Hidden Privatisation in Public Education*. London: Institute of Education.

Ball, S.J. 2012. *Global Education Inc: New Policy Networks and the Neoliberal Imaginary*. London: Routledge.

Ball, S.J., M. Maguire, and A. Braun. 2011. *How Schools Do Policy: Policy Enactments in Secondary Schools*. London: Routledge.

Bank, World. 2018. "World Development Report 2018: Learning to Realize Education's Promise." In. Washington, DC: World Bank.

Barnett, M., and R. Duvall. 2005. *Power in Global Governannce, International Organization*. Cambridge: Cambridge University Press.

Barnett, M., and P. Walker. 2015. "Regime Change for Humanitarian Aid." *Foreign Affairs* 94(4), pp. 130–141.

Barrett, A. 2017. Making Secondary Education Relevant for All: Reflections on Science Education in an Expanding Sub-sector. *Compare* 47(6): 962–978.

Barrett, A.M. 2007. "Beyond the Polarisation of Pedagogy: Models of Classroom Practice in Tanzanian Primary Schools." *Comparative Education* 43 (2):273–94.

Barrett, A.M., S. Ali, J. Clegg, E. Hinostroza, J. Lowe, J. Nikel, M. Novelli, et al. 2007. "Initiatives to Improve the Quality of Teaching and Learning: A Review of Recent Literature." In *EdQual Working Paper 11*.

Barrett, B., U. Hoadley, and J. Morgan. 2018. "Knowledge, Curriculum and Equity: Social Realist Perspectives." In. London: Routledge.

Bartlett, L., and F. Vavrus. 2017. "A Vertical Case Study of Global Policy-Making: Early Grade Literacy in Zambia." In *The Handbook of Global Education Policy*, edited by K. Mundy, A. Green, B. Lingard, and A. Verger, 554–72. Oxford: Wiley Blackwell.

Battiste, M. 2009. "Indiegneous Knowledge: Foundations for First Nations." *World Indigenous Nations Higher Education Consortium-WINHEC Journal* (June) 13.

Bayart, J. 2009. *The State in Africa: The Politics of the Belly*. 2nd English Edition ed. London: Polity Press.

Bengtsson, Stefan. 2019. "Engaging with the Beyond – Diffracting Conceptions of T-Learning." *Sustainability* 11 (12):3430.

Benson, C. 2014."Desingning Effective Schooling in Multi-Lingual Contexts: Going Beyond Bilingual Models. In *Social Justice Through Multilingual Education*, edited by T. Skutnabb-Kangas, R. Phillipson, A. K. Mohanty, and M, Panda. Toronto: Multilingual Matters.

Bermingham, D. 2010. "Scaling up Aid for Education: Lessons from the Education for All Fast Track Initiative (FTI); Background paper for the Education for All Global Monitoring Report 2010: Reaching the Marginalized; 2009." Paris: UNESCO.

———. 2011. "The Politics of Global Education Policy: The Formation of the Education for All – Fast Track Initiative (FTI)☆." *Journal of Education Policy* 26 (4):557–69. doi: 10.1080/02680939.2011.555002.

Bernal, M. 1989. *Black Athena The Afroasiatic Roots of Classical Civilisation: The Fabrication of Ancient Greece 1785–1985*. New Brunswick, NJ: Rutgers University Press.

Bernstein, B. 1962a. "Linguistic Codes, Hesitation Phenomena and Intelligence." *Language and Speech* 5 (1):31–46.

———. 1962b. "Social Class, Linguistic Codes and Grammatical Elements." *Language and Speech* 5 (4):221–40.

———. 1990. *Class, Codes and Control*. Vol. 4. London: Routledge and Keegan Paul.

———. 2000. *Pedagogy, Symbolic Control and Identity: Theory, Research, Critique*. Revised Edition ed. Lanham, MD and Oxford: Rowman & Littlefield.

Berry, R. 2008. *Assessment for Learning*. Hong Kong: Hong Kong University Press.

Bhaskar, Roy. 2011. *Reclaiming Reality: A Critical Introduction to Contemporary Philosophy, Classical Texts in Critical Realism*. London and New York: Routledge.

Bhaskar, R., C. Frank, K.G. Hyer, P. Naess, and J. Parker. 2010. *Interdisciplinarity and Climate Change [electronic resource]: Transforming Knowledge and Practice for Our Global Future, Ontological Explorations*. Hoboken: Taylor & Francis.

Biko, S. 1978. *I Write What I LIke*. London: Bowerdean Press.

Blewitt, J. 2018. *Understanding Sustainable Development*. 3rd Edition ed. London: Routledge.

Blewitt, J., and R. Cunningham. 2014. *The Post-Growth Project: How the End of Economic Growth Could Bring a Fairer and Happier Society*. London: London Publishing Partnership.

Bloch, Carole. 2014. "The Project for the Study of Alternative Education in South Africa (PRAESA)." *Bookbird: A Journal of International Children's Literature* 52 (4): 156–160. doi:10.1353/bkb.2014.0156.

Boas, M., and D. McNeill. 2004. *Global Institutions and Development – Framing the World?* London: Routledge.

Bonal, X. 2011. "Plus ca Change . . . The World Bank Global Education Policy and the Post-Washington Consensus." *International Studies in Sociology of Education* 12 (1):3–22. doi: 10.1080/09620210200200080.

Bond, P. 2001. "Fanon's Warning: A Civil Society Reader on the New Partnership for Africa's Development." Trenton, NJ: Africa World Press.

Brautigam, D., and S. Knack. 2004. "Foreign aid Institutions and Governancne in Su-Saharan Africa." *Economic Development and Cultual Change* 52 (2):255–85.

Brehm, W., and I. Silova. 2019. "Five Generations of NGOs in Education." In *Routledge Handbook of NGOs and International Relations*, edited by T. Davies. London: Routledge.

Bretherton, D., J. Weston, and V. Zbar. 2003. "Peace Education in a Post-Conflict Environment: The Case of Sierra Leone." *Prospects* 33 (2):219–30.

Brock-Utne, Birgit. 2015. "Language-in-Education Policies and Practices in Africa with a Special Focus on Tanzania and South Africa." In, 615–31. Dordrecht: Springer Netherlands.

Brock-Utne, Birgit, and Halla B. Holmarsdottir. 2004. "Language Policies and Practices in Tanzania and South Africa: Problems and Challenges." *International Journal of Educational Development* 24 (1):67–83. doi: 10.1016/j.ijedudev.2003.10.002.

Brown, P. 1999. "Globalisation and the Political Economy of High Skills." *Journal of Education and Work* 12 (3):233–51.

Bude, Udo. 1983. "The Adaptation Concept in British Colonial Education." *Comparative Education* 19 (3):341–55. doi: 10.1080/0305006830190308.

Bush, K., and D. Salterelli. 2000. "The Two Faces of Education in Ethnic Conflict: Towards a Peacebuilding Education for Children." Rome: UNICEF.

Byrne, D., and G. Callaghan. 2014. *Complexity Theory and the Social Sciences: The State of the Art.* London: Routledge.

Cairney, P. 2012. *Understanding Public Policy: Theories and Issues.* Basingstoke: Palgrave Macmillan.

Capra, Fritjof. 2005. "Complexity and Life." *Theory, Culture & Society* 22 (5):33–44. doi: 10.1177/0263276405057046.

Carney, S. 2008. "Negotiating Policy in an Age of Globalisation: Exploring Educational 'policyscapes' in Denmark, Nepal and China." *Comparative Education Review* 53 (1):63–88.

CEDefop. 2014. *Terminology of European Education and Training Policy.* Luxembourg: Publications Office of the European Union.

Chafer, T. 2007. "Education and Politial Socialisation of a National-Colonial Political Elite in French West Africa, 1936–47." *Journal of Imperial and Commonwealth History* 35 (3):437–58.

Cheru, Fantu. 2002. *African Renaissance.* London: ZED Books.

Chisholm, Linda. 1999. "The Democratization of Schools and the Politics of Teachers' Work in South Africa." *Compare: A Journal of Comparative and International Education* 29 (2):111–26. doi: 10.1080/0305792990290202.

———. 2005. "The Politics of Curriculum Review and Revision in South Africa in Regional Context." *Compare: A Journal of Comparative Education* 35 (1):79–100.

Chisholm, Linda, and Ramon Leyendecker. 2008. "Curriculum Reform in Post-1990s Sub-Saharan Africa." *International Journal of Educational Development* 28 (2):195–205.

Choudry, A., and S. Vally. 2018. "Reflections on Knowledge, Learning and Social Movements – History's Schools." London: Routledge.

Clarke, J. 2015. "Stuart Hall and the Theory and Practice of Articulation." *Discourse: Studies in the Cultural Politics of Education* 36 (2):275–86.

Clegg, J., and O. Afitska. 2011. Teaching and Learning in Two Languages in African Classrooms. *Comparative Education* 47 (1): 61–77. doi:10.1080/03050068.201 1.541677.

Clegg, John, and John Simpson. 2016. "Improving the Effectiveness of English as a Medium of Instruction in Sub-Saharan Africa." *Comparative Education* 52 (3):359–74. doi: 10.1080/03050068.2016.1185268.

Cobern, William W., and Cathleen C. Loving. 2001. "Defining 'Science' in a Multicultural World: Implications for Science Education." *Science Education* 85 (1): 50–67. doi: 10.1002/1098-237x(200101)85:1<50::Aid-sce5>3.0.Co;2-g.

Coleman, David, and Phillip W Jones. 2004. *The United Nations and Education.* New York: Routledge.

Coloma, R. 2009. "Postcolonial Challenges in Education." In. New York: Peter Lang.

Comoroff, J., and J. Comoroff. 2011. *Theory From the South: Or, How Euro-America is Evolving Towards Africa.* Boulder, CO: Paradigm Publishers.

Connell, R. 2007. "Southern Theory: The Global Dynamics of Knowledge in Social Science." In. London: Allen and Unwin.

———. 2012. "Just Education." *Journal of Education Policy* 27 (5):681–83.

———. 2014. "Using Southern Theory: Decolonizing Social thought in Theory, Research and Application." *Planning Theory* 13 (2):210–23.

Cornwall, R. 1998. "The African Renaissance: The Art of the State." *Indicator South Africa* (Winter):9–14.

Coumou, D., et al. 2016. "Climate Change Impacts in Sub-Saharan Africa: From Physical Changes to Their Social Repercussions." *Regional Environmental Change* 17 (6):1585–600.

Cowan, L., J. O'Connell, and D. Scanlon. 1965. *Education and Nation Building in Africa.* New York: Frederick A. Praeger Publishers.

Crossley, M. 2014. "Global League Tables, Big Data and the International Transfer of Educational Research Modalities." *Comparative Education* 50 (1):15–26. doi: 10.1080/03050068.2013.871438.

Crossley, M., P. Broadfoot, and M. Schweisfurth. 2007. *Changing Educational Contexts, Issues, and Identities: 40 Years of Comparative Education, Education Heritage Series.* London and New York: Routledge.

———. 2011. *Changing Educational Contexts, Issues and Identities: 40 Years of Comparative Education,* Education heritage series. Paperback ed. Abingdon and New York: Routledge.

Crossley, M., and P. Jarvis. 2001. "Context Matters." *Comparative Education* 37 (4):405–8.

Crossley, M., and L. Tikly. 2004. "Postcolonial Perspectives and Comparative and International Research in Education: A Critical Introduction." *Comparative Education* 40 (2):147–56.

Cummins, J. 1979. Cognitive/Academic Language Proficiency, Linguistic Interdependence, the Optimum Age Question and Some Other Matters. *Working Papers on Bilingualism Toronto* 19: 197–202.

———. 1981. The Role of Primary Language Development in Promoting Educational Success for Language Minority Students. In *Schooling and Language Minority*

Students: A Theoretical Framework, edited by M. Ortiz, D. Parker, and F. Tempes, 3–49. Los Angeles: Evaluation, Dissemination and Assessment Centre, California State University.

———. 1984. Wanted: A Theoretical Framework for Relating Language Proficiency to Academic Achievement among Bilingual Students. *Multilingual Matters* 10 (1984): 2–20.

———. 2008. BICS and CALP: Empirical and Theoretical Status of the Distinction." In Encyclopedia of Language and Education, edited by Nancy Hornberger, 487–499. Boston: Springer US. doi:10.1007/978-0-387-30424-3_36.

———. 2011. Putting the Evidence Back Into Evidence-based Policies for Underachieving Students. *Babylonia* 1 (11): 34–38.

———. 2015. How to Reverse a Legacy of Exclusion? Identifying High-impact Educational Responses. *Language and Education* 29 (3): 272–279. doi:10.1080/095 00782.2014.994528.

Danermark, B. 2002. *Explaining Society: Critical Realism in the Social Sciences, Critical Realism – Interventions.* London: Routledge.

Davies, L. 2004a. *Conflict and Education: Complexity and Chaos.* London: Routledge.

———. 2004b. *Education and Conflict: Complexity and Chaos.* London and New York: Routledge.

———. 2008. Interruptive Democracy in Education. In J. Zajda, L. Davies and S. Majhanovich (eds)., *Comparative and Global Pedagogies: Comparative Education and Policy Research.* Dordrecht: Springer.

Davis, B., and D. Sumara. 2006. *Complexity and Education.* New York: Routledge.

DBE. 2011. "Curriculum and Assessment Policy Statement (CAPS) Life Sciences: Grades 10,11 and 12." Pretoria: Department for Basic Education.

DeJaeghere, J. 2017. *Educating Entrepreneurial Citizens: Neoliberalism and Youth Livelihoods in Tanzania.* London: Routledge.

de Sousa Santos, B. 2002. Toward a Multicultural Conception of Human Rights. In Hernández-Truyol, Berta (ed), *Moral Imperialism. A Critical Anthology.* pp 39–60. New York: New York University Press.

———. 2012. "Public Sphere and Epistemologies of the South." *Africa Development* 37 (1):43–67. doi: 10.4314/ad.v37i1.

Dei, G. 2017. *Reframing Blackness and Black Solidarities Through Anti-colonial and Decolonial Prisms.* Cham: Springer International.

Dei, G., and A. Kempf. 2006. "Anti-colonialism and Education: The Politics of Resistance." In. Rotterdam: Sense Publishers.

DeJaeghere, J., and A. Baxter. 2013. "Entrepreneurship Education for Youth in Sub-Saharan Africa: A Capabilities Approach as an Alternative Framework to Neoliberalism's Individualizing Risks." *Progress in Development Studies* 14 (1):61–76. doi: 10.1177/1464993413504353.

Desai, Zubeida. 2016. "Learning Through the Medium of English in Multilingual South Africa: Enabling or Disabling Learners from Low Income Contexts?" *Comparative Education* 52 (3):343–58. doi: 10.1080/03050068.2016.1185259.

Editorial. 2015. "The 169 Commandments." In *The Economist.* Retrieved 5th November 2019 https://www.economist.com/leaders/2015/03/26/the-169-commandments

El-Hani, Charbel Niño, and Fábio Pedro Souza de Ferreira Bandeira. 2008. "Valuing Indigenous Knowledge: To Call it 'science' Will Not Help." *Cultural Studies of Science Education* 3 (3):751–79. doi: 10.1007/s11422-008-9129-6.

Elliot, J. 2013. *An Introduction to Sustainable Development.* 4th Edition ed. London: Routledge.

Ellis, S., and I. Kessel. 2009. "Movers and Shakers: Social Movements in Africa." Boston: Brill Leiden.

Elmore, R. Improving the Instructional Core. Retrieved 12 November 2019 from http://teacher.justinwells.net/Downloads/improving_the_instructional_core_elmore_2008.pdf

Elmore, R. Improving the Instructional Core. Retrieved November 12, 2019, from http://teacher.justinwells.net/Downloads/improving_the_instructional_core_elmore_2008.pdf

Eltis, D., and D. Richardson. 2008. "Extending the Frontiers: Essays on the New Transatlantic Trade Database." Newhaven: Yale University Press.

Enslin, P., and Horsthemke, K. 2004. Can Ubuntu Provide a Model for Citizenship Education in African Democracies? *Comparative Education*, 40:4, 545–558.

Escobar, Arturo. 1995. *Encountering Development: The Making and Unmaking of the Third World: With a New Preface by the Author.* Princeton, NJ: Princeton University Press, 2012.

Fanon, F. 1961. *The Wretched of the Earth.* London: Penguin.

———. 1986. *Black Skins White Masks.* London: Pluto Press.

Ferguson, J. 2006a. *Global Shadows: Africa in a Neo-liberal World Order.* London: Duke University Press.

Fien, J., R. Mclean, and M. Park. 2009. "Work, Learning and Sustainable Development: Opportunities and Challenges." Netherlands: Springer.

Forestier, Katherine, and Michael Crossley. 2015. "International Education Policy Transfer – Borrowing Both Ways: The Hong Kong and England Experience." *Compare: A Journal of Comparative and International Education* 45 (5):664–85. doi: 10.1080/03057925.2014.928508.

Forum, World Economic. 2015. "The New Vision for Education: Unlocking the Potential of Technology." Geneva: World Economic Forum.

Foster, Philip. 1965. "The Vocational School Fallacy in Development Planning." In *Education and Economic Development*, edited by A.A. Anderson and M.J. Bowman, 142–66. Chicago: Aldine.

Foucault, M. 1989. *Order of Things.* London: Routledge.

———. 1991. "Governmentality." In *The Foucault Effect: Studies in Governmentality*, edited by G. Burchell, C. Gordon, and P. Miller. Hemel Hempstead: Harvester Wheatsheaf.

Frank, A. 1970. *Latin America: Underdevelopment or Revolution.* New York: Monthly Review Press.

Fraser, Nancy. 2008. *Scales of Justice: Re-imagining Political Space in a Globalising World.* Cambridge: Polity Press.

Fullan, M. 1993. *Change Forces: Probing the Depths of Educational Reform.* London: Falmer Press.

———. 1999. *Change Forces: The Sequel.* London: Routledge.

———. 2003. *Change Forces with a Vengeance.* London: RoutledgeFalmer.

———. 2005. *Leadership and Sustainability.* Thousand Oaks: Corwin Press.

Gaitskell, D. 1988. Race, Gender and Imperialism: A Century of Black Girls' Education in South Africa. Unpublished seminar paper presented at African Studies, University of the Witwatersrand.

Garcia, O., and Li Wei. 2014. *Translanguaging: Language, Bilingualism and Education*, 1–402. Basingstoke: Palgrave Macmillan.

Gardner, V., A. Barrett, M. Joubert, and L. Tikly. 2018. "Approaches to Strengthening Secondary STEM and ICT Education in Sub-Saharan Africa." Bristol: University of Bristol.

Geyer, R., and P. Cairney. 2015. "Complexity and Public Policy." Cheltenham: Edward Elgar.

Ghai, D. 1992. "Conservation, Livelihood and Democracy: Social Dynamics of Environmental Changes in Africa." Geneva: UNRISD.

Glewwe, P., and M. Kremer. 2010. "Teacher Incentives." *American Economic Journal: Applied Economics* 2 (3):205–27.

Gould, S. 1996. *The Mismeasure of Man*. London: W.W. Norton.

Gove, A., and A. Wetterberg, eds. *The Early Grade Reading Assessment: Applications and Interventions to Improve Basic Literacy*. Research Triangle Park, NC: Research Triangle Institute.

Gramsci, Antonio. 1992. *Prison Notebooks Volume 1*, translated by J.A. Buttigieg and A. Callari. New York: Columbia University Press.

Grant, J.A., and F. Söderbaum. 2003. *The New Regionalism in Africa*. Aldershot: Ashgate.

The Guardian (2015) *Sustainable development goals: all you need to know*. Retrieved January 15, 2019, from https://www.theguardian.com/global-development/2015/jan/19/sustainable-development-goals-united-nations

Guthrie, G. 2003. "Cultural Continuity in Teaching Styles." *Papua New Guinea Journal of Education* 39 (2):57–78.

Guthrie, G. 2018. *Classroom Change in Developing Countries: From Progressive Cage to Formalistic Frame*. London: Routledge.

Haas, P. 1989. "Do Regimes Matter? Epistemic Communities and Mediterranean Pollution Control." *International Organization* 43:377–403.

Habib, A., and P. O'poku-Mensah. 2009. "Speaking to Global Debates Throguh a National and Continental Lens: South Africa and African Social Movements in Comparative Persective." In *Movers and Shakers: Social Movements in Africa*, edited by S. Ellis and I. Kessel, 44–62. Boston: Brill Leiden.

Haggard, Stephan, and Beth A Simmons. 1987. "Theories of International Regimes." *International Organization* 41 (3):491–517. doi: 10.1017/S0020818300027569.

Haggis, T. 2008. " 'Knowledge Must be Contextual': Some Possible Implications of Complexity and Dynamic Systems Theories for Educational Research." In *Complexity Theory and the Philosophy of Education*, edited by M. Mason, 150–68. West Sussex: John Wiley & Sons.

———. 2009. "Beyond 'Mutual Constitution': Looking at Learning and Context from the Perspective of Complexity Theory. " In *Rethinking Contexts for Learning and Teaching: Communities, Activities and Networks*, edited by R. Edwards, G. Biesta, and M. Thorpe, 1–14. London: Routledge.

Hall, S. 1985. "Signification, Representation, Ideology: Althusser and Hte Post-Structuralist Debate." *Critical Studies in Mass Communication* 2 (2):91–114.

Harber, Clive. 1988. "Schools and Political Socialisation in Africa." *Educational Review* 40 (2):195–202.

Harvey, David. 2003. *The New Imperialism*. Oxford University Press.

———. 2011. *The Enigma of Capital and the Crises of Capitalism*. London: Profile Books.

Head, B.W., and J. Alford. 2015. "Wicked Problems: Implications for Public Policy and Management." *Administration & Society* 47 (6):711–39. doi: https://doi.org/10.1177/0095399713481601.

Held, David, Anthony McGrew, David Goldblatt, and Jonathan Perraton. 1999. *Global Transformations – Politics, Economics and Culture*. Cambridge, UK: Blackwell Publishers and Polity Press.

Heller, M. 2007. *Bilingualism: A Social Approach*. New York: Palgrave Macmillan.

Herbst, J. 2000. *States and Power in Africa: Comparative Lessons in Authority and Control.* 2nd Edition ed. Princeton, NJ: Princeton University Press.

Hettne, B., and F. Soderbaum. 2000. "Theorising the Rise of Regioness." *New Political Economy* 5 (3):457–72.

Heugh, K. 2005. "The Case for Additive Bilingual/ Multilingual Models." *ADEA Newsletter* 17 (2):11–2.

———. 2015. "Epistemologies in Multilingual Education: Translanguaging and Genre – Companions in Conversation with Policy and Practice." *Language and Education* 29 (3):280–85. doi: 10.1080/09500782.2014.994529.

Hewson, M., and M. Ogunniyi. 2011. "Argumentation-Teaching as a Method to Introduce Indigenous Knowledge into Science Classrooms: Opportunities and Challenges." *Cultural Studies of Science Education* 6 (3):679–92.

Hickey, S., and N. Hossain. 2019. "The Politics of Education in Developing Countries: From Schooling to Learning." In. Oxford: Oxford University Press.

Hickey, S., N. Hossain, and D. Jackman. 2019. "Identifying the Political Drivers of Quality Education." In *The Politics of Education in Developing Countries: From Schooling to Learning*, edited by S. Hickey and N. Hossain, 172–96. Oxford: Oxford University Press.

Hickling-Hudson, Anne, Julie Mathews, and Annette Woods. 2004. "Disrupting Preconceptions: Postcolonialism and Education." In. Flaxton, Queensland: Post Pressed.

Hoogvelt, Ankie. 1997. *Globalisation and the Postcolonial World.* London: Macmillan Press.

Hook, S.W., and J.G. Rumsey. 2015. "The Development Aid Regime at Fifty: Policy Challenges Inside and Out." *International Studies Perspectives.* doi: 10.1111/insp.12101.

Hopkins, David, and Rob Higham. 2007. "System Leadership: Mapping the Landscape." *School Leadership & Management* 27 (2):147–66. doi: 10.1080/13632430701237289.

Hoppers, C. 2002. *Indigenous Knowledge and the Integration of Knowledge Systsmes: Towards a Philosophy of Articulation.* Claremont: New Africa Books.

Horn, I. 2009. "Learner-Centredness: An Analytical Critique." *South African Journal of Education* 29:511–25.

Hungi, N. 2011. "Accounting for Variations int he Quality of Primary School Education." Paris: SACMEQ.

Ilon, L. 1994. "Structural Adjustment and Education: Adapting to a Growing Global Market." *International Journal of Educational Development* 14 (2):95–108.

Inkeles, A., and D. Smith. 1974. *Becoming Modern: Individual Change in Six Developing Countries.* Cambridge, MA: Harvard University Press.

Jackson, T. 2016. *Prosperity Without Growth.* London: London: Routledge.

Jansen, J. 2018. *As By Fire: The End of the South African University.* Cape Town: Tafelberg.

Jegede, Olugbemiro J. 1995. "Collateral Learning and the Eco-Cultural Paradigm in Science and Mathematics Education in Africa." *Studies in Science Education* 25 (1):97–137. doi: 10.1080/03057269508560051.

———. 1997. "School Science and the Development of Scientific Culture: A Review of Contemporary Science Education in Africa." *International Journal of Science Education* 19 (1):1–20. doi: 10.1080/0950069970190101.

Jegede, Olugbemiro J., and Glen S. Aikenhead. 1999. "Transcending Cultural Borders: Implications for Science Teaching." *Research in Science & Technological Education* 17 (1):45–66. doi: 10.1080/0263514990170104.

Jickling, Bob. 1992. "Viewpoint: Why I Don't Want My Children to Be Educated for Sustainable Development." *Journal of Environmental Education* 23 (4):5–8. http://dx.doi.org/10.1080/00958964.1992.9942801.

Jones, Phillip W. 2007. *World Bank Financing of Education*. London: Routledge.

Kallaway, P. 1984. "Apartheid and Education: The Education of Black South Africans." Johannesburg: Raven Press.

Keane, Moyra. 2008. "Science Education and Worldview." *Cultural Studies of Science Education* 3 (3):587–621. doi: 10.1007/s11422-007-9086-5.

Keevy, J., and R. Matlala. 2016. "Global Citizenship Education in Southern Africa." Johannesburg: Jet Education Services.

Keohane, Robert O. 2011. "Global Governance and Legitimacy." *Review of International Political Economy* 18 (1):99–109. doi: 10.1080/09692290.2011.545222.

Khor, M. 2002. *Rethinking Globalisation: Critical Issues and Policy Choices*. London: Zed Books.

Khupe, C. (2014). Indigenous knowledge and school science: Possibilities for integration. Doctoral dissertation, University of the Witwatersrand, South Africa.

King, K. 2007. "Multilateral Agencies in the Construction of the Global Agenda on Education." *Comparative Education* 43 (3):377–91.

———. 2013. *China's Aid and Soft Power in Africa*. The Case of Education and Training.

King, K., and R. Palmer. 2013. "Post-2015 Agendas: Northern Tsunami, Southern Ripple? The Case of Education and Skills." In. Geneva: NORRAG.

Kitaev, I. 1999. *Private Education in Sub-Saharan Africa: A Re-examination of Theories and Concepts Related to Its Development and Finance*. Paris: International Institute for Educational Planning/UNESCO.

Klesmer, H. 1994. Assessment and Teacher Perceptions of ESL Student Achievement. *English Quarterly* 26 (3): 8–11.

Koehler, Gabriele. 2015. "Seven Decades of 'Development', and Now What?" *Journal of International Development* 27 (6):733–51. doi: 10.1002/jid.3108.

Koff, D., and G. Von der Muhll. 1967. "Political Socilisation in Kenya and Tanzania – A Comparative Analysis." *The Journal of Modern African Affairs* 5 (1):13–51.

Kraemer, K., J. Dedrick, and P. Sharma. 2009. "One Laptop Per Child: Vision Versus Reality." *Communication of the ACM* 52 (6):66–73. doi: 10.1145/1516046.1516063.

Krasner, S.D. 1982. "Structural Causes and Regime Consequences: Regimes as Intervening Variables." *International Organization* 36 (2):185. doi: 10.1017/S0020818300018920.

Kraus, J. 2007. "Trade Unions and the Coming of Democracy in Africa." New York: Palgrave Macmillan.

Kuchah, Kuchah. 2016. "English-Medium Instruction in an English – French Bilingual Setting: Issues of Quality and Equity in Cameroon." *Comparative Education* 52 (3):311–27. doi: 10.1080/03050068.2016.1185257.

Kuhn, T. 1962. *The Structure of Scientific Revolutions*. Chicago: University of Chicago Press.

Land, M. 2013. "Full STEAM Ahead: The Benefots of Integrating the Arts into STEM." *Procedia Computer Science* 20:547–52.

Latouche, S. 2007. *Le pari de la de´croissance*. Paris: Fayard.

Launey, R. 2016. "Islamic Education in Africa: Writing Boards and Blackboards." Indiana: Indiana University Press.

Leach, Fiona. 2004. "School-Based Gender Violence in Africa: A Risk to Adolescent Sexual Health." In *The HIV Challenge to Education: A Collection of Essays*, edited by C. Coombe, 221–46. Paris: UNESCO IIEP.

Le Grange, L. 2007. "Integrating Western and Indigenous Knowledge Systems: The Basis for Effective Science Education in South Africa?" *International Review of Education* 53 (5):577–91. doi: 10.1007/s11159-007-9056-x.

———. 2008. "Challenges for Enacting an Indigenised Science Curriculum: A Reply to Ogunniyi and Ogawa." *South African Journal of Higher Education* 22 (4):817–26.

Lélé, Sharachchandra M. 1991. "Sustainable Development: A Critical Review." *World Development* 19 (6):607–21. doi: 10.1016/0305-750x(91)90197-p.

Lewin, K. (2018). The Education Outcomes Fund for Africa and the Middle East: Is It a Game Changer? Retrieved from https://worldsofeducation.org/en/woe_homepage/woe_detail/15981/%E2%80%9Ceducation-outcomes-fund-for-africa-and-the-middle-east-is-it-a-game-changer%E2%80%9D-by-keith-m-lewin

Loomba, A. 2005. *Colonialism/ Postcolonialism: The New Critical Idiom*. 2nd Edition ed. Abingdon: Routledge.

Lotz-Sisitka, H., M.B. Ali, G. Mphepo, M. Chaves, T. Macintyre, T. Pesanayi, A. Wals, et al. 2016. "Co-designing Research on Transgressive Learning in Times of Climate Change." *Current Opinion in Environmental Sustainability* 20:50–55. https://doi.org/10.1016/j.cosust.2016.04.004

Lotz-Sisitka, H., O. Shumba, J. Lupele, and D. Wilmot. 2017. "Schooling for Sustainable Development in Africa." Switzerland: Springer.

Lotz-Sisitka, H., A.E.J. Wals, D. Kronlid, and D. McGarry. 2015. "Transformative, Transgressive Social Learning: Rethinking Higher Education Pedagogy in Times of Systemic Global Dysfunction." *Current Opinion in Environmental Sustainability* 16:73–80. https://doi.org/10.1016/j.cosust.2015.07.018

Lyotard, J. 1986. *The Postmodern Condition: A Report on Knowledge*. Minneapolis, MN: University of Minnesota Press.

Maclean, R., and D. Wilson. 2011. "International Handbook of Education for the Changing World of Work: Bridging Academic and Vocational Learning." Netherlands: Springer.

Makalela, L. 2015. "Moving Out of Linguistic Boxes: The Effects of Translanguaging Strategies For Multilingual Classrooms." *Language and Education* 29 (3):200–17. doi: 10.1080/09500782.2014.994524.

Maldonado-Torres, Nelson. 2007. "On The Coloniality Of Being." *Cultural Studies* 21 (2–3):240–70. doi: 10.1080/09502380601162548.

Mamdani, M. 1996. *Citizen and Subject: Contemporary Africa and the Legacy of Late Colonialism*. Princeton, NJ: Princeton University Press.

Mangan, James. 1988. "Benefits Bestowed? Education and British Imperialism." Manchester: Manchester University Press.

Manji, F., and C. O'Coill. 2002. "The Missionary Position: NGOs and Development in Africa." *International Affairs* 78 (3):567–83.

Mason, M. 2008. "Complexity Theory and the Philosophy of Education." Chichester: John Wiley & Sons.

———. 2014. "Compleixty Theory in Education Governancne: Initiaitng and Sustaining Systemic Change." In *Understanidng Complexity: The Future of Education Governancne*. Oslo: UNESCO International Bureau of Education.

Masson-Delmotte, V. et al. 2018. "Global Warming of 1.5°C: An IPCC Special Report on the Impacts of 1.5°C Above Pre-Inductrial Levels and Related Global Greenhouse Gas Emissions Pathways, in the Context of Strengthening the Global Response to the Threat of Climate Change, Sustainable Development, and Efforts to Eradicate Poverty." Switzerland: International Panel on Climate Change.

Maware, M., and T. Mubaye. 2016. *African Philosophy and Thought Systems: A Search for a Culture and Philosophy of Belonging.* Mankon: Langaa RPCIG.

Mayer, M. 1998. "Towards an African Renaissance: The Role of Trade Integration in the Southern African development Community." *Indicator SA* (Winter):27–31.

Mazrui, A. 1999. *The African Renaissance: A Triple Legacy of Skills, Values and Gender.* Paper presented at the The African Renaissance – From Vision to Reality Conference, The Barbican Centre, London, 23 November.

Mbembe, A. 2016. "Decolonizing the University: New Directions." *Arts and Humanities in Higher Education* 15 (1):29–45.

Mbembe, A., and D. Posel. 2005. "A Critical Humanism." *Interventions: Internaitonal Journal of Postcolonial Studies* 7 (3):283–86.

McClelland, D. 1961. *The Achieving Society.* New York: Van Nostrand.

McCowan, T. 2015. "Theories of Development." In *Education and International Development: An introduction,* edited by T. McCowan and U. Unterhalter, 31–48. London: Bloomsbury.

McGrath, S., and L. Powell. 2016. "Skills for Sustainable Development: Transforming Vocational Education and Training Beyond 2015." *International Journal of Educational Development* 50 (September):12–19. https://doi.org/10.1016/j.ijedudev.2016.05.006

McLennan, Gregor. 2003. "Sociology's Complexity." *Sociology* 37 (3):547–64. doi: 10.1177/00380385030373009.

Meadows, D., D. Meadows, J. Randers, and W. Behrens. 1972. *The Limits of Growth.* New York: Univrse Books.

Melber, H. 2018. "Knowledge Production and Decolonisation – Not only African Challenges." *Strategic Review of Southern Africa* 40 (1):4–15.

Milligan, L.O., J. Clegg, and L. Tikly. 2016. "Exploring the Potential for Language Supportive Learning in English Medium Instruction: A Rwandan Case Study." *Comparative Education* 52 (3):328–42.

Milligan, L.O, H. Koornhof, I. Sapire, and L. Tikly. 2018. "Understanding the Role of Learning and Teaching Support Materials in Enabling Learning for All." *Compare: A Journal of Comparative and International Education* 44 (1):1–19. doi: 10.1080/03057925.2018.1431107.

Milligan, L.O., and L. Tikly. 2016. "English as a Medium of Instruction in Postcolonial Contexts: Moving the Debate Forward." *Comparative Education* 52 (3):277–80.

Milligan, L.O., L. Tikly, T. Williams, J-M. Vianney, and A. Uworwabayeho. 2017. "Textbook Availability and Use in Rwandan Basic Education: A Mixed-Methods Study." *International Journal of Educational Development* 54:1–7. doi: 10.1016/j.ijedudev.2017.01.008.

MINEDUC. 2015. "Innovation in Education: A Roadmap for Rwanda." Kigali: MINEDUC.

Mittelman, James H. 2000. *The Globalisation Syndrome; Transformation and Resistance.* Princeton, NJ: Princeton University Press.

Mkandawire, T. 1996. "Stylising Accumulation in Africa: The Role of the State." In *New Directions in Development Economics: Growth, Environmental Concerns and Governments in the 1990s*, edited by Mats Lundhal and Benno Ndulu, 323–51. London: Routledge.

Moe, T., and S. Wiborg. 2017. "Introduction." In *The Comparative Politics of Education*, edited by T. Moe and S. Wiborg, 1–23. Cambridge: Cambridge University Press.

Mohan, G. 2013. "Beyond the Enclave: Towards a Critical Political Economy of China in Africa." *Development and Change* 44 (6):1255–72.

Mohanty, A.K. 2009. Perpetuating Inequality: Language Disadvantage and Capability Deprivation of Tribal Mother Tongue Speakers in India. In *Language and Poverty*, edited by W. Harbert, S. McConnell-Ginet, A. Miller, and John Whitman, 102–118. Toronto: Multilingual Matters.

Moore, R., and M. Young. 2001. "Knowledge and the Curriculum in the Sociology of Education: Towards a Reconceptualisation." *British Journal of Sociology of Education* 22 (4):445–61.

Morin, E. 1999. "Seven Complex Lessons in Education for the Future." Paris: UNESCO.

———. 2008. *On Complexity*. Cresskill, NJ: Hampton Press.

Morrison, M. 2002. *School Leadership and Complexity Theory*. London: Routledge.

Mourshed, M., C. Chijioke, and M. Barber. 2010. *How the World's Most Improved School Systems Keep Getting Better*. London: McKinsey.

Moyo, D. 2009. *Dead Aid: Why Aid Is Not working and How There Is Another Way for Africa*. London: Penguin.

Moyo, S. 2015. "The Land Question and Land Reform in Southern Africa." In. Harare: Sam Moyo African Institute for Agrarian Studies.

Muller, J. 2009. "Forms of Knowledge and Curriculum Coherence." *Journal of Education and Work* 22 (3):203–24.

Mundy, K. 2007. "Education for All and the New Development Compact." *International Review of Education* 52 (1–2):23–48.

Mundy, K., A. Green, R. Lingard, and A. Verger. 2017. "The Handbook of Global Education Policy." In. Hoboken: NJ: Wiley Blackwell.

Mundy, K., & Manion, C. (2015). The Education for All initiative: history and prospects post-2015. In: T. McCowan & E. Unterhalter (Eds.), *Education and international development: practice, policy and research* 49–68. London: Bloomsbury.

———. 2015. "The Education for All Initiative: History and Prospects Post-2015." In *Education and International Development: An Introduction*, edited by T. McCowan and E. Unterhalter, 49–68. London: Bloomsbury.

Mundy, K., and L. Murphy. 2001. "Transnational Advocacy, Global Civil Society? Emerging Evidence from the Field of Education." *Comparative Education Review* 45 (1):85–126.

Murphy, M., L. Stark, N. Wessells, and A. Ager. 2011. "Fortifying Barriers: Sexual Violence as an Obstacle to Girl's School Particaption in Northern Uganda." In *Education, Conflict and Development*, edited by J. Paulson, 167–84. Oxford: Symposium.

Ndlovu-Gatsheni, S.J. 2013. *Coloniality of Power in Postcolonial Africa*. Senegal: CODESRIA.

———. 2015. "Decoloniality as the Future of Africa." *History Compass* 13 (10): 485–96. doi: 10.1111/hic3.12264.

NEPAD. 2001. "The New Partnership for Africa's Development." Retrieved November 12, 2019, from http://www.avmedia.at/nepad/indexgb.html

Ngcobo, Thandi, and Leon Paul Tikly. 2010. "Key Dimensions of Effective Leadership for Change: A Focus on Township and Rural Schools in South Africa." *Educational Management Administration & Leadership* 38 (2):202–28. doi: 10.1177/1741143209356359.

Nkrumah, K. 1966. *Neo-colonialism: The Last Stage of Imperialism*. London: Thomas Nelson and Sons.

Nordtveit, B. 2007. "Complexity Theory in Development Theory." *Comparative Education Bulletin* 10:19–28.

Novelli, M. 2010. "The New Geopolitics of Educational Aid: From Cold Wars to Holy Wars?" *International Journal of Educational Development* 30 (5):453–59.

Ntuli, P. 1998. "Who's Afriad of the African Renaissance?" *Indicator South Africa* (Winter):15–18.

Nussbaum, M. 2006. "The Moral Status of Animals." *The Chronicle of Higher Education* 52 (22):B6–B8.

Nyerere, Julius. 1967. "Education for Self-Relaince." Accessed 6 August 2012. www.swaraj.org/shikshantar/resources_nyerere.html.

Obi, C. 2005. "Environmental Movements in Sub-Saharan Africa: A Political Ecology of Power and Conflict." Geneva: UNRISD.

OECD. 2003. "OECD Policy Brief; Policy Coherence – Vital for Global Development." *OECD Policy Brief* (July).

———. 2014. Report on the OECD Framework for Inclusive Growth. Paris: OECD Publishing.

Ogunniyi, M.B. 2011. "Exploring Science Educators' Cosmological Worldviews through the Binoculars of an Argumentation Framework." *South African Journal of Higher Education* 25 (3):542–53.

Okolie, A.C. 2003. "Producing Knowledge for Sustainable Development in Africa: Implications for Higher Education." *Higher Education* 46 (2):235–60.

Olmedo, A. 2014. "From England with Love . . . ARK, Heterarchies and Global 'Philanthropic Governance'." *Journal of Education Policy* 29 (5):575–97.

———. 2017. "Something Old, not Much New, and a Lot Borrowed: Philanthropy, Business, and the Changing Roles of Government in Global Education Policy Networks." *Oxford Review of Education* 43 (1):69–87.

Omi, M., and H. Winant. 2015. *Racial Formation in the United States*, 3d ed. London: Routledge.

Orlove, Ben, Carla Roncoli, Merit Kabugo, and Abushen Majugu. 2010. "Indigenous Climate Knowledge in Southern Uganda: The Multiple Components of a Dynamic Regional System." *Climatic Change* 100 (2):243–65. doi: 10.1007/s10584-009-9586-2.

Orsini, A., J.F. Morin, and O. Young. 2013. "Regime Complexes: A Buzz, a Boom, or a Boost for Global Governance?" *Global Governance: A Review of* . . . . doi: 10.5555/1075-2846-19.1.27.

Ottevanger, W., J. Akker, and L. Feiter. 2007. *Developing Science, Mathematics, and ICT Education in Sib-Saharan Africa: Patterns and Promising Practices*. Washington: World Bank.

Òtúlàjà, F.S., A. Cameron, and A. Msimanga. 2011. Rethinking Argumentation-teaching Strategies and Indigenous Knowledge in South African Science Classrooms. *Cultural Studies of Science Education* 6: 693. https://doi.org/10.1007/s11422-011-9351-5

PASEC. 2015. "PASEC2014: Education System Reform in Francophone Sub-Saharan Africa: Competencies and Learning Factors in Primary Education." Dakar: PASEC.

Paulson, J. 2011. "Education, Conflict and Development." Oxford: Symposium.

Pawson, R. 2002. Evidence-based Policy: In Search of a Method. *Evaluation* 8 (2): 157–181.

———. 2013. *The Science of Evaluation: A Realist Manifesto*. London and Thousand Oaks, CA: SAGE.

Peck, J., and N. Theodore. 2007. "Variegated Capitalism." *Progress in Human Geography* 31 (6):731–72.

Pennycook, A. 2009. Postmodernism in Language Policy. In *An Introduction to Language Policy: Theory and Method*, T. Ricento (ed), 60–76. Oxford: Blackwell.

Phillipson, Robert. 1996. "Linguistic Imperialism: African Perspectives." *ELT Journal* 50 (2):160–67. doi: 10.1093/elt/50.2.160.

Phillipson, R., T. Skutnabb-Kangas, A.K. Mohanty, and M. Panda. 2014. *Social Justice Through Multilingual Education*. Bristol: Multilingual Matters.

Pinkney, R. 2009. *NGOs, Africa and the Global Order*. London: Palgrave Macmillan.

Pritchett, L. 2013. *The Rebirth of Education: Schooling ain't Learning*. Washington, DC: Centre for Global Development.

Probyn, M. 2015. "Pedagogical Translanguaging: Bridging Discourses in South African Science Classrooms." *Language and Education* 29 (3):218–34.

Ramalingam, B. 2013a. *Aid on the Edge of Chaos: Rethinking International Cooperation in a Complex World*. Oxford: Oxford University Press.

———. 2013b. *Aid on the Edge of Chaos; Rethinking International Co-operation in a Complex World*. Oxford: Oxford University Press.

Rassool, N., K. Heugh, and S. Mansoor. 2007. *Global Issues in Language, Education and Development*. Multilingual Matters.

Raworth, K. 2017. *Doughnut Economics: Seven Ways to Think Like a 21st Century Economist*. London: RH Business Books.

Reed, M., A. Evely, G. Cundill, I. Fazey, J. Glass, A. Laing, J. Newig, et al. 2010. "What Is Social Learning?" *Ecology and Society* 15 (4).

RESA. 1988. *Bantu Education as a Reformist Strategy of the State*. London: Research on Education in South Africa.

Riddell, R. 2007. *Does Foreign Aif Really Work?* Oxford: Oxford University Press.

Rist, G. 1997. *The History of Development: From Western Origins to Global Faith*. London: Zed Books.

Rittel, H.W.J., and M.M. Webber. 1973. "Dilemmas in a General Theory of Planning." *Policy Sciences* 4:155–69.

Rizvi, F. 2007. "Postcolonialism and Globalization in Education." *Cultural Studies Critical Methodologies* 7 (3):256–63. https://doi.org/10.1177/1532708607303606

Rizvi, F., and B. Lingard. 2006. "Edward Said and the Cultural Politics of Education." *Discourse: Studies in the Cultural Politics of Education* 27 (3):293–308. doi: 10.1080/01596300600838744.

Rizvi, F., B. Lingard, and J. Lavia. 2006. "Postcolonialism and Education: Negotiating a Contested Terrain." *Pedagogy, Culture & Society* 14 (3):249–62. doi: 10.1080/14681360600891852.

Robertson, Susan, Karen Mundy, and Antoni Verger. 2012. *Public Private Partnerships in Education*. Cheltenham: Edward Elgar Publishing.

Robertson, Susan, Mario Novelli, Roger Dale, Leon Tikly, Hillary A Dachi, and Ndibalema Alphonse. 2007. *Globalisation, Education and Development: Ideas, Actors and Dynamics*. London: DFID.

Robeyns, I. 2005. "The Capability Approach: A Theoretical Survey." *Journal of Human Development and Capabilities* 6 (1):93–117.

———. 2017. *Wellbeing, Freedo and Social Justice*. Cambridge: Open Book Publishers.

Rodney, W. 1973. *How Europe Underdeveloped Africa*. London: Bogle-L'Ouverture Publications.

Romero, M., J. Sandefur, and W.A. Sandholtz. 2017. "Can Outsourcing Improve Liberia's Schools? Preliminary Results from Year One of a Three-Year Randomized Evaluation of Partnership Schools for Liberia." Washington, DC: Center for Global Development.

Rostow, W. 1960. *The Stages of Economic Growth*. Cambridge: Cambridge University Press.

Rubagumya, C. 2003. "English Medium Primary Schools in Tanzania: A New Linguistic Market in Education." *Language of instruction in Tanzania and South Africa*, edited by Birgit Brock-Utne, Zubeida Desai, and Martha Quorro, 149–169. Dar es Salaam: E&D Publishers.

Rubagumya, Casmir M., Oksana Afitska, John Clegg, and Patrick Kiliku. 2011. "A Three-tier Citizenship: Can the State in Tanzania Guarantee Linguistic Human Rights?" *International Journal of Educational Development* 31 (1): 78–85. doi: 10.1016/j.ijedudev.2010.06.007.

Rudolph, S., A. Sriprakash, and J. Gerrard. 2018. "Knowledge and Racial Violence: The Shine and Shadow of Powerful Knowledge." *Ethics and Education* 13 (1):22–38.

Rychen, D., and L. Salganik, eds. 2003. *Key Competencies for Successful Life and Well-Functioning Society*. Cambridge, MA: Hogrefe and Huber Publishers.

Sabar, G. 2001. *Chuirch, State and Society in Kenya: From Mediation to Opposition*. London: Routledge.

Sachs, J.D. 2012. "From Millennium Development Goals to Sustainable Development Goals." *The Lancet* 379 (9832):2206–11. doi: 10.1016/s0140-6736(12)60685-0.

———. 2015. *The Age of Sustainable Development*. New York: Columbia University Press.

Said, E. 1978. *Orientalism*. New York: Pantheon Books.

Samoff, J. 1992. "The Intellectual/Financial Complex of Foreign Aid." *Review of African Political Economy* 53:60–75.

———. 1994. "Coping with Crisis: Austerity, Adjustment and Human Resources." London: Cassell.

———. 1996. "Which Priorities and Strategies for Education." *International Journal of Educational Development* 16 (3):249–71.

———. 2007. "Education Quality: The Disabilities of Aid." *International Review of Education* 53 (5):485–507.

Samoff, J., E. Molapi Sebatane, and M. Dembele. 2005. *Going to Scale: Nurutring the Local Roots of Education Innovation in Africa*. Paper presented at the The 8th UKFIET International Conference on Education and Development: Learning and Livelihood, University of Oxford, 13–15 September.

Santos, Boaventura de Sousa. 2002. "Towards a Multicultural Conception of Human Rights." In *Moral Imperialism*, edited by Berta Hernández-Truyol, 39–60. New York: New York University Press.

———. 2007. "Beyond Abyssal Thinking: From Global Lines to Ecologies of Knowledge." *Review* XXX (1):45–89.

———. 2012. "The Public Sphere and Epistemologies of the South." *African Development* XXXVII (1):43–68.

———. 2017. *Decolonising the University: The Challenge of Deep Cognitive Justice.* Newcastle Upon Tyne: Cambridge Scholars Publishing.

Sayed, Y. 2019. "The SDGs and the Global Education Agenda: Promises and Possibilities." *Sussex Development Lectures.* Sussex: University of Sussex.

Sayed, Y., and A. Kanjee. 2013. "Assessment in Sub-Saharan Africa: Challenges and Prospects." *Assessment in Education: Principles, Policy & Practice* 20 (4):373–84.

Sayed, Y., and M. Novelli. 2016. "The Role of Teachers in Peacebuilding and Social Cohesion." Sussex: University of Sussex.

Schlosberg, D. 2001. Three Dimensions of Environmental and Ecological Justice. Prepared for the European Consortium for Political Research Annual Joint Sessions, Grenoble, France, 6–11 April 2001. Workshop: The Nation-state and the Ecological Crisis: Sovereignty, Economy and Ecology.

———. 2004. "Reconceiving Environmental Justice: Global Movements and Political Theories." *Environmental Politics* 13 (3):517–40.

———. 2007. *Defining Environmental Justice: Theories, Movements and Nature.* Oxford: Oxford University Press.

Scholte, J.A. 2006. "Globalisation: Crucial Choices for Africa for ESRC." In *Africa After 2005: From Promises to Policy*, edited by ESRC Swindon: Economic and Social Research Council.

Schudel, I. 2017. "Deliberations on a Changing Curriculum Landscape and Emergent Environmental and Sustainability Education Practices in South Africa." In *Schooling for Sustainable Development in Africa*, edited by H. Lotz-Sissitka, O. Shumba, J. Lupele, and D. Wilmot, 138–82. Switzerland: Springer.

Schultz, T. 1961. Investment in Human Capital. *The American Economic Review* 51 (1):1–17.

Schweisfurth, M. 2011. "Learner-Centred Education in Developing Country Contexts: From Solution to Problem?" *International Journal of Educational Development* 31 (5):425–32. doi: 10.1016/j.ijedudev.2011.03.005.

———. 2013a. "Learner-Centred Education in International Perspective." *Journal of International and Comparative Education* 2 (1):1–8.

———. 2013b. *Learner-Centred Education in International Perspective: Whose Pedagogy for Whose Development?* London: Routledge.

Scott, D. 2010. *Education, Epistemology and Critical Realism.* Abingdon: Routledge.

Sen, A. 1999. *Development as Freedom.* Oxford: Oxford University Press.

———. 2002. "'Basic Education and Human Security.' A Backgroundpaper Prepared for the Kolkata Meeting." In *Kolkota Meeting on Human Security.* Kolkota.

———. 2009. *The Idea of Justice.* London: Penguin.

———. 2011. *The Idea of Justice.* Cambridge, MA: Harvard University Press.

———. 2013. "The Ends and Means of Sustainability." *Journal of Human Development and Capabilities* 14 (1):6–20. doi: 10.1080/19452829.2012.747492.

Senge, P., H. Hamilton, and J. Kania. 2015. "The Dawn of System Leadership." *Stanford Social Innovation Review* (Winter):27–33.

Shalem, Y. 2018. "Scripted Lesson Plans: What Is Visible and Invisible in Visible Ped-agogy." In *Knowledge, Curriculum and Equity: Social Realist Perspectives*, edited by B. Barrett, U. Hoadley, and J. Morgan, 545–48. London: Routledge.

Shizha, E., and N. Makuvaza. 2017. *Re-thinking Postcolonial Education in Sub-Saharan Africa in the 21st century*. Rotterdam: Sense Publishers.

Siekmann, G., and P. Korbel. 2016. "Defining 'STEM' Skills: Review and Synthesis of the Literature." Adelaide: National Centre for Vocational Education Research.

Simon, D. 2003. "Regional Development-Environment Discourses, Policies and Practices in Post-apartheid Southern Africa." In *The New Regionalism in Africa*, edited by J.A. Grant and F. Söderbaum. Farnham: Ashgate.

Skutnabb-Kangas, Tove. 2009. *Social Justice Through Multilingual Education*. Multilingual Matters.

Smith, A. 2010. "The Influnece of Education on Conflict and Peace Building." In *Background Paper Prepared for the Education for All Global Monitoring Report 2011 The Hidden Crisis: Armed Conflict and Education*. Paris: UNESCO.

Smith, Michèle C., and Angeline M. Barrett. 2011. "Capabilities for Learning to Read: An Investigation of Social and Economic Effects for Grade 6 Learners in Southern and East Africa." *International Journal of Educational Development* 31 (1):23–36.

Sneddon, Chris, Richard B. Howarth, and Richard B. Norgaard. 2006. "Sustainable Development in a Post-Brundtland World." *Ecological Economics* 57 (2):253–68. doi: 10.1016/j.ecolecon.2005.04.013.

Snowden, D.J., and M.E. Boone. 2007. "A Leader's Framework for Decision Making." *Harvard Business* 85 (11):68.

Snyder, S. 2013. "The Simple, the Complicated, and the Complex: Educational Reform Through the Lens of Complexity Theory." In *OECD Education Working Papers*. Paris: OECD.

Sparr, P. 1994. "Mortgaging Women's Lives: Feminist Critiques of Structural Adjustment." London: Zed books.

Sriprakash, A., L. Tikly, and S. Walker. 2019. "The Erasures of Racism in Education and International Development: Re-Reading the 'Global Learning Crisis'." *Compare*. doi: 10.1080/03057925.2018.1559040.

Steer, L., and K. Smith. 2015. *Financing Education: Opportunities for Global Action*. Washington: Brookings Institute.

Tabulawa, R. 1997. "Pedagogical Practice and the Social Context: The Case of Botswana." *International Journal of Educational Development* 17 (2):189–204.

———. 2003. "International Aid Agencies, Learner-centred Pedagogy and Political Democratisation: A Critique." *Comparative Education* 39 (1):7–26.

Takayama, K., A. Sriprakash, and R. Connell. 2017. "Towards a Postcolonial and Comparative International Education." *Comparative Education Review* 61 (S1):S1–S24.

Thiong'o, N. 1986. *Decolonising the Mind: The Politics of Language in African Literature*. London: James Currey.

Thomas, Sally M., and Massoud Salim. 2011. "The Case for Longitudinal Datasets, EdQual Policy Brief no. 11." Bristol: EdQual.

Tikly, L. 1994. "Education Policy in South Africa Since 1947." University of Glasgow.

———. 1999. "Postcolonialism and Comparative Education." *International Review of Education* 45 (5):603–21.

———. 2001. "Globalisation and Education in the Postcolonial World; Towards a Conceptual Framework." *Comparative Education* 37 (2):151–71.

———. 2003a. "Governmentality and the Study of Education Policy in South Africa." *Journal of Education Policy* 18 (2):161–74.

———. 2003b. "The African Renaissance, NEPAD and Skills Formation: An Identification of Key Policy Tensions." *International Journal of Educational Development* 23:543–64.

———. 2003c. "The African Renaissance, NEPAD and Skills Formation: An Identification of Key Policy Tensions." *International Journal of Educational Development* 23 (5):543–64. doi: 10.1016/S0738-0593(03)00059-2.

———. 2004. "Education and the New Imperialism." *Comparative Education* 40 (2):173–98.

———. 2013. "Reconceptualizing TVET and Development: A Human Capability and Social Justice Approach." *Revisiting Global Trends in TVET: Reflections on Theory* . . . .

———. 2015. "What Works, for Whom, and in What Circumstances? Towards a Critical Realist Understanding of Learning in International and Comparative Education." *International Journal of Educational Development* 40:237–49. doi: 10.1016/j.ijedudev.2014.11.008.

———. 2016. "Language-in-Education Policy in Low-Income, Postcolonial Contexts: Towards a Social Justice Approach." *Comparative Education* 52 (3):408–25. doi: 10.1080/03050068.2016.1185272.

———. 2017. "The Future of Education for All as a Global Regime of Educational Governance." *Comparative Education Review* 61 (1):22–57.

Tikly, L., and A. Barrett. 2013. "Education Quality and Social Justice in the Global South: Challenges for Policy, Practice and Research." Abingdon: Routledge.

Tikly, L., and A.M. Barrett. 2011. Social Justice, Capabilities and the Quality of Education in Low Income Countries. *International Journal of Educational Development*. doi:10.1016/j.ijedudev.2010.06.001.

Tikly, L., and H.A. Dachi. 2008. "The New Regionalism in African Education: Possibilities and Limitations for Developing South-South Collaboration." In *South-South Co-operation and Transfer in Education and Development*, edited by Linda Chisholm and Gita Steiner-Khamsi. New York: Teachers College Press.

Tikly, L., M. Joubert, A. Barrett, D. Bainton, L. Cameron, and H. Doyle. 2018. "Supporting Secondary School STEM Education for Sustainable Development in Africa." In *Bristol Working Papers in Education*. Bristol: University of Bristol.

Tikly, L., J. Lowe, M. Crossley, H.A. Dachi, R. Garrett, and B. Mukabaranga. 2003. *Globalisation and Skills for Development in Rwanda and Tanzania*. London: DfID.

Tikly, L., and L. Milligan. 2017. "Learning from Innovation for Education in Rwanda." *Bristol Working Papers in Education*. Bristol: University of Bristol.

Tollefson, J.W. 2013. *Language Policies in Education*. Routledge. doi:10.4324/9780203813119.

Trudell, Barbara. 2007. "Local Community Perspectives and Language of Education in Sub-Saharan African Communities." *International Journal of Educational Development* 27 (5): 552–563. doi:10.1016/j.ijedudev.2007.02.002.

Trudell, B. 2009. "Local Community Perspectives and Language of Education in Sub-Saharan African Communities." *International Journal of Educational Development* 27 (5):552–63.

———. 2016. "Language Choice and Education Quality in Eastern and Southern Africa: A Review." *Comparative Education* 52 (3):281–93. doi: 10.1080/03050068.2016.1185252.

Truman, H.S. 1949. Inaugural Address. Retrieved November 5, 2019, from www.bartleby.com/124/pres53.html

UN. 1945. "Charter of the United Nations and Statute of the International Court of Justice." San Fransisco: UN.

———. 2013. Communiqué Meeting of the High-Level Panel of Eminent Persons on the Post-2015 Development Agenda in Bali, Indonesia, 27 March 2013, New York: United Nations.

———. 1972. "Declaration of the United Nations Conference on the Human Environment." New York: United Nations Environment Programme.

———. 1975. "The Cocoyoc Declaration." *International Organization* 29 (3): 893–901. doi: 10.1017/S0020818300031805.

———. 1998. "Kyoto Protocol to the United Nations Framework Convention on Climate Change." New York: United Nations.

———. 2002. "Johannesburg Declaration." New York: United Nations.

———. 2012. "The Future we Want: Outcome Document of the UNited Nations Conference on Sustainable Development." New York: United Nations.

———. 2015a. "Paris Agreement." New York: United Nations.

———. 2015b. "The Millenium Goals Report." New York: United Nations.

———. 2015c. "Transforming our World: The 20130 Agenda for Sustainable Development." New York: United Nations General Assembly.

———. 2017. "Progress Towards the Sustainable Development Goals." In. New York: United Nations Economic and Social Council.

UNCED. 1992. "United Nations Conference on Environment & Development Rio de Janerio, Brazil, 3 to 14 June 1992 AGENDA 21." New York: United Nations.

UNDP. 2015. "Human Development Report: Work for Human Development." New York: UNDP.

UNESCO. 1977. "The Tbilisi Declaration." New York: UNESCO.

———. 1990. *Education for All – Framework for Action; Meeting Basic Needs – Guidelines for Implementing the World Declaration on EFA.* New York: UNESCO.

———. 2000. *EFA – Meeting Our Collective Commitments.* Dakar, Senegal: UNESCO.

———. 2003. *Education in a Multilingual World.* Education.

———. 2011a. "EFA Global Monitoring Report 2011: The Hidden Crisis: Armed Confict and Education| Education | United Nations Educational, Scientific and Cultural Organization." *Global Monitoring Report.* Paris: UNESCO.

———. 2011b. "The Hidden Crisis: Armed Conflict and Education." *Global Monitoring Report.* Paris: UNESCO.

———. 2014a. "Global Education for All Meeting; 2014 GEM Final Statement: The Muscat Agreement; 2014." Paris: UNESCO.

———. 2014b. "Shaping the Future We Want: UN Decade of Education for Sustainable Development (2005–2014)." Paris: UNESCO.

———. 2015. EFA Global Monitoring Report 2015: Education for All 2000-2015: Achievements and Challenges. Paris: UNESCO.

———. 2015a. "Education 2030 Incheon Declaration and Framework for Action." Paris: UNESCO.

———. 2015b. "UNESCO TVET Strategy 2016–21." Paris: UNESCO.

———. 2017a. "Global Action Programme on ESD." New York: UNESCO.

———. 2017b. "Global Education Monitoring Report: Accountability in Education: Meeting our Commitments." Paris: UNESCO.

———. 2018. "Local Knowledge Global Goals." New York: UNESCO.

———. 2019. Global Education Monitoring Report: Migration, Displacement and Education: Building Bridges, Not Walls. Paris: UNESCO.

United Nations Development Programme. 2017. *UNDPs Strategy for Inclusive and Sustainable Growth*. New York: UNDP

Unterhalter, E. 2007. *Gender, Schooling and Global Social Justice*. London: Routledge.

———. 2017. "Negative Capability? Measuring the Unmeasurable in Education." *Comparative Education* 53 (1):1–16. doi: 10.1080/03050068.2017.1254945.

Unterhalter, E., and A. North. 2017. *Education, Poverty and Global Goals for Gender Equality: How People Make Policy Happen*. London: Routledge.

Vale, P., and S. Maseko. 1998. "South Africa and the African Renaissance." *International Affairs* 74 (2):271–85.

Vally, S., and E. Motala. 2014. *Education, Economy & Society*. Unisa Press.

Vally, S., and C.A. Spren. 2012. "The Curriculum and Citizenship Education in the Context of Inequality: Seeking a Praxis of Hope." *Perspectives in Education* 30 (4):88–97.

Vare, P., and W. Scott. 2007. "Learning for a Change: Exploring the Relationship Between Education and Sustainable Development." *Journal of Education for Sustainable Development* 1 (2):191–98.

Vavrus, F., and L. Bartlett. 2006. "Making Sense of the Vertical Case Study." *Current Issues in Comparative Education* 8 (2):95–103.

Verger, A. 2009. "The Merchants of Education: Global Politics and the Uneven Education Liberalization Process within the WTO." *Comparative Education Review* 53 (3):379–401. doi: 10.1086/599341.

Verger, A., H. Altinyelken, and M. Novelli. 2018. "Global Education Policy and International Development." London: Bloomsbury.

Verger, A., C. Fontdevila, and A. Zancajo. 2016. *The Privatization of Education: A Political Economy of Global Education Reform*. New York: Teachers College Press.

Verger, A., and M. Novelli. 2012. "Campaigning for 'Education for All'." Rotterdam: Sense Publishers.

Verger, A.L., and S. Robertson. 2012. "The GATS Game-Changer: International Trade Regulation and the Constitution of a Global Education Marketplace." Edward Elgar Publishing.

Vladimirova, K., and D Le Blanc. 2015. "How well are the links between education and other sustainable development goals covered in UN flagship reports? A contribution to the study of the science-policy interface on education in the UN system." *DESA Working Paper*. New York: Department for Economic and Social Affairs.

Wagid, Y., and N. Davids, eds. 2018. *African Democratic Citizenship Education Revisited*. London: Palgrave Macmillan.

Wagner, D. 2018. *Learning as Development: Rethinking International Education in a Changing World*. New York: Routledge.

Walby, S. 2009. *Globalization and Inequalities: Complexity and Contested Modernity*. London: Sage.

———. 2015. *Crisis*. Cambridge: Polity Press.

Waldrop. 1992. *Complexity: The Emerging Science at the Edge of Order and Chaos*. New York: Simon and Schuster.

Walker, M. 2019. "Why Epistemic Justice Matters in and for Education." *Asia Pacific Review of Education*. https://doi.org/10.1007/s12564-019-09601-4.

Wals, A.E.J. 2007. "Special Learning: Towards a Sustainable World." Wageningen: Wageningen Academic Publishers.

Wals, A.E.J., and G. Kieft, G. 2010. *Education for Sustainable Development: Research Overview*. Stockholm, SIDA.

WBG. 2017. "Africa Competitiveness Report 2017." In. Washington, DC: World Bank Group.

WCED. 1987. "Our Common Future." Oxford: Oxford University Press.

Wells, J. 2013. *Complexity and Sustainability*. London: Routledge.

Westbrook, J., N. Durrani, R. Brown, D. Orr, D. J. Pryor, J. Boddy, and F. Salvi, F. (2013) Pedagogy, Curriculum, Teaching Practices and Teacher Education in Developing Countries. Education Rigorous Literature Review. London: Department for International Development.

White, Bob. 1996. "Talk About School: Education and the Colonial Project in French and British Africa (1860–1960)." *Comparative Education* 32 (1):9–26.

Whitehead, C. 2003. *Colonial Educators: The British Indian and Colonial Education Service 1858–1983*. London: I B Tauris & Co Ltd.

Whitehead, Clive. 2007. "The Concept of British Education Policy in the Colonies 1850–1960." *Journal of Educational Administration and History* 39 (2):161–73. doi: 10.1080/00220620701342296.

Williams, D., and T. Young. 2009. "The International Politics of Social Transformation Trusteeship and Intervention in Historical Perspective." In *Empire, Development and Colonialism: The Past in the Present*, edited by M. Duffield and V. Hewitt. London: Boydell and Brewer, James Currey.

Williams, P. 2007. "From Non-inteference to Non-indifference: The Origins and Development of the African Union's Security Culture." *African Affairs* 106 (423):253–79.

Wilson, K. 2013. *Race, Racism and Development: Interrogating History, Discourse and Practice*. London: Zed books.

Wolpe, H. 1988. *Race, Class and the Apartheied State*. Paris: UNESCO.

WorldBank. 2008. *The Growth Report: Strategies for Sustained Growth and Inclusive Development*. Washington, DC: World Bank.

———. 2011. "Learning for All: Investing in People's Knowledge and Skills to Promote Development: World Bank Group Education Strategy 2020." Washington, DC: World Bank.

———. 2018. *Learning to Realize Education's Potential*. Washington: World Bank.

World Economic Forum. 2015. *New Vision for Education: Unlocking the Potential of Technology*. Geneva: World Economic Forum.

Young, M. 2008. *Bringing Knowledge Back In*. Abingdon: Routledge.

———. 2013a. "Overcoming the Crisis in Curriculum Theory: A Knowledge-Based Approach." *Journal of Curriculum Studies* 45 (2):101–18.

———. 2013b. "Powerful knowledge: An analytically useful concept r just a sexy sounding term?: A response to John Beck's 'Powerful knowledge, Esoteric Knowledge, Curriculum Knowledge'." *Cambridge Journal of Education* 43 (2):195–98.

———. 2014. "The Curriculum and the Entitlement to Knowledge." In *Cambridge Assessment Network*. Cambridge: Cambridge Assessment.

Young, M., and J. Muller. 2013. "On the Powers of Powerful Knowledge." *Review of Education* 1 (3):229–50.

Yu, G., and S. Thomas. 2008. "Exploring School Effects Across Southern and Eastern African School Systems and in Tanzania." *Assessment in Education: Principles, Policy & Practice* 15 (3):283–305. doi: 10.1080/09695940802417525.

Zazu, C. 2017. "The Culture Hut Concept as Curriculum Innovation: Engaging the Dialectic Nature of Heritage in Zimbabwean Schools to Support ESD Learning." In *Schooling for Sustainable Development in Africa*, edited by H. Lotz-Sisitka, O. Shumba, J. Lupele, and D. Wilmot, 285–30. Switzerland: Springer.

Index

Page numbers in *italic* indicate a figure and page numbers in **bold** indicate a table on the corresponding page.

Printed in Great Britain
by Amazon